Birthpangs and Blessings

A Commentary on the Book of Genesis

— CLARE AMOS —

Sacristy Press

Sacristy Press
PO Box 612, Durham, DH1 9HT

www.sacristy.co.uk

First edition published in 2004 by Epworth Press, Peterborough
This edition published in 2022 by Sacristy Press, Durham

Copyright © Clare Amos 2022
The moral rights of the author have been asserted.

All rights reserved, no part of this publication may be reproduced or transmitted in any form or by any means, electronic, mechanical photocopying, documentary, film or in any other format without prior written permission of the publisher.

Scripture quotations, unless otherwise stated, are from the New Revised Standard Version Bible: Anglicized Edition, copyright © 1989, 1995 National Council of the Churches of Christ in the United States of America. Used by permission. All rights reserved worldwide.

Every reasonable effort has been made to trace the copyright holders of material reproduced in this book, but if any have been inadvertently overlooked the publisher would be glad to hear from them.

Sacristy Limited, registered in England & Wales, number 7565667

British Library Cataloguing-in-Publication Data
A catalogue record for the book is available from the British Library

ISBN 978-1-78959-194-1

Birthpangs and blessings have we here;
journeys, encompassed in the fear
and love of God, and more:
the rivalry of brothers, the score
of wrongs revenged, but heaven
uneclipsed by hate calls us to wait,
read, discover, find the tears
that summon us to start again,
to grasp the blessing hidden in our pain.

Alan Amos

Contents

Preface to the first edition vi
Preface to the second edition viii
Introduction 1

The story of beginnings 1:1–6:8 15
The song of the seven days 1:1–2:4a 16
Fruits of the earth 2:4b–3:24 31
Brothers and sons 4:1–6:8 45
Theological reflections 57

The story of the flood—and its aftermath 6:9–11:26 67
Washing the world clean 6:9–9:28 71
Peoples and languages 10:1–11:26 82
Theological reflections 87

The story of Abraham 11:27–25:18 101
The journey starts—and a detour 11:27–13:18 104
The stranger in our midst 14:1–16:16 113
Abraham not Abram 17:1–27 129
Entertaining angels unawares 18:1–19:38 135
The endangered future 20:1–22:24 147
A wedding and two funerals 23:1–25:18 169
Theological reflections 183

The story of Jacob 25:19–36:43 203
  Double trouble 25:19–34 204
  His father's son 26:1–35 210
  The stolen blessing 27:1–28:9 216
  Visions of the night 28:10–22 227
  Tricksters tricked 29:1–31:5 231
  Touching God 32:1–33:20 248
  A troublesome brood 34:1–31 262
  Deaths and births 35:1–36:43 267
  Theological reflections 273

The story of Joseph and his brothers 37:1–50:26 287
  Going down ... and up 37:1–41:57 289
  Lives bound together 42:1–45:28 310
  Hints of the future 46:1–50:26 325
  Theological reflections 345

Notes 353

Preface to the first edition

It has been an enjoyable, though also challenging, experience to work on this commentary over the past few years. I would particularly like to thank Ivor Jones and the Epworth Committee for the confidence they showed in me in asking me to attempt it. I am also very aware of how much I owe to Cyril Rodd and Natalie Watson of the Epworth Committee and Press for the assistance they have given. They both demonstrated exemplary care and interest, and gave support which went well beyond what one might justifiably expect from an editorial team. In particular, I am grateful for Cyril Rodd's detailed scrutiny of the work as it progressed. His amazing eye for detail was invaluable.

I also owe an immense debt of gratitude to the École Biblique in Jerusalem where I did my post-graduate studies. Unlike many institutions of higher learning the École Biblique was a place where one was encouraged first of all to look closely at the biblical text rather than books about it! My teachers there, especially Father Jerry Murphy O'Connor, were an inspiration for the way in which they held together scholarly wisdom and religious commitment.

I would like to thank Ted Todd, Verne Fletcher, John McCullough and Rupert Hoare for all having the courage at various times to appoint me to teaching situations in which I could discover how much I enjoyed communicating my love of the Bible. I also remember the many students in Jerusalem, Beirut, Cambridge, Kent and South London, from whom I have learned as much as I have shared.

In recent years, I have had the privilege of working in the field of interfaith relations. This commitment and concern is apparent, I believe, in the commentary. I am grateful to colleagues such as Michael Ipgrave, David Marshall, Susanne Mitchell and Andrew Wingate, who have given me the confidence to believe that my exploration of the Bible could help to resource thinking about the Christian approach to other faiths.

If there is one thing I hope about this commentary, it is that it is not divorced from the experience of my whole life so far, including a significant number of years spent in the Middle East. My husband Alan was my companion through several of those years, and all the time since. It is in company with him, and more recently with our son Robin, that my theology has been worked out and wrestled over. Together with Alan I am still in the process of discovering what may be the full meaning of Genesis 2:24.

Clare Amos
March 2004

Preface to the second edition

When this commentary was originally published in 2004, it was well received and reviewed. However, two factors perhaps meant that it was less widely available or used than would be ideal from the author's (my) viewpoint. The first was the restructuring of the Methodist Publishing House which led to the closure of the Epworth Press only a few years after the commentary was published. In turn, this meant that copies were and are rarely available, and then only at an inflated price.

The second factor was the link between the Epworth commentary series and the Revised English Bible (REB). All the commentaries in the series, including this one, were directly linked to this translation of the Bible. Personally, I appreciate the REB and consider it an excellent translation into modern English. However, for a variety of reasons the REB "lost out" to the much more widely used New Revised Standard Version (NRSV), which was published virtually contemporaneously in 1989. The NRSV is now known and used far more than the REB in both church and academic contexts. For a commentary such as this one whose methodology involves a close reading of both the Hebrew and English text the lack of popular recognition of the REB text was a definite handicap. So I decided a few years ago, that when I retired from full-time work and had the opportunity, I would seek to publish a "new edition" of the original commentary, this time using the NRSV as the base English text. This is the result. I have taken the opportunity to make a few changes and additions, largely at points where my continued fascination with the book of Genesis over the last fifteen years has given me further insights into this biblical book. Our increased commitment to ecological concerns in recent years is also reflected in the current text. On the whole, however, I am pleased with how little I did want to alter, because I felt that my original work had largely succeeded in conveying what I wanted to say about Genesis, this book which is so seminal both to the rest of the Bible, and to western culture as a whole.

One "theme" that ran through the original commentary was the influence that Genesis continues to have in the life of the current Middle East, and in the dynamics of the relationships between Judaism, Islam and Christianity. Over the last fifteen years, I have worked widely in the fields of Middle Eastern and interreligious concerns, and I am even more convinced now than I was when the first edition appeared that the book of Genesis has vital wisdom that can speak in these concerns—though sometimes subversively and offering unexpected insights.

In the first edition of this commentary, I expressed my thanks to a number of former colleagues to whom I felt I owed much. I would like to add to that list some of those who during the years since 2004 have also been supportive and affirmative of my work. Without them I would not be exactly where I am today. They include Michael Doe, Kenneth Kearon, John Peterson and Rowan Williams, as well as many colleagues and interreligious dialogue partners from my years working at the World Council of Churches. They have my gratitude.

Clare Amos
February 2021

Introduction

One of the defining and most memorable moments of the history of the twentieth century was the day, a few months before Neil Armstrong set his "small step" on the surface of the moon, when Apollo 8 circled the moon for the first time on Christmas Eve 1968. Television cameras on board the spaceship beamed back to earth awesome pictures of our planet as it appeared from the perspective of space, and a disembodied voice began to read from the Bible.

The passage that was chosen was not the account of the birth of Christ, nor even the prologue of John's Gospel which sets Christ within a cosmic context. Instead, the astronaut on that small spaceship, set in the skies by all the scientific skills and technical knowledge of the twentieth century AD, read the first chapter of a book that was more than 2,000 years old, and came from what would normally be considered a pre-scientific culture. He read Genesis 1, a chapter which recounts in solemn cadences the story of the creation of those heavens and that earth.

I, like many others who heard those words being read to us from a quarter of a million miles away, was deeply moved. There was a rightness to the choice of the book of Genesis, not simply because Genesis 1 is a story of "heavens and earth", but also because Genesis is an inheritance which belongs to humanity as a whole, even those who would not consider themselves to be overtly religious. There is a "tingle factor" to Genesis that is wider than church or cult, which reaches beyond those whose faith is expressed within an institutional framework. For Genesis continues to point human beings towards the eternal dimension which underpins all human existence, to challenge us to ask the fundamental questions about the origin and meaning of life.

So it is a privilege and a responsibility to write a commentary on the book of Genesis precisely because it is a book of such potential (and actual) power. It can be a tool for good; it has also been dreadfully misused. It can kill faith as well as help to create it. Those who teach or preach from the book of Genesis need to be acutely aware of this.

Genesis begins with an ambiguity. Its title in the Hebrew Bible is *bere'shit* (the opening phrase of the book in Hebrew). But does that mean "In the beginning", which is how it is usually read, or "When God began to create", which is how the New Jewish Publication Society translation takes it? Is the ambiguity significant? Perhaps it helps to remind us that Genesis was never simply a piece of writing about the remote past, about *the* beginning of things. It is always a living kerygma, a proclamation about God's redeeming activity. References back to creation are inspired by a concern to know the creator in the present: to know the way of God's working with humankind.

Genesis is a story which is continually reborn in every age. The existentialist movement has freed up our thinking and allowed a new access to the Genesis stories. We are enabled to see that it is a telling of "beginnings": of the forces of creation and renewal in the here and now.

Genesis speaks to us first of a Middle East, and then of a world, which is ridden with violence and radically unhealed. To address this violent world of reality, it holds up a number of powerful "myths", the very telling of which is a way of singing hope into existence, of recalling humankind to remembrance of the overarching wings of the creator God and pointing us forward to the new possibilities and potentialities which derive from grace.

One of the ironies of Genesis is that this book of "beginning" probably owes a great deal to times in Israel's history when the people's future existence was in question. Further comments on dates and sources can be found in the notes about "Structure, sources, dates and contexts" on p. 6, but the basic premise which undergirds this commentary is that the first impetus to gather together in a connected written form the traditions which now make up Genesis took place during the exilic period. The text was then edited and re-edited over a number of centuries and may have assumed its *very* final form in another epoch of national threat, the Maccabean period. Genesis' retelling of the "beginning" at times when the "end" seemed likely was a statement of hope for the future. It may be that Genesis has a message for our age too, a time when the relevance of tradition is called into question and when the Christian churches sometimes feel that they can do little more than carry on carrying "Joseph's bones".

The standpoint of this commentary

1. I write as an Old Testament scholar working from within the Christian tradition and with an intended audience of those who broadly speaking also live and work within this context. There are two implications to be drawn from this statement:

a) I regard it as a legitimate part of my remit to address the question of the relevance of Genesis within the life of the church today. The story of the interpretation of Genesis in the Christian and Jewish communities over the last 2,000 years is a key part of the interpretative process. If Genesis was originally written "from faith to faith", such an approach is truer to the spirit of its composition than a merely archaeological and historical survey of the book.

b) I write as a Christian scholar of the Old Testament rather than a Jewish scholar of the "Hebrew Bible". This is not to say that I am unaware of Jewish interpretation of the book of Genesis. At many points in this commentary, it will be clear how much I am indebted to such interpretation. I firmly believe that Jews and Christians need to study what we Christians call the "Old Testament" in an ongoing ecumenical dialogue with each other. At the same time, I believe that studying Genesis as the first book of the Old Testament is a qualitatively different exercise from reflecting on it as the keystone of the Jewish Torah. The very terminology "Old Testament" is a reminder that Christians read Genesis as part of a whole which includes, for example, the Gospel of John and the book of Revelation (both of which impact upon a reading of Genesis).

2. This commentary is not intended to compete with Westermann's magnum opus, the great three-volume commentary on the book of Genesis, nor even Westermann's cut-down one-volume version! They are both superb works, and those who are encouraged by using the current book to explore Genesis further could not do better than to turn in Westermann's direction (see suggestions for further reading on p. 12).

But the scope and purpose of this commentary is different. Although it is a commentary on an English translation of Genesis (the first edition based on the Revised English Bible version, this second edition on the New Revised Standard Version), I have where appropriate also referred to Hebrew words, expressions and phrases, partly because one of the fascinating features of Genesis is the writer's delight in wordplay, punning on the meaning of a Hebrew word in a manner that is inevitably lost through translation. It is a particular characteristic of the Hebrew language to draw connections between words that share the same fundamental two or three consonants. If you look at the standard footnotes of the NRSV text you will find that some of these wordplays are actually noted in the footnotes, which helps to justify my decision to refer to them.

3. This commentary reflects some of the important developments in Old Testament and Pentateuchal scholarship which have come about since Westermann's commentary first appeared in German in 1974. There has been an increased concern to look at the Bible and its individual books more holistically, exploring the story they are trying to tell us as a whole rather than engaging in the kind of "excavative" scholarship which was overconcerned to break down the material into smaller units and spend time continually delving for sources.

As a part of the more holistic nature of biblical scholarship in the last thirty years, a concern with the literary or story qualities of the material has become significant. I have found this an illuminating and refreshing approach and have tried to reflect this in the course of this commentary (though steering clear of the very technical vocabulary of some of the more modern literary critics). It is a challenge to any commentary writer to encourage, rather than impede, people in "reading the story whole". Reading the story is not simply an intellectual activity. Rather, the reader is caught up imaginatively by the story, and enters into the story and its world. The reader becomes a participant in its drama. By reading the story in this way, we assimilate the world of the story so that it becomes a world in which, progressively, we feel ourselves to be at home. One of the nicest things that a reader of the first edition said to me was that in reading my commentary she had a powerful sense of enjoying a novel.

Alongside this recent interest, both academic and popular, in "story" there have also developed particular hermeneutical concerns such as feminist perspectives on Genesis and the use of the book in liberation studies.

I certainly write as a woman, and I have been affected and stimulated by the work of scholars such as Phyllis Trible. I am sure that this commentary would read rather differently if I were a man. But I feel that it would be unhelpful and untrue to Genesis to segment out "women's insights" or "feminist perspectives" into a separate section, and so I have not done so. From the first chapter of the book, we hear about "male and female" together, and it is through the dynamic interaction of men and women that much of the story is carried along.

There is a tension here that it is important to acknowledge. Part of the rebirthing of Genesis in each age must be that each age's concerns are and can be reflected. I have found that to be true in my own experience. My early adulthood was spent in the Middle East, both Jerusalem and Lebanon. It was a formative experience for me. I cannot now read the Old Testament without being reminded of modern Middle Eastern attitudes, practices and political concerns. When I say that Genesis is potentially a *dangerous* book, this is certainly part of what I have in mind. In the Middle East today real people really get killed in part because of beliefs some human beings may hold about the book of Genesis. I will never forget my incredulity at being told by a Palestinian friend of mine, an educated Christian woman from Ramallah, a town on the West Bank, how on a visit to Jerusalem she had had a conversation with a Western tourist. On discovering that she was a Christian living on the West Bank, this person had informed her, quite categorically, that "she couldn't be a real Christian, because if she were a real Christian, she would of course have been willing to leave her home town, since she would know that God had given the land to the descendants of Abraham, Isaac and Jacob". One of the features of Genesis is the way in which it seeks to draw together universality and particularity: and the Middle East today is a region where the "scandal of particularity" can feel truly scandalous.

The Middle Eastern context is in my bones, and I make no apology for the way that it has impacted upon this commentary. But once again I have sought to explore this dimension as part of the whole picture rather than regarding it as a separate hermeneutical starting point.

If there is one overriding hermeneutical principle that undergirds this commentary, it is that our interpretation and understanding of Genesis must be linked in some way to the God who is I AM WHO I AM (Exodus 3:14), the one who refuses to become a puppet for human beings yet from the beginning has been gracious in revelation. The mysteriousness and at times illogicality of God and of Genesis are not to be despaired of but are there for wonder and for hope. In the questions themselves are the answers that the writers of Genesis have provided.

Structure, sources, dates and contexts

It continues to be an exciting time to be producing a commentary on Genesis. This is largely due to the fact that the source-critical theory about the origin of the Pentateuch associated with the names of Karl Heinrich Graf and Julius Wellhausen, which dominated Old Testament scholarship for more than a century and which was the foundation-stone of my own university Old Testament studies, has, during the last generation been seriously challenged. The scholarly consensus has almost completely broken down. No longer is it appropriate for example, when producing work on Genesis, to assume the existence of a tenth-century "J" (Yahwist) source. Similarly there have been questions about the dates or existence of the other sources, "E" (Elohist) and "P" (Priestly). Indeed, the issue of whether we can talk about sources at all, or whether we should rather think of one creative mind producing this great work, perhaps drawing on well-known tales and traditions, has been raised by a number of scholars, most notably R. N. Whybray in *The Making of the Pentateuch*.[1] The only thing that is certain is that we are in a time when certainties have disappeared.

The corollary of this, however, is that there has been considerable interest in the "final form" of Genesis—as it appears in our Bibles. The format of this present commentary highlights the "final form" and structure of the biblical book.

One of the features of Genesis is that the word *toledot* appears at ten key points in the narrative and seems to be designed to mark where one section ends and another begins. This word *toledot*, which is variously translated as "generations", "list", "descendants", "story", appears at 2:4; 5:1; 6:9; 10:1; 11:10; 11:27; 25:12; 25:19; 36:1 (repeated 36:9) and 37:2. Of these ten instances of the word, five introduce a narrative section (often lengthy) and five a genealogy, or genealogy with a short narrative. Five of them appear in 1:1–11:26, the part of Genesis often designated as the "primeval story" and five in 11:27–50:26, the part of the book which focuses on the story of Israel's ancestors. Given the interest of Genesis in number patterns, this is probably not accidental. The shape of the book is constructed for us by this word.

Genesis at a glance

(In this table, the word *toledot* is designated by the letter "T".)

Primeval Story

Section 1: Creation and the antediluvian period
1:1–2:4   Prologue
2:4 T   Introducing story (2:4–4:26)
5:1 T   Introducing genealogy and short narrative (5:1–6:8)

Section 2: The flood and its aftermath
6:9 T   Introducing story (6:9–9:29)
10:1 T   Introducing genealogy and short narrative (10:1–11:9)
11:10 T   Introducing genealogy (11:10–11:26)

Story of Israel's Ancestors

Section 3: The story of Abraham (Terah's descendants)
11:27 T   Introducing story (11:27–25:11)
25:12 T   Introducing genealogy (25:12–18)

Section 4: The story of Jacob (Isaac's descendants)
25:19 T   Introducing story (25:19–35:29)
36:1 T (repeated 36:9)   Introducing genealogy (36:1–43)

Section 5: The story of Jacob's sons
37:2 T   Introducing story (37:1–50:26)

By taking this pattern as our starting point for understanding Genesis we gain some important insights:

1. The English (and Greek) name of the book of Genesis is highly appropriate. Genesis literally means "birth", and the word *toledot* comes from a Hebrew root which means to "beget" or "give birth to". Genesis is a tale in which "birth" will be important. The first instruction of God to humanity is "Be fruitful and multiply" (1:28). Genesis tells the story of how this instruction, and God's blessing which accompanies it, operates in the story of creation and especially humanity. Life, of which birth is such a central part, will survive flood, divine curse, infertility and famine.
2. It is remarkable that several of the genealogies relate to a wider or different group than the leading characters featured in the narrative material. Genesis 25:12–18 lists the descendants of Ishmael and 36:1–43 those of Esau. Genesis 10:1–32 includes the descendants of Ham and Japheth as well as Shem. Genesis is interested in their destinies, as well as the fate of the offspring of Abraham, Isaac and Jacob. The very structure of Genesis therefore challenges any narrow focus on a chosen family or race. It is particularly striking that this point is made specifically through the use of genealogies, since genealogical status seems to have become a key marker for membership of the Jewish community during the post-exilic period. To employ a "genealogical" device to structure the overall book in this way feels subversive. It raises important questions about inclusivism and exclusivism for both Judaism and Christianity.
3. If there are five examples of the word *toledot* in each of the primeval and ancestral parts of Genesis, it may well be that the *middle* example is particularly important in each case. Ancient narratives were often structured to direct their readers' attention to a midpoint. In Genesis, this certainly seems to be the case for specific sections of the book (see further on the Abraham story on p. 103 and Jacob on p. 204). It has been suggested that this feature also applies to the overall structure of Genesis, and therefore the story of the flood (in the primeval story) and that

of Jacob (in the ancestral history) are both thrown into particular focus. Both sections may be particularly important therefore if we want to explore the impetus and context that brought Genesis to birth.

The origins of Genesis: a working hypothesis

Notwithstanding the work of scholars such as R. N. Whybray, it is likely that the book as a whole was composed over several centuries. The following is a possible description of the history of the book:

1. The kernel of the book originated among the Jewish community in Babylonia, during or slightly after the period of the exile (c.586–538 BC), drawing on memories of physical realities, folk traditions and religious practices of pre-exilic times in Palestine which had been cherished by the community during the years of exile. However, motifs such as the Garden of Eden and the flood have clear links to a Babylonian context, and may at times show dependence on Babylonian or Mesopotamian literature. This could also have been the time when the figure of Abraham first became important as a "national" figure—it is notable how little Abraham appears in those parts of the Old Testament which seem to be definitely pre-exilic in origin. It is also clear that the adoption of Abraham as national ancestor was not universally popular (see Isaiah 63:16) and may have been due to the influence of a particular group among the exiles with links to Hebron, or the royal house of Judah. Stories about Jacob, however, seem to have been told widely as traditional tales over several centuries before the Exile, particularly in the Northern Kingdom (see Hosea 12:3–4). They too are reworked at this time so that, in what eventually becomes this book, the adventures of this ancestor increasingly reflect the fortunes of the nation whose name he came to bear (32:28). The Exile is a time when both "flood" and the story of an ancestor who was forced to travel to Mesopotamia and travel back again would be very relevant.

2. The book continues to be developed during the Persian period (538–332 BC) and reflects some of the tensions and struggles of this time. In particular, this was a period when the relationship between "Israel" and the people of Edom was highly ambiguous, with an awareness on the one hand of the close affinity of the two peoples, but, on the other, intense hostility. Yet it was recognized that YHWH himself was a deity with close links with Edom (Deuteronomy 33:2; Judges 5:4). The enmity with Edom was exacerbated as a result of ongoing Edomite control over Southern Palestine and the increasing emphasis on Abraham's association with Hebron/Beer-sheba may be intended as a counterweight to this.

3. Even within the community of "Israel" there were varied viewpoints at play. It is far from certain that the primacy of Jerusalem and its temple was universally accepted at this period. There seems to have been worship offered to YHWH at both Bethel and Shechem/Gerizim, and the importance given to these sites within Genesis may reflect the voice of "priestly" groups who were not Jerusalem orientated. In particular, the rigorous exclusivism that seems to have been practised at Jerusalem (e.g. Ezra) appears to have been gently challenged at points of Genesis. Stories such as those of Hagar (Chapters 16 and 21) or Dinah (34) are told with an awareness that "Israel" needed to co-exist with other peoples of the land.

4. At some point, the developing book was edited by an individual or group who moved it a long way towards its final form. This stage was also the time when further material was produced or incorporated into the existing narrative, e.g. 1:1–2:4; some of the genealogical material; parts of the flood story; 17:1–27; probably 23:1–20; 27:46–28:9; 35:9–15; and probably 46:1–27. The "style" of these sections is distinctive and would traditionally be described as "priestly", though again their location was not necessarily Jerusalem. They may have been based in Babylon/Mesopotamia (see especially 27:46–28:9). This group may well have been responsible for the overall *toledot* structure of the book.

5. The extensive story of Joseph was added after most of the rest of the book was complete. This could have happened during the Hellenistic period, probably between 300 and 200 BC, a time when Palestine was ruled by the Ptolemies of Egypt. See further in the introductory material for the section "The story of Joseph and his brothers" (p. 287). In adding this story, an earlier, briefer account of Jacob and his sons may have been displaced. (Traces of this earlier account may be found, for example, in Chapter 46.) The purpose of the additional material about Joseph was partly to explain how and why the family of Jacob came to be in Egypt and thus act as a bridge into the book of Exodus. In this section the figures of Judah and Joseph seem to jostle for hegemony among the brothers. This may reflect both the ancient rivalry in pre-exilic times between the kingdoms of Israel ("Joseph") and Judah, and also its post-exilic manifestation reflected in the uneasy relationship between the Jewish community of Jerusalem and groups located in Samaria and Shechem (eventually known as the "Samaritans"). There are points where the story of Joseph seems to echo or contrast with the opening chapters of Genesis. If the earlier sections of the book had largely been composed before the story of Joseph was added, these echoes may be intentional.

6. Finally, the chronological data (ages of the ancestors, etc.), in the form in which we now have them was added either in the late third century BC or, more likely, in the first half of the second century BC. The chronology of the patriarchs' ages is intricately worked out—apparently to a precise schema. Detailed analysis of the numbers and dates involved suggests a) that they may be linked to a calendar which was only introduced in Egypt by the decree of Canopus in 238 BC;[2] b) that the key dates of Genesis seem to form part of an elaborate time frame in which the Exodus happens in the year 2666 (after the creation of the world), and the year 4000 (the length of a "great year" in ancient astronomy) would fall in 164 BC—the date when the temple was rededicated by the Maccabees and the Feast of Hanukkah was established.[3] It is unlikely that this is accidental—and the chronology of Genesis as we now have it seems designed to point to this event in the

Hasmonean period as the culmination of history. Some would also link the story of the adventures of Abraham in Genesis 14 to this time. It is, however, important to point out that the chronology in the Septuagint (Greek translation) and the Samaritan version of the Pentateuch both differ from that in the Massoretic text (the Hebrew version on which our English translations are based) and that the chronology as we now have it in our English Bibles may therefore be a later revision of what was found in a previously existing earlier version.

In summary, the book of Genesis came into existence during the exilic and post-exilic period, and its content reflects concerns and challenges that were faced by the community during this time. It is written during a period when Judaism had spread beyond the boundaries of Palestine: the voices of the Jewish community in Babylonia, and perhaps also Jews who had close links with Egypt are heard, as well as those living within Palestine itself. The story and challenges of post-exilic Judaism are echoed in its pages. Indeed, part of its fascination lies in the fact that no other portion of the Bible addresses the tension between universality and particularity quite as compellingly as does Genesis.

For further reading

Among commentaries the following may be noted:

- Claus Westermann's commentaries on Genesis have a "classic" status and provide an essential point of reference, even if certain of the conclusions about dating and sources would now be challenged. His three-volume commentary on the Hebrew text: *Genesis 1–11* (Minneapolis, MN: Augsburg, 1984); *Genesis 12–36* (Minneapolis, MN: Augsburg, 1985); *Genesis 37–50* (Minneapolis, MN: Augsburg, 1986) is unrivalled, but is probably too detailed for those relying entirely on English translation. However, the one-volume abridged version *Genesis* is accessible in paperback, published by T. & T. Clark in 1988.

- Gerhard von Rad, *Genesis* (London: SCM, 1961, revised edition 1972) is notable for the way in which it interweaves biblical scholarship and Lutheran theological reflection.
- Similar in intent to von Rad but more recent is Walter Brueggemann, *Genesis* (Atlanta, GA: John Knox Press, 1982).
- Not precisely a commentary, the two Sheffield Old Testament Guides on Genesis address a number of key issues in an accessible way. John Rogerson, *Genesis 1–11* (Sheffield: Sheffield Academic Press, 1991) and R. W. L. Moberly, *Genesis 12–50* (Sheffield: Sheffield Academic Press, 1992). They are now also published as part of a composite volume, along with the Old Testament Guide on Exodus.
- For those who wish to know more about the Pentateuch as a whole, the following three books can be recommended:
- Joseph Blenkinsopp, *The Pentateuch: An Introduction to the First Five Books of the Bible* (London: SCM Press, 1992).
- David J. A. Clines, *The Theme of the Pentateuch* (Sheffield: Sheffield Academic Press, 2nd edn 1997).
- E. W. Nicholson, *The Pentateuch in the Twentieth Century* (Oxford: Clarendon Press, 1997).
- Two translations that are particularly designed to help the English reader feel closer to the Hebrew idiom of Genesis:
- Mary Phil Korsak, *At the Start . . . Genesis made new* (Louvain: Leuvense Schrijversaktie, 1992) aims to provide a translation as literal as is possible in English.
- Robert Alter, *Genesis* (New York, NY: W. W. Norton & Company, 1996) is a translation with short commentary notes.
- The following deal with particular parts of the book or themes raised within it:
- M. G. Brett, *Genesis: Procreation and the Politics of Identity* (London and New York, NY: Routledge, 2000) provides a "reading" of Genesis which understands it as resistance literature against the ethnocentrism of the Persian period.
- W. Lee Humphreys, *The Character of God in the Book of Genesis: A Narrative Appraisal* (Louisville, KY: Westminster John Knox

Press, 2001) considers how God functions as a character in the story of Genesis.
- Trevor Dennis, *Looking God in the Eye: Encountering God in Genesis* (London: SPCK, 1998) contains very accessible reflections on the interrelationship between God and human beings at key points of Genesis.
- Ellen Van Wolde, *Genesis 1–11 and Other Creation Stories* (London: SCM Press, 1996) looks at the creation stories, particularly aware of the interaction between human beings and the earth.
- Norman C. Habel and Shirley Wurst, *The Earth Story in Genesis* (The Earth Bible Vol. 2) (Sheffield: Sheffield Academic Press, 2000) bears witness to the importance of the interpretation of Genesis for our ecological engagement.
- Karl-Josef Kuschel, *Abraham: A Symbol of Hope for Jews, Christians and Muslims* (London: SCM Press, 1995) offers a reflection on the various ways the figure of Abraham is used in the faiths that are often linked to his name.
- Jon D. Levenson, *Inheriting Abraham: The Legacy of the Patriarch in Judaism, Christianity and Islam* (Princeton, NJ and Oxford: Princeton University Press, 2012) also addresses the use of "Abraham" in these faiths, building on the work of Kuschel, noting that it is important to be aware of differences as well as similarities.
- Jon D. Levenson, *The Death and Resurrection of the Beloved Son: The Transformation of Child Sacrifice in Judaism and Christianity* (New Haven, CT and London: Yale University Press, 1993) offers an exquisitely written, profound but accessible reflection on the motif of the actual or metaphorical sacrifice of a son as it appears in the biblical tradition, and especially in Genesis.
- Thomas Mann, *Joseph and his Brothers* (London: Vintage, 1999) is a classic novel which elucidates the Jacob and Joseph stories in some unexpected ways. The details given are for the paperback edition.
- Craig A. Evans, Joel N. Lohr and David L. Petersen, *The Book of Genesis: Composition, Reception and Interpretation* (Leiden, Boston, MA: Brill, 2012) explores in more detail some of the themes and topics linked to Genesis that are touched upon in this commentary.

The story of beginnings

1:1–6:8

As we begin to read Genesis 1:1–6:8, we find ourselves listening to a song of creation. It is as though the writers of these chapters are part of a choir singing the song, standing in a line with others behind and in front of them. They borrow images and themes from other creation narratives in the Ancient Middle East, in particular from the Babylonian geographical milieu. But even though Genesis transforms much of what is received, we are still allowed to hear echoes of earlier viewpoints, both Israelite and non-Israelite. Sometimes as in Genesis 1:1–2:4a these echoes are muted; at other points, as with the cherubim of Genesis 3:22 or the strange story of the sons of the gods in Genesis 6:1–4, they can ring loudly or even discordantly in our ears.

The early chapters of Genesis provide a model for those in every age who are prepared to deepen their own faith by listening to the sounds that other religious traditions can sing. The attitude they contain also acts as an implicit critique to those who would treat these pages as an absolute and unqualified statement of how the world scientifically came into being. For if you seek to read them flatly, on the one prosaic level, you are not really hearing the subtle orchestra of tones that empower them. Genesis will be a book in which the need for "true" listening will be very important. These chapters offer us the overture.

The song of the seven days
1:1–2:4a

This magnificent chapter was deliberately composed as a prologue to the book of Genesis. It is also significant that it has come to introduce the Old Testament and the whole of the Bible. It is the intended starting point of the biblical story. It is deliberately placed before what is apparently an alternative account of creation in Genesis 2:4b–3:24.

Whoever wrote the measured and solemn "liturgical" prose of Genesis 1 was fully aware of what was to come next. They knew that the picture offered of the story of Eden to be in the next chapter was coloured very differently. But they chose to give us first what we have received in Genesis 1.

It is likely that Genesis 1:1–2:4a and 2:4b–3:24 stem from different hands, possibly writing several centuries apart, and that this can help us explain the different style and feel of the two accounts. But the authors of Genesis 1 purposefully gave us this first chapter with its contrasting feel, not because they were careless or unaware of surface inconsistencies.

The creation of the world and of human beings within it includes paradox, and by setting Genesis 1 alongside Genesis 2 we are being reminded of this. We are both in the "image of God" (whatever that may mean, see p. 60) and of "the dust of the earth". It is the glory and the tragedy of the human condition that this is so. By beginning Genesis with these two contrasting pictures, the authors of Genesis have set out the vision that Psalm 8:4–5 expressed in a brief poetic couplet: "What are human beings, that you are mindful of them ... Yet you have made them a little lower than God."

When we read Genesis 1:1–2:4a, we can imagine that we are standing in a vast cathedral. Soaring above us are the heavens and their luminaries. Around us the walls are coloured with pictures of the varieties of plant and animal creation. There is an ethereal choir humming almost wordlessly, and there is a voice which, as so often in a cathedral, you cannot see, declaiming solemnly, chanting creation into being.

It is no accident that such a picture might spring to mind. The authors of this passage inhabited a world in which cathedrals—or rather temples, their ancient equivalent—were at the heart of religious, intellectual, cultural and economic life. It is possible that this chapter was originally written for use in temple worship. It is prose which stands on the borders of poetry and liturgy. We know that other ancient creation stories were closely linked to worship. Such stories told of the activities of the gods, and temple liturgies offered the place and the time for human beings to come into contact with the divine and be blessed.

Those who composed Genesis 1 probably knew the Babylonian creation story, *Enuma Elish*, which formed part of the temple liturgy in Babylon, though they also offer a challenge to it. Creation stories, such as *Enuma Elish*, were primarily interested in the past in order to understand and sustain the present. "Order" was what was desired: order over against the chaos and unpredictability of much of ancient life. People in the ancient world were confronted with the turbulence of the annual floods of the Tigris-Euphrates rivers which could be both life-giving and death-dealing, with impotence in the face of most human illnesses, with the fragile veneer which constituted stable civilization. Kings and temples had key roles in society to act as the guarantors of longed-for order. Reciting creation stories was also a way of bringing about stability, their telling reinforcing the "order" of the present and dreaming hopes for the future into being.

So too those who authored Genesis 1 were concerned to portray or even help to create an ordered cosmos. We can debate their precise geographical and chronological context. Because of their connection with the world of priests they are often referred to as "P". Writing either in an exilic, or more likely post-exilic, context, they were very aware of what a chaotic experience the exile had been: cherished theological and political traditions had been challenged, the people's very existence had been called into question. Some of the ways in which this concern for "order" (and specifically the priestly view of "order") is expressed in Genesis 1 include:

- A fascination with numbers and number patterns, linked to the way that numbers form part of the fabric of the regular pattern of human life and of the structure of the universe. The numbers ten (ten fingers), seven (the traditional seven planets) and three were regarded as key elements of life. The number two also had a particular importance, because it was the natural product of "dividing".

- A concern that different features of the universe should be "separated" from each other. The very word "separate" used in this chapter is characteristic of priestly vocabulary. It was a key task of priests to ensure that different elements with different qualities should be kept apart (e.g. the clean/unclean, the holy/common), and so God as creator is being described in priestly terms. The process of separation is good—creation proceeds by the recognition and naming of opposites, which in turn enables new forms of existence to take shape.
- The complementary patterning of the six days in which creation takes place in two sets of three.
- The structuring of time and the narrative to emphasize the importance of the Sabbath day.
- The interest in genealogies hinted at in 2:4a and which runs through the book of Genesis will also be a symptom of these authors' quest for "order". Genealogies help to link people to their roots, particularly rootless people who have experienced exile, or are in diaspora. They can also help to ensure that only the right kind of people are chosen for a role: for example, priests needed to prove their fitness by tracing their ancestry. The time of Ezra and Nehemiah in the post-exilic period saw great interest in genealogies, in order to ensure ethnic purity.

And yet despite this desire for an "ordered" world, both Genesis 1:1–2:4a itself, and the rest of Genesis, will help to subvert it. The neat patterns of numbers and words will almost work—but not quite; the outsiders, who one would not expect to be cherished if purity is paramount, will not only be allowed a place in the story, but become fundamental to it. Such is the God of Genesis, who will insist on being allowed to work in some surprising and unexpected ways.

1:1–2 *In the beginning* There is no end to the beginning of Genesis. The book begins with a conundrum. How should we translate the first Hebrew phrase *bere'shit* which does not actually include the word "the" before "beginning"? The NRSV seeks to reflect this by making this first verse with its verb "created" subordinate to verses 2–3 rather than treating verse 1 as a separate sentence, which is what is suggested in older translations such as the Authorized ("King James") Version, "In the beginning God created the heaven and the earth. And the earth was without form, and void . . . "

Underlying this debate about language is an important theological issue. What is the grammar of creation? Is God here creating everything absolutely out of nothingness, *ex nihilo*, or is God's creation rather the bringing of form and order to an already existing chaotic morass? Was there already an earth, in the shape of a "formless void", before God began the process of creation that is being described here? The *Enuma Elish*, for example, speaks of creation in such a manner. The squelchy seamonster Tiamat is torn apart to provide the raw material out of which the god Marduk fashions the world and its creatures. The "deep" (Hebrew: *tehom*) that is covered by darkness (1:2) may well be a word deliberately chosen to remind us of the Babylonian Tiamat, so are our writers of Genesis also thinking of creation in similar terms, even though the fierce conflict between the gods which is part of the Mesopotamian myth is totally absent from Genesis? This is what the NRSV is seeking to convey by subordinating verse 1 to verse 2 as it does. However, it is arguable that such a translation fails to do complete justice to the way that the authors of Genesis wanted to frame the whole of creation as taking place within the power and providence of God. God needs to be more than the subject in a subordinate clause! The traditional translation offered by the Authorized Version preserves an ambiguity about the exact process and timing of creation, which may well be what the original authors intended.

Indeed, one way of understanding verse 1 might be as a prologue summary to the rest of this chapter, rather as Genesis 1 is itself a prologue for the rest of the book. We are metaphorically standing outside our world and its creation—looking at it from a distance, as did those Apollo 8 astronauts as they circumnavigated the moon in December 1968. But the telescope that we are peering through in this chapter collapses time as well as space. Can we properly speak of *the* beginning before time itself has begun ("time" will not be created until Days One and Four)? Perhaps that is the reason why "the" is absent in the Hebrew text, though the limitations of English do not fully allow us to reflect this. And perhaps it is *a* rather than *the* beginning precisely because it is the start of a process that will be ongoing. We are being offered a perspective on the ultimate goal of creation—as well as its development. In the New Testament, John 5:17 draws on this part of Genesis to reflect that creation is not yet complete—for the father is working still.

It may well be that the "formless void" and "deep" were believed to exist in some fashion before the word of God spoke to it and shaped it. And yet, did it ever really exist apart from God? For even before God spoke, a "wind" from God hovered over the chaos. The NRSV translation "swept" does not quite capture the continuous sense of the underlying Hebrew participle which somehow takes us out of time. The Hebrew word *ruah* can mean "wind", "spirit" and "breath". It expresses and sums up the force of life. It can be intensely personal spirit—or impersonal power. Yet even if we picture what is happening as a mighty wind swirling like a storm on the surface of the planet, it is still an intended sign that God is and always has been intimately involved with all that is, whether good or evil.

Perhaps those who composed this chapter wanted to begin their story with a mystery. There certainly will be others to come. The God we meet in the first verses of Genesis both transcends the created universe, and yet also eternally cherishes it, sweeping or hovering over it like a mother bird (cf. Deuteronomy 32:11—which uses the same Hebrew word, though there translated as "hovers" to describe the Lord's care for his people). The participle translated as "swept" is expressed in a feminine form, reflecting the grammatical gender of the Hebrew *ruah*. Eventually the feminine gender of *ruah* will influence understanding of the nature of God, especially in the Christian tradition.

It is paradoxical but important both to say that God created *ex nihilo* and to acknowledge God as working with and through chaos. The one affirms that nothing in the universe is outside the will and power of God. The other is a reminder that God can bring good out of whatever mess human beings and the created order find themselves in.

The language of the beginning of Genesis is echoed at various points in the New Testament. Most clearly in John 1:1–18 but also in Colossians 1:15–20, and probably in the use of the word "beginning" in Mark 1:1

and the description of the "first" of Jesus' signs in John 2:11. When the word *beginning* occurs in several of these New Testament examples, it is clear that what is meant is a process rather than a particular point in time. May not this be helpful as we reflect on that mysterious "beginning" at the start of Genesis 1:1? For all the emphasis of the words that will be used to describe the completion of creation (2:1–3), this account encourages us to look to the future rather than cast our eyes solely on the past.

God created   The world as we now know it owes its shape to God. "Create" (Hebrew: *bara'*) in the Old Testament is a word that is only ever used with God as its subject. It has been deliberately chosen by the author of this chapter to affirm God's absolute responsibility for the entire created universe, and it will appear a significant seven times in the narrative up to 2:4a. The word which is used for God, *'elohim*, itself reminds us of God's universality. This is a generic word for "God" rather than the name of Israel's own special deity. In many creation stories in the Ancient Middle East, there was a focus on the author's own people or particular god. But that nationalistic element is largely missing from this account. So too is any real sense of struggle between God and other divine figures, which is remarkable when Genesis 1 is compared with other texts such as *Enuma Elish*, which link creation to a heavenly war. It is also suggestive that the word *'elohim* is formally plural, even though it normally appears in the Hebrew Bible accompanied by a singular verb. It teases us straightaway to begin to reflect on God's unity—and God's plurality. Genesis 1 offers a majestic monotheistic vision, which shames us when so often our conception of God still seems unashamedly tribal. Yet there is also a plurality in unity of the divine which will be hinted at in 1:2 and 1:26 and act as a reminder that we cannot easily grasp this God (*'elohim*), either intellectually or as a convenient divine talisman.

Formless void   It is difficult to capture the sound play of the Hebrew words *tohu wabohu* although the translation offered by the Revised English Bible, "vast waste", is a good effort. Probably a lifeless, dark and moonless desert is envisaged. In the next moment, the picture of chaos switches to a vast "deep" or watery abyss. In the verses that follow, this "formless void" and "deep" and the "darkness" will not be consigned in their turn to non-existence or destruction; instead, they will form part of God's new and emerging order. The "darkness" will be named as "night" and help to structure the boundaries of time; the "deep" will become "seas", eventually teeming with life.

1:3-5 *God said* Something that will happen a perfect ten times in the course of this creation account. God creates through his word. In Old Testament thinking, words were powerful, had a concrete reality to them and could effect what they spoke about. The words of prophets were feared, precisely because if they predicted doom there was an inevitability about it happening. Yet like Isaiah 44:26; 55:10-11, this chapter suggests that the proven power of God's words can also be an effective source of hope. If God can speak and everything come into being, then the corollary is that God's word is surely powerful enough to redeem and restore.

We too know God through his words, words are an essential part of self-communication and tell us something about the real core of a person as John 1:1-18 will later remind us.

Light is the first thing to be created. This light is something apart from the sun and the moon which still remain to be created on Day Four. This is a primal energy, a metaphor for the sense of consciousness that God has granted to the universe. Light will be used in the making of the later elements of creation, but not used up, even when the sun and moon have been formed.

As God "separated" the light from the darkness, he implicitly created time, through the division between light and darkness. The emphasis on time will become more overt on Day Four. It is an indication of the importance of time in the worldview of Genesis.

The phrase "God saw ... was good" will recur seven times during creation. God is like an artist; it is only as an artist feels satisfaction with a painting or a sculpture that he or she is empowered to go on and create further. So with God: God's pleasure in each stage of the creative process will help the conception of the next stage. This affirmation of creation as "good" or beautiful is fundamental. The Old Testament is at its heart gloriously world-affirming and acts as a rebuttal to elements of the Christian tradition that have had an escapist or negative attitude to the world. If the world is created as "good", it is important that humanity continues to keep it so: concern for justice, peace and the integrity of creation ultimately stems from this chapter. In the New Testament, we are reminded of God's intentions by Peter's words on the Mount of Transfiguration. "Rabbi, it is good for us to be here" (Mark 9:5) suggests that on that mountain for a brief moment creation was restored to its intended harmony.

Although the NRSV concludes verse 5 by referring to "the first day", it is notable that unlike the numbers which are linked to the later days of creation, we have here uniquely a cardinal, not an ordinal, number, "one day". Perhaps, as we have already hinted above, this might suggest that what has taken place on "Day One" cannot simply be described in sequential temporal terms.

1:6-13 Creation proceeds apace in the second and third days. Again, it takes place through a process of separation. Notice that when the "dome" is created, "God said" is reinforced by "God made". The double way that God's creative activity is described helps to emphasize that what is made fits precisely into God's prior intention.

A traditional understanding of the cosmos is present here, with waters both beneath and above the vault that marks out heaven. The process of separating out the waters into their proper place is quite complicated and lengthy even for God (it takes two days before the dry land can appear!). Water is difficult to deal with: the ultimate chaotic element, as anyone who has experienced a Middle Eastern flash flood would know. The waters that are now being separated out are part of that primordial deep referred to in verse 2, and perhaps there is just a hint of their ambiguous status. Are they a force that stands over against God, or are they rather part of the "good" of creation?

In many other Middle Eastern cultures, the sea was personified as an evil god or goddess who had to be defeated and killed by the power of divine order. That is a central motif in the *Enuma Elish*. It is remarkable how Genesis demythologizes the ancient stories: the waters are no longer seen as having the characteristics of a person or god. Sea is here even specifically called "good" (1:10), even though there are other parts of the Bible which do come close to personifying seas and waters as an evil power that God has to defeat (e.g. Isaiah 51:9–11; Revelation 21:1). "Who then is this, that even the wind and the sea obey him?" mused Jesus' disciples as he stilled the storm (Mark 4:41). Throughout the Bible, reaching back into the folk memory of Israel the sea was viewed as a potentially hostile force, and, as here in Genesis, one of the supreme marks of divine power in the Bible was that God alone was able to control its waters.

It reads strangely to our modern eyes that plants should be produced by mother-earth before sun and moon appear, since they would have had problems with photosynthesis. However, from the perspective of the authors of Genesis the important distinction is that between creatures that move (created in Days Four to Six), and things that do not, which includes plants (created in Days One to Three). Plants are also (according to the thinking of Genesis 1) asexual: their reproduction did not depend on the merging of male and female. Rather they had the power of renewal within themselves, through their ability to propagate by bearing "fruit with the seed in it". Plants form part of the milieu which will support the life to be created on Days Five and Six. The third day has been a particularly busy one, seeing both the appearance of the earth and this summons to the earth itself to produce plant life. If the *Enuma Elish* provided a pattern for the writers of Genesis 1, they needed to conflate what takes eight days to happen there into six days. This may be part of the reason for the increased activity on Days Three and Six.

The Pattern of the Days

Non-moving creation	Moving creation
Day 1: Light	Day 4: The moving lights (sun, moon, stars)
Day 2: Waters and the heavens	Day 5: Creatures that live in the waters and heavens
Day 3: Earth Vegetation	Day 6: Earth creatures Humans (who are allotted vegetation to eat)

1:14–25   With the creation of the sun and the moon, we start the second set of three days of creation, which correspond to the first set.

Yet the objects created by God are not named as sun and moon, but rather "two great lights". In Mesopotamian culture, the sun was venerated as a god, and sun worship also featured in Israel's own previous history (e.g. Ezekiel 8:16–18). The guarded language of this chapter is intended to emphasize that these heavenly bodies are themselves merely a part of creation, with ironically one of their main functions being to ensure the proper worship of God.

This day, the fourth, is the midpoint of the seven days, which have both begun and will end by God's shaping of time. Here too a focus on time is apparent: the heavenly bodies will serve "for signs and for seasons and for days and years". This is a reflection of the "priestly" concerns of the authors. It was important to ensure that religious festivals happen on the correct dates. In the post-exilic period, there was bitter and ongoing debate over calendrical systems—whether the year should be organized on a solar or lunar calendar. This affected the writing of Genesis, indeed it may explain some of the chronological data in the book (see e.g. 5:22–24). The authors of Genesis believed that the calendar was built into the fabric of the universe.

Day Five corresponds to Day Two: the waters and the vault of the heavens are filled with their appropriate living beings. Once again, the word "create" is used, for the first time since 1:1, to mark the appearance of "living creatures" (1:20: Plants were not considered "living creatures", see comment above on 1:11–12). "Create" is a key word: a sign that what is happening now is a critical fresh stage in the orderly development of creation, and part of the deliberate intention of God.

It is remarkable that the "great sea monsters" are mentioned first among the animal creation, and indeed that the actual verb "created" is used in relation to them, as the only other life form for which it is used in this chapter are human beings. We hear of Leviathan in Psalm 104:26, described almost as God's giant bath toy! Such semi-divine sea monsters appeared in the mythologies of Israel's neighbours. They summed up in animal form the terrifying and hostile nature of the sea. Yet in Genesis by contrast they are included in God's power and God's care. God's delight in the goodness of creation extends even to such as these.

God's act of blessing is also a sign of the new stage that has been reached. Sea creatures and air creatures are blessed. (It is interesting to speculate why land creatures are not blessed on the following day: probably the writer wanted to save up this important word to use it later that day of human beings.)

Blessing at its heart is connected with the love of and gift of life. Life has always been important in Old Testament and Jewish culture: preservation of life supersedes even the Sabbath. God's presence is to be desired precisely because in him is the fullness of life. Full life, however, in Old Testament thinking depended upon sufficient health and wealth to enjoy it, and the possibility of having the gift of life in oneself, exemplified by having descendents. Animals (unlike plants) need to be blessed to ensure their ability to reproduce and thus continue the chain of life. So here and in 1:28 blessing and the command to "be fruitful" are closely connected. Throughout Genesis, the author will repeatedly show us how this first command of God works itself out both in creation as a whole, and more especially in the world of human beings.

As we move into Day Six, the parallel with Day Three becomes apparent. In both cases, the earth "brings forth" the plant and animal life that inhabits it—perhaps a dim reflection of the ancient belief in the earth as a kind of mother. And once again there is a great deal happening. Important though the creation of terrestrial animal life may be, it is slightly squeezed as we move on towards humanity, since the whole of creation needs to fit in to a seven-day pattern.

1:26–31 Suddenly the chapter reaches a crescendo as the creation of human beings is reached. Genesis 1 makes it clear that this creation of humanity is a crowning moment in several ways. The plural "Let us" draws sudden attention to the plurality in unity of God. In Christian tradition, this has been understood as a moment when God deliberates within the Trinity before taking this step, while several parts of the Old Testament speak of a divine council surrounding God, made up of heavenly beings, "sons of gods" or angels. In the book of Job, their involvement with creation is majestically related: "Where were you when I laid the foundation of the earth . . . when the morning stars sang together and all the heavenly beings shouted for joy?" (Job 38:4,7) demanded God of Job. In our author's eye, it is this divine council who is being invited to share in this particular moment of creation—perhaps because it may affect their own relationship with God.

For God states that human beings are to be created "in our image, according to our likeness". It was brave, even dangerous, language to use. For many who heard it the word "image" would have brought to mind statues and idols. Genesis takes a traditional concept and fills it out with a revolutionary meaning. It is no longer statues of wood or stone that best represent God but living, breathing human beings. But how exactly are we human beings able to do this—represent God?

At the heart of the author's thinking seems to be the possibility of a relationship or partnership with God. Great emperors in the ancient world set up images of themselves in far-flung corners of their realms to remind their subjects that they still ruled even if they were not there in person, and to help reinforce the authority of the governor of the region. Similarly, if human beings are in the image of God they are being offered the responsibility of being God's viceregents over creation (e.g. 1:28).

Yet "imaging God" also has consequences for how human beings relate to one another. There is an intrinsic connection between the plural verb used by God ("Let us make") and the vocation of human beings to live as the "image" of God. God desires to exist in relationship rather than isolation. In so far as human beings then mirror or image God they too need to be in relationship, with God and with one another. It is human beings alone to whom God speaks directly as "you" in this chapter (1:29)—but it is in the plural that they are addressed. It is also notable that the other points in Genesis where God deliberates using the plural (3:22; 11:7) are both moments where the issue of human relationships—with God, and with one another—is to the fore.

One fundamental aspect of relationship is that of gender. Human beings are the only creatures that are described in Chapter 1 as "male and female". Partnership involves complementarity, and there is no more basic form of complementarity than that which exists between male and female. If human beings are to fulfil their God-given task to "be fruitful and multiply", then both male and female are essential to this process. And both sexes are created in the image of God, despite later traditions reflected for example in 1 Corinthians 11:7.

Could the writer be hinting that the "plurality" of God in these verses is a plurality that transcends the normal boundaries of gender? Back in Genesis 1:2, the "wind from God" which hovered over chaos was described in feminine terms. Throughout the rest of the chapter, the God who speaks creation into being is grammatically male and singular. Is there a hint being offered at this moment of "Let us" that the creative working together of male and female human beings might image the working together of male and female within divinity?

1:27, the actual moment when God's plan to make this special creature is enacted, repeats the key word "created" three times, and is set out as poetry in the NRSV. Poetry in Genesis is reserved for significant moments in the story, and is particularly used to emphasize a relationship, for good or ill, between a "pair" of individuals or groups. The form of Hebrew poetry facilitates this, with the structure of Hebrew poetic parallelism naturally inviting comparison and contrast between the two halves of a couplet. In 1:27, we have our attention drawn to two different sets of pairs: God and human beings form one pair; male and female the other (see further on image and creation on p. 60).

God blessed them   The fivefold form of blessing of human beings offered in 1:28 contains key concepts which reappear in other parts of Genesis, and provide themes which will recur throughout the story. One or more phrases from the blessing appear at critical moments (see e.g. Genesis 9:1; 17:6). The various elements of the blessing seem to represent the opposite of the situation that early readers of Genesis must have experienced: they felt themselves to be few in number, "barren" (see e.g. Isaiah 54:1), subjugated and dominated by the great empires which had controlled the Middle East for hundreds of years. Was the author's vision written in the faith that God wanted to turn this situation around, and create a new creation in which all people would have their rightful place?

Genesis 1:28 contains forceful language. The word translated "subdue" is elsewhere used to describe the rape of a woman, and it is sometimes felt that texts such as this bear considerable responsibility for the lack of concern for the environment in parts of the Judaeo-Christian tradition throughout history. But the control of human beings over the rest of creation is actually restricted by these verses: the gift of plants for human food (1:30) implies that the eating of animals is off limits. The final verses of Chapter 1 tie human beings firmly into the network of creation as a whole; God gives attention to the food of animals as well as human beings; and *all* creation, not simply humanity, is pronounced as "very good".

2:1–4a Human beings may be the crown of creation, but they are not also its goal. The creation story does not finish until the consecration of the seventh day. And when human beings begin to keep the Sabbath (Exodus 20:8–11), the very act of keeping this day holy will return ultimate control of the world to God. The Hebrew text states that God brought everything to an end on the seventh day, which is the understanding followed by the NRSV. However, this implies that God himself worked on the Sabbath, a theological conundrum which John 5:17 also seems to be addressing. Probably due to this "problem" the Septuagint (Greek translation) chooses to suggest that God finished his creative work on the sixth day.

Creation gets thoroughly finished off in these few verses! In Hebrew, the verb translated "finished" is closely related to the word translated "all". Both words are repeated within the first two verses of this chapter. The use of so many similar sounding words so close together at this point is for deliberate emphasis. What God has desired God has now brought to pass. All is completed.

Although the noun "Sabbath" is not used, no one could have read these verses without being reminded of it. In Hebrew, the verb "rested" is *shabat* and the number "seventh" is *shebi'i*. They are similar in sound and also similar to the word "Sabbath" (*shabbat* in Hebrew). By the time this chapter of Genesis was written, the keeping of the Sabbath had become a distinctive mark of members of the Jewish community, both within Palestine and outside it (e.g. in Babylon or Egypt). To write the Sabbath into the very rhythm of the cosmos, as Genesis 2:1–4a does, was an extraordinary statement of self-confidence on the part of the writer. Since the Jewish community were the only people who kept the Sabbath, their existence must be as sure as creation. Even if the appearance of things at times looked very different, even if the people felt themselves to be few and getting fewer, in consecrating the seventh day God had acted to guarantee their present and their future.

The language describing how God "hallowed" the Sabbath is reminiscent of descriptions of temples being consecrated. Indeed the whole account of creation in Genesis 1:1–2:4a is subtly echoed in the description of the setting up of the Tabernacle in Exodus 39–40 (see e.g. Exodus 40:9, where the word "consecrate" uses the same Hebrew word that is translated here as "hallowed"). It is also probable that the pre-exilic Temple in Jerusalem was decorated with motifs which helped to emphasize its role as a microcosm of the created world.[4] Yet unlike the gods of pagan nations the God of Genesis had no absolute need of a temple—perhaps the very universe itself was his shrine. So instead of selecting a sacred space he has chosen for himself a sacred time to which all people can have access wherever on earth they are. And it will also offer liberation for all. Other ancient creation stories, such as *Enuma Elish*, often concluded with the gods taking a rest—after they had created human beings to order to do the work in their stead. By contrast, the biblical tradition will suggest that God's rest on the seventh day provides a model of rest for his human creation—and a model which human beings are required to emulate as they too ensure that the humans and animals whose lives they control (Deuteronomy 5:12–14) can also share in this privilege.

These few verses about the seventh day do not follow the ordered structural pattern of the previous six days. That is deliberate. Genesis will be a book in which patterns and order will be important. But it will be precisely the individuals and the events that flout the moulds which will be highlighted and give meaning to the whole. The seventh day is a foretaste of this. And this seventh day is a day without end.

These are the generations of the heavens and the earth when they were created. The short sentence at the beginning of 2:4 is a kind of seam. It reiterates the phrase "heavens and earth" and the concept of creation/created from Genesis 1:1 and was intended to round off this initial section of Genesis. At the same time, it probably points forward to what is coming next. The word "generations" used here is telling of a birth story of the earth (some other English translations actually use the word "story" at this point); elsewhere in Genesis this word often refers to a genealogical list of fathers and sons (see comments about the *toledot* in the introduction p. 6). The word might have jarred with those who first read this passage. It is an implicit reminder of how different this particular creation story is. Ancient creation accounts normally began with the—generally unhappy—family history of the gods, and the world and its population resulted from their infighting in a haphazard fashion. However, here we have not been given a prehistory or genealogy of the gods, but instead the created world has become the beloved "child" of God (although see also comments on 2:4b below).

Genesis 1:1–2:4a has set the stories shortly to come—small and large—of struggling humanity within a cosmic and transcendent framework and introduced a God whose ultimate sovereignty seems assured. It has presented us with an ideal ("very good") that the other forty-nine chapters of this book (and the rest of the Bible!) will continually struggle to realize.

Fruits of the earth
2:4b–3:24

As we turn to these chapters, it is like putting our eye to a keyhole in the middle of creation. We are being given a snapshot enlargement that focuses on one aspect of the panorama which flashed before us through Genesis 1. If Genesis 1:1 can be described as a summary of the rest of that chapter, so in turn we can think of Genesis 1:26–31 as being unpacked in Genesis 2–3.

Of course, this picture looks and feels very different from Genesis 1. The story of Genesis 2–3 is a traditional tale with ancient roots that must have been told and told again. Each time it was told the story grew, adapted and changed to fit new circumstances, yet at the same time conserved elements that had come to form an important part of the tale. The tale is rich with features such as wordplays and aetiologies, which aided this oral retelling. Most commentators also point to the anthropomorphic way in which God is pictured in these chapters: he "forms" human beings like a potter working with clay (2:7) and then is prepared to walk with them in the garden (3:8). This God feels very different from the transcendent and all-powerful creator of Genesis 1, and he is named differently as well.

Until forty (or so) years ago, mainstream biblical scholars usually suggested that these chapters came at the beginning of what was called the "J" or Yahwist section of the Pentateuch, a telling of Israel's history that was sometimes dated as early as 950 BC, the era of David or Solomon. However, the Documentary Hypothesis (J, E, D, P) on which this identification was based is now being widely questioned, and in particular there is considerable discussion of the likely date of the parts of the Pentateuch traditionally credited to the Yahwist. For example, although it was frequently suggested that Genesis 2–3 implies a Palestinian geographical context, the themes and images in Genesis 2–3 actually seem to find their closest parallels in literature written in Mesopotamia, either found within the Old Testament or coming from extra-biblical sources. Ezekiel 28:12–16 reminds us strongly of Genesis 3, while outside Genesis 2–3 the description "Eden" as a name for paradise occurs mainly in the writings of Ezekiel and Deutero-Isaiah which seem to have a Babylonian context. Among extra-biblical writing, the Epic of Gilgamesh and the Adapa myth (both from Mesopotamia) contain close thematic links to these two chapters of Genesis (see further p. 63). Does this imply that the story itself underwent substantial development and was perhaps first written down during the exile, even if it may have roots reaching back into pre-exilic Israel?

Those who incorporated these chapters within Genesis in its present form, who were probably the authors of Genesis 1:1–2:4a, wanted them to be read against that other account of creation for which they themselves were responsible. They acted as a counterpoint to and expansion of Genesis 1:1–2:4a. Genesis 3:22 with its divine plural is purposefully reminiscent of God's deliberation in 1:22. We are thus challenged to look at Genesis 1–3 as a whole, puzzling over the irony and tension that is implicit in the relationship between human beings and God.

As against the measured stateliness of Genesis 1:1–2:4a, this section has an untidy and awkward feel to it both as a literary creation and as theological reflection. Does it all hang together? Has, for example, the mention of the "tree of life" been dragged into an account that originally referred only to one tree, that of knowledge? And what about the theological ambiguities: a God who seems to want to keep his human creation in a kind of infantile ignorance to preserve his own standing?

As we read through Genesis, we will find this feature recurring at key points: two literary strands set alongside each other, ordered genealogies and stately tableaux contrasting with messy stories which reflect real life. Together they make up what for Israel was the thread of faith; a certainty regarding God's purposes and his ability to fulfil them, and an awareness that doubt, ambiguity or paradox was the friend rather than foe of true faith.

One of the features of Genesis in which 2:4b–3:24 is particularly rich is a delight in wordplays. It is difficult to understand the story fully without being aware of these. This feature of the narrative is linked to the biblical belief in the effective power of words which sound similar even if they are not technically "related" to each other.

2:4b–9 *In the day that the LORD God ...* We are immediately confronted with the different way God is named in this section: "LORD God" rather than "God" as in 1:1–2:4a. "The LORD" represents the Hebrew YHWH, the personal name of Israel's own god. It is probable that it was pronounced Yahweh (with short vowels as in "cat" and "get"). Out of reverence and to avoid taking God's name in vain, later Jews did not pronounce the name and substituted *Adonai* (= the LORD) wherever it occurs, and this was followed by the Old Greek translation. The NRSV adopts the traditional practice, reaching back to the AV, of printing LORD with small capitals when it represents the name YHWH. Throughout this section, with the exception of 3:1–7 (see below), it is YHWH God we meet.

The different namings of God were, for at least two centuries, one of the key reasons for the division of Genesis on the basis of sources. According to the classic Graf-Wellhausen version of the Documentary Hypothesis, the sections where God is called YHWH were identified as coming from the Yahwist. Yet here in Genesis 2–3 the deity is called not simply YHWH, but YHWH God. This particular designation occurs nowhere else in Genesis. So even if we argue on the basis of the presence of the name YHWH in Chapters 2–3, that these chapters come from the same source as for example in 4:1–26; 11:1–9; 15:1–21, we need to explore why it is that in these two chapters we consistently have *'elohim* (God) written alongside YHWH. Perhaps this story originally used the name YHWH, but *'elohim* was added by the final editors who placed Genesis 1:1–2:4a before it. It was a device to help to weave the two different sections together and suggest that they needed to be read alongside each other to be properly understood.

But it may also be that a theological point is being expressed when God is named as *'elohim* or as YHWH or both together.

By the time Genesis 1 was produced, the plural *'elohim* had become the generic word for "God" in Israelite and Jewish theological writings. The plural helped to convey a sense of both the universality and the transcendence of the only God of the whole world.

YHWH, the personal name of God, special to the people of Israel, conveyed a sense of intimacy, and of close interaction between YHWH and human creation and human history. The word YHWH is closely related to the Hebrew verb for "be" or "become" (see Exodus 3:14). Is YHWH used to speak of God when in immanent relationship with that which he has brought into "being", while *'elohim* reminds us at the same time that God cannot be bound and limited by creation, but also stands outside it, rather like an emperor ruling from afar? In Chapters 2–3, the dual form YHWH *'elohim* reflects the tension between these two aspects of God, which perhaps lies at the heart of the story.[5]

Made the earth and the heavens The order, the reverse of the way creation was described in 1:1–2:4a, is significant. What we are now going to read is a story that will be concerned mainly with life on earth, and even with the potential well-being of the earth itself.

Earth and its ground or soil form the foundation on which these chapters are based—quite literally. The introductory comment about the "generations" in 2:4a may even contain a veiled hint that heaven and earth are in some way the progenitors of who and what is then made. The role of the human being is preordained: it is to "serve" (NRSV: till) the ground (2:5). The destinies of humanity and ground are intertwined. When the human beings are punished for their eating of the forbidden fruit, it is the ground that suffers as much as they do themselves (3:17).

The rather long and ungainly sentence that runs from 4b to 5 accurately mirrors the Hebrew, which is equally awkward. The geography of the scene is redolent of the Middle East. Water is precious—and one possible understanding of 2:5–6 is that throughout these early chapters of Genesis it does not rain. Rain will be a new phenomenon which arrives—with a vengeance—only when the great flood begins (7:5). Until then the fertility of the ground depends completely on primeval underground springs, such as the moisture referred to in 2:6. It is when the ground is dampened by this moisture that God, the divine potter, can get to work—perhaps like all potters he needs wet rather than dry clay or earth to work with. Out of the earth God then forms a human being: the link between human and the earth is then reinforced by the deliberate punning between *'adam* ("human being", "Adam") and *'adamah* ("ground"). It is difficult to reflect this pun in English although Robert Alter's human and humus is a good try![6] Other writers have sought to express the pun by calling the human being a "groundling" or "earthling". Note that it is the human being who derives his name from the ground—rather than vice versa. This human creature is verbally as well as physically dust of the earth.

The intimacy of the mouth-to-mouth respiration with which God coaxes the human being into life is remarkable: never again in Genesis can a human being be as close to God. From now on, for better and for worse, human beings will have to work out their existence as separate beings from God. Separation can have its positive side—the whole of Genesis 1 has presented a series of separations which have resulted in a good creation. But it also has its flipside—and this biblical book will be an exploration of both its positive and negative implications. Life has originated in and come from God, how will it be sustained when humans and God travel their separate ways?

There is not a fully worked out Hebrew anthropology in these verses, but for a human being to become "a living being" both the material "dust of the ground" and the God-given "breath of life" are essential. Human beings are not immortal souls temporarily imprisoned in material bodies. We are intrinsically bodily people, and the *'adam/'adamah* pun reminds us of this.

Next Eden is made—literally a garden of "Delight" (the meaning of the word "Eden") for human beings. It is "in the east". It is unlikely that the writer had any specific place in mind, but the east, the place of sunrise and also a region known for its wisdom (e.g. 1 Kings 4:30), was the appropriate region to locate this garden of new beginning. Among all the trees of this garden two are singled out: "the tree of life", and "the tree of the knowledge of good and evil" (see further on these two trees on p. 63).

Like all good storytellers, the writer whets our appetite at this point—by telling us just a little before diverting into the luscious description of Eden's rivers. He will return to the subject of the tree of knowledge later on. The phrase "pleasant to the sight and good for food" with which the trees are described, seen as through God's eyes, anticipates the thoughts that the woman will have in 3:6. We are being prepared for what will shortly happen in the story.

A feature of 2:4–9 is the number of pairs mentioned: earth/heavens, earth/ground, shrub/plant, tree of life/tree of knowledge, good/evil. At the moment, there is only one human being, although perhaps the human being is to be paired with God. But the pairing of nature seems to act as an example for human life. There will shortly be two human beings, how will they relate? Constructive opposition can clearly be part of God's purposes, but will it be so in the case of humanity?

2:10–14 Our snapshot now opens out into a panorama. In case we felt that Eden was an insignificant far away place of which we know nothing, the picture suddenly enlarges to encompass the whole earth. The four rivers of these verses between them "skirt" the whole of the significant known world as it was known from the writer's perspective. The Tigris and Euphrates were the great rivers that made possible Mesopotamian civilization. The Pishon may stand for the Nile or may represent a smaller river in Mesopotamia. The Gihon has the same name as the spring at the foot of the hill on which Jerusalem stood (see e.g. 1 Kings 1:33). Despite the link to the land of Cush (southern Egypt/Ethiopia) which might encourage us to think about the Nile, the original readers of this text would probably also have recalled that stream in Jerusalem, "a river whose streams make glad the city of God" (Psalm 46:4). What a compliment to such a small spring—to compare it with the Tigris and Euphrates! Yet this exaggeration is a reminder that this water was the lifeblood on which Jerusalem, the biblical holy city, depended. Biblical writers such as Ezekiel (47:1), Zechariah (14:8) and the author of Revelation (22:1) link to these images in Genesis to look forward to the days when a spring will gush so copiously from the heart of Jerusalem that it will make even the Dead Sea fresh.

2:15–25 *The Lord God ... put him in the garden* The story picks up again where it left off at 2:11, yet the repeated comment that God "put" the human being in the garden makes an important new point. For the word "put" is here (unlike 2:8) translating the Hebrew root *nuah* (from which Noah will take his name) which also expresses the concept of "rest". God may have put the human being in the garden to "till" the ground, but it is certainly not the harsh back-breaking labour that human beings will later experience outside the garden. Several biblical texts which come from the time of the Babylonian exile speak longingly of entry/re-entry into Canaan as a time of "rest" (e.g. Deuteronomy 12:9). Perhaps the garden is being envisaged as a kind of long-lost promised land.

You may freely eat ... you shall die. Both eating and dying appear in the text using an emphatic Hebrew idiom. A death sentence is here being uttered if the human being contravenes Yhwh's command. It is paradoxical that so shortly after having discovered life, the human being is now threatened with death. Indeed, since he was not to eat of "the tree of the knowledge of good and evil" could he be expected to know what death meant?

What was "knowledge of good and evil"? Many different suggestions have been made: a key component seems to be that the knowledge of good and evil is something that comes with human maturity. Young children do not possess such knowledge (see Deuteronomy 1:39). Such knowledge contains various elements: common sense, appropriate judgement, moral attentiveness and consciousness of human mortality. But it also seems to include sexual maturity and awareness.

It is no accident that Hebrew regularly uses the verb "know" to describe sexual intercourse. This sexual dimension of the knowledge of good and evil will play a key part in Genesis 3; the story will not make sense without it.

Why is there this link made between human acquisition of sexual knowledge and human death? On the one hand, sexual maturity allows human beings to procreate, and allows for an increase in the human race. Without death, over population would ensue, and even God's own position might be threatened (see 3:22). And from the human perspective the nature of sexual love inevitably has a bitter-sweet aspect to it: our feelings of love for another exacerbate the pain of loss. Song of Songs 8:6 eloquently reflects on this relationship between love and death. Those who love passionately long for the immortality of the loved one.

To eat "of the tree of the knowledge of good and evil" then is to acquire all the aspects of wisdom that human adulthood implies.

When God's command is uttered in 2:16 the solitary human being is in no position to know "good and evil"—precisely because he is solitary! It is ironic that God then immediately sets about providing him with the companion that will facilitate the transgression. "It is not good that the man should be alone" is a significant statement when read in the light of the repeated pronouncement in Genesis 1 that all aspects of creation are "good".

God's first efforts don't exactly work out: though they do result in the creation and naming of the animals. The task of naming the animals is a sign of human control over them. But none of them is "a helper as his partner" (2:20; cf. 2:18) for the human being. Their very lack of human speech emphasizes the loneliness of the human being. They are almost like toys with which the child-like human plays in God's garden.

Helper as his partner is a very precise expression. The traditional translation "help meet for him" does not bring out the equality of the two beings that stand before God. The woman is the counterpart of the man. "Helper" does not equate with "assistant": God is frequently described as the helper of Israel (e.g. Exodus 18:4; Psalm 33:20). Ancient commentators such as Philo and Ephraem the Syrian suggested that until the making of the woman in 2:22-23 the human being was in some sense androgynous. He had not been diversified by sexuality. That individuation now takes place, as the woman is made (literally "built") out of the original human being by God, and man and woman greet each other. "At last", God gets it right: the words with which the man begins to speak perhaps suggest a degree of frustration with God's previous fumblings. And now the man's attention seems to be focused on the woman to an extent that must inevitably lead to him drifting away from God.

This is the first time the human being has used direct speech in Genesis. The ability to speak is what marks off human beings from the animals (and enables them to become close to God). It is appropriate that the first human speech relates to another human being.

The words are few but exquisitely measured, drawing attention to the way that the one has now become two. They are also poetry, and as above (see p. 28) the formal parallelism of Hebrew poetry draws attention to the interplay of one and two. The human being now speaks of himself as *'ish* (= man/male) rather than *'adam*, and with a pun that is fortuitously possible also in English addresses the *'ishshah* (= woman). Male and female are intertwined in the phrases of 2:23. The unity between the two is further reinforced by the writer's explanatory comment in 2:24.

Yet is this unity enough in the relationship of man and woman? It is only when we are aware of differences from others that a real partnership with them becomes possible. It is the difference as well as the similarity of man and woman that will make procreation possible. For the moment, they play together child-like in Eden, as happily naked together as toddlers splashing in a paddling pool. But the final words of the chapter suggest that there is more to come, as the description *'arummim* (= naked) points us towards the *'arum* (= cunning) serpent whom we will meet so shortly. Is it not the very infantile innocence of the man and the woman which will leave them open to the wiles of the serpent?

3:1–7 We now meet a talking serpent. Although later reworkings of Genesis 3 personified this serpent as Satan, that is not how he is portrayed here. Wriggling "Satan" into this passage has encouraged the reading of this story as a "fall". But snakes are sinister enough. They played an ambiguous role in Israel's religion, ranging from the plague of serpents in the wilderness (Numbers 21:6–9), to the mysterious snake-statue of Nehushtan that was kept in the Jerusalem temple for centuries until eventually expelled in Hezekiah's reform (2 Kings 18:4). It is telling that the Hebrew word for snake or serpent (*nahash*) comes from the same root as the word for "divinization", an activity which is referred to in the stories of Jacob and of Joseph, there too with an ambiguous feel (see p. 320 and p. 240). Snakes also have an ominous role in other Middle Eastern myths and legends: in the Epic of Gilgamesh a snake snatches the plant of eternal youth out of Gilgamesh's grasp—an intriguing parallel to the snake's role in the Garden of Eden.

Physical features of the snake help to explain its role in such stories. The snake renews its own skin, an apparent sign of its ability to recreate life. The skin looks naked—which would remind a Hebrew speaker of its "cunning" (see notes on 2:25 above). Its obvious resemblance to the male sexual organ facilitated its association with both life and sexuality, as in Genesis 3. And as one of the few poisonous creatures in the Middle Eastern world, it was most definitely feared.

The serpent engages the woman in conversation. Suddenly the name YHWH disappears; in 3:1–7, they speak only of God. The closeness and intimacy with YHWH God that had once been part of life in the garden has gone.

The conversation between the two parties has an opaqueness about it. Is the woman telling the truth when she tells the serpent that God told them not "to touch" the fruit of the tree of knowledge? That was not precisely what was stated in 2:16. So is the woman being super-cautious, or is it a lie which is the first stage of her determined journey to make her own decisions without reference to God? And as for the serpent, are his seductive words in 3:5 true or false? After eating the apple, the man and woman do know good and evil, and they do not die—at least not immediately.

What happens is in large measure an allegory of the maturing of human beings both as individuals and as society (in Romans 7:7–12, Paul seems also to suggest this). As the episode progresses, the woman seems to be experiencing a sexual awakening. One by one the senses come into play, and the words "delight" and "desired" with which the fruit is described have a deliberately erotic quality to them. The serpent with its phallic shape is an appropriate instructor for this topic. It may also explain why the woman eats of the fruit before the man, since girls normally mature sexually at an earlier age than boys. And the desire of the woman and the man then to conceal their genitals is an understandable one for these now sexually mature adults, who are being constrained by the expectations of society.

There is of course a wider awakening. As suggested above sexual maturation is an important part of a wider development that takes place as humans reach adulthood. Human beings long to be wise: "... the tree was to be desired to make one wise". There was an extensive wisdom tradition in Israel linked to the name of Solomon that is reflected in the Old Testament. Wisdom sought to enable people to make sense of and control their lives, and the society in which they lived. Yet the Old Testament also reflects a somewhat uneasy attitude towards such wisdom. Did not wisdom seek to encourage human beings in their autonomy? Where was the place for God, and particularly the God of Israel in wisdom's scheme of things? Did not this quest for wisdom ultimately lead Solomon himself astray? Can human beings really understand the deepest mysteries of their existence, the problem of suffering, the issues of life and death or does the fullest wisdom belong only to God (Job 28:12–24)? The book of Job presents such dilemmas with which Israel's history sought to wrestle.

Here in Genesis 3, a similar ambiguity about wisdom comes to the fore, as the woman and the man gain knowledge only to become aware of the nakedness and vulnerability of human wisdom. As human beings grow up, we learn about our mortality. We know enough to know that we are going to die, but we do not know enough to prevent it. That is both our glory and our tragedy.

The eyes of both were opened, and they knew that they were naked ... they ... made loincloths for themselves. The very first thing that human beings come to "know" after eating of the fruit of the "tree of the knowledge of good and evil" is that they are "naked". The sound link between the words "naked" and "cunning", a concept that could be described as the perversion of knowledge and wisdom, makes this consequence punningly appropriate (see above, 2:25). The motif of clothing, especially clothing used with cunning to conceal truth and reality, will become increasingly important in Genesis, especially in the stories of Jacob and his sons. It is thus bitterly ironic that "clothing", this indirect "fruit" of the tree of knowledge, becomes eventually a means to hide genuine wisdom (see also p. 350).

It is quite rare in the Bible to find the phrase "eyes ... opened" in the passive voice. One of the few other occasions is in Luke 24:31, when, at Emmaus, the eyes of the disciples are opened during the course of a meal and they realize who their companion is. Whether or not Luke was intentionally drawing a link to Genesis the congruence of opened eyes, the eating of food, and a foundational story about life and death is intriguing.

3:8–19 *Where are you?* is the first question in the Bible. God has never needed to ask a question before. The question reflects the increasing alienation between God and human beings. Yet at the same time asking and answering questions is one of the best ways for human beings to develop. The pathos of what is happening is emphasized by the way that Yhwh God (the name is now back again for a few more verses until the couple are sent out of Eden) is "walking in the garden" as he asks that question. It is the moment in Genesis when God is depicted most anthropomorphically, most like a human being himself. Human beings are so near to God—and yet soon so very far. The sense of alienation develops as the man uses a repetitious sentence in an attempt to blame both God and the woman for what has happened: "The woman whom you gave to be with me, she gave me fruit." In turn, the woman's efforts to throw the blame on the serpent symbolize the lack of solidarity between the animal world and humanity that will exist from now on and which will form part of God's curse. The verbs in 3:10–14 are starkly singular (the "I"s contrasting with the earlier "we" used by the woman in 3:2–4). "Naked" (*'arummim*) "crafty" (*'arum*) ... and now "cursed" (*'arur*) (3:14,17): the three words are linked by their sound in Hebrew. There has been a circuitous but perhaps inevitable journey which has led from one to the other.

In three brief poems, one after another God confronts in turn the serpent, woman and man. The parallelism of each poem helps in each case to emphasize a once close pair now divided and disunited. First the woman and the serpent, then the woman and the man, and finally the man (here *'adam*) alienated from the earth (*'adamah*). Each of the parties has a penalty to pay—and the penalty for each one impinges upon others than themselves. Our actions always have consequences which affect others. The serpent's penalty will lead to danger for the woman and her brood, the woman's penalty will involve a change in the man's relationship with her, and the man's penalty will affect the earth or *'adamah*. The earth is the only party who had not taken part in what has just happened, yet the buck seems to stop with it!

Two of the poems allude to childbirth or descendants. That is appropriate in view of the new knowledge that the man and the woman have just gained.

Two of the poems speak of labour deliberately using the same Hebrew word, although unfortunately the NRSV does not preserve the link in its translation. The woman's "labour" ("pangs") in childbirth is compared to the man's "labour" ("toil") in the fields. Yet this equality of language does not reflect a future social equality between the sexes. The parity that was implied by 1:27 and 2:23 and by the expression "helper as his partner" (2:20) has been profoundly dislocated. Now a hierarchy has developed, and the man will "rule over" the woman.

On the face of it the future looks bleak. These verses were certainly written in the knowledge of the harsh agricultural conditions that prevailed in much of the Ancient Middle East, and in awareness of the dangers of childbirth for women (perhaps 50 per cent of adult women died through giving birth). But if the original blessing of Genesis 1:28 was to "Be fruitful and multiply", is it a curse or a blessing that the man and the woman are now adult enough to begin to live out God's first hopes for humanity? The woman's childbearing pains may have been multiplied, but at least that meant that she could now multiply as God had wished!

3:20-24 When the man named his wife Eve (*hawwah*) because she was the mother of all who live (*hay*), did he do so ironically—in view of her responsibility for this new era in which difficulty and death would predominate? Or did he do so in truth, since it was only through the woman's initiative in eating the fruit that procreation had now become possible? Perhaps the writer wants us to keep both possibilities in mind.

And what of the gesture of Yhwh in giving the couple animal skins for clothes? Was it a generous action, showing care for his human creation and enabling them to survive the rigours of life outside the garden? Or is it rather a making permanent of the situation that had been initiated by the couple themselves when they made themselves temporary clothing of leaves (3:7) and thus effectively segregated themselves from God? Once again, the ambiguity may be deliberate. At any rate, the verbal punning which began in 2:25 with the word "naked" reaches its conclusion here with "skins" (*'or*), which sounds similar in Hebrew. We have travelled through naked . . . crafty . . . cursed . . . finally to land up with the human beings clothed yet also banished permanently from the garden where a naked innocence had been possible and human beings had nothing to conceal from God.

A defining moment is being reached. The divine plural of the statement "the man has become like one of us" recalls the moment of the original creation of humanity in 1:26–27 when God also spoke in the plural (see p. 26). There are other deliberate similarities between what God says now and what he said then. In both cases, the likeness between human beings and God is referred to. Yet something strange has happened. Then it was at God's initiative and with God's blessing that human beings were created in God's image and likeness. Now Yhwh God seems to be jealous of and threatened by such a similarity. Indeed, Yhwh God at this point resembles the gods of Greek and Babylonian myths who feel threatened and disturbed by the increase in the human population and decide to take vindictive action against humans. In now knowing good and evil, human beings have gained the ability to create/procreate which up till then has been a prerogative of the divine.

Procreativity and immortality added together would be a recipe for imminent overcrowding of the earth! There is a logic in Yhwh God's action, in sending forth the human beings from the one place where they would have been able to eat of the "tree of life" and defy the mortality that the Old Testament believed was intrinsic to human beings, and which is emphasized once again by the description of the man's role "as to till the ground from which he was taken".

But is it a total disaster for humanity? Some English translations load the situation with particular theological weight by using the verb "banish" to speak of humanity leaving the garden. The NRSV's "sent him forth" has a more neutral ring to it. Certainly, there is no going back to Eden, since

God had stationed the "cherubim", fierce winged beasts whose statues traditionally guarded temples, to prevent their return. The man and the woman have indeed been driven out from Yhwh God's presence, as Cain will be in 4:14. But perhaps the writer's comment at 2:24 can also stand as a reflection on what takes place in Chapter 3. The man has now grown up and left his parent God, and as he cleaves to Eve his wife, the two together prepare to face the challenge of their new life.

Brothers and sons
4:1–6:8

Genesis 4 is in many ways the continuation of Genesis 2–3 and deliberately spirals round to revisit some of the themes that were introduced in the garden of Eden. The verbal echoes of the earlier narrative remind us that our actions are influenced both by previous history and our environment. Correspondingly most of Chapter 5 has a close affinity with 1:1–2:4, though it was also written in a knowledge of the text now found in Genesis 4. There are some strange links between the two chapters themselves—note some names given in the genealogy of Cain in 4:17–24, which are similar or identical to the names given in the list of Seth's descendants in 5:1–26.

The two streams finally knit together in the announcement of the birth of Noah (5:28–32). They are complementary and together they are setting the parameters which will help us—and the later characters of Genesis—work out the meaning of our humanity once Eden has been left behind. There are also clear verbal connections between 5:29 and 6:5–8, verses which offer the first of two explanations for God's decision to bring the flood. Taken together the connections between the chapters encourage us to see the history of humanity from creation to flood as connected pieces within an overall pattern—albeit a largely pessimistic one.

4:1–16 The story of Cain and Abel conveys several messages, some explicit, others almost subliminal. It suggests that the hostility between the farmer and the shepherd, which has traditionally been a feature of

Middle Eastern life, goes back to the beginning of human existence. The sharp differences in climate in a small area such as east of Jerusalem, where the rainfall differential in a space of only ten miles is striking, accentuated this hostility, for it meant that groups with contrasting lifestyles lived in close proximity to one another. The antagonism of the biblical tradition to aspects of Canaanite agricultural and urban culture may also be reflected—Cain has connections with both agriculture and city-dwelling. There is a hint that sacrifice may not be totally desirable. But above all it is a story of two brothers, and as such could be said to act as an introduction to the rest of the book of Genesis, which spends Chapters 12–50 digging deep into the meaning of brotherhood. The teasing out of the implications of the benefits and stresses of "duality" to which we have been introduced in Genesis 1–3, is focused in this archetypal relationship.

4:1 dives in with the consequences of what has happened in Genesis 3. "The man knew his wife Eve"— To describe sexual relations in this way suggests one important consequence of eating from the tree of knowledge. And the one named as the "mother of all living" in 3:20 starts to live out her role. She is very sure of herself: "I have produced (*qaniti*) a man with the help of the LORD", punning on the name of Cain (see above). She seems to be claiming a kind of equality with YHWH in the role of creation—indeed simply "with the LORD" may more accurately convey the sense of the Hebrew here, though too daring for most translators. The word "man" (*'ish*) to describe the newborn Cain is striking since both in Hebrew and English this normally refers to an adult male. It may deliberately recall the triumphal cry of 2:23, when YHWH God's making of *'ish* and *'ishshah* was celebrated. But Eve's exclamation seems almost designed to exclude her husband. Is it a symptom of the lack of harmony that has developed between the couple (3:16) and will such imbalances in creation that have resulted from the action of the man and the woman in Genesis 3 also have their effects on the next generation?

Cain, the firstborn, seems to have everything going for him: the focus of his mother's attention. By contrast, Abel seems an afterthought. There is no obvious rejoicing in his birth, and his very name Abel means "nothingness"! (It is the word translated "vanity" in the famous opening passage of Ecclesiastes.) Is this the reason that "the LORD had regard for

Abel and his offering"—because the God of the Bible does have a bias towards those whom the world regards as of little account? Throughout Genesis we will discover a marked disposition in favour of younger sons. Perhaps it is significant also that Abel brought the choicest parts of his animals, "their fat portions". But it is notable too that it is the sacrifice of the brother who worked the land (*'adamah*) and who offers its fruits which is rejected. Is this the "curse" pronounced on the earth in the previous chapter working itself out?

This is the first time human beings have offered sacrifice. Sacrifice created communion with a deity: were Cain—and Abel—born outside Eden, intending by their actions to try and restore for themselves a closeness with Yhwh that their parents had lost? Adam and Eve had "grown up" and become independent of their parent God, but perhaps Adam and Eve's own children wanted to revert to being children before God once again. If so, then Yhwh clearly needs to go on a parenting course! His way of dealing with the two brothers, and particularly with Cain, does not on the surface show him as the ideal father. The theme of sibling rivalry runs through the Bible, often provoked by a father's favouritism. Yhwh seems as inept a parent as Jacob and David are later to be (see e.g. Genesis 37:3; 2 Samuel 13–20), and the consequences are as dramatic as occurred among Jacob's and David's sons.

Yet maturity demands that we leave behind us jealousy of our brothers and sisters—perhaps what Yhwh is doing is forcing Cain to "grow up" before he is ready or able to do so. Life *is* unfair but it is the mark of an adult to be able to accept this. Cain is an angry adolescent.

The metaphor of sight resonates through these verses. Yhwh "had regard for"—literally "looked upon"—Abel and his offering but did not "regard" Cain. In consequence Cain's "countenance fell", so that he looked at neither Yhwh nor his brother Abel. Yhwh in response seems to be challenging him to continue to look upon his brother. Instead, he kills Abel, believing that he has thereby removed his rival from Yhwh's presence. But in doing so he ironically removes himself too, as he is forced to confess "I shall be hidden from your face". He discovers too late that if we want to look upon the face of God the route to do so is via the face of our brothers and sisters, who have been created in God's own image—a theme that will be revisited in the story of Jacob and

Esau, Genesis 32–33. Alienation from our fellow human beings results inevitably in alienation from God, just as the separation from God in Chapter 3 has led ultimately to this separation between the brothers. The first question of God, the "Where are you?" of 3:9 leads inevitably to the second question "Where is your brother Abel?" of 4:9.

There is another progression that climaxes in this chapter. In Genesis 1:18,28, the destiny of human beings is to rule over the earth, in the same way as the sun and moon ruled over day and night. In Genesis 3:16, the man rules over the woman, a symptom of the new disordering of relationships. In 4:7, the expression is recapitulated once again as Cain is warned that he must "master" or rule over sin. Unless human beings can master themselves, they cannot master their world!

The consequence of this is expressed in the other aspect of the punishment of Cain. Cain will be "cursed from the ground", a stark fate for a child of Adam who had been created from the ground or *'adamah* (see 2:7), especially one whose life's work had been to tend it. The breach between Cain and the earth, a breach that leads on from the original fracture of 3:17, is described vividly and concretely. Then it had been the earth which was cursed, and now it is Cain. It is as though the earth (*'adamah*), polluted with the blood (*dam*) of Abel, cannot "stomach" Cain anywhere near it. Our actions do not simply have repercussions upon our fellow human beings—they affect the environment in which we live.

Does the description of Cain as "a fugitive" and "a wanderer", two words which alliterate in Hebrew (*na'*, *nad*), imply that he is being condemned to life as a nomad? Since Genesis is generally positive about the nomadic life, more probably we should think of the perpetual moving and shaking of the earth itself in an earthquake, along with the terror of those who try to flee it. Cain's eventual destination is the "land of Nod"; but even there he will not find rest, for "Nod" is related to the word for "wanderer" and so means something like "Land of the Restless Life". He has lost his way, spiritually as well as physically. This land "east of Eden" would have reminded early readers of Genesis of Israel's own time and place of exile. Yet it is also a place where hope is possible. In this faraway land, which was away "from the presence of the Lord", his writ still runs. His will to protect this murderer is a statement that his power extends beyond his "home" territory. The "mark" of Cain is ambiguous:

both blessing and curse. No one, not even the first murderer, stands outside God's grace. The special "seven" makes its first reappearance since Genesis 1, with God's pledge of "sevenfold vengeance" on anybody who attacked Cain. Yet there must have been times when Cain wished his restless and guilt-ridden life could be ended by the release of death. Is it significant that Cain is one of the few male characters of Genesis whose death is not recorded?

4:17-26 The rest of this chapter will offer a pessimistic but realistic assessment of how the violence begun by Cain then multiplies by geometric progression—assisted by the development of human technologies. The ghosts of Cain have floated around the corridors of the Middle East ever since.

In the writer's mind, Cain may have been associated with the Kenites—a tribe of metal workers who were associated with the Israelites in later history (see 4:22). Cain's is an untidy genealogy—contrasting with the much more ordered list in Genesis 5. The untidiness accentuates the sense of chaos that is a result of a lack of control among Cain's offspring.

Was it Cain or was it his son, Enoch, who built the first city? It is not clear but the link between cities and the family of Cain is notable. Cities were a development out of the agricultural mode of life, and the first great cities originated in the east from Israel's geographical perspective. The Old Testament is ambiguous about the benefits and drawbacks of city or urban life. Cities could aid civilization—but they could also become the locus of oppression, violence and even murder.

Back in 4:7, Cain's sin had been identified as a force of "desire" almost outside himself. Freud wrote of something similar which he identified as the "id". Without the "id" of desire there would not be the energy for human progress or creative activities. Yet desire also needs to be controlled; otherwise it is ultimately destructive.

Cain's descendants witness to these characteristics of humanity. They discover new technology, they evolve the performing arts, all of which are important in the development of city life, but in the person of Lamech, the seventh generation from Adam, they give vent to unbridled violence. A city is a place of blessing if brothers and sisters dwell there together in unity—but perhaps it would be too much to expect the descendants of Cain to take to heart the meaning of brotherhood. The last words that are said about the family of Cain are ones of violence (4:23–24). The exaggeration of the number seven in Lamech's boastful speech threatening violence "seventy-sevenfold" jar when we remember what seven signified in Genesis 2:1–4a. Have we reached a dead end?

But God starts again—as happens often in this book. Another son is born to Eve, and once again she makes a play on his name. He is called Seth because God had "appointed" (Hebrew: *shat*) her a son. This time her jubilation is muted in comparison with the words used at the birth of Cain. Has Eve discovered that there is more to creating than merely giving birth? Cain, her first "creation" had himself brought death rather than life. This time, God's rather than Eve's own role in the birth is emphasized. According to the NRSV, she refers to "another child", but the literal meaning of the Hebrew here is "other seed". The term both reminds us of the disaster in the garden and the fact that the serpent would strike at the seed (NRSV: "offspring") of the woman (3:15), but also looks forward to the patriarchal narratives (e.g. 12:7; 15:18), where the term "seed" will feature as a sign of hope in the promises to Abraham, although it is not always apparent in English translations (since it is often translated "descendants"). Is there a wistfulness in Eve's use of the word "God" (4:25)—a longing for the immanent Yhwh who had walked with her in the garden, who has been replaced by the more distant "God", creator of the universe? Human beings are gradually moving away from their original intimacy with Yhwh, but they will shortly find a new way of relating to him.

To Seth also a son was born, and he named him Enosh. Enosh is an alternative Hebrew word for "human being", often used in contexts of weakness. In Enosh's time, "people began to invoke the name of the Lord", a biblical idiom for worship. Is it the sense of human frailty reflected in the name Enosh which has led to a sense of dependence on God which needs now to be expressed in worship? It was a need that could only have been discovered by Seth's heirs, since Cain's descendants were so confident in their own strength. Yhwh is now a god to be worshipped rather than a friend and sparring partner walked with in the garden.

Yet the very name—Y$_{HWH}$—by which Enosh and humanity choose to worship suggests a God with them.

5:1-27 The clue to reading Genesis 5 is found in the first verse of the chapter. We are led back to 1:26-28, when human beings were created in God's likeness and blessed by him. The ten remarkably long-lived generations (once again a perfect number) of the genealogy in this chapter suggest that humans are living out this blessing by "filling" the earth—although we will shortly hear that this "filling" has a negative side to it as well (6:11).

The similarity between the names in this list and those of the descendants of Cain in Chapter 4 may suggest that there was a common oral tradition which gave the names of people of "ancient" days, or perhaps more likely, that the author of Genesis 5 has chosen to adapt the list of names found in the previous chapter as a means of emphasis that the responsibility for moral choices rests firmly with humanity—we cannot use biological difference as a justification for evil choices. The genealogy, introduced by a phrase including the strategic word *toledot* ("list of the descendants", 5:1), which last appeared in 2:4a, is one of the dividing points of Genesis, telling us that one part of the story is closing while another is soon to begin.

Although the lifespans given to these figures seem fantastic, there are Babylonian texts which give heroes living before the flood even longer lives such as 20,000+ years. Methuselah therefore is a mere stripling at only 969! The assignation of dates in Genesis has a logic to it—even if the numbers are unrealistic (see below on Enoch, Lamech and Noah).

Adam ... became the father of a son in his likeness, according to his image, and named him Seth. Since Adam was himself made in the divine likeness this means that Seth was also. (Genesis nowhere suggests that the divine image was lost to humankind as a result of the events of Genesis 3.) On the basis of this comment, a wealth of traditions about Seth developed in later Judaism and early Christianity. Many of these were heretical in flavour: the name of Seth crops up frequently in the Gnostic writings discovered at Nag Hammadi in Egypt.

Enoch walked with God; then was seen no more, because God took him. Enoch is a mystery. He is the seventh, a sacred position, in the list from Adam with a far shorter lifespan than the other patriarchs: only 365 years!—the link with the 365 days of the solar year is no accident. His name means something like "Dedicated", and along with Noah he is the only person who "walked with God". In Enoch's case, the result of this was that he did not die as did other humans (see e.g. Hebrews 11:5–6), because God removed him. Against the stark backcloth of the repeated phrase "and he died" applied to every other figure in this list, Enoch's alternative destiny is a reminder that God too lives in the tension between life and death.

There is an extensive literature in which the figure of Enoch is prominent. 1 Enoch is the most important example (the book seems to have been considered scripture by early Christians, e.g. Jude 14–15), but the name of Enoch also crops up in Sirach 44:16 and 49:14 and in the Book of Jubilees. The strange story of Enoch clearly fascinated people. Not surprisingly he seems to have been a particular hero for those (like the writers of the Dead Sea Scrolls) who sought to follow a solar calendar rather than the lunar calendar employed by official Judaism in the post-exilic period.

It is likely that when Genesis 5:22–24 was written, there were already stories and legends circulating about Enoch and these verses are the tip of an iceberg, most of which remains hidden from our eyes (although the stories would probably have been known to the first readers of Genesis and would have helped them make sense of this curt and cryptic note). A similar situation applies to the strange story of the intermarriage between the "sons of God" and the "daughters of humans" in 6:1–4. 5:22–24 and 6:1–4 seem to be in some way related, and both reflect the undercurrents of the tension between human knowledge and human immortality that is a central theme in Genesis 1–11.

The days of Methuselah were nine hundred and sixty-nine years; and he died. The lifetime of Methuselah, the longest lived of the patriarchs, has been nicely timed to ensure that he lived almost to the moment when the great flood began.

The days of Lamech were seven hundred and seventy-seven years. Lamech's lifespan, which is shorter than most of his ancestors, is explained by two factors. He needs to be dead before the flood starts(!), and there is an apparent cross-reference to 4:24, where another figure also called Lamech is associated with multiples of the number seven. But this Lamech speaks with a piety (verse 29) which contrasts with his counterpart, and his age suggests completeness. Seven has been restored to its honoured place in God's schema.

5:28-32 *Noah ... Out of the ground that the L*ORD *has cursed this one shall bring us relief from our work and from the toil of our hands.* Verses 28-32 not only conclude the genealogy of Genesis 5, but also allude to the earlier story of Genesis 2-4, the curse that is referred to in 3:17 and the "pangs/toil" to which Eve and Adam are condemned in 3:16 and 17.

Noah is an exceptional person. He is the representative of the perfect tenth generation, the first of the patriarchs to be born after Adam had died, and the first to be born in a new millennium. A new start is going to begin with him. He waits far longer than any of the other patriarchs (exactly half a millennium) before becoming a father. Like Enoch, he "walked with God" (6:9, see notes below p. 72).

There is an elaborate "pun" on the name of Noah worked into 5:29 and 6:5-8. Noah is so called because he "will bring ... relief" (Hebrew: *naham*) (5:29). The two words sound similar, although they are not etymologically related. In fact, the name Noah comes from a Hebrew root *nuah* meaning "rest". Words that come from this root *nuah* are used at key points in Genesis 1-11, although the English translations often conceal this. The ark "came to rest" (8:4) on Mount Ararat; Noah offered a "pleasing" (8:21) sacrifice, while back in Genesis 2:15 the LORD God had "put" the man (again from this same verbal root) in the garden of Eden to till it. To be "at rest" seems, in the eyes of the biblical writers, to be in a place where one rightly belongs, and where the earth will respond to the human beings who till it, without making them "weary". In 5:29, we are being given a hint of Noah's agricultural prowess which will come to the fore after the flood.

But the puns do not stop there. The sound-link made between *nuah* and *naham* allows for another set of connections. When God "was sorry" (6:6) that he had made human beings, the Hebrew verb used here also comes from the same Hebrew root, *naham*, even though in English "was sorry" and "bring ... relief" do not seem to have much in common. A link is being drawn between the emotions of God and those of human beings; indeed the one results in the other, for an ironic consequence of the flood is that the earth will from now on be easier for human beings to work, because it will have regular rainfall, and regular seasons. Similarly, in another play on words, the "toil" from which Noah will relieve humankind (which was imposed on Eve and Adam in 3:16 and 17) is also picked up in the Hebrew word that lies behind the word "grieved" which describes God's regret for the creation of human beings (6:6). Teasingly Genesis is reminding us that God and human beings belong together, and their fates and emotions are interwoven—whether either party likes it or not!

6:1–4 After the genealogy which has told us of the productivity of human beings comes the consequence: God's blessing of humanity given in 1:26–28 is being fulfilled as "people began to multiply on the face of the ground".

What comes next feels one of the strangest episodes in the whole of Genesis, and as suggested in the notes on 5:22–24, may well be the summary of a traditional legend already widely known to both the writer and his readers. There is a lot bubbling away under the surface of these few cryptic sentences, and quite possibly the narrator was embarrassed by their polytheistic undercurrent.

We are told of divine beings, members of Yhwh's heavenly court, "the sons of God" (see also Psalm 29:1; 89:5–7; Job 38:7)—who choose to intermarry with human women. Their offspring are half-divine and half-human and far larger than normal humans—in Numbers 13:33, these *Nephilim* (6:4) are described as giants. Should this offspring count as mortal along with humans, or immortal, along with Yhwh and his heavenly court? Yhwh decrees that they will be mortal—with a lifespan of "one hundred and twenty years". Probably the original implication was that this is the normal lifespan for humans—although it will not explicitly fall to that limit until the final chapter of Genesis (50:26). An alternative view is that the "hundred and twenty years" refers to the timelag between these events and the coming of the flood—which will wash away this offspring altogether! The positioning of these verses, sandwiched here between an introduction to Noah and an explanation for the flood, suggests that as Genesis was edited connections were drawn to link this episode more closely to the following deluge.

The union of heavenly beings with human women is a common motif in both Greek and Mesopotamian mythology. There are also Mesopotamian stories which explain that the great flood was caused by the excess of number and noise of the human population, and this is perhaps being hinted at here too. The narrator seems to disapprove of what has been taking place, and to choose his words accordingly. Does "took wives for themselves of all that they chose" hint at unbridled lust? The reference to polygamy may be telling; marrying more than one wife seems to bring trouble and violence in its train as with Lamech (4:19–24), Jacob, and possibly even Abraham. The story of these heavenly beings is further developed in the Enoch literature (see 1 Enoch 6–11), where a link is made between the fact that the sons of gods "knew" human women sexually and that, rather like malevolent Prometheuses, they transmitted "knowledge" of evil to human beings, leading to the flood. It is likely such legends were already in existence before Genesis reached its final form.

We have here a story about breaking boundaries set between humanity and divinity, and in that sense the story is parallel to Genesis 3. Both touch on the limited length of human life. In fact, the expression "saw that they were fair ... took" (6:2) employs the same Hebrew words chosen in 3:6 to describe the woman's perception and taking of the fruit. (The word translated in 6:2 as "fair" is the same as that translated as "good" [to eat] in 3:6.) And it is striking that on each occasion when the plurality of the divine is emphasized in Genesis 1–11 (Genesis 1:26; 3:22; 11:7 and here as "the sons of God" in 6:2) the issue at stake is the relationship between God and human beings, their closeness, but also the necessary distinction that God imposes. The descendants of this mingling of earth and heaven may be "warriors of renown" (literally "of name", Hebrew: *shem*), but as we will discover later, a "name" is a gift from God rather than humanity's possession as of right.

Jewish writings from around the New Testament period tended to prefer to use stories based on Genesis 6:1–4 rather than Genesis 3 to explain the origin of evil in the world—it is perhaps more comforting to suggest that evil originates from outside human beings rather than from within!

6:5–8 It is a bleak picture of the state of humanity in these few verses. The naïve hopes for humanity with which the story of Genesis 2:4b began are turned on their head. There God had "formed" (*yatsar*) human beings, but now the inclination (*yetser*) that he had made was apparently only evil. God who in Genesis 1 had seen so much that was good, now sees only "wickedness" (6:5) or "bad".

The language used is intensive and emphatic—two words get used, in phrases such as "inclination of the thoughts" or "was sorry ... grieved", when one would have done. The punning word-links (see comments on 5:29) draw together the human condition, the reaction of Yhwh and the role of Noah as the person who will bring relief (*naham*) to human beings as well as becoming the agent through whom Yhwh's "regret" over the creation of humanity is tempered with his compassion. Relief, regret and compassion all come from the same Hebrew stem. The ebb and flow of the different meanings somehow foreshadows the chaos that is shortly to befall the earth.

Then the confusion stops abruptly, as does this first section of Genesis, with the briefest sentence and verse in Genesis so far. "Noah (from the Hebrew verb *nuah*) had won the Lord's favour (*hen*)." This final (for the moment) pun which inverts Noah's name both links us to what has gone before (e.g. 5:29) but also provides a much needed glimmer of hope for the future.

Theological reflections

1. The One and the Two

The first word of Genesis in Hebrew is *bere'shit*. There are many stories told in Jewish tradition to explain why the story of the world's creation begins with the letter "B", the second letter of the Hebrew alphabet. One response sometimes offered was that "B" (Beth) was the letter which also begins the word for "blessing"—*berakah*. And why not with an "A" (Aleph)? Answer: Because that is the first letter of the Hebrew word for "curse" (*'arur*). A more widespread tradition, however, drew attention to the fact that Beth as the second letter of the alphabet is also used to represent the number two. The tradition suggests that Beth was chosen for this honour precisely because duality permeates the created universe. That is certainly an insight that resonates through Genesis: creation in Genesis 1 is effected through a series of divisions or bifurcations; in Genesis 2 the animals are clearly "paired"—contrasted with the human being whose aloneness is "not good"; later the animals will enter the ark two by two. And then there will be the brothers whom we will meet—often in pairs—throughout most of Genesis.

Yet rabbinic tradition also held that behind this duality of creation lay the fundamental unity of God. The unifying aloneness of God is proclaimed through the Shema: "Hear, O Israel, the Lord is our God, the Lord alone" (Deuteronomy 6:4), in biblical passages such as Isaiah 44:24, and in the great medieval Jewish hymn "Lord of the world, he reigned alone".

These first few chapters of Genesis introduce us to the theme with which the entire book will be wrestling, both explicitly and implicitly. How can, or should, the "one" and the "two" relate to each other—so that neither dominates nor disappears? Both unity and duality are necessary. And human beings are required to live at the very heart of this conundrum—precisely because we are "in the image of God". The concept of image itself locates us somehow between the one and the two. An image is not identical to that which it "images"—yet at the same time it cannot be wholly apart from it. The task is to live properly in the world of duality—for that is the world in which God has set us—but at the same time to perceive and focus within ourselves the underlying unity of God. Commenting on the eating of the fruit of the tree of the knowledge of good and evil, Carol Ochs writes:

> The real problem represented by the tree is . . . that the serpent so focuses us on duality that we lose sight of the underlying unity. When we age, we need bifocal eye glasses. One sort of bifocal vision—seeing both duality and deeper unity at the same time—opens us to the context in which we have been set down and the awareness of the creator in and with the creation . . . our capacity to recognize both differences and underlying unity allows us to experience perspective and depth. We need both kinds of vision.[7]

A Talmudic "number poem" about the commandments is also suggestive. It begins from the traditional Jewish statement that Moses received 613 commandments from God and goes on: David reduced them to eleven (Psalm 15), Micah to three (Micah 6:8), Isaiah to two (Isaiah 56:1), and Amos to one (Amos 5:4). It then observes that Rabbi Akiva said that this one most important principle in the Law was "Love your neighbour as yourself: I am the LORD" (Leviticus 19:18), but finally oberves that Rabbi Ben Azzai taught a greater principle even than this: When "God created humankind in his image, in the image of God he created them" (Genesis 1:27). The rabbis were surely right that this "greater principle" underlies all the commandments. It is because we "image" God that we must honour other human beings who are also made in his "image". This will have important moral consequences, spelt out explicitly in Genesis 9:6 with its prohibition against murder. Elias Chacour's challenging comment (see p. 285) suggests what this might mean in one of the most intractable hostilities of the modern age.

The Jewish philosopher Emmanuel Levinas has worked extensively to explore the concept of "the other". He comments:

> Men [sic!] are not only and in their ultimate essence "for self" but "for others," and this "for others" must be probed deeply ... Nothing is more foreign to me than the other, nothing is more intimate to me than myself. Israel would teach that the greatest intimacy of me to myself consists in being at every moment responsible for others, the hostage of others.[8]

It is only when we acknowledge the radical otherness of the other, and yet our own responsibility towards that "other", that we cease to make an idol of ourselves.

That is the challenge to which Genesis will keep on returning throughout its fifty chapters. Already in this first section it is met with in the relationship between man and woman, and between two brothers. The delineation of the relationship between man and woman is a key motif of Genesis 2–3. The natural world described in 2:4b–9 includes a number of "pairs". This is what is intended by the creator. It is clearly "not good" for the human being, the crown of creation to be "alone". What life could he have if not life in community? His isolation is emphasized. When woman is created as a "helper as his partner", the man rejoices. But the terms in which he speaks suggest overidentification. Before man and woman can properly become one flesh of each other, they need to become completely themselves and discover their identity in relation to God. The fourth-century Syriac poet and theologian St Ephraem caught something of this in his remark, "Adam was both one and two; one in that he was man (adam), two in that he was created male and female" (Commentary on Genesis).

Perhaps there is even a similar dynamic in the life of God for it is interesting that although the fundamental image of God in Genesis 1 is one of unity, the moment when human beings are created "male and female" is precisely the time when there is a hint of a plurality in God, "Let us ... ". Writing from the Christian perspective, one can suggest that we are not far from the mystery of the Trinity, that doctrine which without compromising the unity of God holds that "life in relationship" is an essential part of the nature of God.

The challenge of the "other" also appears of course in the sibling rivalry between Cain and Abel, the first of a series of such struggles which will dominate this biblical book. The theme of "brotherhood" is discussed in more detail on p. 200 and p. 282 But in relation to this specific story, it is interesting to ponder whether the essence of Cain's sin was that he wanted God (Yhwh) for himself alone? The first act of religious worship led to the first murder. Yet he can only have God if he also has his brother. And the isolation to which he is condemned is a fitting punishment. Though he seeks to overcome this by building a city—he (and we) soon discover that there is no real community in a place where human beings have not learned what it is to be a brother or a sister.

2. The image of God: being and becoming

Though we have already touched upon the concept of "image of God" in the previous section, it is a concept that is so fundamental in Jewish and Christian theology that it deserves further exploration.

Quite literally, the "image" is remade in every age.

There are two closely related questions. What is it about human beings that means they are made in God's image? And what are the consequences of this?

A prior issue is the relationship between the two words "image" and "likeness" (1:26). Are they the same or not? Although there have been attempts, particularly in Catholic theology, to suggest a distinction, with "image" referring to the natural image, and "likeness" a supernatural characteristic, it is probable that as originally written the two terms were considered largely synonymous—and the use of both is for emphasis.

So what is it about human beings that means we can be described as "the image of God"? Answers have included:

- the physical appearance of God and human beings
- the spiritual qualities of human beings
- the human mind and ability to reason
- the capacity for human beings to have a relationship, with God, with one another and with creation.

This last, which perhaps includes elements of the two previous suggestions, is supported by Karl Barth and Claus Westermann, and has become influential in both doctrinal and Old Testament studies. That is broadly speaking the view that is taken in this commentary. Barth in fact explicitly draws out the connection with the creation of humanity as male and female. "By the divine likeness of man [sic!] in Genesis 1:27 f. there is understood the fact that God created them male and female, corresponding to the fact that God himself exists in relationship and not in isolation."[9] As Angela Tilby put it, "[t]he image of God is enfolded in our sexuality".[10] Others would challenge this as too narrow, suggesting that the "image of God" is to be found in the interrelatedness of a human being with others, regardless of whether that other is male or female. Certainly at a time of very considerable discussion about gender and sexuality in the churches, it is a reminder that Genesis is a book still with power to impact on the present.

But if we are people of relationship, with God and with each other, a primary reason for this is, as we reflect in the comments on Genesis 1:26–28, to be God's representatives or viceregents in creation (the implications of this for Christian ecological reflection are explored further on p. 91). We noted that the language of image is probably partly drawn from the practice of setting up statues of an emperor throughout the length and breadth of his realm as reminders of his power. It has been suggested that Genesis 1:26–31 could be read as a liturgy for the "enthronement" of human beings as rulers of creation. Psalm 8, where very similar ideas are stated, certainly uses the word "crowned". At a marriage service in the Eastern Orthodox tradition, the bride and groom, representing the "male and female" of Genesis 1:27, wear crowns during the ceremony to express this concept.

However, to speak of human beings as the "image" in this way has a revolutionary feel to it. There is an attractive story told about the Rabbi Hillel that vividly illustrates this. Hillel used to go to bathe regularly, and when asked why he did so, he commented that since the images (statues) of the Caesars were washed so regularly he (Hillel) also needed to wash. Because he was made in the image of God, he was greater even than a Caesar!

It is therefore telling that modern Christian (and to some extent Jewish) theological underpinning of human rights draws on the language of "image" from Genesis 1:26–28 as a fundamental cornerstone, and since the 1940s, these verses have been widely quoted in official Christian statements about human rights. Indicative examples include:

- The dignity of man is the dignity of the image of God. (Pius XII, Christmas Broadcast of 1944)
- Our concern for human rights is based on our conviction that God wills a society in which all can exercise full human rights. All human beings are created in the image of God, equal and infinitely precious in God's sight and ours. Jesus Christ has bound us to one another by his life, death and resurrection, so that what concerns one concerns us all. (World Council of Churches, Fifth Assembly, Nairobi, 1975)
- All theological statements on human rights derive from the Christian anthropology of the human person made in the image of God. (World Alliance of Reformed Churches, approx. 1975)
- According to the teaching of the book of Genesis, man is made in the image of God (cf. Genesis 1:26–27). This signifies that every human being is endowed with intelligence, will and power which exist in this full perfection, free of contingency: only in God. These gifts of God constitute the essential basis of the rights and dignity enjoyed by man as such, independent of his particular personal talents, background, education or social status. (The Church and Human Rights, Pontifical Council for Justice and Peace, 1975, 2nd edition, 2011).

It was not only the people of Israel who reflected on the nature and role of humanity. Many peoples in the Ancient Middle East did so, and these chapters are imprinted with the richness of their reflections. There are mythic images and symbols used, particularly in Genesis 2–3, that we cannot fully appreciate the significance of, perhaps because the Old Testament itself was always ambiguous about how far the mythology of other peoples should be offered space on its own pages.

So, for example, the serpent may have meant more to those readers of Genesis who had neighbours who worshipped a serpent god, while the guardian cherubim are close cousins to the Karibu who protected the entrances to the temples of Assyria. In particular, the mysterious "tree of life" would have expanded its meaning in a culture where wooden tree-like figures were venerated as sources of life and perhaps even identified by many as a representation of Asherah, the female goddess. Similarly, it is possible that the "tree of the knowledge of good and evil" may represent a parallel male principle to balance the tree of life's female one. The play and dynamics of the relationship of male and female is undoubtedly a theme in the story, but we cannot totally comprehend this because we are not fully conversant with the writer's code.

Even within the Old Testament itself there is a parallel passage which tells the human story and in which mythological elements seem to be given greater prominence than in Genesis 2–3. Ezekiel 28:1–17 tells of a creature who arrogantly seeks to become a god but who is unceremoniously flung out of God's garden.

There are also at least two extra-biblical stories about humanity that can be helpfully read alongside the early chapters of Genesis. The Sumerian Adapa myth tells of Adapa, "the man" who is bold enough to break the wing of the south wind and is summoned to the divine court to account for his actions. As he arrives in heaven, he is offered the bread and water of life, but refuses them because he has been tricked by a god into believing that they are the food and drink of death. He catches a glimpse of heaven, but then is returned to his earthly and mortal existence.

In the Babylonian Epic of Gilgamesh, Gilgamesh who is mourning his dead friend Enkidu, seeks eternal life. After a long quest he is directed by Utnapishtim (the Babylonian flood hero) to pick the precious plant of eternal life. He does so, but then it is snatched from his grasp by a serpent, and Gilgamesh like Enkidu before him is doomed to mortality.

What Genesis and these stories have in common is a recognition of the ambiguity of the human condition. In the image of God, greater than the animals, and "a little lower than God" (Psalm 8:5)—but that little lower is ultimately an unbridgeable gap. The story expresses wistfully the almosts and the might-have-beens. The interplay of human and divine wisdom adds poignancy to the ultimate acceptance that the human destiny is death. In Genesis 2–3, we can see a kind of arch: the link between the human being and the dust of the earth is categorically made clear both at the beginning and the end. But in the middle human hopes soar and for one brief moment we wonder if human beings can have it all, wisdom as well as eternal life. It is not to be. Yet perhaps it is not a "fall" that human beings experience (although Ezekiel 28 comes closer to suggesting this) but an overabrupt rise, a too hasty transition from naïvity and innocence to maturity. Human beings are children who grew up too quickly.

We can never return to Eden, and the Old Testament is aware that the way forward for humanity should not be to try and keep one foot standing there. Nor are we to become gods, for there are boundaries between divinity and humanity which must not be transgressed. But Genesis 2–3 can only properly be understood if Genesis 1:26–27 is read first. Human beings *are* created in the image and likeness of God and for relationship with him, and nowhere in the Old Testament is it stated that we have lost this image (Genesis 9:6 makes this clear; Sirach 17:3–7 even links a comment about the image with a positive appreciation of humanity's acquisition of knowledge): if we are banned now from eating from the tree of life in the garden we will need to discover a different way of reflecting God's image. God needs this no less than we do, and the pages of Genesis will seek to work out this fraught but essential relationship.

This interpretation may come as a surprise to many readers, who, coming at Genesis wearing the Christian spectacles provided by Augustine of Hippo (with the help of St Paul) have been encouraged to view the beginning of Genesis as an account of the creation followed by a "fall" of humanity. Careful analysis of Genesis 2–3, however, throws this interpretation into question and leads one to ask whether we are being presented with a story of the necessary maturing of the human race. Such a discovery has felt like a liberation to many and is a model of interpretation increasingly being explored.

Augustine's view of this story as a "fall" was never the only (though it may have been the dominant) viewpoint in Christian history. The second-century theologian Irenaeus commented on Genesis 2–3 in a way that was probably far closer to the mind of the original writers. "Being but recently made, they had no knowledge of procreation of children; they had to grow up first, then in this way to propagate themselves" (*Adv. Haer.* III, 32).

The language of image clearly has important implications for Christology. The New Testament explicitly describes Christ as the "image" of God (e.g. 2 Corinthians 4:4; Colossians 1:15; cf. Hebrews 1:3). A similar understanding is embedded in the discussion in John 1 of the revealing of God's glory through the Word become flesh. But the celebration of Christ as the "image of God" does not imply its removal from the rest of humanity. Christ bears the image precisely because he is humanity's perfection. Our problem may not be that we are too human, but that we are not human enough. The task of humanity is to show God's "glory", his visible presence "imaged" in us. This image may be marred in us, but it is our potential birthright. The New Testament episodes of Christ's transfiguration on the mountain and his ascension represent this birthright coming to fruition.

Within Christian tradition, the Eastern Orthodox theology of iconography owes a great deal to the concept of image in Genesis 1:26–28; the very word "icon" is simply the Greek translation of "image". As the material and visible icon enables the invisible and immaterial God to be sacramentally present on earth, so too human beings are his moving and breathing "icons". Irenaeus summed it up in a way that cannot be bettered: "The glory of God is humanity alive, and the life of humanity is the vision of God." Both halves of this statement are important, both belong together, and the story of Genesis takes us on a voyage of discovery to discover the potential of both.

For to speak of human beings as in the image of God says something important about God as well as about human beings. One of the features of other Middle Eastern creation stories is that they normally begin with a complicated story of interaction between different gods well before the creation of the world ever gets started. Human beings appear in the story very much as an afterthought, and normally not in the most complimentary of terms! The *Enuma Elish* pictures human beings as being made from the blood of Kingu, one of the minions of the evil goddess Tiamat.

The monotheism of the Old Testament forced God into a different relationship with human beings when compared with these polytheistic stories: despite the sense of divine transcendence that runs through Genesis 1, God still needs human beings to form relations with—even as human beings need God!

The story of the flood—and its aftermath

6:9–11:26

What is it about the story of the flood that has made it probably the Old Testament story best known to children? On the surface, a story about the almost total catastrophic destruction of the entire world seems hardly to be an appropriate tale for tender years—and yet for generations of children it has been a particular favourite. In part, it must be the dramatic possibilities of the story which have been evident at least since the time of the medieval mystery plays. In part, it must be because children (and others) can relate well to a story which focuses on the interaction between humans and animals.

The popularity of the flood story is not a modern phenomenon. The story of a great flood is one of the most widespread of all folk tales or myths. Peoples from many parts of the world have told of the inundation of the earth by a deluge. It is likely that many of these stories grew up independently, reflecting the common human dread of uncontrolled and uncontrollable water. A feature they have in common is that they remind us in a pure form of the reason for myth: we tell the story precisely because we believe that by doing so, we will prevent such a flood from coming again. This is a feature that is a part of the biblical flood story (see Genesis 9:9–16), which ends with a solemn promise on the part of God never again to visit flood on the earth.

And yet, of course, flooding would recur. The biblical flood story cannot be understood apart from the Mesopotamian accounts of the flood to which it owes several significant features, even though it also reworks the Mesopotamian tales to accommodate its own theological viewpoint. The geography and climate of Mesopotamia encouraged reflection on a "flood": civilization in Mesopotamia, the land between the great Tigris and Euphrates rivers, was only possible because of the annual flood of these rivers, swollen with waters brought down from the Taurus Mountains. Without the annual flood the elaborate irrigation systems of the Mesopotamian cities would dry up: yet in years when there was an excess of water destruction and death would result. Water brought both death and life, and that tension is there also in the biblical story, where the destruction wrought by the flood is interwoven with the thread of new creation.

There are at least three differing Mesopotamian accounts of the flood. The best known is that set within the Epic of Gilgamesh. Gilgamesh in his quest for eternal life seeks out the survivor of the flood, Utnapishtim, who has been privileged to have been granted eternal life by the gods. Utnapishtim recounts to Gilgamesh the story of his experiences, and why it is that he was specially chosen. A much older story (on which the saga of Utnapishtim itself depends) was told by the Sumerians, whose civilization in southern Mesopotamia flourished in the third millennium BC. The name of the hero in this account was Ziusadra. There is also a third version, which is in some ways the closest to the biblical tale. In this version the hero who escapes the flood is Atrahasis—"the exceeding wise".

There are also apparently two accounts of the flood in Genesis, in Chapters 6–9. Unlike the creation stories of Genesis 1 and 2, we are not given two consecutive accounts; rather two versions are interwoven with each other throughout, including, for example, two apparently different sets of instructions as to the number of animals to be taken onto the ark, two different chronologies for the period of the flood, and two different conclusions.

The two versions of the flood story

	A	B
Chronological information about Noah		6:9–10; 7:11
Reason for flood	6:5–8	6:11–13
Noah told to build Ark		6:14–18a
Number of animals to take	7:1–5	6:18b–22
Entry into the Ark	7:7–10	7:13–16a
Y<small>HWH</small> closes the Ark	7:16b	
Description of flood	7:22–23	7:18–21
Length of rain/flood	7:12,17	7:24; 8:4–5; 8:13–14
Flood stops	8:2b–3a	8:1–2a
Sending out of birds	8:6–12	
Exit from Ark		8:15–19
Noah sacrifices/new relationship with God	8:20–22	9:1–17

The material in column A has affinities with Genesis 2:4b–4:26 and that in column B with Genesis 1:1–2:4a and Genesis 5. This apparent doubling in the narrative complicates and challenges the assumptions of source-criticism. On the one hand, it *is* difficult to accept that one writer could be solely responsible for what appear to be two versions of the same story intertwined together; on the other hand, it is not feasible that any final editor would weave together the two strands without noticing the kind of discrepancies that also perplex modern readers. The question is: accepting the possibility that Genesis 6–9 features two different retellings of the traditional story of the Flood, what is the reasoning behind this apparently confused conflation of them in the final edition of Genesis? The setting of Genesis 1:1–2:4a alongside Genesis 2:4b–3:24 provided us with alternative and contrasting views about the nature of humanity:

what does the intermingling of their counterpart narratives in Genesis 6–9 suggest to us?

We need to remember that the interaction between "duality" and "unity" is a focus throughout the whole of Genesis. The working together of "one" and "two" is presented as the ideal goal of creation. This is expressed perfectly by the ordered narrative of Genesis 1:1–2:4a in which number plays such an important part in the establishment of the "good" creation. Conversely the "breakdown" or dissolution of creation, which is how the flood is portrayed in Genesis, is aptly reflected in the numerical confusion in these chapters and the very fact that we have two narratives that are woven rather uncomfortably together. This jarring sense of de-creation is emphasized particularly through the contradictory references to time in the narrative. Since the establishment of time was such a central focus of Genesis 1:1–2:4a, it is appropriate that "creation undone" is marked by it ceasing to work properly. Yet for all these inconsistencies Genesis 6–9 does have an underlying structure—noted by Bernhard Anderson, it is a chiastic or concentric form, in which the beginning corresponds to the end—and the narrator encourages us to work towards the middle, the most important moment.[11] In this case, that is Genesis 8:1, and the moment when "God remembered Noah". Similar chiastic structures mark out other sections of Genesis—the story of Abraham and that of Jacob.

We have included the "post-flood" episode of the Tower of Babel, again reflecting a Mesopotamian geographical context, and the two genealogies which surround it, both introduced by the *toledot* formula, in this section. There is uncertainty as to where precisely they belong, and they seem to be used within the structure of Genesis both to conclude the primeval history and to open up the story of Abraham which follows. The focus on unity in the story of the Tower of Babel provides an intriguing contrast with the dualities which permeate the story of the flood.

Taken as a whole this section seems to "replay" similar themes and motifs to those which were introduced in Genesis 1:1–6:8. The parallels have often been noted.

Parallels in Genesis 1–11

1:1–2:25	6:9–9:17	Creation/uncreation/re-creation
3:1–24	9:20–21	Problems with a fruit
4:1–16	9:22–27	Competition between brothers
4:17–5:32	10:1–32; 11:10–26	Genealogies
6:1–4	11:1–9	Breaking human/divine boundaries
6:5–8	11:27–32	Interlude introducing next section

By "replaying" the first section of Genesis in this way the material in Chapters 6 to 11 implicitly poses a key question about God's dealings with creation, and particularly humanity. The flood is God's statement that his first efforts had "gone wrong" so drastically that he felt the need to start afresh. But when the new world that emerges from the deluge seems to have so many of the same problems as did the old, what will God do this time? Will he need to start over again—again—or is there another, and better, way forward?

Washing the world clean
6:9–9:28

The introductory comments about the story of the flood which have been given above emphasizes how this long narrative dominates the second section of Genesis.

6:9–22 *These are the descendants of Noah.* A new section of Genesis has begun—introduced by the key word *toledot*—which contains within itself the idea of "birthing" or giving life. Yet this new section will start with so much death.

"Noah was a righteous man, blameless in his generation." This is the first time in Genesis that anybody has been described as "righteous", and it is a term that will be used very sparingly in the future. Abraham's bargain with God over the fate of Sodom suggested that a few righteous men might be able to save a whole community (19:23–32). Noah's righteousness at least allowed him to save all his household (7:1)—and the future, even if not the present, of the world.

Blameless is an expression used frequently of "perfect" sacrificial animals. Perhaps it is apposite, since Noah's muteness throughout the entire flood story is remarkable. He is no Abraham pleading for those whom God has decided to destroy.

Like Enoch his great-grandfather before him, Noah "walked with God". Yet there will be an important difference. Enoch was mysteriously "taken" by God and seems to have avoided death. A similar fate was met by the Mesopotamian flood hero Utnapishtim whom Gilgamesh consulted in his quest for eternal life. Despite the correspondences that link Noah to both Enoch and Utnapishtim, Noah will definitely die (9:29) albeit at 950 years.

Noah had three sons, Shem, Ham, and Japheth. These three sons tell us that a new era in humanity's history is about to begin (cf. 11:26).

Now the earth was corrupt in God's sight, and the earth was filled with violence provides verbal reminders of Genesis 1. There God had told humanity to "fill" (1:28) the earth—and now he "sees" just what they have chosen to fill it with. The word "corrupt" (*shahat*) occurs three times in two verses. The identical Hebrew verb, though translated as "destroy", occurs as God pledges "I am going to destroy them". It is like for like, quid pro quo.

One of the striking aspects of the judgement is the interplay it presupposes between human beings and the earth. It is acknowledged that human beings are responsible for the violence on the earth (6:13), but due to this the world itself "was corrupt". Underlying this is a belief that blood shed violently (e.g. 4:10) physically polluted the earth. Such a contamination had also to be physically eradicated. The flood is when the earth is washed clean.

Make yourself an ark. The detailed description for the making of this ark is reminiscent of the even more elaborate description in Exodus 25–27 of the making of the Tabernacle. That is not accidental. The welfare of the entire human race will depend on both being properly built. The Hebrew word used for the ark (*tebah*) is rare: the only other time it is used in the Old Testament is in Exodus 2:3 where it describes the floating basket of reeds in which the baby Moses was kept safe. In both ark and basket, the future of God's relationship with humanity is cradled with fragility.

I am going to bring… The tense of the Hebrew emphasizes how soon the flood will come. The drops of rain are virtually starting to fall!

… flood of waters The "flood" was the name given to the heavenly ocean on which God was enthroned (Psalm 29:10), divided from the earth by the vault (Genesis 1:6–7). So for this "flood" to come "on the earth" was a mark of the dissolution of creation.

All flesh in which is the breath of life. It is deliberate that language so associated with humanity's creation (2:7) is re-spoken by God at this time of total obliteration.

But I will establish my covenant with you. At this precise moment when all is as dark as possible, the word "covenant" is introduced into the Bible. Against all the odds there will be hope for the future. And it is a future that will involve a concrete relationship between God and human beings. (See further on "covenant" on p. 95)

And of every living thing, of all flesh, you shall bring two … into the ark. The focus on pairs helps to reinforce the sense of duality which pervades this narrative.

Noah did this; he did all that God commanded him. Now that the verb "command" has been introduced into Genesis it will reappear twice within the next ten verses. (7:5,9). It will then disappear again. It is an appropriate verb to reflect the situation of the mute Noah and the lengthy monologue by God.

7:1–23 *The LORD said to Noah, "Go into the ark".* The instructions are repeated again, with some differences. Though these differences are probably due to the incorporation of material from two different sources, the repetition of the divine commands further emphasizes Noah's obedience and God's determination.

Take with you seven pairs ... and a pair. This is one of the most readily noted discrepancies between the two strands in the narrative. In 6:19–20, Noah had been told to save two of each kind of animal, now it is seven pairs for animals that are ritually "clean". There is a logic to this larger number; it will allow for sacrifice, and for the fact that after the flood humanity is allowed to eat the flesh of "clean" animals. 7:8–9 offers a still further variation.

Noah was six hundred years old when the flood of waters came on the earth. It is remarkable how many precise chronological notes there are in this story (e.g., 7:10,11,24; 8:4,5,13,14. See further below, p. 76, for comments on 8:13–14).

The fountains of the great deep burst forth, and the windows of the heavens were opened. The flood is not simply caused by the rain referred to in 7:4,12: rather the whole cosmos seems to break up as the work of the second day of creation is reversed. "The great deep" is the primeval ocean which as a result of God's creative activity had been confined beneath the dry earth. Underground springs were points at which it could still break through, and now these springs were surging up with overwhelming force. Water came from above as well. As in 6:17, we are reminded that the "vault" of heaven had waters confined above it (cf. 1:6): the opening of the windows in the vault threatened to release the destructive power of these waters too. This was no ordinary rain shower.

The LORD shut him in. The quaint, almost anthropomorphic, description reminds us of the deity who had once walked with Adam and

Eve in Eden. It is an intimate gesture which suggests that despite God's determination to destroy almost everything, he was equally determined to ensure the safety of Noah and those entrusted to his care.

Coming at the end of a section (7:7–16) which habitually uses the word "God" rather than "LORD", these words have always been a problem for division of the flood narrative along traditional source critical lines (see comments above). Perhaps the choice of the word "God" or "LORD" (i.e. YHWH) to describe the deity may (at least in part) depend on the precise role God is playing in the story at any given point.

The waters ... increased greatly upon the earth. Another reversing reminder of the creation story. Then humans had been commanded to "increase" (1:28)—but now the "increase" of the waters ensures a dramatic and almost total decrease in their numbers!

7:24–8:19 *God remembered Noah.* This is the midpoint of the story around which the waters of the flood may swirl but they cannot overwhelm. It is the tiny pinprick of hope which will allow a new future to be inaugurated. Later on, the same Hebrew verb *zakar* will often be linked to a covenant. God will "remember" how he is bound in covenant relationship with human beings and act accordingly (e.g. 9:15). But at this point in time, there is no covenant yet inaugurated. God's remembering of Noah stems from the very nature of God.

God made a wind blow. The re-creation is beginning. "Wind" or "Spirit"—the same word *ruah* in Hebrew—had hovered over the deep in Genesis 1; so now it marks the beginning of God's new adventure with his world.

The ark came to rest on ... Ararat. The dramatic peaks of this mountain on the borders of present-day Turkey/Armenia made it a suitable location for the grounding of the ark. Appropriately the verb *tanah* ("came to rest") used here comes from the same Hebrew root as Noah's own name.

Noah ... sent out the raven ... the dove. This is one of the points where there are very close links with the Mesopotamian versions of the flood story. In these, a dove or a raven are also used as "scouts". Indeed the mention of the two birds perhaps suggests that more than one traditional source was in the writer's mind and there has been an attempt to collate them. The raven is rather redundant to the story as it now stands. The dove's first unsuccessful journey is curtailed because it "found no place to set its foot" (Hebrew: *manoah*)—yet another pun linked to Noah's name. Her later return with an olive branch in her mouth is the first time that a part of a tree has been mentioned since humanity was in the garden of Eden.

In the six hundred and first year, in the first month, the first day of the month … In the second month, on the twenty-seventh day. The chronology of the flood plays an important part in the story. It is quite confusing, but it seems likely that the author wants to suggest that the flood lasted exactly a year. It is possible that the two chronological references in verses 13 and 14 are referring to the same day: in one case measuring it in terms of Noah's life, in the other in terms of the calendar. Back in 7:11, we had been told that the flood had been begun "in the second month, on the seventeenth day", so at first sight it looks as though the flood must have lasted a year and ten days. It has been plausibly suggested that this apparent discrepancy is due to the use of two different calendrical systems "playing together" in this one text. During the post-exilic period there was fierce controversy about calendars. There is little contemporary evidence about the "official" Jewish calendar, but 1 Enoch 72–82, Jubilees and Qumran show that in some circles two systems were known, a "lunisolar" calendar with a year of 354 days (adding an extra month every thirty-six months), and a solar calendar with a year of 364 days (presumably with the addition of an extra month at intervals), though a 365-day year was also known. Perhaps the interweaving of the two calendrical systems in this one story reflects this debate and is an additional example of the "confusion" of time which has symbolized the breakdown of creation throughout the flood.

But with the ending of the flood, the "right" time will be restored. The new beginning of the world on this day implicitly lays the foundation for the annual observance of New Year's Day, just as the creation of the world in Genesis 1:1–2:4a had laid a similar foundation for the keeping of the Sabbath.

Bring out ... so that they may abound ... and be fruitful and multiply. Almost identical words had been spoken in blessing in 1:22 (to animals) and 1:28 (to humans). The flood had transparently undone the hope expressed in the earlier blessing—will humanity and the animal world fare any better this time?

8:20-22 *Noah built an altar... When the Lord smelt the pleasing odour.* The version of the flood story in the Mesopotamian Epic of Gilgamesh tells us that Utnapishtim too offered sacrifice to mark the end of the flood and "the gods smelled the sweet savour, they gathered like flies over the sacrifice". However, the choice of the word "pleasing" (Hebrew: *nihoah*) to describe this particular sacrifice links it to the very reason for Noah's own existence. The linguistic connection between *nihoah* and Noah's own name, with its basic meaning of "rest" is deliberate. Noah was celebrated as the one who "shall bring us relief from our work and from the toil of our hands" (5:29). And so with this sacrifice the wordplays on Noah's name which underpinned the flood narrative (see p. 53) come to their resolution: the promised rest to be brought by Noah is now actualized through this sacrifice, which "rests" the anger of Yhwh. The earth will no longer be cursed: its seasons and times will have a regularity which will allow it to be productive. Perhaps too productive ... (see 9:20–21).

I will never again curse the ground. It is God who has changed—not humankind. The "inclination" of human beings is still "evil" at the end of the flood, just as it had been at the beginning (6:5), when it had provoked God to take his devastating action. In this verse the entire relationship between God and his creation has shifted. God's very graciousness now means he forsakes his absolute power (see further p. 88). The internal wrestling within the divine heart is emphasized by the way that Yhwh "said in his heart".

As long as the earth endures. The rhythms of this short verse aptly express the rhythms of the seasons which it is promising. The divisions of time, which had broken down so completely during the flood's uncreation, are now restored. This is the first of three short poems (the other two in 9:6 and 9:13–14) which highlight in turn the modus operandi to apply to the earth, to human beings, and to God, in this brave new post-flood era.

9:1–17 *God blessed Noah and his sons.* Even more explicitly than in 8:17 the blessing of Noah recapitulates the original blessing offered to humanity in 1:28. Noah is presented as a "second Adam" in this new creation. The fruitfulness of this tiny group of survivors will repopulate the earth. There are differences: human beings are no longer simply vegetarians. Animals, as well as plants, can now legitimately be consumed as food. Not surprisingly therefore the original trust between humanity and the animal creation pictured in Genesis 1–2 no longer exists. It is replaced by "fear and dread".

But there are still prescribed limits to humanity's dominance of the animal creation. The eating of animals with their blood, where it was believed their life was concentrated, is prohibited. This is the foundation text for the Jewish (and indirectly the Muslim) food laws which prescribe a particular method of animal slaughter.

But it is to humanity itself that God then explicitly turns, with the punning in 9:6 between *dam* (blood) and *'adam* (human) strengthening his pronouncement. The phrase "for the blood of another" (literally "brother") immediately recalls Cain's killing of Abel, that primeval sin which had been multiplied by Lamech (4:23–24). This new creation is not to be marred by similar violent death.

Is this new creation to be an inclusive or exclusive one? Is it marked by diversity—or uniformity? It is striking how a connection is made between humanity's status in the image of God and respect for the sanctity of human life (9:6). Cain by his actions against his brother Abel had defaced the image of God in himself. The statement of Genesis 9:6 offers a remarkably wide-ranging vision of what it means to be human. The formulaic way in which it is set out implies that all human beings have a similar right to equality of protection. Protection is owed to all descendants of Noah, which means everyone. There is no place for preferential treatment or discrimination over this fundamental human right. Any who wage war today, justifying their actions on the basis of the Judaeo-Christian tradition, do well to remember this. Western lives are not more valuable than those of the peoples of Africa or Asia.

The requirements laid upon humanity in this chapter underlie the later concept of the "Noachide commandments", which rabbinic Judaism considered to be imposed on all humanity. According to this understanding Jews and Gentiles alike were required to abstain from murder, idolatry and sexual sins. The requirements laid upon Gentile converts in Acts 15:20 by the church in Jerusalem may also be linked to this.

Yet the inclusive vision does not stop there—for the covenant that is then granted by God is made not only with human beings, but "with every living creature" (9:10,15,16) and between God "and the earth" (9:13) After the flood, just as before it, human beings cannot separate themselves from the rest of creation of which they are a part.

God said ... I am establishing my covenant. Seven times the word "covenant" occurs between verses 8 and 17, a powerful echo of the days of creation and a symbolic reminder of completeness. Something fundamentally new—and creative—has entered the relationship between God and creation. The hidden commitment which God had made in 8:21 is now out in the open. The dualities which have dominated the flood narrative throughout finally come to their resolution in this one covenant made for all time and with all creatures. Unlike the Sinai covenant, which is presented in conditional terms and could be potentially terminated (Exodus 19:5) through human disobedience, the covenant offered by God in Genesis 9 establishes a relationship which God binds himself to—whatever the cost to himself, and however deep the intransigence of human beings. The reference to this covenant in Isaiah 54:9–10 captures perfectly the overwhelming grace of God contained within it: "My steadfast love shall not depart from you, and my covenant of peace shall not be removed". Through 9:1–17, Noah remains completely mute, accentuating the one-sided obligation which God is placing himself under (see further on "covenant" on p. 95).

The choice of the rainbow as the sign of this covenant may owe something to Mesopotamian traditions, but it is also very apposite here. By placing his bow (with its seven colours!) in the sky God had put aside his weapon of war and was offering a covenant promising peace. Formed like an arc it echoes the shape of the vault of heaven. It was a visible reminder that this barrier, so essential to the well-being of creation, would never be dissolved. God's "remembering", which had initially sprung freely out of his own heart and on which the whole flood story had turned (8:1), is now linked irrevocably to the concept of covenant (9:15,16).

At the end of the Mesopotamian flood stories, the flood hero is removed from the rest of humanity and taken to live with the gods as an immortal. In this biblical equivalent, Noah very definitely remains a man of the earth. Unlike Utnapishtim the "life" that results from his experiences is not for him alone—his task rather is to be an agent of life for the entire world.

9:18–28 This final episode in the story of Noah feels, on the surface, rather like a comic contrast with the world-shattering events which have just taken place. But just as after Genesis 1–2 creation took some inopportune paths, so here too, the "new creation" presents problems as well as possibilities. The actions of Noah recall Genesis 3. In both stories, the eating of fruit has unforeseen consequences, and the theme of nakedness plays a part in each. There are also echoes of the fraternal rivalry of Genesis 4. Genesis 9:18–28 in fact has a key role in concluding the story of Noah, and it may be no accident that the name of the son Ham, who is responsible for the outrage against his father, recalls the Hebrew word *hamas*, "violence", mentioned in 6:11 as the primary cause of the flood.

The strange elliptic tale contains inconsistencies. Why is it implied at one point that Ham is the middle son of Noah, but elsewhere his youngest son (9:24)? Why is Canaan apparently unfairly cursed for his father Ham's actions? Perhaps there was a more extensive well-known tale of which this is a fragment. The story also points forward to what will transpire shortly: the comment that the whole earth will be "peopled" by the descendants of Noah's three sons (9:19), prefigures the "scattering" (same Hebrew verb) that occurs after the Tower of Babel (11:8,9), though here in Chapter 9, perhaps significantly, the verb does not appear to have the negative connotations with which it is often loaded in Chapter 11.

With the curse now lifted from the ground, Noah can become a productive "man of the soil". Too successfully, as his imbibing of the wine from his vineyard leaves him in a pathetic drunken stupor. What exactly did his son Ham see—or do? Was it more than simply looking on his father's genitalia? Suggestions have included the possibility that he engaged in incest with him or even castrated him. But even "looking" might well have offended social taboos, certainly in an Old Testament culture that disapproved profoundly of Canaanite fertility cults, in which drunkenness and sexual licence played a part. The specific mention of "Canaan" as the object of Noah's curse may hint that this was partly what was in the writer's mind. However, a glance at Ham's descendants in the following genealogy (10:6–20) also suggests they represent nations that were feared either for their empires or for their aggressive expansionism, just as Ham's misguided actions had earlier seemed to give him inappropriate control over his father. In the eyes of the writer of Genesis, the curse of slavery would seem an appropriate reversal.

His curse of Canaan and blessing of Shem and Japheth is the first time that Noah has uttered a word throughout his entire story from 5:28 onwards. Back in 6:9, Noah had been described as "righteous" and "blameless", and he had mutely followed God's instructions all through the lengthy narrative of the flood. But in this post-flood era righteousness needs to be more than that. God will begin to withdraw from direct involvement in human society. It will not be enough for human beings simply to relate to God, they need to discover how to relate to each other in a way that fosters justice and peace between peoples, rather than inappropriate competition. Noah, whose words were used for centuries to justify the slavery of millions of Africans (the putative descendants of Ham) may not be the hero we need for this new time.

All the days of Noah were nine hundred and fifty years; and he died. This then is all there is left to say about Noah. He died at a great age, older even than Adam, and with a far longer lifespan than any of his descendants. He lives—just—into the third millennium, but he will have died by the time that the new era inaugurated by Abram has begun (12:1)

Peoples and languages
10:1–11:26

The two genealogies (10:1–32; 11:10–26) form an envelope around the story of the Tower of Babel, and the whole section acts as a bridge between the primeval stories and the tales of the ancestors. Structurally it is debatable where the primeval narrative ends and the ancestral saga begins: some commentators regard 11:10–26 as beginning and belonging to the Abram saga which follows it. Others would suggest that the primeval story ends with 9:29 and see the "Table of Nations" (10:1–32) as setting the scene for the call of Abram. The analysis of Genesis' structure is affected by the theological presuppositions brought to it. Certainly, both genealogies and the story of the Tower of Babel look forward in the overall tale of Genesis, as well as back.

10:1–32   The *toledot* formula reappears (10:1) to introduce what is often called "the Table of Nations", which illustrates how quickly the blessing of 9:1 has come to fruition.

It is marked by its expansive diversity, setting out the entire "family of the nations" as known to the writer of Genesis. One of its intriguing features is that it mentions three times (10:5,20,31) how each nation had its own language. Set, as it is, immediately before the story of the Tower of Babel, this feels a contradiction, but perhaps it is also a hint that we should not take the "confusion of language" in the tale of Babel as negatively as is often done.

If one brackets out the reference to Nimrod which feels like an intrusion, designed perhaps to hint at the story of the Tower of Babel which comes next, the list contains exactly seventy names—a number which symbolically reflected completeness. It is not neat and tidy. Some names appear twice, e.g. Havilah 10:7,28. It includes the offspring of all three sons of Noah. Note that Ham, whose family is cursed as a result of his actions in 9:20–25, is still included in the list. However, Ham's descendants do not have a particular ethnic profile. Genesis has no truck with an ethnic apartheid.

The use of the -*im* plural form for some of the names (10:13–18) is a reminder that we have moved away from a focus only on individuals or a family, to human communities and civilizations. Though the saga of Abram/Abraham will revert to concentrating specifically on one small group, this table encourages us to set those doings of Abraham's family in a wider political and social context.

Some of the names are clearly identifiable with specific geographical localities, for example: Javan (Greece), Tarshish (Spain), Kittim (Cyprus), Rodanim (Rhodes), Cush (Ethiopia), Egypt, Put (Libya), Canaan, Seba and Havilah (areas of Southern Arabia), Asshur (Assyria), Lud (Lydia) and Aram (Syria). In the case of others, we can often guess the general area that is meant. Broadly speaking the family of Japheth is linked with regions north and west of Palestine, the family of Ham, Africa, and the family of Shem is located in Arabia and Mesopotamia.

But "untidiness" creeps in. Why, for example, is Canaan, son of Ham— the eponymous ancestor of the land along the east Mediterranean coast to which Abram would journey—a "brother" of those who are associated in this table with Africa? And why does Nimrod, son of Cush, migrate from Africa to Mesopotamia—and in the process overlap with a region and places (e.g. Assyria in 10:11 and Asshur in 10:22) associated with the family of Shem?

Ellen Van Wolde suggests that the divisions are not so much geographical as sociological.[12] The descendants of Japheth were primarily coast-dwellers and seafarers, those of Ham primarily urban and sedentary, and those of Shem largely nomads. This may explain the emphasis clearly placed on "Eber". Although he was only the great-grandson of Shem, he is mentioned alongside his great-grandfather in 10:21, where Shem is described as "the father of all the children of Eber". Eber's name is related to the word for "Hebrew", and comes from a word which means to "pass by", "travel" or "cross over". His name implies his nomadic lifestyle. It is from Eber that Abram will descend. Is being a "wanderer" or "migrant" therefore being "written in" as a necessary characteristic of the branch of the family on which the story will soon focus?

Two references in the list linked to Ham hint at negative episodes that will shortly take place. Nimrod's kingdom includes Babel in "the land of Shinar" (10:10) just where the Tower will be built. And we are very carefully told that Canaan's border included Sodom and Gomorrah (10:19, see 19:1–29).

Yet although the "Table of Nations" reflects the hostility between the different lifestyles of the ancient world, and in particular fear of the power of the great urban empires and kingdoms in Egypt, Mesopotamia and Canaan, the impression it creates is of a blessed diversity. And a question: where in all this is the nation Israel?

11:1–9   It is difficult to read the account of the building of the Tower without recalling modern skyscrapers, and perhaps particularly the Twin Towers of New York. Since September 2001, the analogy has often been pointed out. We have already had a hint that cities may not be the healthiest of locations—it was Cain or his son Enoch who built the first one (4:17). Another clue that something is amiss is found in the location, Shinar (where Nimrod's kingdom was). There are also verbal indicators that link this story with earlier episodes (3:1–24; 6:1–4) in which humanity had overreached itself and transgressed the boundaries between humanity and divinity.

Indeed, it is remarkable that the builders set about their task with an exhortation in the first person plural "Come . . . let us make . . . " (11:4) that recalls God's own use of the first person plural when he created humanity (1:26). Equally telling—God's reaction, a few verses later "Come, let us go . . . " (11:7) both echoes the builders' own turn of phrase and also reclaims for God the majestic plurality used at that moment of creation. These people may think that they can "make" something—and a "name" for themselves (11:4), but they completely fail to realize the awesome gap between themselves and the Lord of all Creation, however high their tower might be.

Yet God's first instruction to humanity after their creation and repeated after the flood was to "fill" the earth. That is precisely what these builders have forgotten. In their quest for unity and homogeneity focused on one small space of earth they have tried to obliterate God's creative vision of duality and diversity. To no avail—God's purposes will not be defeated. The ironic result of God's intervention is that they do receive a name—Babel/babble (11:9)—though presumably not the one they sought. And their "scattering" (11:9) across the earth is not only a punishment but also the fulfilment of God's will in creation.

The story "dances" with wordplays to reinforce its point: fittingly appropriate in a tale about language. As well as that between Babel and "babble" (Hebrew: *balal*) which is apparent in English as well as Hebrew, the narrator plays with the words for "build" (*banah*), "brick" (*lebena*) and "son" (*ben*), which sound similar in Hebrew. The Hebrew of 11:5 literally speaks of Yhwh coming down to see what "the sons of the human being had built", and this choice of words to describe the builders both hints at the puny competition they seek to offer Yhwh ("What is the son of a human being that you should take notice of him?" [Psalm 8:4]) and reminds us of the original human challenge to the deity in Genesis 3. And it is surely not accidental, as Michael Fishbane suggests, that with a subtle ironic twist, the "babbling" or confusing of language which Yhwh proposes in verse 7 (*nabelah*) inverts the same letters as the builders used in their bricks (*lebenah*).[13]

But there is a further set of wordplays associated with "name" (*shem*), which links the tale to what has immediately preceded it—and will shortly follow it. The basic pun is now between *shem* and *sham* (= there), which is emphatically used on five occasions in these verses to designate the place where the tower was built. A "name" is not made for oneself by doing something "there", in "that place". Rather Shem, the son of Noah (with a name which means "name"!), who will be mentioned again in the very next verse, shows us what a name is all about. It is associated with a nomadic life rather than city dwelling, and it will be given par excellence to Shem's descendant—Abraham (12:3) as he sets off on a journey in obedience to Yhwh's command.

11:10-26   Once again the *toledot* formula appears, this time to introduce a vertical genealogy of Shem's descendants. The list of ten names has a similar function at the end of this section of Genesis as the genealogy of 5:1-32 with its ten names had at the end of the preceding section. It bridges the generations to take us speedily to the next important initiative in God's dealings with humanity.

Although the deaths of the ancestors are not specifically mentioned this time (unlike 5:1–32) their apparent lifespans are getting shorter. Shem in fact outlives all his descendants except Eber. Eber is the last ancestor to have a lifespan of more than four hundred years. Is the diminution after this due to the association of his son Peleg with the time when "the earth was divided" (10:25—presumably a reference to the Tower of Babel)? Eber is the fourteenth ancestor (counting from Adam), a position that reinforces his symbolic significance (i.e. 7 × 2).

Though only one son is named for each ancestor the regular comment that they had "other sons and daughters" makes apparent the fruitfulness of humanity in response to the blessing of 9:1. It contrasts with Abram's lack of progeny, a theme which will shortly dominate the narrative of Genesis.

Finally we reach Terah—like Noah (5:32), he breaks the pattern by having three named sons, in his case Abram, Nahor and Haran. And the fact that they were born when he was a "perfect" seventy years old is another clue telling us that once again something important is going to take place.

Theological reflections

1. The chaos of exile

The story of the flood is by far the longest episode in the "primeval history" of Genesis 1–11, and it lies at the midpoint of these chapters. This may mark its importance from the perspective of those whose own experience was formative in the writing of the book—those who were living through exile in Babylon. In these chapters we hear the echoes of their own story and their sense of being "overwhelmed" by the chaos of exile. The Old Testament explicitly draws a comparison between flood and exile. In the exilic section of Isaiah, 40–55, Yhwh proclaims "This is like the days of Noah to me" (Isaiah 54:9). The exilic community felt acutely the sense of almost total loss that the flood narrative portrays, loss of land, identity, religious and social institutions, of hope and relationship with God. Everything had changed. All had apparently been swept away. The community had also experienced the "violence" which had been the flood's precursor. The uncreation of which the flood story tells mirrored Israel's own.

Yet it was also as a result of the exile that they were able to discover the possibilities for new beginning. It was precisely the flood myths told and retold in Mesopotamia that provided the source for the Old Testament telling of the story of the flood—which did not ultimately end with destruction, but with new creation and the promise of God to sustain the future. To paraphrase T. S. Eliot's famous words, the flood story was an acknowledgement that having faced "the end" they were gifted a "beginning" in which they might know themselves properly for the first time. Isaiah 40–55 once again provides commentary, in its wrestling both with the reality of sin and the assurance of God's ultimate refusal to abandon the people: "When you pass through the waters, I will be with you." (Isaiah 43:2) The relationship between God and his people is being hammered out afresh, and at a new depth:

> In overflowing wrath for a moment I hid my face from you;
> but with everlasting love I will have compassion on you,
> says the LORD, your Redeemer...
> Just as I swore that the waters of Noah
> would never again go over the earth,
> so I have sworn that I will not be angry with you
> and will not rebuke you.
> For the mountains may depart and the hills be removed,
> but my steadfast love shall not depart from you,
> and my covenant of peace shall not be removed,
> says the LORD, who has compassion upon you.
>
> *Isaiah 54:8–10*

Recent writers have pointed out how the motif of exile is one which speaks to our time in the early twenty-first century. Ralph Klein, in a thought-provoking monograph, *Israel in Exile*, has argued that the literature that springs out of the "exile" has a peculiar power to address us in these days when a spirit of alienation, change and rootlessness is widespread, and the relevance of tradition is called into question. Along with the psalmist many of us might say, "I have come into deep waters, and the flood sweeps over me" (Psalm 69:2).[14]

Through the flood narrative, Genesis recalls humankind to remembrance of God's power to re-create. The story delivers us to resonances of hope which we desperately need.

2. The grieving of God

It is important to draw attention to the "grace" which is written into the story of the flood (see further the play on "grace" and Noah's name, p. 56), because at first sight the picture of God that this story offers is very dark indeed. Can we really worship a God who is prepared actively to wage total destruction on creation? Trevor Dennis comments that the only way he finds himself able to preach on the passage is by suggesting that the ocean on which the ark finds itself adrift is that of God's own tears.[15] He goes on, however, to suggest that that is not how Genesis itself presents it. Yet perhaps the grief of God lies closer to the heart of the narrative of Genesis than we initially realize?

One of the features of the intricate wordplays in 5:29 and 6:6-8 (see p. 53 and p. 56) is that they bind together God and humanity with words of power and pathos. They thus contain a hint, albeit a tentative one, that God is not a stranger to human pain. This is accentuated by the double use in Hebrew of the word *leb* (which can be translated as "heart") in 6:5-6 where a literal translation might be that the "thought of the heart" of human beings was wicked (6:5) and that God was "grieved ... to his heart" (6:6). As Walter Brueggemann puts it, "this is indeed 'heart to heart' between humankind and God".[16] In these verses, we are being presented with a deity who wishes to stand alongside his human creation rather than over against them in judgement. Yhwh is not detached from this decision. He is intimately caught up in it, as we all are when we take difficult and perhaps painful decisions which impact on those we love. Indeed, the very word "sorry" used twice in connection with Yhwh's intention to destroy comes from a Hebrew root (*naham*) that more usually means "have compassion", "console", "pity". It is used with that sense at the powerful opening of Isaiah 40:1, "Comfort my people". Even while we translate it in 6:6-7 as "sorry", perhaps the word hints at Yhwh's ultimate "compassion" for humanity, and the "relief" (5:29, a word from the same Hebrew root) which Noah will ultimately bring.

Admittedly 6:11-13 feels rather different. No longer is there the need for deliberation. God here is assured. "I am going to destroy them." Yet it is important to note that the name of the deity has also switched here from Yhwh, to *'elohim* (God) and this switch seems to reflect a different face of God. It is Yhwh that is used when the divine relationship to human beings is emphasized. And the placing of the two names, and two moments of decision together like this could even suggest a struggle in the very being of the divine, such as is expressed in Hosea 11:8-9, where God argues within himself about the fate of Israel, and even speaks of his change of heart.

But whatever we make of God before the flood, when we come to its aftermath, we certainly discover a God who has changed. Not so human beings; the language used to describe their attitude after the flood is deliberately reflective of the words used to describe them beforehand. Once again, we have the double use of *leb* to reflect the "heart" of both God and humanity. The "thought of the heart" of humanity is still evil (8:21, NRSV, "the inclination of the human heart is evil"). Yet as Yhwh speaks "in his heart" once again, his, his own heart has moved from regret to compassion. The flood "has effected an irreversible change in God, who now will approach his creation with an unlimited patience and forbearance".[17] He will continue to grieve over human wickedness but has pledged himself to show forbearance. And this means that the promise that God offers to Noah and all creation is one which will be of great cost to God and which will necessitate divine suffering. He will allow his love to be wounded—again and again. God will voluntarily limit his power, but in giving humanity this new freedom he will open up the possibility of a real relationship with them.

Back in Eden, God had been fearful of allowing human beings to "grow up" and make decisions for themselves. Their childish disobedience had been duly punished—for God had not yet realized that if he wants a real relationship with humanity, it would inevitably involve confrontation. The flood is the moment when that original mode of relating reaches its climax—and God learns that it is not enough. In the world begun anew after the flood God will try another way, that will allow us to reflect back God's love. This is the paradox at the heart of Genesis: God has to allow human destructiveness to exist and take its course in order for there to be such a thing as divine love incarnate.

3. Our good and fragile globe

The first eleven chapters of Genesis offer us both resource and challenge for faith-based reflection on our human responsibility for the well-being of creation.

The fundamental premise of Genesis is that creation is "good", indeed "very good" (Genesis 1:31). This positive affirmation of the physical world is characteristic of the Old Testament as a whole. Such an attitude was not necessarily prevalent in other parts of the ancient world. The widespread influence of Platonic philosophical ideas encouraged a view that this material earth was merely a shadow of the ultimate "reality".

The Christian Church came to birth in the tension that these two opposing worldviews produced, and sometimes found itself struggling to give space to the world-affirming strands of Christian incarnational and biblical faith alongside the dominant world-denying intellectual currency of the era.

Such conflict was one of the primary roots of Christian Gnosticism, an ideology that suggested that salvation, frequently portrayed as escape from this material world, was to be gained by knowledge or *gnosis*. The discovery of a substantial number of ancient Coptic papyri in Egypt at Nag Hammadi in 1946 has provided a rich resource for the study of such Christian Gnosticism. It is interesting how many of these manuscripts include a retelling of the early chapters of Genesis from a Gnostic perspective (e.g. *Reality of the Rulers*; *On the Origin of the World*; *Apocalypse of Adam*). In such reworkings of the biblical story, it is an evil demiurge who creates the world (sometimes accidentally!) and who wants to stop Adam and Eve from eating of the fruit of the tree of knowledge in order to prevent humanity from escaping his clutches. Although the manuscripts are written in Coptic (a dialect of Ancient Egyptian), it is clear that they have been translated from earlier Greek versions. But close attention to the Gnostic texts that explore Genesis 1–3 suggests that these Greek versions depend in turn on a version that was originally written in a semitic language (either Hebrew or Aramaic), because there are a number of puns that only "work" in such languages. All of this suggests that a discomfort with affirming the "goodness" of creation dated back to very early years of the Christian era and may have been quite pervasive in parts of the Christian Church.

It is important to insist that Genesis itself cherishes the created world and affirms it as "good". It is a vital starting point for any Christian theological reflection on ecological concerns. It is more difficult to make the effort to care for what one does not value.

Genesis 1:26–28, which speaks first of human beings as being created in the image of God and then grants them "dominion" over the earth, has often been treated as the axiomatic biblical text for exploration of the relationship between humanity and the rest of creation. However, as noted earlier (see p. 28) the verbs "subdue" and "have dominion" may suggest a degree of violence in this relationship. Indeed, recent reflection sometimes lays the blame for the ecological crisis on this particular biblical text. "The idea of human stewardship of creation is 'sheer hubris'" (James Lovelock). "Especially in its western form, Christianity is the most anthropocentric religion the world has seen" (Lynn White).

There are, however, two factors that can be pleaded in mitigation to Lynn White's charge. The first is that the diversity of the Old Testament is reflected in the diversity of views it contains about the relationship between humanity and the rest of creation. The book of Job, for example, markedly displaces humanity from any place at the centre.

The second is that, from a Christian perspective, a celebration of Christ as the "image" of God (see p. 65) should affect our understanding of this term so that its focus is on service rather than privilege and control, and this in turn feeds into our perception of the relationship between humanity and creation.

It is also important, as we are now doing, to reflect on creation, not only from the perspective of Genesis 1–5, but also in the context of the following story of the flood. As we noted, the flood is described as a sort of "uncreation".

However, the shift in the relationship between God and humanity at the end of the account of the flood has implications also for the relationship with creation. The responsibility for this world and its future now rests firmly with humanity. No longer can we "merely" consider ourselves serfs who can blame a divine "master" if things go wrong. God has limited his power to bequeath it to humanity. But the covenant in which he has done so is one that is deliberately couched in terms that remind humanity that the welfare of the entire creation depends upon them. The *'adam* (= human being) whose story we have been hearing in Genesis 1–11 is still to be responsible for the *'adamah* (= earth).

There was a tradition in apocalyptic writings that there would be another great cataclysm—but that this would be of fire, not water (see 2 Peter 3:10). God had apparently pledged himself merely to refrain from bringing another flood (9:11,15). As a folk song puts it, "No more water, but fire next time." But this is to misunderstand the climax of the story of the flood. If there is another world disaster, another cataclysm, it will probably be due to humanity, not God. The fact that often such feared disasters are described in language that is reminiscent of the flood or other early parts of Genesis emphasizes their profundity and awfulness but also twists the knife of the irony. We cannot blame God—comforting though it might be to do so.

We cannot blame God for the nuclear holocaust of which Edith Sitwell writes in her startling poem, "The Terrible Rain", an image which was echoed in the protest songs of the 1960s.

We may speak of Schindler's Ark when we hear about the activity of Oskar Schindler in saving hundreds of people from the Nazis—but we cannot blame God for the holocaust from which he was seeking to save them.

We cannot blame God for the violence that infests our world today, whether it be the direct violence of terrorism or the indirect violence which comes in the train of a certain kind of globalization. We need to remember the words of Martin Luther King spoken in Memphis the night before he was killed in April 1968, "It is no longer a choice between violence and non-violence in this world; it is non-violence or non-existence." But it is our choice—not God's.

And above all, we cannot blame God for potential and actual ecological disasters in our fragile world—for those who have seen an ecological significance in the "rainbow covenant" that is offered in Genesis 9 have perceived something which is true to the heart of the story. Just as Chapters 6–7 seem to suggest an "uncreation", so too does the following anonymous poem:

> In the beginning was the earth.
> And it was beautiful.
> And man lived upon the earth. And man said:
> "Let us build skyscrapers and expressways."
> And man covered the earth with steel and concrete.
> And man said: "It is good."

On the second day,
man looked upon the clear blue waters of the earth.
And man said, "Let us dump our sewage
and wastes into the waters." And man did.
The waters became dark and murky.
And man said: "It is good."

On the third day,
man gazed at the forests on the earth.
They were tall and green. And man said:
"Let us cut the trees and build things for ourselves."
And man did. And the forests grew thin.
And man said: "It is good."

On the fourth day,
man saw the animals leaping in the fields
and playing in the sun. And man said: "Let us trap
the animals for money and shoot them for sport."
And man did. And the animals became scarce.
And man said: "It is good."

On the fifth day,
man felt the cool breeze in his nostrils.
And man said: "Let us burn our refuse
and let the wind blow away the smoke and debris."
And man did.
And the air became dense with smoke and carbon.
And man said: "It is good."

On the sixth day,
man saw the many kinds of people on the earth—
different in race, colour and creed.
And man feared and said: "Let us make bombs
and missiles in case misunderstandings arise."
And man did. And missile sites and bomb dumps
checkered the landscape.
And man said: "It is good."

On the seventh day, man rested.
And the earth was quiet and deathly still.
For man was no more.
And it was good![18]

God has offered us the freedom and privilege of a covenant with him. That is our blessing and our bane.

4. The challenge of covenant

What about the "covenant" referred to above? In this section of Genesis, the concept of "covenant", so central to the entire Bible, is introduced for the first time. God has made a covenant with Noah and with "all living creatures". The motif of covenant will recur again in the coming chapters, most particularly of course in the account of God's making of a covenant with Abraham (15:18; 17:1–14), but also in the agreements that will be made between Abraham and Abimelech (21:27–31), then between Isaac and Abimelech (26:28–31) and finally between Jacob and Laban (31:44–54). What is the essential meaning of this concept?

There has been a great deal written about "covenant" in Old Testament scholarship over the past sixty years. Most of it, however, has focused on the Mosaic or Sinai covenant and has drawn analogies with the international treaty system in the Ancient Middle East, whether focusing on second millennium Hittite treaties, or first millennium Mesopotamian ones. But while such analogies *may* make sense of the Sinai covenant—presenting it as in effect a "treaty" between Yhwh and the people of Israel, they are far less satisfactory as an explanation of the covenants made between God and Noah or Abraham in Genesis. Unlike the Sinai covenant whose continuance apparently depended on Israel's willingness to keep the commandments, these two covenants seem to have an unconditional nature: God "oaths" himself to Noah and his living creation without apparently making any corresponding demands upon them. The case of Abraham is slightly more complicated partly because of the two versions of the covenant; in Genesis 15 and Genesis 17 each has a slightly different emphasis. But even in Genesis 17, where there is a link made between covenant and circumcision, it is likely that the covenant itself was perceived as eternal and irrevocable and that circumcision was effectively a sign of those who had agreed to identify themselves as partners in the covenant which God had established.

Studies of the actual Hebrew word for covenant, *berit*, have not been altogether fruitful, although there is a general consensus that there is a close relationship between a covenant and the pledge of an oath. Certainly, an oath seems to be an intrinsic part of a covenant-making ceremony, and it is probably not accidental that the first and second covenants recounted in Genesis between two human parties both take place at Beer-sheba, a site apparently with the word "oath" in its name.

An article by F. M. Cross published in 2000, "Kinship and Covenant in Ancient Israel", has, however, revived a view about the essential nature of a covenant which, while never completely forgotten, has often been overshadowed by the focus on the treaty analogy. Cross argues that we should understand a covenant as a

> legal means by which the duties and privileges of kinship may be extended to another individual or group... kinship relations defined the rights and obligations, the duties, status, and privileges of tribal members... kinship was conceived in terms of one blood flowing through the veins of the kinship group. If the blood of a kinsman was spilled, the blood of the kinship group, of each member, was spilled. Kindred were of one flesh, one bone.[19]

He also comments that marriage in ancient Israel should be understood in a similar way: the bride enters into a relationship of kinship with the family of the groom.

Cross's suggestion implies that when God makes a covenant with Noah and creation, or with Abraham and his descendants, he is, in effect "adopting" the other party as kin and agreeing to accept the mutual obligations inherent in kinship:

> He leads in battle, redeems from slavery, loves his family, shares the land of his heritage... provides and protects. He blesses those who bless his kindred, curses those who curse his kindred.[20]

He becomes "the Divine Kinsman". It is likely that such a concept of "covenant" was initially applied to a specific national or tribal group (e.g. the descendants of Israel, or Abraham), and it was perhaps only during the exile that it was radically extended to relate to Noah and all creation. Given the link between kinship relations and marriage, it is telling that the analogy of the deserted, but now reinstated, wife of Isaiah 54:1–8 appears immediately before the mention of a covenant with Noah in Isaiah 54:9–11. Perhaps this was in fact one of the points where the biblical tradition said more than it realized, or even intended, in suggesting such a wide-ranging covenant, and we have been tasked with working out its meaning ever since.

For the corollary is that there is a family likeness in all humanity, a concept that perhaps may seem so obvious that it is redundant to state, until one remembers how the genocides of the twentieth century were facilitated by the belief that the "other" was somehow sub-human. It is on this "familial" assumption that the prohibition of murder in 9:6 is based. This is why it will be so important in the stories to come that brotherhood is "got right" because ultimately it will be a pattern for relationships not simply between the descendants of Abraham, but also between the descendants of Noah—everyone.

5. Faith in the city

Cities do not, on the whole, get a good press in the Old Testament, or at least in Genesis. It was Cain, or perhaps his son, who built the first one (4:17). Our analysis of the "Table of the Nations" (10:1–32) suggested that the great cities of the day were regarded as being inhabited by the family of Ham, again presumably a connection viewed negatively. And then there is the Tower of Babel, where not only a tower, but also a city, is built (11:4)—and destroyed. The French theologian Jacques Ellul has famously described the city as being a focus of evil throughout human history, an example of humanity's declaration of independence from God.[21]

Yet it is no accident that the Bible, which begins in a garden, will end in a city (Revelation 21:2–22:5). This is all the more striking since the "tree of life", originally associated with the Garden of Eden, will end up being planted in the middle of this city (22:2). In the transference of the symbol, there has been a deliberate shift from the garden to the city: the implication is that life can, or should, be found in the city. Even within the confines of the Old Testament itself the language with which the new Jerusalem is pictured, particularly in Isaiah 56–66, offers us an alternative vision of the city as the place where God dwells. Cities are recognized as the places where human life can be lived with a particular fullness and intensity, for good or for ill.

So what are the dangers, and the possibilities, inherent in city life? One of the features of the city described in Revelation 21:25 is that "its gates will never be shut by day—and there will be no night there". Is this significant? In the Ancient Middle East, what marked out a city over against, for example, a village, was the fact that it had walls. The primary image associated with a city, therefore, was defence, and possible warfare. And this sense of defensiveness is surely in the minds of the builders of Babel too, "Let us build ... otherwise we shall be scattered" (11:4). Their first reaction to an apparent technological advance, the ability to make bricks, was a concern for self-defence.

Throughout human history, there has frequently been a connection between the desire for security and the ordering of society along totalitarian models, in which difference is prohibited from being expressed. There are plenty of examples from the infamous "evil empires" of the twentieth century. Most of these have now disappeared, but they have been replaced by the "globalization" of our world, which itself might be viewed as an ideology. Indeed, since we are thinking about the Tower of Babel, it is relevant to note that there is a strong link between the rapid spread of globalization and the use of the English language. Whether intentional or not, this has privileged one language and culture over all others. In turn, this has led this particular culture to a sense of defensiveness about itself. In view of the way that the events in America on 11 September 2001 have been read alongside this biblical narrative, it is pertinent to observe that there was an implicit arrogance in the title "World Trade Centre". It begs the question, whose "world" is it anyway? Who has the right to appropriate for themselves such a sweeping title?

Has our post-9/11 world really considered that the way forward for the future is to find new ways to respect "The Dignity of Difference"? It is telling that Jonathan Sacks' book of that name, with its subtitle, "How to avoid the clash of civilizations" has a sixteenth-century picture of the Tower of Babel on its cover. Sacks argues that the meaning of this biblical story is, at least in part, how God insists that people "make space for difference. God may at times be found in the human other, the one not like us."[22]

Since Christians often read the story of Pentecost (Acts 2:1–36) as an undoing of Babel, it is important to observe that the gift of the Spirit there does not make people identical—but facilitates their mutual understanding, while still preserving their differences. "In our own languages we hear them speaking about God's deeds of power" (Acts 2:11). As our churches have wrestled with the fact of globalization and its significance, positively or negatively, for their mission, they have increasingly come to realize that their task may be to provide an alternative model which encourages inculturation and values difference.

The walls of the traditional city were a powerful symbol of the fear of the "other". Yet the story of Pentecost, which took place in the city of Jerusalem, itself showed how cities can be places where different cultures can meet and learn from each other in a way that would be impossible in rural or small-town life. The last biblical word on the city, with its gates continually open (Revelation 21:25), invites us to find in the city a place of hospitality rather than defence.

The story of Abraham

11:27–25:18

With the journey of Abraham in Genesis 12 a "New Start" begins: quite literally. It is the first significant event to happen in the third millennium (2021) counting from the creation of the world, and just as Noah's birth had announced a new beginning at the start of the second millennium, so Abraham's journey will also mark a new departure for humanity. We are now entering an epoch and dealing with people who have a basic familiarity about them: they will live lives comparatively close to the normal human lifespan, and the boundaries between the divine and the human worlds will gradually be fixed in a shape with which we are comfortable (though it will take till the story of Joseph and his brothers to get this sorted out completely!).

The stories of the ancestors which fill the next chapters of Genesis have a strange homeliness about them: they are the accounts of the loves and hates of a family, with emotions such as jealousy, greed, passion and longing all to the fore. A witty friend of mine referred to these tales as "the Middle East-Enders". They remind us of some of the incidents in Genesis 1–11 (perhaps particularly the episode of Cain and Abel), but the figures we are going to meet are no longer cardboard cut-outs from a faraway time, but characters with whom we can begin to empathize, despite their obvious differences of lifestyle and social mores.

Over the last seventy-five years, a variety of approaches have been taken to the ancestral stories linked to Abraham.

The 1950s and 1960s saw "the quest for the historical Abraham". Working backwards from the later history of Israel, the time of the patriarchs was hypothetically located in the eighteenth to the fifteenth centuries BC. The stories were then quarried for examples of economic and social institutions which were regarded as particularly characteristic of this period in the mid-second millennium BC. W. F. Albright and others used their knowledge of extra-biblical Middle Eastern cultures to provide parallels: one often quoted example is the practice in the Hurrian city of Nuzi, whereby a husband could adopt his wife as his sister and thus also gain the status of her brother. This is linked by Albright with the occasions when both Abraham (twice) and Isaac (once) attempt to pass off their respective wives as their sisters (Genesis 12:11-13; 20:2,12; 26:7). Another comparison frequently made between extra-biblical texts and Genesis is the use of a slave-girl by a barren wife to provide her husband with children (Genesis 16:1-2; 30:1-4).

But during the last fifty years, such an approach has been challenged: first by Tom Thompson in *The Historicity of the Patriarchal Narratives*[23] and shortly afterwards by John Van Seters in *Abraham in History and Tradition*.[24] Both writers have called into question the methodology used by Albright, which tended to overemphasize similarities between Genesis and extra-biblical material and did not pay adequate attention to the context of these extra-biblical sources themselves. (Nuzi is actually far from the presumed trajectory of Abraham, as he journeyed round the Fertile Crescent from Ur to Haran and thence to Canaan, while the Nuzi texts themselves stem from a period several centuries after the supposed "patriarchal age".) The views of Thompson and Van Seters have grown increasingly influential, and there would now be considerable scepticism about the validity of a "quest for the historical Abraham", arguing that the stories reflect rather the social and religious context of the first millennium BC in which they were written down.

As with the primeval history of Genesis 1-11, these chapters have also been explored from a source-critical perspective. Source criticism has been employed to explain the number of apparent doublets in the chapters—the twice that Abraham attempts to pass off Sarah as his sister, and the fact that Abimelech, King of the Philistines, suffers the same gambit from Isaac as well as Abraham. In this part of Genesis too, the differing ways that God is named were believed to provide a guide to distinguish the different sources.

However, the comments about recent developments in Pentateuchal studies made on p. 6 also apply here. Although it is almost certain that the final author(s) of this part of Genesis made use of earlier oral and written sources in compiling their work, it is now difficult to be confident as to the precise date and provenance of these earlier sources. In particular, the apparent "doublets" in the story may not reflect two parallel sources which have been combined, but may have been developed as part of a story-telling device. And the rationale for the different names of God, which in this section of Genesis extends beyond the words Yhwh and *'elohim* met in Genesis 1–11 to include titles such as *El Shaddai* (e.g. 17:1) and *El Roi* (16:13), may be primarily due to the different modes with which God interacts with the variety of characters in the tales.

A recent approach to the Abraham material, which owes a debt to traditional Jewish scholarship, is to concentrate on the quality of the narrative, and explore it from the perspective of literary criticism. Apart from helping us to understand just why certain incidents in the lives of the ancestors were apparently repeated, it allows us to make sense of the stories as part of a greater whole. The core of this section of Genesis is 12:1–22:19, which is begun and ended by two stories in which God calls Abraham, in both cases using the unusual Hebrew expression *lek leka* to do so. If we look at Genesis 12–22 in this way, the following structure seems to emerge:[25]

The literary structure of the story of Abraham

A1 12a The call (*lek leka*). Blessing promised.
  B1 12b Abraham in Egypt. Wife-sister motif.
    13 Controversy over livestock.
    C1 13–14 Lot in danger. Sodom.
      D1 15 Covenant.
        E 16 Hagar and Ishmael.
      D2 17–18a Covenant.
    C2 18–19 Lot in danger. Sodom.
  B2 20 Abraham in Gerar. Wife-sister motif.
    21b Controversy over livestock.
      [21a Birth of Isaac/Hagar and Ishmael.]
A2 22 The call (*lek leka*). Blessing confirmed.

By omitting for the moment the stories of Isaac's birth and Ishmael's expulsion in Chapter 21, this provides us with a perfectly concentric or chiastic pattern in which Genesis 12a is balanced by 22, 12b by 20, moving steadily inwards until we reach the account of the flight of Hagar and the birth of Ishmael in Genesis 16. This acts as the linchpin of the structure. It is intriguing that the story of Hagar should have this role in the narrative (see further on pp. 123–4). It also helps to explain the further story of Hagar and Ishmael in 21 which breaks the concentric pattern. Chapter 21 *ought* structurally to be the ending of the literary unit—the fact that it isn't increases our anticipation as we wait for Chapter 22 (to which it is closely related, see p. 154)

Within this overall structure it seems that the two Hagar-Ishmael stories in Chapters 16 and 21 form a further envelope surrounding the announcement of Isaac's birth in 17–18 and his actual birth at the beginning of 21. So the Hagar-Ishmael stories both provide the structural centre for the cycle, and also point away from Hagar-Ishmael ultimately to Isaac. This ambiguity reflects the place of Ishmael and his mother in these stories.

Although Chapters 12:1–22:19 form the core of this section, they are in turn further framed by 11:27–32 and 22:20–25:18 which offer an introduction and conclusion to the saga of Abraham.

Note: Although we use the name "Abraham" to describe the patriarch at points when we are considering his story as a whole or looking back on his life from the perspective of his descendants, within the commentary below we have deliberately used the name "Abram" to refer to him up till the point where his name is changed by God in 17:5.

The journey starts—and a detour
11:27–13:18

The rest of Genesis will be dominated by a sense of "travel". So the motif is introduced at this key and opening point in the story of the ancestors. The description of Abram's movements in 12:8–9 deliberately uses words which draw upon the technical vocabulary of nomadic life. But we are reminded that there are various kinds of journeys, those like

Terah's (11:31), which appear to stem from his own initiative, and those like Abram's in which divine initiative plays a leading role. We are also reminded that it is possible to take wrong paths, and potentially get lost. Within the space of a chapter a major diversion will occur, which will require a speedy backtrack—and bring problems in its wake.

11:27-32 Once again the word *toledot* (here translated "descendants") appears, to mark out a new section of Genesis. Note that it is the "descendants of Terah". Although the chapters that follow will focus on one particular descendant—Abram/Abraham—before the section finally concludes (25:18), other members of the family will have had their part to play in the story. Our appetite is being whetted.

Since the excavations of Leonard Woolley at Ur, on the banks of the Euphrates in Southern Iraq, "Ur of the Chaldeans" has often been linked to this location. It is, however, perhaps more likely that a town in northern Mesopotamia was meant—perhaps modern Urfa (Edessa). "Haran" was an ancient city in what is now north-east Syria.

The overall impression created by these few verses is of death and sterility. Haran dies (11:28), Terah dies (11:32) and Sarai is barren (11:30). It is a negative picture with which to begin this section of Genesis, even if on a more domestic scale than the utter destruction of the human race with which the previous section of the book had begun. If there is to be the life and fruitfulness which creation had promised (1:28; 9:1), a new initiative is clearly going to be necessary.

12:1 *Now the* LORD *said to Abram, "Go from your country and your kindred and your father's house to the land that I will show you."* The main part of Abram's story begins with a summons and a peremptory one at that, particularly in the original Hebrew. The first of the two appearances of the alliterated expression *lek leka* (translated "Go from") demands of Abram that he must sacrifice his entire past. (The second in Genesis 22:2 requires of him that he be willing to sacrifice his future.) And for what? "The land that I will show you" is an unbearably vague geographical expression, which calls straightaway for an absolute trust in YHWH.

I will show you translates a Hebrew word that literally means "I will make you see". Sight, or the lack of it, is going to be a key motif in the Abraham cycle: from its beginnings here in Haran Abraham will journey "to the mount of the LORD" (22:14), where he will eventually discover that there is vision.

The threefold list of what Abram is compelled to leave behind sharpens the sense of loss: it would not have been too great a burden for him to leave his country—after all, he was only a temporary and recent visitor to Haran. But "your kindred" and then "your father's house" builds up the tension and increases the sense of isolation, particularly if we remember what we have been told only a few verses previously: "Sarai was barren; she had no child" (11:30).

Abram is summoned by God speaking intimately as YHWH. YHWH will continue to use this name for his dealings with humans throughout most of the following chapters, though he will name himself as "God Almighty" in 17:1 at precisely the moment when Abram becomes Abraham (17:4). Names for humans and the divine are important in these chapters, though not necessarily as a marker for different sources.

12:2-3 In Genesis 1, God had spoken and called creation into being. The words now being spoken (particularly because of their close connection with blessing) recall that genesis and are equally as powerful. They are a new "divine initiative in a world where human initiatives always lead to disaster, and are an affirmation of the primal divine intentions for humanity".[26] God's promises to Abram are to be as sure as creation.

In line with the vagueness of YHWH's command, the promises themselves have a lack of specificity about them—at least to begin with. They will be fleshed out as Abram's story continues.

To be a "great nation", which means both numerically great, and politically significant, will require both offspring and land.

The promise that God will "make your name great, so that you will be a blessing" is written with one eye on the previous story of the Tower of Babel. The builders had set about their work in order to "make a name for ourselves" (11:4); now a great name is being freely offered to Abram by God. The secret is of course, as it is throughout Genesis, that when human beings seek to assert their own wills against God they are doomed to failure; when they acknowledge their dependence upon God, they gain more than they would have ever dreamed possible. Abram, descendant of Shem (a word which means "Name") is to fulfil the destiny to which Shem's very name points.

Although not set out as such in the NRSV, the promises move from prose into a poetic couplet as what is meant by "I will bless you" is elucidated. Abram is not merely himself the recipient of Yhwh's blessing, but through his relationship with God is to become the source and means of blessing for others. This is a new initative in God's relationship with humanity: once again a snippet of poetry marks out a milestone in God's adventure with the human race. As with other points when poetic forms appear (see p. 28), they help to emphasize a relationship, in this case between Yhwh and Abram, and between Abram and "the families of the earth".

Resonances of the blessing offered to Abram surface again later in the stories of the ancestors, particularly at points of transition or difficulty (e.g. 22:18; 26:4). However, even when no direct verbal links are expressed, many of the stories of the later patriarchs seem designed to show this blessing practically working itself out in action.

I will bless those who bless you. God's promise of blessing will extend to those who support and work alongside Abram and his descendants, such as Laban the Aramaean whose flocks multiplied while Jacob was working for him. The other side of the coin, "The one who curses you I will curse", is not clearly demonstrated in Genesis, but the language is echoed in Numbers 24:9 when the Moabite opposition to the people of Israel after their escape from Egypt rebounds upon the Moabite king's own head.

In you all the families of the earth shall be blessed is one way to make sense of an ambiguous piece of Hebrew. There is an alternative translation noted in the NRSV footnote: "By you all the families of the earth shall bless themselves", which is suggested by some modern translators to be a more accurate rendering of the Hebrew. However, Christian tradition has cherished the primary reading offered by the NRSV which of course, makes explicit that Abram becomes the channel of Yhwh's blessing for others. Paul's New Testament theology of Abram (e.g. Galatians 3:8–9 and comments on p. 189) depends upon this translation.

Genesis 12:2–3 are in essence the narrowing down of the blessing given at creation, and repeated to Noah. The blessing focuses now on one person, in order that it might eventually be shared by all humanity as had originally been intended. It is, of course, ironic that the outworking of a blessing which had insisted that human beings should "be fruitful and multiply" (1:28) should depend on this one, childless man.

12:4–9 Abram's age is mentioned at key points in his story, as here.

Significant times in Abram/Abraham's story

12:4 Abram is seventy-five years old when he leaves Haran.
16:3–4 Abram had been in Canaan for ten years when Ishmael was conceived.
16:16 Abram is eighty-six years old when Ishmael is born.
17:1,24 Abram is ninety-nine years old when the covenant of circumcision is given.
21:5 Abraham was one hundred years old when Isaac is born.
23:1 Sarai died aged 127 (Abraham would have been 137 years old).
25:7 Abraham was 175 years old when he died.

This means that the life story of Abram from the moment when God called him spanned exactly one hundred years.

If he was "seventy-five years old when he departed from Haran", then his father must have been alive when he did so, even though Terah's death has already been referred to (11:32). If Terah was still alive, the command given in 12:1 to leave "your father's house" makes better sense.

Was it intended by Yhwh that "Lot went with him"? On the surface it suggests that Abram was not fully obeying the instruction to leave "your kindred". Certainly Lot's presence on the journey and in Canaan creates problems and acts as a diversion and sub-plot before Abram's ultimate destiny is fulfilled. There is quite a lot of baggage which travels with Abram to Canaan: some, at least, of it will need to be stripped away before Abram is made ready to be the instrument of God's purpose.

Abram originally travelled to the major Canaanite sanctuary of Shechem, a key location in the story of the patriarchs, and throughout the later history of Israel (e.g. Joshua 24:1–32; 1 Kings 12:1,25). Magnificent trees such as terebinths (a form of oak) often marked out significant sanctuaries in Canaanite culture. They were a sign of abundant life, in a potentially arid land. Although worship "under every green tree" is condemned by prophets as syncretistic (Isaiah 57:5; Jeremiah 3:6), the ancestral stories suggest that there were those who believed that it was not impossible for Canaanite religious practices to be "baptized" into the faith of Yhwh.

Once again Yhwh speaks to Abram and what had been a vague location when he spoke in Haran now is made precise: one of the criteria for the fulfilment of Yhwh's promise that Abram would become a great nation is now made more explicit with the promise of land.

Shechem is an appropriate place for the ancestral story to begin: the same location implicitly ends the book of Genesis, for it is where Joseph's bones will eventually be buried (50:25–26; Joshua 24:32). First here at Shechem, then next between the significant cities of Bethel and Ai Abram builds an altar, and standing in a line that goes back to Enosh, the grandson of Adam, calls upon Yhwh by name (see 13:4, and notes on 4:26). In effect, he thereby stakes out his and Yhwh's claim to this land, although the comment "At that time the Canaanites were in the land" helps to remind us that God's promise to Abram is still far from being fulfilled. (It also makes it clear that the narrator is telling the story from a perspective considerably later than the supposed era of Abram.)

Abram journeyed on by stages towards the Negeb. We can assume that he is en route for the sanctuaries of Hebron (Mamre) and Beer-sheba to build altars there and to complete the "claim" to the land. Shechem, Bethel/Ai, Hebron and Beer-sheba would mark out a very neat "Promised Land". But it doesn't work out like that, for something else intervenes!

12:10-20 *There was a famine in the land*—a frequent event in the hill country of Canaan where the variable and fragile annual rainfall pattern often meant that land used for agriculture one year became semi-desert the next. Where better to go than Egypt, a byword in the ancient world for food in abundance (Numbers 11:5)?

But in the Old Testament people cannot go to Egypt without going *down* there—with all the negative connotations the word implies. To travel to Egypt is to undo the Exodus (Deuteronomy 17:16), and that applies to Abram the forefather just as much as to kings who might rule Israel and Judah centuries later. There is a hint of lack of faith in Abram's decision to leave the land of promise and migrate Egypt-wards: it is certainly not a move sanctioned by Yhwh.

Abram's next actions don't cover him with glory either. He is selfishly far more concerned with his own safety ("they will kill me") than with protecting his wife Sarai or preserving her dignity. Abram acknowledges that her life would never have been in danger: "they will let you live". Sarai is treated merely as a chattel to be traded for Abram's own advantage. Perhaps it is fortunate that she is still barren, for otherwise (in the patriarchal culture of the day) Yhwh's promises to Abram could go seriously askew, since the inference that Sarai had sexual relations with Pharaoh is clear. Does Sarai herself know about those promises that God made to her husband? There is no hint that she does—yet. Abram's hope "that it may go well with me" is reminiscent of the expression that God uses when people are blessed for keeping the commandments (see e.g. Deuteronomy 6:18): it is ironic that Abram should use it of himself when he is where Yhwh doesn't want him to be, and when he is doing what Yhwh presumably doesn't want him to do!

Pharaoh on the other hand is presented reasonably positively. "He dealt well with Abram." The gifts that he offers Abram are almost excessive. He is an innocent party, who is justifiably annoyed when Yhwh, hitherto notably absent from these verses, has to step in and sort out the situation to prevent his promise to Abram from going adrift. There is a hint of the Exodus story around: "the Lord afflicted Pharaoh...with great plagues". Pharaoh apparently has his wits about him and realizes straightaway the reason for the disaster (cf. 20:3). But unlike the attitude shown by the Pharaoh of the Exodus towards Abram's descendants this Egyptian treats Abram with decency even when his deception is uncovered. It may be the first triumph over Egypt recorded in the Old Testament, but Abram has hardly as yet proved a blessing to the "families of the earth" (12:3)—rather the opposite.

Yet he does quite satisfactorily out of his Egyptian adventure—he is allowed to keep all that Pharaoh has given him and has become very rich (a point reiterated in 13:2). Of course among the "male and female slaves, female donkeys, and camels" that Abram took with him as he departed from Egypt we can assume that there was a female slave called Hagar, who will appear so prominently in Abram's later misadventures. In these ancestral stories one thing so often leads on to another.

13:1-9 The aftermath of the Egyptian escapade had other consequences too. It meant that Abram and Lot between them risked overloading the fragile land of promise. Too much cattle, too many possessions. The situation is exacerbated because other people are also around with their rights and their demands on the land. The comment first made in 12:6 is repeated: "At that time the Canaanites and the Perizzites lived in the land."

Abram and Lot are still on their travels together, for due to their diversion into Egypt they haven't yet completed their stakeout of the land. It takes them some time even to get back to the spot between Bethel and Ai "where his tent had been at the beginning". They then have to pick up the story again from the point where they left it before the detour to Egypt.

There was strife between the herders of Abram's livestock and the herders of Lot's livestock. The rancour hasn't yet infected the relationships between Abram and Lot themselves, which is fortunate for otherwise we could be retreating back to the story of Cain and Abel. But it risks doing so: "Let there be no strife between you and me." The risk and reality of fraternal strife runs throughout Genesis. Even though Abram and Lot are uncle and nephew it can still infect them too: "we are kindred" (the literal meaning of the Hebrew is "we are brother people").

Opportunely Abram takes an initiative to ensure harmony. If Yhwh's blessing of humanity is going to work brothers will have to learn to live in some kind of peace. It is up to Abram to start this process, even though he is going to make many mistakes before he is through. He generously suggests that Lot should settle in part of the land of promise, while he will choose another part for himself. "If you take the left hand, then I will go to the right; or if you take the right hand, then I will go to the left." From the perspective of where they were standing "left hand" meant a northwards direction, and "right hand" southwards. But Lot chooses to go neither north nor south—but rather east, to the plain of Jordan. He removes himself from the promised land. (It is interesting how in Genesis going "east" often means travelling in a direction that takes one away from God, see 3:24, 25:6.) In case we have not taken the hint from the direction in which Lot goes, it is made clear. The place that Lot chooses was "like the land of Egypt". And though it is here described as "well watered ... like the garden of the Lord", presumably a reference back to the garden Yhwh planted in Eden, we know all too well that things can go wrong in Eden. The first readers of Genesis who were aware how barren was the landscape near Sodom must have appreciated the irony of the description.

Harmony has thus been secured at a cost—the exclusion of Lot from the promises. We were not sure if the reason that the childless Abram brought Lot with him from Haran in the first place was for Lot to take the role of his heir. But if so, what has now happened must rule it out. We are back to square one again, or even perhaps in minus territory, because the unspecified wickedness of Sodom, the place where Lot had chosen to settle hints at menace and disaster to come. There would be another occasion when Lot would look "in the direction of Zoar" (see 19:20–22). One thing certainly leads to another in the stories of the ancestors.

13:14–18   After Lot and Abram had parted, Yhwh speaks to Abram again. It is as though Yhwh couldn't really have a proper conversation while Lot was still around. Now we can really get down to the serious business of the promise. Yhwh requests Abram politely (using the Hebrew particle *na* which will appear again in Genesis 22) to "Raise your eyes now". The relationship between Yhwh and Abram is growing closer. Yhwh does not command Abram to receive the promise; he invites him to.

The symbolism of seeing is a powerful motif throughout Genesis 12–22. But when Abram is told to "raise your eyes", there is something special to look at. (In Genesis 22:13, he "looked up", literally "raised his eyes", and saw a ram which took the place of his son as a sacrifice.)

It is a spectacular vista for him to glance at now. The Genesis Apocryphon (a reworking of part of Genesis that has been discovered among the Dead Sea Scrolls) suggests that Abram stood on top of Ramat Hazor, a magnificent hill near Bethel, from which even today you can see clearly as far as both the Mediterranean Sea and the Jordan Valley. This might well have been the very spot in the writer's mind. The land has been promised to Abram before (12:7) but not in such detail. He is instructed to complete the stakeout that he had begun before he had got diverted to Egypt. "Walk through the length and the breadth of the land." He does so and finally, near Mamre, in the south of the country, near the ancient city of Hebron, he settled.

At this point in his story the working out of Yhwh's promise to make Abram "a great nation" (12:2) takes another tentative step forward. The picture of the land which is to be granted to Abram is painted in with more detail. We also hear Yhwh pledge to make Abram's descendants as countless as "the dust of the earth": a paradoxical announcement to this childless man who was now effectively bereft even of his nephew.

The stranger in our midst
14:1–16:16

Although the three next chapters feel disparate, with their scope ranging from the international to the domestic, and may well come from different sources, as they now appear in Genesis they are linked together through a series of wordplays and motifs, which encourage us to read them alongside each other.

14:1–12   The tempo and the panorama changes. We are looking at things on a completely different scale. Not the familial, but almost a global perspective. The first four of the kings named here are not local lords of small city states, but emperors of massive realms that created the history of the Ancient Middle East. Abram himself will be very different too: no longer the cowering husband who hid behind Sarai's skirts when he met Pharaoh, but a courageous warlord who refuses to allow his "nephew" (14:14, literally his "brother") to be held prisoner whatever the personal cost to himself. One might wish that Abram had showed as much concern for Sarai as he now does for Lot.

Such differences have led some scholars to suggest that this chapter was written by an entirely separate hand from the rest of Genesis 12–22. They believe that although it may contain early source material it was appended to the rest of Genesis at a very late date, perhaps even the Maccabean period. Others, however, have suggested that this story of an encounter between Abram and Melchizedek may contain traditions dating from the days of the monarchy designed to justify the way in which aspects of Jerusalem's pre-Israelite and Canaanite religious roots influenced the religious practices of the nation.

It is "four kings against five". But the four emperors far outweigh the petty princelings who are their opponents. They are the rulers of Shinar (Babylon), Ellasar (possibly the kingdom of Larsa south-east of Uruk), Elam (a powerful kingdom east of Babylon and to the north of the Arabian Gulf) and Goiim (which means simply "nations" but may stand here for the kingdom of the Hittites). We cannot identify for sure any of their names with known historical figures, though Amraphel may refer to "Hammurabi", the almost legendary ruler of Babylon, and Tidal could be linked to Tudhalia which is known as the name of a Hittite king. There is an intrinsic unlikeliness to such a powerful group of emperors uniting in coalition to attack insignificant communities far from their home territory. Certainly there is no record of cities in the area being subject to Chedorlaomer, the King of Elam.

Their opponents hardly deserve the title king in comparison: they rule the petty towns that are strung along the southern part of the Jordan Valley. Sodom and Gomorrah's eventual fate is well known from Genesis 19. Zoar was a nearby village that provided a temporary refuge for Lot as he escaped the destruction of Sodom; Admah and Zeboyim were also bywords for towns in the region of the Dead Sea destroyed by Yhwh's wrath (Hosea 11:8).

The process that led to the war would have been a familiar one to the inhabitants of the small nations along the Mediterranean coast throughout much of the first millennium BC. Years resentfully spent paying tribute and when it became too burdensome a rash decision to throw off the imperial yoke—all too temporarily and inviting swift retribution. It was a pattern that dominated the history of Israel and Judah for centuries. The story which follows needs to be read in this light.

The battle is recounted using expressions of military vocabulary that are not found elsewhere in Genesis: "rebelled" (14:4); "subdued" (14:7); "joined battle" (14:8).

The list of those defeated in 14:5–7 includes some obscure names but makes it clear that the four kings were being opposed by a much wider group than merely the rulers of cities in the Jordan Valley. The war seems to have spread to a wide area of southern Transjordan and the Negev and may reflect authentic military scenarios in the region.

Then the story shifts back suddenly to focus on the Valley of Siddim, and Lot himself. Although this takes place before the destruction of Sodom and Gomorrah, the "bitumen pits" into which the defenders fell seem to anticipate the later destruction. They hardly remind us of the "garden of the LORD" (13:10) which was the vista that Lot had first seen. Although Lot had attempted to settle in Sodom, clearly he is not going to find there the security and riches which he had craved.

14:13–17 Abram now returns suddenly to the story. He is introduced almost as though we have never met him before: "Abram the Hebrew". This is the only time he is designated in this way. The term "Hebrew" is used sparingly in the Old Testament, to describe the Israelites while slave labourers in Egypt (e.g. Exodus 1:22), or during the time of the wars with the Philistines (e.g. 1 Samuel 13:3). It is also used to refer to "Hebrew slaves"—people who were forced through debt to sell themselves into temporary slavery (e.g. Deuteronomy 15:12). The use of the term here seems to reflect the way the term *Habiru* (surely connected in some way to "Hebrew"?) is used in a wide range of Ancient Middle Eastern texts to refer to social groups of people who could be categorized as "outsiders" or even "outlaws". So "Abram the Hebrew" is a kind of Robin Hood figure, leader of an armed resistance group who sticks up for the underdog against the powers that be. But in view of the fact that the Egyptian slavery of Abram's descendants will be mentioned in 15:13, the description "Hebrew" at this point may also act as a foreshadowing of what is to come. The biblical tradition also links the expression Hebrew to the name Eber, the descendant of Shem (10:21). So Genesis 14 may contain a veiled allusion to the supremacy of Abram, descendant of Shem and of Eber, over the inhabitants of Sodom and the other cities who were descendants of Canaan (9:25–27; 10:19).

Abram's companion Mamre has also changed—from being a place in 13:18 he is now somewhat unexpectedly a person. He and his brothers were "allies" (literally "lords of the covenant") of Abram. This unusual description of them perhaps hints at the "covenant" which will be the major focus of Genesis 15. It is one of a number of wordplays that link together Genesis 14 and 15.

The pursuit of the four kings and the rescue of Lot takes Abram beyond Dan. Not only does this allow for a pun on the Hebrew word for "punish" (*dan*, see also 15:14), but it is the traditional far northern boundary of the land of promise (see e.g. Deuteronomy 34:1). Abram's control therefore extends over the entire land, even if only on a temporary basis.

14:18–24 A tenth king now makes his appearance in the story—and this number is surely significant. Earlier on (14:9), the fact that there were nine kings had been emphasized, now this tenth king perfectly completes the story (as the number ten often does!).

He is very different from the others. They had brought war. He "brought out bread". There is a pun on the two words, both of which in Hebrew contain the letters *lhm*.

The mysterious Melchizedek only appears in the Old Testament here and in Psalm 110:4. Since that psalm is very difficult to interpret, it simply increases the enigma. Based on these Old Testament texts the Epistle to the Hebrews devotes considerable attention to Melchizedek, further emphasizing his strangeness: he is "without father, without mother, without geneaology, having neither beginning of days nor end of life" (Hebrews 7:3). An angelic figure called Melchizedek is also referred to in a Qumran text (11Q Melch) although it is not clear how much the Qumran text owed to Genesis 14 and Psalm 110.

Melchizedek is both a king and a priest: that much is apparent both here and in Psalm 110. Kings of the ancient world often had priestly, sacral roles, acting as a channel for the divine among their people. Early Israel seems to have been hesitant about adopting the institution of kingship, probably partly because of its sacral, religious overtones. But the accounts of David's capture of Jerusalem in 2 Samuel suggest that after its capture such rituals were embraced by the Davidic ruling house, perhaps based on the pre-existing royal cult of Jerusalem (2 Samuel 6:17–19).

Melchizedek is King of Salem, which is probably to be identified with Jerusalem. Perhaps it is here referred to as Salem to stress the link with peace (*shalom*) and the contrast with the warlike activities of the other kings. Names containing the Hebrew root *tsadaq* which means "righteous" often seem to have a close connection with Jerusalem (Adonizedek in Joshua 10:1,3; Zadok in 1 Kings 1:8; Zedekiah in 2 Kings 24:18. Note that 'ts' and 'z' are two different ways in English of writing the same Hebrew letter.)

Melchizedek blesses Abram by "God Most High" (*'el 'elyon*). The deity, a manifestation of the chief Canaanite God El, creator of the world, seems to have been worshipped particularly in Jerusalem (see e.g. Psalm 82:6; 87:5; Isaiah 14:14). In Abram's response to the King of Sodom he identifies this God with YHWH: "I have sworn to the LORD, God Most High." The identification facilitated the process by which YHWH, originally perhaps the tribal god of a small ethnic group, came to be viewed as lord of creation.

The story is also an extraordinarily powerful portrayal of a non-Israelite. For Abram, by allowing Melchizedek to bless him and by offering him tithes, is effectively acknowledging him as a superior, and accepting his legitimate authority as a priest of a major sanctuary in Canaan.

We are also being prepared for what comes next: Melchizedek's very name hints at righteousness (15:6); the oath that Abram swears (14:22) prepares the way for the oath that YHWH proffers as he makes a covenant, and even the unusual designation of Melchizedek's city as Salem leads us towards this event, for covenants and peace (*shalom*) often belong together (e.g. 26:31; Isaiah 54:10); whether by chance or design, in 15:15 we have the direct first mention of *shalom* in the Bible.

By the end of this story, Abram himself has changed. No longer is he the willing recipient of unethically gotten gains from a ruler (cf. 12:16,20). Now he refuses to accept gifts from the King of Sodom: not "a thread or a sandal-thong", but is therefore prepared for the "reward" Yhwh is going to give him (15:1).

15:1–5 As with Genesis 14, so also with this chapter, widely disparate views have been expressed about the origin of the material it contains. Is this one of the earliest parts of Genesis, or one of the latest?

On the one hand, the description of the covenant made in Genesis 15:9–20 with its features such as the cutting up of the animals and the sight of the flaming torch has a primitive quality to it. This has led some to suggest that there was an "ancient" memory of a covenant between Yhwh and Abram preserved at Hebron (possibly dating back to the second millennium) which may have been used as a model for the Davidic covenant tradition, and that is reflected in the portrayal of the covenant made here in Genesis 15. The very name Hebron, in fact, suggests a connection with some group bound together in an "alliance".

Others, however, would suggest that the tradition of a covenant made between God and Abram probably depends on, rather than pre-dates, the concept of a covenant made between God and David. The description of the covenant offered in this chapter then comes from the time of the exile and addresses many of the same concerns as Deutero-Isaiah for whom Abraham was an important figure of faith (see e.g. Isaiah 51:2). There are apparent links in this chapter to the situation of the exiles in Babylon (15:13), as well as verbal allusions to the Sinai covenant tradition (e.g. 15:7,17). It is significant that this chapter follows directly on from Genesis 14, in which the King of Babylon (Shinar) is defeated, and, as we have already noted, contains wordplays that links it to the earlier chapter. The placing of these two chapters in proximity could help to provide a message of hope for Abram's exiled descendants. Broadly speaking this second view is the one adopted in this commentary.

A further issue is the relationship between verses 1–5 and verses 6–21. Possibly rather than reading them sequentially (as we do below) we should see them as alternative descriptions of the same event.

It is night. It must be if God is able to ask Abram to "count the stars". It is also metaphorically dark. Abram is enduring a dark night of his soul. He sounds now like a prophet: "The word of the Lord came to Abram in a vision." But like many a prophet he is afraid, doubts his vocation, and needs reassurance from Yhwh (cf. 1 Kings 19:1–18; Jeremiah 1:6–8). This is the first time that Abram has spoken to Yhwh. Previously the conversation had always been one way—the other way. Abram needs to be stripped, even vulnerable, before a real two-way conversation can start, and a proper relationship between God and this human being can begin.

God's words "I am your shield" (Hebrew: *magen*) straightaway makes a punning connection with Chapter 14, where in verse 20 Melchizedek had celebrated how God Most High had "delivered" (Hebrew: *miggen*) Abram from his enemies.

Yhwh has promised Abram a "reward". This is understood primarily as a promise of land, but as Abram immediately points out, land without descendants to share it is meaningless. It is a useless gift which will have no significance beyond Abram's own lifetime.

Note the way that Abram addresses God: "Lord God" (literally "Sovereign Yhwh"). It is repeated in 15:8, but it is not used elsewhere in Genesis. There is a movement in Abram's relationship with God. Previously he had been known as the comfortable, almost familial Yhwh for whom Abram had built a series of altars (e.g. 12:7). Through his meeting with Melchizedek, he has learned that this Yhwh is also "God Most High, Maker of heaven and earth". The terms on which he now speaks to Yhwh suggest that his concept of God has deepened and become more aweful. In other places where the rare expression "Sovereign Yhwh" is used, e.g. Deuteronomy 3:24 and Isaiah 30:15, it describes a powerful God in whom it is right to trust. Since Abram now understands Yhwh to be "Maker of heaven and earth", it is particularly appropriate that he should come to faith by being taken to look at the stars. Psalm 8 reads almost like a commentary on Abram's experience that night: the psalmist reflects on how he has become aware of the immeasurable power of God by looking at the stars in the heavens, and how it helps him to put human worries in their proper perspective. (The psalm, incidentally, also uses the designation "Sovereign" to address God.) Isaiah 40:26 also resonates with this story—there looking at the stars is an explicit reminder to the exiles in Babylon that Yhwh is able to accomplish what seems to human beings to be impossible.

15:6-8 Day now dawns in the life of Abram, although night will come again shortly (15:12). There is a strange shift between night and day in this chapter, which seems to reflect the mood of the words.

Abram "believed the Lord; and the Lord reckoned it to him as righteousness". Abram's trust was hard won, but Yhwh didn't seem to mind. He is now considered by God as a righteous man. Noah had been described as "righteous" once (6:9); it seems to have come more easily to him and without the struggle Abram has gone through. Noah was also called "blameless" (6:9) at the same moment in time. Abram will one day be exhorted to be "blameless" as well (17:1), but that is yet to come. God is learning something as Genesis goes on—that if you want human beings to have a relationship with you, you have to keep faith with them through all the mistakes they make and the wrong turnings on the journey to their land of promise.

The verb "believed" derives from the Hebrew root *'aman* (from which "Amen" comes). It is a root used most characteristically when the logical human response would be to do the opposite (see Isaiah 7:9). But whether it was due to the stars, or the meeting with Melchizedek (who had "righteousness" in his own name), Abram has made a breakthrough—at least for the moment.

The "righteousness" with which Abram is credited probably refers both to the right relationship with God he has now established, and to Abram's justness of character (which God discovers to his cost in Genesis 18, see p. 140). It may also hint at something else. In Isaiah 51, a chapter of the book of Isaiah in which the figure of Abraham appears, words from the root *tsadaq* are used five times. They have there an active sense and can even be translated as "victory" or "deliverance". Is it then possible that when Abram's faith is "reckoned . . . to him as righteousness", we are hearing that Abram (and perhaps also his exiled descendants in Babylon) are being promised victory or deliverance?

I am the LORD who brought you from Ur of the Chaldeans. YHWH does quite a lot of "bringing out" in this chapter. First he brings Abram out of his tent in order to look at the stars (15:5), then there is this formula which is curiously reminiscent of the way God describes himself at the Exodus ("I am the LORD your God, who brought you out of the land of Egypt" Exodus 20:2), and finally there is his role in the departure of Abram's descendants from Egypt (15:14). The "bringings out" from the past, present and future belong together, and may link too to the latter-day exodus of Abram's later descendants from Babylon (which was, like Ur of the Chaldeans, also a part of Mesopotamia).

Lord GOD, how am I to know that I shall possess it? Is Abram's newfound faith dissipating so fast? Yet the Lord GOD of his address stills leaves him within the circle of trust.

15:9–21 An extraordinary scene now unfolds. It is YHWH's response to the uncertainties expressed by Abram. A selection of animals is dissected and set out by Abram. The cutting up of animals was often used to ratify a covenant or solemn agreement between two parties. By cutting up the animals the parties to the agreement were in effect binding themselves by an oath—if I break this covenant may I become like one of these cut up animals! When 15:18 reports "On that day the LORD made a covenant with Abram", the literal meaning of the Hebrew verb is that "the LORD cut a covenant". YHWH is the clear initiator in this covenant, for Abram is actually asleep when the ritual is completed. The strange description of "a smoking fire pot and a flaming torch [which] passed between these pieces" is a symbolic portrayal of YHWH himself, whose presence is often signified by flame (see e.g. Exodus 40:38). By passing through the dissected pieces in this way YHWH is binding himself by the oath of the covenant. He has promised to give this land to Abram irrevocably. The verbal promise uttered in 12:2–3 has now been incarnated in deed. For the first time YHWH uses the perfect tense of the verb in the Hebrew (15:18), "I *have* given to your descendants this land", as he speaks to Abram, although this is not apparent in the NRSV translation. Previously it had always been a promise made in the future tense. Moreover, the geographical detail of the map of promise is now sketched in. It is as though YHWH has drawn up a legal title deed. The borders given for the land, as also the list of the peoples whose territory it is, are reminiscent of similar lists and descriptions in Deuteronomy (see e.g. Deuteronomy 7:1; 11:24). Unlike Deuteronomy, however, it is not stated that Abram's right to possess will necessarily require the dispossession of these people, the land's original inhabitants. Indeed, since the previous chapter demonstrated Abram's willingness to work with and for the people of this land, co-existence rather than confrontation seems to be hoped for.

But it isn't all good news.

As the sun was going down, a deep sleep fell on Abram. The same Hebrew word is used in 2:21 to describe the deep sleep into which Adam fell, when the first woman was drawn from him. As with Noah and the re-creation after the flood, this is a "new beginning". Abram is almost a "new Adam", being made ready to face the challenges which lie ahead. Here the trance emphasizes the dark and fearsome history that awaits. The Egyptian experience of Abram's descendants has already been hinted at by Yhwh's self-designation in verse 7; here it is made explicit—"Know this for certain".

The prediction is made that Abram's descendants will be "aliens" and "slaves" in Egypt. This is the first use of the Hebrew noun *ger* (= alien) in Abram's story, although the related verb appeared in 12:10 (translated "live"). Both times so far the root has referred to a stay in Egypt. That corresponds to comments later in the Pentateuch e.g. Exodus 22:21. Egypt was the place par excellence where Israel knew what it is to live life with the insecurity of a *ger*, and Israel's Egyptian experience is also used as the justification in the lawcodes to demand generous treatment of other people who lived with the status of *ger* among the Israelites in Canaan.

What was a *ger*? The word has been variously translated as "resident alien", "stranger", "immigrant", "migrant". Older translations spoke of "sojourner". It is difficult to find an English equivalent which conveys the exact sense of the Hebrew word: unfortunately perhaps the NRSV's choice of "alien" has been undermined by the extra-terrestrial associations of the word in modern usage. A *ger* was a person who resided in a country or a town of which they were not a full, native, land-owning citizen.

They (or their forbears) might well have migrated to this country or town from elsewhere.

Is there a reason why the alien status of Israel in Egypt is referred to here? Is it perhaps Hagar herself, an Egyptian, whom we are going to meet in the next chapter? Whatever the actual etymology of Hagar's name (and it may well be linked to a semitic word for "flight" from which also comes the Arabic and Muslim Hijra, the archetypal flight of Muhammad) to any Hebrew-speaker it sounds curiously similar to *ha-ger* (= the alien). The shadow of the next chapter seems to be casting itself back to darken Abram's dream. Is there perhaps a connection between the way that Abram and Sarai will treat Hagar their Egyptian slave-girl, and the fact that their descendants too will one day know what it means to be a *ger* and enslaved in Egypt? This is made more likely when we look at the other comment made here on Israel's stay in Egypt: they "shall be oppressed" (*'innu*). The only other occasions when this particular verb occurs in Genesis 11:27–25:18 are in 16:6 and 16:9, where it describes how Sarai ill-treated Hagar. (The related noun is also used in 16:11.) Daringly, the writer hints at the reason for Israel's own later afflictions.

Yet ironically these threats are also words of hope—for if there are descendants to be enslaved, this must mean that one day Abram will be no longer childless. Adam's sleep had given birth to Eve, and the beginning of procreation between husband and wife. Does Abram's trance hint that the childlessness of Abram will soon be overcome as well?

16:1–6 With Genesis 16 we have reached the middle of the concentric circles into which Genesis 12–22 falls (see p. 103). Logically then we expect a kind of climax. And we are given one, but it is not quite the apparently intended solution. For we are now to meet Hagar, who has been described as "the woman who complicated the history of salvation".[27]

The central role of this chapter in the Abram/Abraham cycle is also hinted at by the use of the motif of sight: here and in Genesis 22 it assumes particular prominence.

"Sarai, Abram's wife, bore him no children." The hint of hope with which the previous chapter had concluded appears damned by the bleak sentence at the beginning of this one. But no, because in the very next line there is an implicit "however". "She had an Egyptian slave-girl whose name was Hagar." Hagar must have been one of those slave-girls given to Abram by Pharaoh (12:16), so Abram's apparent deception in that escapade is going to have long-term consequences in his family life. As we have suggested above, names matter in Genesis and Hagar's name offers a clue to what lies ahead: whether linked by sound to the Hebrew word for "alien" or related to a word for "flight" (see comments above, p. 123), by the end of her story here and in Chapter 21 the name will seem almost unbearably appropriate.

Sarai suggests a solution to her own inability to bear a child—that her slave Hagar should act as a substitute wife. Ancient Mesopotamian parallels have been suggested for this practice, but it is not clear how close these parallels actually are. (They seem particularly to relate to the situation of women who are priestesses.) The inference seems to be that any child born to a "surrogate" slave-wife counted legally as the child of her mistress.

What are we supposed to think about this scheme of Sarai? Should we commend her altruism? She is offering her husband the opportunity to be delivered from the state of childlessness which so clearly grieved him (15:2), even though by doing so her own barrenness will become even more transparent. We wonder what Abram has yet shared with Sarai. Does she know about the promise of countless descendants that has been made to him? There is no sure indication that she does—and certainly it has not yet been made clear to the couple that the countless descendants of Abram will also be those of Sarai. And yet her use of language is striking: "It may be that I shall obtain children (literally "sons") by her." Even in her despair, she manages to produce a pun: the literal Hebrew meaning is "perhaps I shall be built up through her", but the Hebrew words for "build" and "son" both contain the same letters, *bn*. Is Sarai's role as the eventual matriarch being hinted at here? For "building up" is something that happens par excellence to Israel as the people of God. Does Sarai then know about those promises, and is she seeking by her own actions to participate in them? After all, "Abram had lived ten years in the land of Canaan". Sarai's agony of infertility had gone on a long time. Even God's promises may need human machinations to chivvy them into fulfilment.

Whatever Sarai's motivation might be it is immediately made clear that YHWH does not sanction this scheme of Sarai, for Abram is now about to play Adam to Sarai's Eve, as subtle textual connections are made that link this narrative to what had happened in Eden.

There is the foreboding phrase: "Abram listened to the voice of Sarai." The precise Hebrew expression translated "listened to" normally appears in the Old Testament only when people listen to God—if human beings listen to other human beings trouble usually lies ahead! Abram is listening to Sarai, just as once Adam had "listened to" Eve, his wife, and eaten the fruit, and later Jacob will "listen to" his mother Rebekah and deceive his father.

Our suspicions of a parallel are reinforced by the verbs of 16:3 which draw our memories back to the fateful actions of Eve. Sarai/Eve took ... and gave ... to her husband (cf. 3:6). Can anything good come out of this—or will it all go wrong once again?

At one level, Sarai's efforts are successful—Hagar conceives immediately. On another level it is disastrous for "when she [Hagar] saw that she had conceived, she looked with contempt on her mistress". In offering her to Abram as a secondary wife, Sarai had elevated Hagar's status—but this has not resulted, as she had hoped, in her own elevation but rather her diminishment. Psychological tensions surround surrogacy even today: whatever the intentions may be, the process of pregnancy alters relationships. With this verse the motif of sight that runs through the story has now begun; corresponding to the motif of hearing which first appeared with Abram's action in 16:2.

Neither Sarai nor Hagar come out of the situation particularly well. Our instincts are perhaps first to side with Sarai (though see comments on p. 200). Strong words are now used to describe the breaking of their relationship. There is "wrong done" to Sarai by Hagar; in return Sarai "dealt harshly with her". As we suggested (see above, p. 123), that striking Hebrew root, used three times in this chapter ("dealt harshly", 16:6; "submit to", 16:9; "affliction", 16:11) is the same verbal stem as appeared in 15:13 (there translated "shall be oppressed") to describe the situation of the later Israelites in Egypt. That is no accident. What is happening to Hagar is a sort of Exodus in reverse: she, an Egyptian will flee from Israel's ancestors, into the wilderness, back in the direction of Egypt.

Abram has used Hagar, but after his use he washes his hands of her: his passive remark to Sarai "do to her as you please" is identical to that with which Lot will offer his virgin daughters to a baying mob (19:8). The conflict of eyes that had begun with Hagar's pregnancy also continues: his instruction to Sarai is literally "do what is good in your eyes". It is those hostile eyes, in that hostile face of Sarai, that Hagar now flees.

16:7–16 That it is a spring where the next scene takes place is a hopeful sign. For springs in the biblical idiom often speak of fertility and new life. Intriguingly the Hebrew word for spring (*'ayin*) is identical to that for "eye", so the theme of sight still seems to be echoing through the story. A spring is *the* ideal place to see God! And a spring at *Shur* is even better since Shur can be linked to a Hebrew word meaning "behold".

This is the first time that a figure called "the angel of the LORD" has appeared to a human being in Genesis. As 16:13 makes clear, this is really God himself in human form. It is impressive that the first recipient of such an appearance should be a slave-woman, who is apparently not even a descendant of Shem, and who is presently existing outside the land of promise.

There are other firsts associated with Hagar. She is the first woman to receive an annunciation in the Bible (the annunciation form is used, even though Hagar was already aware of her pregnancy). She is the first—and last—person to name God for herself, rather than simply calling upon him by name. No one else in the whole of scripture has this privilege.

Hagar does seem to "complicate the history of salvation". What is YHWH doing, paying such attention to a woman whose son will not be included within the covenant (17:18–19)? Genesis exists in a sort of tension between particularity (God's special care for particular individuals and a particular people) and universality (God's involvement with all humanity). This tension is nowhere more visible than in the two stories of Hagar and Ishmael (16:1–16; 21:1–21). It is as though YHWH (as well as Abram!) cannot quite make up his mind what to do with her.

On the one hand, he finds her "by a spring of water in the wilderness, the spring on the way to Shur". Intriguingly, this is the precise location where the Israelites will wander after the Exodus—though unlike Hagar they are not able to find water for themselves (Exodus 15:22). It sounds like one up for Hagar! On the other hand, she is then immediately told to return to Sarai and submit to the same "affliction" from which she had fled in her "Exodus".

She is promised "I will so greatly multiply your offspring that they cannot be counted for multitude"—almost identical words to those used to Abram (13:16; 15:5). Is this a hint that it will be via Hagar's offspring that the promise and blessing to Abram will come to fruition? Indeed, the Hebrew phrase translated as "I will so greatly multiply your offspring" is "I will greatly multiply your seed", closely recalling the words spoken by God to the woman in 3:16, "I will greatly multiply your pain". Sarai may have sounded like Eve earlier in this chapter, but now it is Hagar's turn: and she seems to be reversing the curse—into blessing. Is it Hagar rather than Sarai, therefore, who is to be "built up" as the matriarch of Israel? Although we know the answer, for the moment the story seems to be leaving the possibility wide open.

It seems even more likely when the angel comments "The LORD has given heed to your affliction", and this is given as a reason that she is to call her son Ishmael (= God hears). For that is exactly what happens when the Israelites are enslaved in Egypt (Exodus 3:7; Deuteronomy 26:6-7). They are oppressed—and God hears. Surely any child with the name Ishmael must be a part of God's own people? But the trouble is, the "hearing" in Ishmael's story did not begin with God, though it may end with him (21:17). Instead, it started with Abram "hearing" a desire of Sarai (16:2).

Ishmael stands so close: but his place in the story of the ancestors is ultimately delimited by another verse from the Exodus tradition: "You shall not wrong or oppress a resident alien; for you were aliens in the land of Egypt ... when they cry out to me, I will surely heed their cry" (Exodus 22:21-22).

God has heard Hagar and Ishmael not because they are part of God's Israel, but because he cares for them as he cares for those who are *gerim* (aliens). Yet they will still impact on the ancestral story: they will be there in the background when Isaac is nearly sacrificed, when Joseph nearly dies, and when the Israelites suffer near extinction in Egypt. God's promise of protection for the *ger* (and for widows and orphans) is immediately followed by his threat of anger for those who fail them: the interplay between 15:13 and 16:6,9,11 suggests that we are not wrong to see Israel's own Egyptian servitude directly related to the treatment of this Egyptian servant.

However, the description of Ishmael himself vividly evokes not servitude but the idealised freedom of Beduin life. This "wild ass" of a child will know the freedom that Hagar lacks with "his hand against everyone". (It is perhaps telling that back in 16:6 the Hebrew literally suggested that Hagar was "in Sarai's hands".) Moreover, "he shall live at odds with all his kin", although this apparent description of intra-family hostility may be more ambiguous than it appears at first sight (see Theological reflections on p. 200).

A misguided sort of seeing had been where it had started to go wrong with Hagar's life: this episode concludes by returning to a truer vision. There is an aetiology here for a place name that will appear again in the ancestral stories (24:62), and (if we accept the NRSV reading of some problematic Hebrew words) a sense of wonder by Hagar that she is still alive after seeing God (cf. Exodus 33:20). But the cryptic phrases of verse 13 remind us that seeing is two-way: YHWH has "seen to" Hagar (i.e. provided for her) as well as being the object of her sight. That same double sense of "seeing" will surface in 22:14. For the moment, Hagar drops completely out of view. We will see her again in Chapter 21, and there too vision will have its part to play in her story.

No human being has spoken directly to Hagar throughout her story nor acknowledged her by name (nor will they do so when we meet her again in Chapter 21). It is right that such a nameless one should have the particular power of giving God a name. That is her final moment of empowerment. For when Hagar returns to her servitude after her brief liberation, it is not she, but Abram, who actually gives the child his name. Even this power is now taken out of her hands.

Abraham not Abram
17:1–27

Language, theology and ideology all link this chapter very closely to Genesis 1 and 9. It is one of the "seams" with which earlier strands of material have been knit together. The fruitfulness which those earlier texts had seen as the destiny of humanity is now about to come to fruition with the establishment of this covenant with Abraham. The use of expressions like "perpetual" (17:8), "everlasting" (17:7,13) helps to collapse time itself, and takes us back to the very beginning of creation—as well as down to the writer's own era.

At the same time, there are connections between this chapter and 15:1–20; 18:1–15. Many similar themes are repeated, albeit in a very different style. It may well be that Chapter 17 was composed deliberately using these other sections as sources, and then positioned at this key point in the Abraham cycle, complementing 15:1–20 as a frame for the story of Hagar.

17:1–22 is one of the few passages in the Abraham stories where the narrative context is lacking. We are not told where Abraham is, or what he is doing when this life-changing dialogue takes place. Should we perhaps imagine 17:1–22 as happening within the context of the story told in 18:1–33? Notice the curiously parallel way in which both passages end (17:22; 18:33).

17:1–8 *When Abram was ninety-nine years old* By beginning the chapter in this way, the passage of time is emphasized. The previous chapter had just concluded with Abram's age when Ishmael had been born. "Abram was eighty-six years old when Hagar bore him Ishmael." Thirteen whole years have come and gone. Ishmael is now an adult by the standards of Jewish legal tradition. He is of the age when a Jewish youth would become "Bar Mitzvah"—take upon himself the obligations of the covenant. In Genesis 15, we read a graphic description of a promise of an heir to Abram "Your very own issue shall be your heir" (15:4) and a covenant made not only with Abram but also his descendants (15:18). This was immediately followed by the birth of Ishmael. Surely after all this time, now that thirteen further years have passed, it must indeed be

Ishmael who will be Abram's heir and the means of fulfilling the promises of the covenant?

The first few verses of Chapter 17 do not discourage us from thinking this. Unless we already knew the story (which of course we do!), we could read 17:1–8 (or perhaps even to 17:14) assuming that Ishmael is going to be the means by which this covenant is going to come to fruition.

It is clear of course that something momentous is unfolding. "The LORD appeared to Abram." Although YHWH had appeared to Abram once previously (12:7), since Abram's misadventures in Egypt, which presented him in a less than "blameless" (17:1) light there had been no repetition of this inaugural appearance. (Genesis 15 comes close but the language used there seems to be deliberately mysterious and guarded: God spoke to Abram in a vision.)

Of course, Hagar too has just seen God, even though in her case it is described as an appearance of "the angel of the LORD". As with Hagar, Abram's theophany leads to the revelation of a new name for God. This time "I am God Almighty". With this new name, or at least new title "God Almighty" (*'El Shaddai*) for God, we have arrived at a defining moment in Genesis, for this name is particularly associated with the era of the patriarchs. Possibly linked to an archaic Hebrew word for "mountain", it seems to be used in contexts which emphasize God's role in fertility, fruitfulness and blessing.[28] Such themes dominate this chapter: they apply to Abraham (17:5–6), Sarah (17:16) and even Ishmael (17:20). The emphatic Hebrew expression, *me'od, me'od*, a repetition of the word for "very", occurs three times in this chapter (17:2,6,20), each time translated as "exceedingly". The first time that it occurs, in the phrase "make you exceedingly numerous" (17:2), it helps to introduce the name change that Abram undergoes, from Abram to Abraham. In Hebrew, there is only one letter difference between the two forms, the addition of the letter *he* (which English reads as "h"). All five letters of Abram's new name are contained within the Hebrew words translated "make you exceedingly numerous". The point is further driven home by the words "ancestor (literally: father) of a multitude of nations" (17:4), which also read like a deliberate pun on the name Abraham. Abraham can only truly be Abraham when he is enabled finally to be *'ab* ("father").

There is a solemn, "priestly" feel to these verses. No longer do we meet the questioning Abram of Chapter 15, but a stately figure who "fell on his face" (17:17) in an attitude of worship (though see the comments on laughter on p. 191). The demand on Abram that he should be "blameless" also echoes cultic ritual: the same word is used elsewhere to describe sacrificial animals (e.g. Exodus 12:5), though then it is usually translated "without blemish". The identical expression was employed to describe Noah (6:9), but there is an important difference between Noah and Abraham. Noah "walked with God" (as did Enoch); Abraham is told in 17:1 to "walk before me [God]". The Hebrew verb is identical in both expressions: but the difference in the preposition helps to suggest that the exceptional nature of the ancient times when human beings could actually walk and talk with the deity is coming to an end. Abraham was a special person (he is sometimes referred to as "the friend of God"), but he is an example for human beings to aspire to rather than a mythological figure who crossed the normal bounds separating humanity and divinity.

What is now said to Abraham goes beyond what he was told in 12:2 (that he would be made into a great nation) and perhaps beyond even the covenant of 15:18–20, which also seems to envisage one, albeit extensive, nation. The "multitude of nations" suggest that he is to be father of a whole new humanity, almost on the scale of Noah.

I will make you exceedingly fruitful. The language deliberately resonates with God's original words to humanity at creation in Genesis 1:28 and his restatement of it after the flood (9:1). There are also resonances of both the Noachic and the Davidic covenant traditions, especially the emphasis given to this being an "everlasting covenant" (cf. 9:16; 2 Samuel 7:16; Psalm 89:29,36,37; Isaiah 54:10; 55:3). Indeed, Abraham is presented here as a royal figure, himself the ancestor of kings, and enjoying a name-change as kings of antiquity often did on their coronation.

There is indeed a political dimension to the covenant with Abraham as those who told the story of Abraham in exilic or post-exilic times were undoubtedly aware. The particularity of the promise that the land of Canaan would be given as a "perpetual holding" to Abraham's descendants sits uncomfortably with the universality implicit in the "multitude of nations". But monarchs need their royal parks, and though

Abraham's descendants may span the world, Canaan was to be a special land grant that effectively signified royal status.

The desire for possession of the land ran deep among those who were either landless exiles or seeking once again to get a toehold in the land of their ancestors. By now in the story, we know all too well how vulnerable it is to be a *ger*, an alien (17:8), whether in Egypt, Canaan or Mesopotamia. Yet the covenant with Abraham cannot be used in a simplistic way to legitimate political and territorial aspirations. On the one hand, there is the inconvenient fact that the covenant with Abraham gave him the privilege of being the ancestor of a "multitude of nations", including some that the exilic and post-exilic Jewish community would have regarded with hostility. On the other hand, the promise to Abraham which overshadows everything else is that I shall "be God to you" (17:7, reiterated 17:8). These words are the first part of what is sometimes referred to as the "covenant formula", which is normally completed by the corollary "And you shall be my people". God's promise to be Abraham's God, and that of his descendants, is a promise that goes beyond land, and can even be fulfilled among a people travelling in the wilderness (see e.g. Exodus 33:15–16) or, we might add, in exile or a diaspora.

17:9–14 Although the other half of the covenant formula is not explicitly verbalized, what it means is now set out: "You will be my people". The mark of circumcision will mark out precisely who are God's people.

Every male among you shall be circumcised. The practice of male circumcision was ancient and widespread in the Middle East. During the pre-exilic period most of Israel's neighbours performed this ritual on their boys or young men. The Philistines were one of the few exceptions. However, by the time of the exile, the practice was not normative in Mesopotamia. From the exilic period onwards circumcision became an important means of preserving the distinctiveness of the Jewish community and this seems to be reflected by the prominence given to it in this chapter.

Originally it is likely that circumcision was an initiation ritual performed on young men as they approached adulthood and in preparation for marriage. Hints of this remain in the mysterious passage Exodus 4:24–26. Interestingly, Ishmael, aged thirteen, would have been about the age at which youths had once been circumcised. We are not sure when the ritual was transferred to a boy's infancy. Perhaps the transfer is linked to the custom described in Exodus 22:29–30 which speaks of giving the first born to God, apparently on the eighth day. But establishing infant circumcision is integral to the meaning of Abraham's story. Taking place "when he is eight days old" meant that it happened at the beginning of the second week of a boy's life—when it would be apparent whether or not he had survived the hazards of birth. It was symbolically the beginning of his "new" creation, as a child of the covenant. It was a visual statement that God was intricately involved with the mysteries of creation, not only of the world but also of each human being. It was also an obvious reminder to each boy as he grew to adulthood and in his turn engaged in sexual intercourse that the blessings of sex and fertility were a gift from God, and that the fruit of them should belong to God as well.

It was therefore an appropriate visible mark for a covenant that promised the provision of an heir supernaturally to an old man and old woman well past the age of normal childbearing. It is only once Abraham has been circumcised that his seed really belongs to God and God can work miracles with it. Isaac could not be born as the child of promise until this sign of the covenant had been inaugurated.

The relationship between what happens now and the covenant described in 15:6–20 is intriguing. The passages do seem to come from different sources, yet it is no accident that they are placed together as a frame around Genesis 16. They are complementary. Genesis 15 had vividly pictured the cutting of animals to inaugurate a covenant between God and a human being. Now the "cutting" has to be internalized in the actual body of the human being before the covenant can come to fulfilment. Anyone who is not "cut" in circumcision "shall be cut off from his people" (see also comments about covenant on p. 95).

17:15-27   But what of Sarai? Up till now she has not been involved. It is far from certain that she knows anything about God's promise (see p. 124), and there has been nothing conclusive to say that it will be any son she bears rather than Ishmael who will be the child of the covenant. Perhaps in 17:9–14, there is a hint that the ideal child will be circumcised at eight days, in which case Ishmael has missed the boat since he is already thirteen years old! But it is no more than an inkling.

If anything, it is outweighed by Abraham's obvious focus on Ishmael. "O that Ishmael might live in your sight." Abraham does not think he needs another son now that he has Ishmael: the transparent pain of his words in 15:2 is replaced by a bout of surreptitious laughter (17:17). This is the first time in the story that the topic of laughter has surfaced, and it will be a recurrent motif through the following chapters (see 17:17; 18:12,13,15; 19:14; 21:6,9; 26:8. "Jesting" [19:14], "playing" [21:9] and "fondling" [26:8] are all translations of the Hebrew verbal root *tsahaq* "to laugh".) Isaac's very name itself means "laughter". The link between laughter and fertility, both human and agricultural, runs deep in the Old Testament tradition (see e.g. Psalm 126). Words from the same root often refer to sexual "play" (see e.g. Exodus 32:6). This first mention of laughter in the Old Testament paints an extraordinary picture of contrasts. Walter Gross comments that "the Abraham prostrate in worship before God and yet laughing at the same time is one of the most inscrutable images in Holy Scripture".[29] Perhaps such a picture tells us that faith can encompass even a laughing doubt of God.

God has not forgotten Sarai even if Abraham has. She too is given a new name—Sarah, which means "princess"—appropriate for one who "shall give rise to nations" (cf. Genesis 12:2 "I will make of you a great nation") and be the ancestor of kings. She is (as was Hagar in 16:10) mentioned specifically as the recipient of God's blessing in words that are redolent of the original blessing of Abram in Genesis 12. "I will bless her and moreover I will give you a son by her". The link between blessing and Sarah's new role as birth-giver is important. In Eden, Eve's curse included the pain of birth-giving: now in this time when God creates new relationships with humanity that curse is reversed into blessing.

And yet? Sarah is still apparently off stage while all this is going on. Her future is being discussed between her husband and his God. She is still effectively a passive bystander. Her only active intervention in the story so far led to the existence of Ishmael who complicated the "history of salvation", and, one might add, Sarah's own life. God's final speech in this chapter, 17:19–21, is in a concentric or chiastic structure. At the centre of the chiasm in verse 20 are not words about Isaac, but words of promise for Ishmael, "I will bless him and make him fruitful". As father of twelve princes, he will be Israel's parallel. Ishmael may not be able to "live in God's sight" in the way that Abraham himself does (17:1), but with a name like Ishmael ("God hears") he cannot be forgotten: God has "heard" Abraham (17:20) as once he had also heard Hagar. Though the life of Abraham is moving convolutedly to its denouement, Ishmael's existence will continue to make its mark upon Genesis till almost the final chapter (see p. 338).

The final few verses of the chapter simply recount the carrying out of God's instructions about circumcision. Yet the detailed information about Abraham's and Ishmael's ages when the ceremony took place helps to reinforce a point. If both Abraham and his son Ishmael were circumcised on the same day, this means that Ishmael cannot be fully a child of the covenant of circumcision even though he has been circumcised himself. Only one conceived after the moment when Abraham has been circumcised can fulfil that role, and we are shortly to hear of the strange circumstances in which his conception takes place.

Entertaining angels unawares
18:1–19:38

Could the story in 18:1–15, which has a folk tale quality about it (there are loose parallels in both Greek and Middle Eastern mythology), be one of the ancient roots of the Abraham traditions? Set in Mamre, the location with which Abraham seems to have the closest links, it presents the pledge of offspring to Abraham in the course of a story. Westermann argued that this was the seed of the promise tradition developed elsewhere in the Abraham cycle: a seed dropped one day by the terebinths of Mamre.

18:1–15   God drops in. We can see it even if Abraham can't. Never before and never again in Genesis will God be quite so homely. The story reads rather like newspaper reports of a monarch dropping in for tea in a council flat. The difference is that most people would recognize the monarch if she called by. Abraham does not seem to realize who his visitor or visitors are, at least not until verse 10. Even though he "saw three men", he doesn't really see who they are (as with Chapters 16, 19, 21 and 22, the motif of sight is prominent).

There is both mystery and comedy here. Mystery because the description of who Abraham saw swerves backwards and forwards between the singular and plural. Is it one figure? Or is it three? Which one is Yhwh? Or are they all? Are two of them simply angels? Is this a story born in other ancient cultures which were not monotheistic, and so it sits uncomfortably transposed into the monotheistic world of the Old Testament? Abraham addresses the men as "Lord"—not aware of who he is speaking to, but ironically uttering the identical Hebrew word that later Israel was to use when people talked reverently about Yhwh. It is not surprising that Christian tradition has viewed this passage as an Old Testament prefiguring of the Trinity, the Three-in-One or One-in-Three. There have been exquisite icons painted of this scene, as Christian artists have used the story to depict the life and work of the Trinity. The best-known example is by Andrei Rublev. The mutual hospitality which is at the heart of the life of the Holy Trinity is drawn forth by Abraham's readiness to show a welcome to three apparently unknown human beings.

Yet there is also comedy. The behaviour of Abraham is almost exaggerated. He is too polite with the courtly style of his greeting: "My lord, if I find favour with you, do not pass by your servant." He is too generous in his offering: it is not a "little bread" he offers. "Three measures of choice flour" is an enormous quantity. He is too quick: how the calf is killed, prepared, cooked and ready within the space of one verse is a culinary miracle in the days before microwaves. He is not, of course, so polite to Sarah. His garbled instructions to her "Make ready quickly" distinctly lack the finesse of his greetings to the visitors. And after Sarah's Herculean efforts at baking, there is no mention of the bread she produced along with the calf which Abraham and his servant offered. Once again, she is sidelined. Is Abraham still the same fumbling figure that has seemed in some times past to be so mismatched with the promises in store for him?

No, for as elsewhere in the Bible the sharing of food becomes the time of revelation. It is impossible to overstate how important hospitality is in the creation of divine and human relationships. Sharing food and drink seems to have been an integral part of establishing a covenant relationship (Genesis 26:30–31; Exodus 24:11). There is a hint that here too, the covenant between God and Abraham has finally taken on a concrete reality only at this moment when Abraham shares food and drink with strangers. Abraham's mode of operations may have been clumsy, but at least they revealed the generosity of spirit for which God had been searching among humanity. Someone who offers hospitality to unknown strangers is indeed a person who is their "brother's keeper". It is significant to remember that this story is placed between several references to the fact that Abraham and his family were vulnerable *gerim*, ("aliens", 17:8; 19:9; 20:1; 21:34) who had received the hospitality of the land of Canaan. It is only when Abraham eventually demonstrates an equal concern for others who are vulnerable that he and Sarah can take root in the land, via their descendants.

The exercise of hospitality has involved Sarah as much as Abraham. She may remain half hidden behind the tent curtain, but it is only when she is involved, albeit indirectly, in the discussion, that the promise of the heir which has so dominated several of the previous chapters can finally be fulfilled. "Where is your wife Sarah?" are the precise words used to Abraham in 18:9. They remind us of the question addressed to Adam (3:9) and even more that spoken to Cain (4:9). It is only when human beings are "guardians" of each other, that the reversal of the ancient curses can proceed apace.

In due season   Sarah will have the child for which she has waited so long. The Hebrew phrase translated in this way in 18:10 and 18:14 is a rarely used expression; it means "about the time of reviving". It is probably a reference to the season of spring, but it perhaps includes a cryptic allusion to Sarah's and Abraham's situation. Old people, "advanced in age" with only the winter of their lives to look forward to suddenly will experience a new spring, a moment of "reviving". She will become a new Eve (whose name also comes from this root).

There is a hint in the passage that it is not simply Sarah's post-menopausal condition which stands in the way of conception. Does Sarah's pointed remark "my husband is old" suggest that by now Abraham himself was impotent, or perhaps that sexual relations had ceased between the pair?

But nothing stands in the way of Yhwh's desire to bless his people, or his ability to bring this about. "Is anything too wonderful for the Lord?" echoes the vocabulary used of the events at the Exodus, and when God's later acts of redemption for his people in Babylon are described.

First Abraham (17:17) and then Sarah had laughed at the ridiculous possibility of a son being born at their time of life. The last verse of the story hints at the uncertainties which still lie ahead. Eventually Sarah's laugh will ring out down the centuries like a shout of triumph, but for the moment it sounds like a cry in the dark. Yet Yhwh himself has the last laugh when Isaac (= Laughter) is born!

18:16-33 God has made a covenant with Abraham, and it is going to have consequences for God as well as for Abraham and his family. If the relationship between Yhwh and Abraham is to be real, he must let Abraham into his plans. No longer can God act totally on his own terms—he must allow himself to be judged by the standard he has set down for others. If Abraham's family is charged "to keep the way of the Lord by doing righteousness and justice", the code of behaviour which is required by the covenant (see e.g. Micah 6:8), then Yhwh too needs to conform to the same standard.

It is not accidental that the original promise to Abraham is hinted at in the language of these verses: he will become "a great and mighty nation, and all the nations of the earth shall be blessed in him" (cf. Genesis 12:2-3). In the rest of this chapter, we are going to discover what that means as Abraham intercedes for others, effectively seeking to become a means of blessing for them.

It is a decisive moment in the story of Genesis. Yhwh deliberates with himself: "The Lord said, 'Shall I hide from Abraham what I am about to do?'" There are only a few other points in Genesis when such divine deliberation is described (1:26; 3:22; 6:6-7; 8:21; 11:5-7). They are all moments of decision/crisis in God's dealing with humanity. All of them, except for this one, occur in the primeval history of Genesis 1–11. That is no accident, for there are hints in the story of Sodom and Gomorrah that it is a kind of "replay" of the primeval history.

> ## Links between the primeval story and the story of Sodom and Gomorrah
>
> **13:10** The plain of Sodom is like the Garden of Eden.
> **13:13** The wickedness of the people is monstrous (cf. 6:5).
> **19:5** Sexual misdeeds are referred to (cf. 6:1–4).
> **18:20–21** God descends and sees what is going on in Sodom (cf. 11:5).
> **18:12–13** Yhwh takes action to save one man and his family (cf. 6:13–14).
> **19:24** It rained (fire and brimstone) (cf. 7:10).
> **19:31** The daughters of Lot believe that there is no man left on the earth (cf. 7:23).
> **19:32–35** Lot gets drunk (cf. 9:21).
> **19:32–35** Incestuous sexual relations (cf. 9:22?).

But this time, unlike in the primeval stories a human being may, just may, affect the outcome, as he is made privy to those deliberations in the heart of God. It is striking that as two of the divine figures turn off towards Sodom, "Abraham remained standing before the LORD". It is as though he is blocking the way of this third and leading figure. At the very least, Sodom cannot be destroyed before Abraham has had his say.

The modern Jewish writer Elie Wiesel describes Abraham's intervention: Abraham "did not hesitate for a moment to take God to task as he tried to save two condemned cities from destruction. How can you—who are justice—be unjust? He was the first who dared to query God. And God listened and answered. For unlike Job, Abraham was protesting on behalf of others, not of himself. God forgave Abraham everything, including his questions."[30]

But, we may respond, did Abraham need to be forgiven? These verses are perhaps Abraham's greatest moment: the high point of his life and his relationship with God (greater even than his ambiguous willingness to sacrifice his sons, Genesis 21 and 22). There are echoes of a typical Middle Eastern barter scene, as God and Abraham bargain for the safety of the cities. "Suppose there are": 50 innocent people ... 45 ... 40 ... 30 ... 20 ... 10 ... ? Voltaire, the French eighteenth-century philosopher, poured scorn on Abraham's intervention—he regarded Abraham as a comic figure, an inveterate haggler who could not resist trying to cut a deal with God even at this moment. Yes, there are comic touches around, as there were earlier in this chapter when Abraham's effusive hospitality was painted, and there will be again when Abraham haggles once more, this time over a burial place for Sarah (Genesis 23). But Abraham's humanity, comic touches and all, is precisely what is going to be important. Because only a real human being will care enough for humanity to be a means of blessing for them, and in the process dare to try and teach God how God ought to behave.

Running through these verses are the keywords *tsaddiq* and *mishpat*, "righteousness" and "justice". They appear together many times in the Old Testament as a summary of the behaviour required by God of Abraham and of the people of Israel (see e.g. Isaiah 5:7). Sometimes, however, *tsedeqah* (righteousness) is contrasted with *tse'aqah* (the cry of distress of an oppressed party). The pun is made clearly in Isaiah 5:7, and perhaps also here as YHWH listens "how great is the outcry" (18:20). By contrast those who do "righteousness" (18:19) must stand alongside the "righteous" (18:23, both words are linked to *tsaddiq*). YHWH, as any good ruler or judge, needs to keep his side of the covenant by showing righteousness to those who are righteous/innocent and therefore in right relationship with him (see Psalm 72). That is the essence of justice. If Abraham is required to do "justice" (*mishpat*), so too must YHWH, as Abraham points out to him. "Should not the Judge (*shophet*) of all the earth do what is just (*mishpat*)?"

Abraham's temerity is disguised by the English translation: the repeated "Far be it from you" literally means "profanation". This is a word often used in connection with cultic worship, where it describes objects or people who are polluted and thus "defile" or render invalid a holy place or ritual. In effect, Abraham is suggesting that if God allows the innocent to suffer along with the guilty not only is he not just, but he is also not holy, and thus not God! (cf. Psalm 82:1-8, where the "gods" are demoted because they have "judged unjustly".)

Perhaps Abraham suddenly realizes how far he has gone with his murmured apology and consciousness of his status as part of creation "I who am but dust and ashes" (see also the comments he makes in verses 30,31,32). But he shows an extraordinary boldness, possibly unique in the pages of the Old Testament. He also moves theology into a new dimension. Never before in the history of humanity has the possibility of vicarious salvation been raised. The righteous may have previously saved themselves (as in the case of Noah) but that is not what Abraham is asking for. He is requesting that they should be the means of saving not only themselves but also their compatriots. He begins with only a few, fifty is not many within the context of a city, and the numbers shrink still further: "suppose ten are found there?"

Why does he stop at ten? Later Judaism would argue that this is the quorum needed in a synagogue. It may also be that the number we are left with must be larger than the family of Lot. The lengthy encounter leaves some unanswered questions hanging over us: it has held us in suspense as we draw near to the moment when we shall arrive in Sodom. Will we find that Abraham has been successful in saving this city after all his pleas?

And the LORD went his way, when he had finished speaking to Abraham. YHWH goes away and he will never again be seen so directly by Abraham. Perhaps such intimacy is too dangerous for Abraham; perhaps it is also too dangerous for YHWH!

Abraham returned to his place. Is the implication of the word "place" that after this strange dialogue when God and a human being speak openly almost on equal terms it is now time for Abraham to "know his place" and return to the normal status of a human being vis-à-vis the creator?

Yet something has changed. We will never again after this in Genesis read of internal deliberations in the heart of God. But perhaps we no longer need to, because the discussion between God and Abraham in this chapter has made it clear that human beings can know how God will behave. For now, there is a covenant, and it binds God and humanity mutually together in righteousness.

19:1–11   Abraham had received the divine messengers with generous hospitality—how will they fare on their visit to Sodom?

The scene at the beginning of Genesis 19 deliberately echoes, and contrasts with, the picture of the previous chapter.

Lot was sitting in the gateway.   Abraham had been sitting by the opening of his tent. It was "in the evening", a time that hints at the sinister dangers that may lie ahead in Sodom, rather than the middle of the day when the visitors appeared to Abraham. Lot bows low to the men and greets them with the same polite "my lords" that echo his uncle Abraham's words. As Abraham had done, Lot offers hospitality. But then subtle differences become apparent: his words are a little more curt, brooking no argument: "he urged them strongly", and the repast he prepared for them wasn't quite up to Abraham's standards. Does that "unleavened bread" hint at the speedy flight that will soon be necessary, as at the time of the Exodus?

It is as though we are re-reading the account of Abraham's hospitality once again, but in a way that is slightly off-key. Lot is doing his best, but he isn't quite Abraham, and he doesn't quite get it right. The previous chapter had ended with the phrase "Abraham returned to his place" (18:33). Even though Abraham is an alien (17:8) and still has some travelling around the land to do (20:1), he has a place where he fits in and which he can call his own. Lot, on the other hand, may look as though he is dwelling in Sodom, a proper city where people could live permanently (13:12; 14:12), but we are soon to discover that he doesn't really belong there. He may think he does—after all, he is settled by the city gate, where the city elders normally met to conduct business and share in judging the affairs of the city. He may even call the inhabitants of Sodom "my brothers", but he soon discovers that he is a rank outsider with no place where he can feel safe. The men of Sodom put him straight: "This fellow came here as an alien, and he would play the judge! Now we will deal worse with you than with them." Intriguingly the intensive form of the words translated "play the judge" creates an echo back to the discussion in the previous chapter between Abraham and YHWH about the importance of justice.

Perhaps Lot really knew that Sodom was no "safe place" all along. Is that why he is so insistent that the strangers accompany him into his house when they are willing to "spend the night in the square"? Is that why the story emphasizes how he goes out into the street to bargain with his fellow-townsmen, being careful to "shut the door after him"? He is trying to preserve his house as an "ark" of safety as hostility rages around him. But even his own personal space is no longer protected, as the men of Sodom "came near the door to break it down". Abraham is far more secure in a flimsy tent among wide open spaces than Lot is in a building in a walled city. It is only through the superhuman efforts of his guests that the safety of Lot, his house and his family is eventually guaranteed.

And what of the men of Sodom, "to the last man", as it emphasizes. What do they really want? The text does not pull its punches. "Bring them out to us so that we may know them." It seems they want to gang-rape Lot's guests. This may well be the meaning, but in fact the Hebrew is somewhat more ambiguous: they want to "know" the men. Is what is being referred to here, a desire simply to "know more about" these strangers: whether, perhaps, they were spies? Could it be that the basic problem in Sodom is not sexual perversion but xenophobia, the abuse of hospitality and fear of, or hostility towards, strangers? It is an intriguing suggestion.

On balance, it seems most likely that the intention of those attacking Lot's house was to make a sexual assault on Lot's visitors. But it is unhelpful to regard the story as a normative description of homosexual practice (for example in the way that the term "sodomy" which obviously derives from this incident has frequently been employed as a term for genital homosexual activity). It is also mistaken to regard the sin for which the whole city of Sodom was soon to be destroyed as being primarily homosexual practice. The sins of Sodom are alluded to in a number of other places in the Old Testament. They include adultery, hypocrisy, lack of charity (e.g. Ezekiel 16:49–50), but at no other point are they specifically stated to include homosexual activity. The sin of the city might best be summed up by the phrase to "do to them as you please". Underlying these words, spoken by Lot to the men of the city as he offers them his virgin daughters, is the well-known Hebrew expression "everyone did what was right in his own eyes". This phrase appears a number of times in the Old Testament (e.g. Judges 21:25) to describe a situation of unbridled anarchy and violence, characteristic of times and places where relationships between human beings have broken down. Like Cain, the inhabitants of Sodom deny the demands of human "brotherhood", explicitly to Lot, and implicitly to the strangers.

And what of Lot's offer of his daughters to the intruders? We are horrified by it today (though till very recently a number of male commentators on this passage were able to write as though it was to Lot's credit!). The silence of the storyteller is suspicious. Though it is not explicitly criticized, like other features of Lot's hospitality it seems distinctly off-key. Does Lot's willingness to see his daughters abused at this point pave the way for his own incest at the end of the chapter?

19:12–30 The end of Chapter 18 had left the issue in suspense: will there be found ten righteous people in Sodom, in order to prevent its destruction? The answer seems to be a resounding "No". Lot and his immediate family are the only ones who could be possibly considered innocent, and they do not add up to ten. Abraham's intercession appears to be ultimately of no avail.

Yet Lot and his family are spared. Is it because of their own innocence, or is it rather because God "remembered Abraham"? For several verses, the question remains unanswered.

It is hard work to rescue this family, and eventually turns into a black comedy. The sons-in-law (which may mean the betrothed fiancés of Lot's unmarried daughters) do not get out at all. "He seemed to his sons-in-law to be jesting"—a Hebrew word cognate to "laughter" appears in this sentence. It is the sound of unbelief. But the joke is on them at the end, as the tragedy unfolds.

As for Lot, his wife and daughters "lingered". The vividly onomatopoeic verb *yithmahmah* alludes to their hesitancy in leaving. In the Hebrew Bible, this word is written with a rare Hebrew musical note called a *shalshelet* set above it. The *shalshelet* instructs a reader to modulate their voice up and down the musical scale three times before moving on to the next word. The word *shalshelet* itself means a "chain", and it is as though

Lot and his family remained "chained" to Sodom which had been their home for so long. Perhaps his wife even more so than Lot: was she a native of Sodom with ties to the city that simply could not be broken? She was to remain there looking back to it for evermore.

The repeated word "flee" (Hebrew: *himmalet*) then puns on the name of Lot. Perhaps it is fitting because once he eventually starts fleeing, he goes all over the place: he cannot make his mind up where to settle. First he wants to go to a *little* city called Zoar ("Little"; Hebrew: *tso'ar*) in spite of the divine instructions to "flee to the hills". He cannot leave city life behind entirely, at least not straightaway. But as soon as he arrives there he is off again, this time to a cave in the hills. The story of Lot is the tale of a man who settles everywhere but cannot settle!

After Lot is finally sorted out the cities are destroyed, in a fashion that provided the raw material for later apocalyptic visions. What, if any, is the history behind the story of this destruction? It is probably a combination of geological observation, folk aetiology, and remembered traditions. There is no clear evidence of once large cities at the southern end of the Dead Sea (the presumed location of Sodom and Gomorrah). However, earthquakes are prevalent in the region, as are sulphur springs (which may have provided components of the description). The almost lunar terrain of the area is dotted with weirdly shaped rocks, a wide selection, from which tourist guides can choose their individually preferred "Lot's wife". Prehistoric archaeological remains do suggest that the climate of the area was once more equable and the terrain more fertile than it is today. It is even possible that the level of the Dead Sea altered suddenly and the tradition of that inundation further coloured the picture. Whatever the historical kernel, it is intriguing that there is no other event in Genesis which is referred to in the rest of the Old Testament as frequently as the destruction of Sodom and Gomorrah.

In the course of this chapter, we seem to have deviated far from the story of Abraham. Indeed the destruction of Sodom reads more like a saga from the primeval history than part of the ongoing story of the ancestors. But now we return to Abraham who is exactly where we had met him last: "the place where he had stood before the LORD". It was there that he had struggled to save Sodom; there now he sees the apparent failure of his efforts. Was it because there weren't enough innocent people in the city, or was it ultimately because God doesn't operate like that, saving the wicked because of the innocent? The question has hung over faith and history ever since.

Yet something has been accomplished, something won. Abraham had not asked for special treatment to save his nephew, but God had rescued him for Abraham's sake all the same. Abraham has begun to be a source of blessing for the nations—of which, as we shall shortly read, Lot is to be the father of two!

19:30–38 Our last sight of Lot reads like the final scene in a "Rake's Progress". The man who once had herdsmen, tents, and so much livestock that the land could not support him alongside Abraham, is now holed up in a cave with only his daughters. What happens next is perhaps intended as just retribution for Lot's willingness to sacrifice these daughters sexually to his fellow-dwellers of Sodom.

In a drunken stupor, he engages in incest with them. He is presented not as evil but simply pathetic. "He did not know", when his two daughters "knew" him. From this performance are born the ancestors of the Moabites and Ammonites. With a punning wordplay the narrator hints that the ancestor of the Moabites was so called because he was born "from our father" (Hebrew: *me'abenu*), and the ancestor of the Ammonites is called Ben-Ammi, because he is "son of my familial people". The actions of the daughters provide an aetiology for these two nations whose mutual antagonism to the Israelites and Judaeans was a constant factor in pre-exilic and post-exilic history. On the one hand, the story seems intended to disparage these ancient enemies: with a birth like that what can you expect! On the other hand, it does not let us forget that these peoples were close kin to Abraham's descendants, and deserve to be treated as such. (See e.g. Deuteronomy 2:9, with its favourable comment on the Moabites as the "children of Lot".) As the story of Ruth will remind us, even King David had a Moabite woman among his ancestors (see also p. 300, the story of Tamar).

The endangered future
20:1–22:24

Although the next three chapters appear diverse, they are subtly linked together. The stories concerning Abimelech are enveloped around the account of the birth of Isaac and the dismissal of Ishmael. In turn, the eventual fate of Ishmael prepares the way for what may happen in the following chapter to Isaac. Running throughout the chapters is the topic of heirs—and their endangering. It is also conspicuous that God is rarely referred to as YHWH in these chapters and the term *'elohim* (= God) seems to be preferred. Is this due to different sources being represented (see p. 33), or is there another reason intrinsically related to the story?

20:1-18 Abraham the "alien" is on the move again. This time he travels south from Hebron to reside "in Gerar as an alien". The pun on the Hebrew word for alien = *ger* which contains the same letters as the name of this city to which Abraham has now moved, Gerar, suggests that Abraham's alien status is going to be particularly important in the immediate future. We have just seen in the story of Lot how insecure life as an "alien" could be (19:9), even for people who had been settled in a particular place for a long time. Is Gerar going to be another Sodom? Perhaps this is why Abraham behaves as he does in the next few verses.

He is up to his old tricks! This time it is not the Egyptian Pharaoh to whom he seeks to pass Sarah off as his sister, but the King of Gerar (who is apparently a Philistine; see 21:34; 26:1). The repetition of this "trick" by Abraham was once considered a significant reason for suggesting that Genesis 12:10–20 and Genesis 20:1–18 come from different sources. But it is not that simple. The very bare way that the writer of Genesis 20:2 introduces the incident: "He said of his wife Sarah, 'She is my sister'", implies that the writer (and the reader) knows the content of Genesis 12:10–20, where the explanation for such a deception is set out. The two incidents, with Pharaoh and with Abimelech, are complementary in their present form. Even if they did originate in different literary circles their "doublet" presence in this part of Genesis is not mere repetition but designed for a narrative purpose.

We read of the incident with a heavy heart—it is really irritating that Abraham should try this one on again. Hasn't he learned anything over the past eight chapters? About trusting Yhwh? About treating Sarah with respect? He had been "getting there", but now it seems as though he is virtually back where he started. It is almost as though he is trying his hardest to jeopardize the promises that Yhwh made to him. In 18:10, Yhwh had promised that Sarah would have a child within a year. By now she must either be pregnant (not the most appropriate state in which to join a harem!) or shortly to become so. And if she were to get pregnant in the next few weeks, nobody would know whether the child was Abraham's or Abimelech's. Some child of promise!

God has to act quickly and authoritatively. In the earlier story we are probably meant to understand that Pharaoh did have sexual relations with Sarah, but this time God acts before Abimelech has a chance! Dreams are an effective way for God to communicate speedily with human beings and will be used increasingly to do so as Genesis develops (see Jacob's dream in 28:12–13). "God came to Abimelech in a dream by night and said to him, 'You are about to die because of the woman whom you have taken; for she is a married woman.'"

Not surprisingly Abimelech is put out! His (and Sarah's) continence is highlighted: "Abimelech had not approached her."

Then in words that remind us again of Abraham's conversation with Yhwh in 18:16–33, he argues, "Lord, will you destroy an innocent people?" Previously Abraham had acted almost as God's teacher; now it is to be this Gentile Abimelech. Words from the root *tsadaq* are rare in Genesis outside Genesis 18, so the appearance of this root once again in the word translated "innocent" surely means that we are intended to see a connection with the last time it had been encountered in that dialogue about divine justice. There is therefore a contrast being drawn, between Abimelech and the inhabitants of Sodom. In Sodom no "innocents" had been found, except from the family of Lot, Abraham's own kin. But lest Abraham (or Abraham's descendants, the first readers of Genesis) believe that no non-Israelite can have "integrity", we have now been introduced to Abimelech, a righteous Gentile, whose responses should shame Abraham, and perhaps even call into question his own righteousness.

"You have done things to me that ought not to be done", says Abimelech to Abraham.

Abraham's responses hardly justify his actions. We are not even sure that he is telling the truth. Is Sarah really his half-sister, as he maintains? This is certainly the first we have heard of this, though it is not impossible, and it is perhaps significant that no ancestry is given for Sarah in 11:29. (Marriages between half-siblings with different mothers were considered acceptable at various times and places in the Ancient Middle East.)

As for Abraham's professed belief that "there is no fear of God at all in this place", not only is it insulting; it is also clearly inaccurate. The story makes it clear that Abimelech does "fear God"—his comments during the divine dream confirm that. And as for Abimelech's retainers, "the men were very much afraid". There is plenty of fear around! Unlike what might have befallen him in Egypt (12:12), here in Gerar, absolutely nothing would have happened to Abraham if it had been known that Sarah was his wife.

The motif of "fear of God" will appear again in Genesis 22, where it will be applied to Abraham himself. But it is paradoxical that the first time that this phrase "fear of God" should appear in the Bible it is effectively linked to a Gentile. The tension between universality and particularity which has pervaded the cycle of Abraham stories still continues. Perhaps that is also why the word God (*'elohim*) has been used (in the main) in this chapter rather than YHWH. The name YHWH seems to be reserved in the Abraham cycle for situations when God is dealing with or on behalf of those who will be his own people, or perhaps (as with Hagar in Genesis 16) in a situation of particular intimacy. In this encounter with Abimelech, a "Gentile" ruler, the designation "God" is more apposite. The writers of Genesis seem to have believed that Gentiles could know God as God even if not as YHWH.

Abraham evidently has one or two things to learn from Abimelech. Instead of "fearing God", he seems distinctly grumpy about his divine call. "When God caused me to wander from my father's house." "Wandering" frequently bears a pejorative sense: people in the Old Testament tend to "wander" when they get lost physically or spiritually. Abraham seems for a moment almost to have lost the plot as well as his way! Is Abraham refuting the promise he was offered, or is he simply showing a certain amount of "savvy"? Abimelech may not be too pleased to hear that his realm is intended as part of a promised land! The generosity of his recompense to Abraham in 20:15–16, offering not only money but the pledge that Abraham can "settle where it pleases you", may be something he might live to regret (see 26:16). Intriguingly, Abraham's self-justification to Abimelech in verse 13 is one of the few places where "God" (*'elohim*) is linked to a plural verb. It is tempting to wonder whether Abraham is accommodating his form of speech to the Gentile Abimelech in this respect also.

Yet even though Abraham's flaws are all too apparent, God still has an important role for him, one that no Gentile could play. "He is a prophet, and he will pray for you." (20:7) This is the first time the word "prophet" appears in the Bible. It will not appear again in Genesis. To refer to Abraham as a prophet is in one sense anachronistic. The writers of Genesis knew this well; the point they want to make here is not historical but theological. One key role of prophets was to intercede with Yhwh on behalf of people. This aspect of the prophetic vocation is referred to in Amos 7:2 and Jeremiah 15:1. It is what is being alluded to here. Earlier in Genesis, 15:1–4, language distinctive to prophecy has been associated with Abraham. At various points, Abraham's story colours him not only as prophet, but also as priest and king. And when 20:7 describes Abraham as a prophet, it is not simply of him as an individual that it is speaking. The original promise of Abraham gave him and his heirs the responsibility of acting as a mediator of God's blessing to the Gentiles: "In you all the families of the earth shall be blessed" (12:3). In Genesis 18, Abraham had interceded for the people of Sodom—ultimately to no avail. But in his prayer on behalf of Abimelech—"Then Abraham prayed to God; and God healed Abimelech"—this vocation was beginning to come to fruition. For all God's willingness to deal with the Gentiles, and the recognition that they may have moral insights, the call and privilege of particularity was to be reserved for Abraham and his descendants.

And what of Sarah? Once again she has been silenced. Abraham does not even speak to her at all, which contrasts with Abimelech's gracious words to her in 20:16. Though is there a touch of pointed irony in his reference to "your brother"? Abraham speaks about the loyalty he has demanded from her (20:13), but he seems to have pushed this loyalty to the limit, and since the word translated as "kindness" (verse 13) is vocabulary that is often used in relation to a covenant, we might wonder whether he is pushing divine loyalty to the limit too.

21:1–8 The sterility with which the previous chapter concluded (20:18) is swept away by fertility and new birth. A son is born who is "a living and walking laugh".[31] Whenever people speak to or about Isaac they will speak "Laughter". Whenever Abraham and Sarah use his name, they will remember how they had laughed in disbelief when his birth was announced to them (17:17; 18:12), and the proof that God can work miracles will be before their faces. "Sarah said, 'God has brought laughter for me; everyone who hears will laugh with me.'" There is a delightful ambiguity about the last words of this sentence: "with me" could equally be translated "at me". Are we being invited to join in her joy, or laugh in amazement at this ninety-year-old mother? Sarah is so happy that it doesn't matter any longer! It doesn't even concern her that Abraham did the naming of this child (21:3), even though mothers in the Ancient Middle East often had this privilege reserved for them, and most other matriarchs of Israel assume this responsibility for their sons. After all, what better name than "Isaac" could there be for this child who had been laughed into life? (The slightly awkward position of 21:6 in the text has led some commentators to suggest that in an earlier version of the story, Sarah actually did name the boy.)

What a hundredth birthday present for Abraham! "Abraham was a hundred years old when his son Isaac was born." As always in the Abraham cycle, when dates are given, momentous events are taking place. What has happened at this unique moment in Abraham's life must be very special indeed. It has been quite a year! The time reference encourages us to look back to the last point that Abraham's age was mentioned, Chapter 17, a year ago, when he was ninety-nine. The link to that earlier passage is intensified by the precise reference to Isaac's circumcision when he "was eight days old, as God had commanded him" (see 17:10–18). (Genesis does not refer to the specific moment when any of the later patriarchs were circumcised.)

Surely the story of Abraham has now reached its climax, as the covenant itself is being fulfilled in the birth and circumcision of Isaac (see 17:10–12; 17:21)? We can also turn our eyes further back to the original formulation of the promise in Genesis 12:1–3: there the word "great" had been repeated in God's pledge. Now that we learn that Isaac is weaned and has survived the dangerous first two or three years of early infancy, we hear that word echoed; for Isaac, the first fruits of this covenant, "grew" (literally "became great"). The famine with which the story of Abraham had begun (12:10) is replaced by feasting, "a great feast", barrenness by abundance. We have commented in the introduction on p. 103 how the concentric patterning of these chapters leads us to expect that we have now reached the conclusion.

21:8–13   Not so. It is not over yet. The laughter turns swiftly sour. Logically we anticipate that the blessing of greatness with which the Abraham cycle began is going to be confirmed. But we will have to wait the best part of two chapters for that (22:17–18), and they are not going to be easy stories to read.

The weaning feast of Isaac is not the story's closure, but the inauguration of further complications.

Sarah saw the son of Hagar the Egyptian, whom she had borne to Abraham, playing with her son Isaac.   It is remarkable how the story cannot bring itself to mention Ishmael by name even once in this chapter, as Sarah herself certainly is unwilling to do.

What was Ishmael doing? Why was it so wrong for him to play with Isaac? The clue lies in that powerful root *tsahaq* which has threaded through the story of Isaac. Normally it has been translated "laughter"; now in a slightly different form it means "playing". Was it that Ishmael was too rough in his play with his younger brother? In view of the possible sexual connotations of the word (see p. 134) was he even sexually abusing him? Was it rather, (since the words "with her son Isaac" do not appear in the Hebrew) that Ishmael was involved in sexual play with the young women of Abraham's household, a visible reminder to Sarah of how much older he was than her own son, and how great a threat he and his potential heirs might be to Sarah's line? Ishmael was, after all, the firstborn, and in the natural way of things the firstborn would inherit the greatest of his father's possessions. And with Abraham already so old

... and Isaac so young? A recent creative suggestion is that the word is a kind of double pun: Sarah objected because she saw Ishmael "Isaacing", playing at being Isaac.[32] There he is, the big brother, laughing and trying to be the centre of attention on what was supposed to be Isaac's big day! He still behaved as though he was the heir! How dare he pretend to be "Laughter" when that should be reserved for Sarah's Isaac alone. If indeed this was the case (and it makes a lot of sense) then Ishmael's laughter is shortly to be turned into weeping (21:16).

Her language is fierce. "Cast out this slave-woman with her son." As in Genesis 16 we have been taken fast forward to Israel's own Exodus from Egypt once more. That harsh "cast out" was the action the Egyptian Pharaoh would take against the Israelites (Exodus 6:1; 12:39).

This slave-woman is repeated. Sarah's relationship with Hagar has altered from 16:2,5 when she was "my slave-girl". "This" can be a damningly distancing word, used, for example, when God disclaims any relationship with the Israelites (e.g. Exodus 32:9; Isaiah 6:9). When God speaks about Hagar to Abraham in 21:12, he will call her Abraham's slave-woman, but she will never be Sarah's ever again. (In fact, the Hebrew word translated "slave-woman" in this episode differs from that used in Chapter 16. It may well be that the word used now implies a lower social status, so that the change further emphasizes the diminishment of Hagar.)

It is striking that Abraham's distress is restricted to anxiety for his son, presumably Ishmael. God's next words to Abraham credit him with wider generosity of spirit than he actually seems to possess. "Do not be distressed because of the boy and because of your slave woman." But then comes the knife that will twist into Abraham's heart "whatever Sarah says to you, do as she tells you"—superficially innocuous, though perhaps strange to listen to in a patriarchal culture. But the phrase contains the identical verb "hear" and identical noun "voice" that was used in 16:2 when "Abram listened to the voice of Sarai" and took Hagar as a concubine. As we suggested then (see p. 125) such an expression in the Hebrew Bible normally means that trouble lies ahead. The seeds that Abraham sowed then are now to be harvested: once he heeded Sarah and Ishmael was born, so now he must heed her again and the child has to be sent away. Since the same verb "hear" appears in Ishmael's own name, there is possibly another twist in God's words. Abraham "heard" Sarah, even though he did not hear her use the name "Ishmael". So now this child of "hearing" has to be silenced; will God hear him one day instead? The echo in 21:13 of the original promise in 12:2 offers Abraham only rueful consolation—were those glorious beginnings really supposed to work out like this?

Early in the morning We will hear this phrase again very soon (22:3), because once one gets in the habit of "sacrificing" one son, one may find that one needs to sacrifice another. There are striking literary parallels between the dismissal of Ishmael and the near sacrifice of Isaac (see chart below).

Parallels between Genesis 21 and 22

Early in the morning	21:14; 22:3
Shoulder	21:14; 22:6
angel of God/LORD	21:17; 22:11,15
He sent/reached out (his hand) (Hebrew: *shalah*)	21:14,15; 22:10
She saw/He saw	21:19; 22:13
Do not be afraid/you fear God	21:17; 22:12
Boy	21:17; 22:5
Bush/thicket	21:15; 22:13
(lit.) Heed the voice of ...	21:12,17; 22:18

21:14–21 *Abraham ... took bread and a skin of water.* It is simply bread and water he offers and not very much of either. They may show Abraham's care, but they are a contrast with the "great feast" we have just celebrated for Isaac.

Putting it on her shoulder, along with the child is a gesture that hints at a regretful tenderness. The Hebrew syntax is convoluted here. It is actually not clear whether it is the provisions or the child or both which is placed by Abraham on Hagar's shoulder. One of the issues is the apparent age of

Ishmael at this time. Practical maternal experience of the writer of this commentary suggests that carrying a child above the age of three or four upon one's shoulders is not feasible! But Ishmael would presumably be fifteen or sixteen at this time according to the chronology of the overall Abraham cycle (see 17:24; 21:8). However, other features of this story (e.g. 21:15,18) clearly picture Ishmael as a young child in this story. One is driven to suggest either that the editing of earlier oral or written material has been uneven, or that strict chronology has been deliberately overridden by a desire to emphasize the pathos of the situation.

She ... wandered about in the wilderness of Beer-sheba. What is significant about Hagar's banishment to this territory is that unlike Shur (to which she fled in Chapter 16) it does not border her homeland of Egypt. It is exile to which she is banished, rather than flight to her homeland. The area is also (and presumably was in ancient times) a particularly waterless terrain. The rare word "wander" appeared also in the previous chapter, when Abraham complained to Abimelech how God had made him "wander" from his father's house (20:13). It is ironic of course that in this present chapter Ishmael could have made the identical comment—if he is old enough to speak.

The water didn't last long. Such a water skin (I write from the experience of leading groups on walks in the Judaean and Negev wildernesses) would only contain enough water to keep two people alive for a couple of days. In normal circumstances, anyone sending out a woman and child into the wilderness with just these supplies would be deliberately condemning them to a lingering and unpleasant death. Abraham presumably believed that he wasn't—because of what God had just told him. He is going to be required to show the same faith in the next chapter, when it comes to his other son, Isaac.

Ishmael is "the child": not her child, not Hagar's. It is as though the narrator dare not let us get too emotionally close to him. However, from the point when we are told that God heard Ishmael's voice the Hebrew switches from *yeled* to *na'ar*, translated as "the boy". The word *na'ar* normally refers to a slightly older child than does *yeled*, so it is as if the angel is giving him a future by altering the way he is described. (It also emphasizes the parallel with Genesis 22, where the angel refers to Isaac as *naʿar* in 22:5,12).

Back in Genesis 16:4, Hagar had "seen" that she was pregnant and had then "looked with contempt" upon Sarai. All that seeing then had eventually led to what has now befallen her. So it is appropriate that verbs of sight come to the fore once again at this crisis point in his life. "Do not let me look on the death of the child." In that other story she had been looking at the quickening of Ishmael's life; now she fears to gaze upon the inertness of his death. Yet it will shortly be through seeing that her salvation will come.

But before sight first comes hearing. "She lifted up her voice and wept." It is fortunate for her that the child has been named Ishmael (= God has heard) since with yet another deliberate play on his name "God heard the voice of the boy". In case we did not get the pun, it is repeated within the confines of the verse. God's response clearly echoes the language (the parallel is sharper in the Hebrew) used to Abraham (21:12, see above). At least we are now assured that if Abraham was then commanded to hear only Sarah, there will be another who will finally hear the child. Have those problematic and harsh instructions of God to Abraham had their sting drawn by the way in which God himself has done the listening to Hagar and Ishmael that he had forbidden to Abraham?

God may listen, but can Hagar still speak? The parallels between the present narrative and Hagar's earlier story (Genesis 16:1–15) draw ironic attention to the differences. Both feature a water source; in both, there is a pun on the name of Ishmael; in both an angel speaks to Hagar. But this time it is the angel of God who has simply called from heaven, rather than the intimate angel of the LORD whom she actually saw (16:13) on that previous occasion. She has become the passive recipient of a message, rather than one who speaks or names a deity. Once she had said "Have I really seen God and remained alive after seeing him?"; now her glance is restricted to a well of water—"God opened her eyes and she saw", though that at least means that she and her son still live. The special dispensation that had been granted to her in that earlier revelation is now subtly withdrawn. Is this in fact why the text uses "God" rather than YHWH in this story? She, like Abimelech, may be close to Abraham's family, but like him she is and will ultimately remain a Gentile. By contrast the narrator emphasizes the closeness between Hagar and her son: "Come, lift up the boy and hold him fast with your hand." The Hebrew words here offer another allusion to her earlier story. There that earlier angel had predicted how Ishmael's hand would be against all, and all against him, but now we see that at least that does not include Hagar's hand. Though he may be alienated from the rest of his kin (16:12), he and his mother form a tight-knit unit together. Growing up in the "wilderness of Paran" (part of the Sinai Desert) it will be logical for his mother to find him a wife from her own homeland of Egypt. Such an alliance distances him from the rest of Abraham's family and also prepares the ground for a later episode linked to Egypt in which Ishmael's descendants will have a part to play (37:25).

21:22-34 It is strange to meet Abimelech again at this point. He feels almost an intrusion between these powerful stories of the two brothers. Since this incident feels very much like the continuation of what happened in Genesis 20, we might ask why it has been separated from that earlier narrative. It is not unreasonable to suggest that the oaths of friendship which Abimelech demands from Abraham (21:23) are a corollary to the generosity he has previously shown in offering gifts and allowing Abraham to settle in his country (20:14-15). After all, Abraham's apparent deviousness has already seriously endangered Abimelech and his household (20:3-5). Appropriately, and perhaps pointedly, Abimelech uses the same Hebrew word *hesed* that Abraham had employed in his somewhat lame justification for his deception (20:13 translated "kindness"; 21:23 translated "loyalty"). Abimelech seems to be rescuing this key biblical word from the dubious use to which Abraham had previously put it (see comments on p. 150). It is a word deeply rooted in Old Testament covenant traditions, expressing the mutual loyalty upon which the covenant relationship (or a marriage relationship) depends and which in turn the relationship should strengthen (e.g. Hosea 6:6, "steadfast love"). Abimelech was offering Abraham greater privileges than those which were his by right as a *ger* or "alien". Yet a powerful *ger* such as Abraham had become could well affect the political stability of the district where he lived, which appears to be on the geographical fringes of Abimelech's realm. It is no accident that now Abimelech is accompanied by "Phicol the commander of his army"; he felt that heavyweight support was necessary. Abimelech is reminding Abraham that with privilege comes responsibility. The vocabulary makes it clear that he is proposing a mutual covenant with Abraham, and that is what transpires a few verses later (21:27).

However, as the story now stands this covenant is also linked to a specific incident in the ongoing saga of Abimelech's relationship with Abraham, a dispute about the ownership of a well, a matter of vital concern for a herder of animals such as Abraham. It may well be that this was originally told as an entirely separate story, for it fits uneasily with the previous verses. But when 21:22–24 was detached from 20:1–18, the incident of the well was incorporated here in order to give a rationale for the making of a covenant at this point.

The oath that formed a vital part of a covenant-making ceremony is particularly emphasized (21:24,30,31). It is used in 21:31 as an aetiology to explain the name Beer-sheba (= Well of the Oath). A link is also made with the number "seven", a Hebrew word which sounds very similar. Abraham set seven ewe lambs apart, probably to be cut up in the covenant-making ceremony (see 15:10). There is a double pun here, for the word "oath" is itself connected to "seven", and to "swear" meant originally to "seven oneself". Because "seven" was a sacred number (see p. 17) it was used for this purpose in solemn ceremonies.

This is the only occasion that Abraham actually plants a tree (at other times he builds an altar next to an already existing terebinth or oak). The "tamarisk tree" is actually a large, long-living evergreen shrub. Notable trees, particularly evergreens, have long been markers of holy places in the Middle East; their greenness acts as a sign of life and fertility amid the arid countryside. Perhaps it is only now, when Abraham has "seed" (15:5; 17:9), that he can actually plant such a tree himself. It is no accident that he should invoke YHWH as "the Everlasting God" (*'el 'olam*) at this point. Not only is there a connection between the "everlasting" God and the "evergreen" tamarisk. More significantly, *'olam*, everlasting, is a word that in Genesis is associated with covenant making (see Genesis 9:16; 17:7). Perhaps the only way for human beings to experience the "everlasting" is through a covenant relationship which includes the divine. The almost throwaway remark of 21:34 that Abraham then "resided as an alien many days in the land of the Philistines" reinforces this conclusion. It is only a covenant that makes long-lasting relationships possible, whether between God and humanity, or different groups of human beings.

This apparently intrusive story of Abraham's covenant with Abimelech has several functions within the overall Abraham cycle. It acts as a foil to the earlier occasion when problems had arisen for Abraham the herder in view of the scarce resources of the land (see Genesis 13:5-11). There in an incident which followed immediately on an occasion when Abraham had passed Sarah off as his sister, such controversy had led to division between Abraham and Lot. Now, by contrast, in another similar incident that also follows upon a wife-sister episode, the problem is resolved not by division but by the unity that is brought about through a covenant.

The reason for the displacement of this incident from its original setting directly after the events of Genesis 20 is probably twofold. First, it allows the threatened sterility of Abimelech's household (20:18) to be placed directly before the birth of Isaac and to contrast with it. Secondly, it also encourages us to compare Abraham's dealings with Abimelech and those with Hagar. Both stories are linked by the place name Beer-sheba and by a reference to a well, and remembering Hagar's name (see comments on p. 123) both seem to be linked to the motif of what it means to be, or treat others as, a *ger*. Is the covenant with Abimelech a better way forward for Abraham and his descendants to deal with non-Israelites? It is certainly a different way in which human beings deal maturely with each other, allowing God to begin to retreat from centre-stage.

22:1-14 This is probably the best-known episode in the Abraham cycle, revisited by literature and theology many times in the more than two millennia since it assumed its current form. It is "central to the nervous system of Judaism and Christianity".[33] Its power is drawn from a variety of factors:

The austerity and restraint with which the story is told: it is remarkable how much is crafted in the short space of fourteen verses (especially if one compares it with, for example, the lengthy retelling of the destruction of Sodom, or the betrothal of Isaac and Rebekah).

The narrative is at least as powerful for what is *not* said as for what is stated. One modern literary critic has described it as being "fraught with background",[34] an element which encourages the readers to empathize emotionally with the story and to seek to interpret for themselves.

It is constructed with an exquisitely painful precision; both literary structure and wordplays help to intensify its telling. "Vision, the seeing that produces understanding, is a central theme in the story, but in the shadow of the all-but-unbearable beginning, Abraham is blind to it until the surprising end."[35]

Its placement, near the end of the Abraham cycle, adds to its pathos and suspense; by now we have been through so much together with Abraham. Is it all going to end like this? Indeed the incident is retold in a fashion which seems to deliberately balance the opening of the cycle with the original call of Abraham back in Genesis 12 (see p. 103).

And then there is the awful and awe-full subject-matter, which challenges our notions of theodicy today, as it did for readers in ancient times. The story could be (and has been) described as the book of Job writ small, and like that other great example of Hebrew literature, it leaves those who read and engage with it profoundly disturbed, despite the apparently "happy" ending.

After these things An innocuous beginning, although the expression suggests that we might read the story now to be told in relation to what has taken place most recently. This, of course, means Abraham's dealings with Abimelech, and perhaps even more so, the experiences of Hagar and Ishmael, Abraham's other son.

God tested Abraham Does this statement relieve us? We know, though Abraham did not, that this is only a "test", and therefore hopefully real life—with Isaac—will be able to proceed once the test is complete. Or does it make us angry, that God should behave in such a cat and mouse fashion with a human being?

This is the only time in the Pentateuch when an individual is tested by God, although it will happen to Israel as a whole on several occasions after the Exodus, and also during the entry into Canaan in the early chapters of Judges (Exodus 20:20; Deuteronomy 8:2; Judges 2:22). When God tests

Israel, it seems to be an attempt to discover if the people are able to show a single-minded loyalty to God, perhaps even love (Deuteronomy 13:3) for him, exemplified by their willingness to trust God to provide for them. It involves them in listening to his voice, showing appropriate "fear" of him, walking in his way, and precisely obeying his commandments. Consistently, if they do this, they will prosper. All these elements of God's testing of Israel can be detected in the story of Abraham, either in this chapter, or in other passages that have a close affinity to it (Genesis 18:19; 26:5). The test is to discover whether Abraham trusts God enough to be single-minded, whether he has sufficient confidence to obey what God tells him to do. One could argue that he has been subject to this test once already—when he followed God's instructions and sent Ishmael and his mother away. But didn't we perhaps wonder then whether Abraham was using God as an excuse, a convenient way of sorting out a family quarrel? We can all hear God speaking to us when it is opportune to do so, and Abraham's loyalty to God has gone through so many twists and turns since we first met him in Genesis 12. Now, by contrast, the purity of Abraham's faith will be discovered as God demands of him the one thing that under no human circumstance would he ever have wished to relinquish.

It can help if we remember Yhwh's conversation with Abraham in Genesis 18. There it is made clear that Yhwh doesn't always know everything (18:21), so perhaps this too is now a genuine enquiry on God's part to discover Abraham's heart: he does not yet know how Abraham will respond. Perhaps this is not a cat-and-mouse god after all. And if we read this story having first listened to Genesis 18, we shall remember that "the way of Yhwh" involves righteousness and justice, and that the character of this God means that he does not glibly destroy the innocent. A small consolation, but one which will help us bear the terror of the story.

There is something else: normally in Genesis when the word *'elohim*, God, is used it appears without the definite article. But here, and in verses 3 and 9 of the story it appears prefixed with "the". It bequeaths upon the deity an intense solemnity as God addresses Abraham. However, it is fascinating that most of the other occasions in Genesis when the word for God is given the definite article (e.g. Genesis 5:22,24; 6:9; 17:18; 48:15) seem to be circumstances when a relationship of special intimacy with God is being portrayed. Is the inference that this test which Abraham is about to undergo is only possible because he is already so dear to God? For the very first time in the whole story cycle, he is addressed by God simply as "Abraham", as a man talks to his friend. This, it seems, is the context in which the "test" should be read.

Abraham's reply, "Here I am", is one of the defining structural features of the story. The single Hebrew word *hinneni* thus translated appears as a refrain twice more in the story (22:7; 22:11). This threefold *hinneni* powerfully builds up the drumbeat of the narrative.

God said, "Take" The untranslatable Hebrew particle *na* added to the imperative verb conveys a note of hesitancy or pleading. God is aware of the enormity of his request.

Reminiscences of Genesis 12 appear at several points. We note them in context.

As with that first call of Abraham the magnitude of what needs to be offered (country, kin, father's house) is gradually reinforced, "Your son, your only son Isaac, whom you love". The following comment by the medieval Jewish scholar Rashi, presented as a hypothetical dialogue between God and Abraham, perfectly captures this stepping up of God's request:

> Your son. He said to him, "I have two sons." He said to him, "Your only one." He said, "This one is an only one to his mother and this one is an only one to his mother." He said to him, "Whom you love." He said to him, "I love both of them." He said to him, "Isaac."

The vocabulary of the sentence is uniquely tender: *yahid* translated "only son", is the normal Hebrew word for an "only child" but seems often to echo parental pain and passion. Like *hinneni*, it will be repeated three times in the story (22:2,12,16), and through its pairing with the cognate word *yahdaw* (22:6,8,19) will carry much of the story's meaning. Some might object that Isaac wasn't Abraham's only son—for there was also Ishmael even if he was not a child of the covenant. But Ishmael had already been dismissed from Abraham's life, and at this point Abraham could not know for sure whether he had survived his ordeal in the wilderness. Isaac was the only son who now mattered.

And as for "love", intriguingly this is the very first time the word has appeared in Genesis. After this story, it will appear again in the book several times. It is fascinating that in Deuteronomy 13:3 the words for "test" and "love" should also appear close together. ("The LORD your God is testing you, to know whether you indeed love the LORD your God with all your heart and soul.") It is as though mutual love between human beings can only begin to flourish when we have first established that human beings can truly love God.

Go For the second time, we meet the unusual expression *lek leka* with which the story of Abraham had begun. Will he now need to sacrifice his future, as he had then been called to give up his past (cf. 12:1)?

The land of Moriah ... on one of the mountains This is the first of the wordplays around "seeing" which will echo through the chapter. The name of this mountain is clearly related to the verb *ra'ah* (= to see). Moriah is "the land of vision" (see chart of wordplays below). Since 2 Chronicles 3:1, Moriah, the mountain of Abraham's sacrifice, has been identified with the temple mount in Jerusalem. Was this identification originally intended by the writer of Genesis 22? This has been frequently disputed, with suggested identifications for Moriah ranging from Moreh (see Genesis 12:6), Jeruel, a town in Judah (see 2 Chronicles 20:16), Beer-lahai-roi (see Genesis 16:14) and Mount Gerizim (the Samaritan tradition). There may well have been various earlier "editions" of this story in which one or other of these sites was intended. However, by the time Genesis reached its final form Jerusalem was established as the pre-eminent cultic location of the people; it was the place one went to "see" YHWH (e.g. Isaiah 6:5). Since the ancestral stories of Genesis contain a number of aetiological stories explaining the origin of various Israelite and Judaean cultic sites (e.g. Bethel, 28:17–19, Mamre, 13:18, Beer-sheba, 21:33), it would be strange if there was no reference in Genesis to worship and sacrifice at Jerusalem, even if obliquely. It is likely therefore that one function of this story (though not necessarily the central one) was to act as an aetiology of the temple site in Jerusalem, and perhaps also to account for the fact that child sacrifice was not practiced there. The shrine that is established after Abraham's sacrifice (22:14), where "The LORD will provide" is the "mount of the LORD" (cf. Isaiah 2:2) in Jerusalem. The pun on "seeing" which runs throughout the chapter strengthens this possibility: most of the verbs of seeing here begin with the form *yer* which inevitably encourages thought of *yerushaliyim* (= Jerusalem).

Wordplays on sight in Genesis 22

Moriah (place of seeing/vision)	22:2
Abraham looked up and saw	22:4
God will provide (literally: will see)	22:8
Fear God	22:12
(The form of the Hebrew verb "to fear" looks very similar to certain forms of the verb "to see".)	
Abraham looked up and saw	22:13
The LORD will provide (literally: see)	22:14
It was provided (literally: was seen)	22:14

Offer him there as a burnt offering   There are several different kinds of sacrifice referred to in the Old Testament. This one is to be a whole burnt offering, in which everything is given to the deity. The totality of what is demanded from Abraham is stressed.

on one of the mountains that I shall show you recalls the similar, apparently vague, language used at the beginning of the story of Abraham ("go... to the land that I will show you", 12:1). It is at least a reassurance that God will accompany him on this journey—as he had accompanied Abraham in the years since he left Haran.

Early in the morning brings to mind the similar setting for the dismissal of Ishmael (see the table on p. 154 with other parallels).

[He] set out and went to the place ... that God had shown him. This phrase, which is repeated in 22:9, makes it clear that Abraham is seeking to obey the instructions he has been given as precisely as possible. In terms of literary structure, it opens a chiasm which leads us to the very heart of the story.

> ## The test of Abraham: Analysis of its literary structure
>
> **A1** He set out and went to the place ... that God had shown him.
> **B1** Abraham looked up and saw the place far away.
> **C1** Abraham took the wood ... and laid it on his son Isaac.
> **D1** The two of them walked on together.
> **E** Isaac said to his father Abraham "Father!" And he said, "Here I am, my son." (Hebrew: *hinneni*). He said, "The fire and the wood are here, but where is the lamb for a burnt offering?" Abraham said, "God himself will provide (literally "see for") the lamb for a burnt offering, my son."
> **D2** The two of them walked on together.
> **C2** He bound his son Isaac, and laid him on the altar, on top of the wood.
> **B2** Abraham looked up and saw a ram, caught in a thicket.
> **A2** Abraham called that place, "The LORD will provide".

On the third day The third day is always a special day in biblical symbolism (e.g. Genesis 40:20; 42:18; Exodus 3:18; Hosea 6:2). Things happen on the third day; perhaps like death, and maybe even resurrection.

We will ... come back to you. Was Abraham really already confident that "both" of them would return, or was he seeking to allay any fears of Isaac and the attendants? The ambiguity is surely deliberate.

Abraham... took the wood... and laid it on his son Isaac, and he himself carried the fire and the knife. The story never misses an opportunity to stress the relationship between Abraham and Isaac: the repetition of "his son" intensifies the agony. Gerhard von Rad comments how Abraham makes sure that he himself carried the fire and the knife which could be dangerous for the child[36]—ironic in view of the child's fate that lies ahead.

The two of them walked on together. This is the first time that the word *yahdaw* appears. The identical phrase will be repeated in verse 8 which intensifies the emotional content. The punning between *yahdaw/yahid* has begun. Both expressions are connected to the Hebrew word for "one". When the father is prepared to offer his "one" son, with the two of them intent on the action "as one", the duality that has been a feature of human existence since Genesis 3 begins to be embedded in the divine unity. "By showing his willingness to give up his only son, Abraham gets him back, and a much deepened togetherness begins, both between father and son, and between the Lord and his obedient follower."[37]

Isaac said to his father Abraham, "Father!" And he said, "Here I am, my son." Structurally verses 7 and 8 form the chiastic heart of the story. Isaac's call to his father suggests the beginnings of his unease with the situation. (Is this why he doesn't mention the knife in his question?) Abraham's response to him is the identical *hinneni*, "Here I am", with which he has already expressed his readiness to God (22:1). It is the response offering security that any parent might give to a frightened child when it calls out upon a dark night. But with bitter irony this father is apparently shortly to become the agent of his child's terror.

Abraham said, "God himself will provide the lamb for a burnt offering, my son." Is this the exact moment when Abraham passes his test? When he shows this absolute trust in God's ability to provide (literally "see"—in the sense of "see to") that God seeks from human beings? In terms of the wordplay that runs throughout this story, it is because he knows that God will "see to" the offering for the sacrifice, that he, Abraham, will be able to "see" the sheep that has perhaps been there all along on that mountain named "The LORD will see to it". The literary structure of the chapter reinforces this conclusion: Abraham's verbal response at this point forms an exact parallel to his acted response of obedience when God addressed him in verses 1–3. Does this mean that the ultimate "test" is not so much whether Abraham is willing to sacrifice his son, but whether he is completely confident in God?

This may well be so, but the tension of the story is not allowed to dissipate immediately. We, the readers, are offered an excruciating choice: are the words "my son" simply a vocative, or are they intended to be in apposition to the expression "lamb for a burnt offering", which has immediately preceded them? Is Abraham obliquely telling Isaac that he will be the sacrificial animal? The writer lets us make that decision for ourselves.

The angel of the LORD *called to him from heaven . . . "Abraham, Abraham".* This is almost a repetition of the divine words with which Abraham's ordeal began. But the doubled use of his name here somehow cancels out the original dreadful command to him: it may also indicate a note of haste—seeking to stop Abraham's action at the very last minute.

It is now "the angel of the LORD" speaking "from heaven". Earlier it was God who spoke. The words *'elohim* (God) and YHWH (LORD) both appear exactly five times in this chapter—which certainly creates problems for assigning this chapter to a particular source on the basis of its use of the divine name! It may well be that the balance in the naming is deliberate, as the story shifts from the distant *'elohim* who instigated the dreadful command, to YHWH with whom Abraham has dealt intimately over the preceding chapters. There is a clear parallel to "the angel of God . . . from heaven" whom we met in the story of Ishmael (21:17); but Ishmael and his mother have now been excluded from the covenant, and because of that they can no longer know God by his familiar name, YHWH. On the other hand, in both stories the angel speaks "from heaven". It would seem that YHWH is now withdrawing from Abraham's direct gaze as well. For now that Abraham has "looked up" and seen a sheep which God has "seen", he no longer will be able to see the God who has appeared to him so directly up till this point! Among the many ironies of this story is the fact that from the time that Abraham reaches Moriah, the "land of vision", he will never again see God in his lifetime. Sight is to be transmuted into fearing ("you fear God" [22:12]; see also notes on 13:14 on p. 113 on "Raise your eyes" and on 20:11 on p. 149, on "fear of God").

22:15-19 *The angel of the* LORD *called to Abraham a second time from heaven.* There had been no second call for Ishmael and his mother. The angel will speak in language that is reminiscent of the prophetic and Deuteronomic tradition but also reminds us of the original and earlier formulations of the blessing of Abraham (12:1-3; 13:16; 15:5) and perhaps even take us back to the beginning of human history. Underlying the word "numerous" is a Hebrew expression which has also appeared in Genesis 16:10 (see comments p. 127) and Genesis 3:16, where it is used to speak of the greatness of the woman's suffering in childbearing. One can wonder whether its reappearance here is intended to suggest that finally that ancient curse is undone, first through Sarah for whom childbirth had been a blessing (17:16), rather than curse, and now through the obedience of Abraham, which has superseded the disobedience of the garden.

That this possibility is likely is reinforced by the last words of the divine voice: "because you have obeyed my voice". Finally Abraham has got it right after listening to the voice of Sarah mistakenly (16:2) and of necessity (21:12; see comments on p. 153). But of course he wasn't the first man to "listen to the voice" of someone other than God—that was Adam's responsibility (3:17). So Abraham is not only repairing his own mistakes but those of humanity before him.

Your offspring shall possess the gate of their enemies. The divine oracle now looks forward as well as back. The words resonate with those that will be pronounced over Rebekah as she leaves her homeland to marry Isaac (24:60). They also have a political and military content which looks forward to Israel's later history.

Abraham returned to his young men. The fact that Isaac is not specifically mentioned here generated considerable speculation among ancient and medieval exegetes. In fact, Isaac is almost certainly intended to be included within the final "together" of the story.

22:20-24 The Abraham cycle is "tailed" by this brief genealogical notice, as it had been "topped" by a similar report in 11:27-30: Abraham's brother Nahor features in both passages.

Two names stand out: Uz, which brings to mind the "man from the land of Uz", Job, and his story so similar to that which we have just read. Yet in Job's experience there had been no substitutionary ram for his children. It is interesting to speculate whether the story of Job, well known by the time of the exile (see Ezekiel 14:14) might have influenced the development of the Abraham cycle.

And besides the twelve sons (surely a significant number!) of Nahor, there is mention of one daughter, "Rebekah". Isaac has emerged from his ordeal not as a boy, but as a man ready for marriage, and we are being prepared to meet his bride. But that's another story...

A wedding and two funerals
23:1–25:18

Chapters 23–24 feel rather different in style to the earlier episodes involving Abraham. They are almost like an epilogue to the rest of the story, perhaps even squeezed in when most of it had already been composed. Their themes—burial and marriage—were pressing concerns to the post-exilic community, both in Palestine and in Babylon.

23:1-20 Jewish rabbinic tradition suggested that the reason for Sarah's death, announced so suddenly at the beginning of this chapter, was that she had heard a (false) rumour that Abraham had killed her son Isaac, and died of the shock. This is nowhere explicitly stated in the actual text but the jarring contrast between the style of Genesis 22 and 23 "shocks" the reader and makes such an interpretation feel entirely plausible. God, who has been so very present in the previous chapter, is almost entirely absent from this one. In the last chapter, God had taken direct action to preserve one facet of the promises (offspring); now it will seem as though Abraham is on his own, at this crisis moment of his life, when his wife has died, and it will be up to him to acquire enough of the "promised" land even to bury Sarah.

The mention of "the Hittites" is strange here; the great Hittite empire of the second millennium BC was centred on Anatolia (modern Turkey), but Hittite power extended into the coast and hill-country of Canaan. However, the term seems to be used to refer in a general way to the pre-Israelite inhabitants of the land.

I am a stranger and an alien residing among you. Abraham's status as a *ger* is at the heart of this story. Normally a "stranger" would not be able to own land outright. The Hebrew terms *ger* ("stranger") and *toshav* ("alien") are paired elsewhere in the Pentateuch (e.g. Leviticus 25:23), although they are there translated slightly differently. Since Leviticus 25:23 strikingly claims the land as belonging to Yhwh and maintains that the Israelites are still to be "aliens and tenants"—albeit now of Yhwh rather than non-Israelites, one can wonder whether Abraham may here be hinting at more than the Hittites realize, or perhaps even more than he realizes himself. The issue of ownership of the land is a major topic in this chapter. Should it belong to the Hittites? To Abraham? Or to Yhwh?

Give me property among you for a burying place. Included in this request is the Hebrew word *'ahuzzah* which means "property". It also appears in 23:9 and 23:20, translated there as "possession". The word had first appeared in Genesis 17:8, when, during the making of the covenant God promised that the land would be given as "a perpetual holding". The repetition of the word three times in this chapter is a verbal clue that the purchase of Sarah's tomb will be in effect a down-payment on that promise.

The Hittites are certainly aware of the significance of what Abraham is asking for. Their apparently kind offer to provide burial space for Sarah in one of their graves neatly side-steps what Abraham is really asking for. Once he has been allowed to purchase land his political status will have been irrevocably altered.

However, the Hittites' offer of shared space is not enough. Not least because the separation of Abraham's family from other peoples which had been symbolized by the covenant of circumcision, would not be able to be properly fulfilled if in death his kin is intermingled with the Hittite dead. From the exile onwards members of the Jewish community sought to maintain their separate identity primarily via rituals celebrated in the family, associated with birth (circumcision, Chapter 17), death (here), and, as we shall see in Genesis 24 and 28, marriage.

Abraham asks respectfully (the elevated level of mutual politeness is one of the features of this chapter) to buy the cave of Machpelah belonging to Ephron the Hittite, "at the end of his field". The location is important: it would allow for access to the grave by Sarah's family without trespassing on Ephron's land. Sarah's welfare after death would partly depend on how well she was physically remembered and her grave was tended by her family.

But Abraham is offered more than he had asked for, in the bargaining scene which follows, with which those who have ever purchased goods in a Middle Eastern bazaar may be ruefully familiar. It all happens "at the gate of his city", the place where trade and official business of a city was conducted. Everyone can see what is going on: this purchase is to be above board and completely legal.

Ephron offers to "give" Abraham both the cave and the land where it was situated. The writer of the story must have chuckled as this verb is repeated in verses 11 and 13. It is an expensive gift—for Abraham. As he is well aware the actual price will shortly be mentioned, in a throwaway fashion. Ephron has taken the opportunity to sell him his land as well as the actual cave. We can only estimate the value of the asking price "four hundred shekels of silver", but a comparison with the price paid by Omri for the whole site of the city of Samaria, two talents or 6,000 shekels (1 Kings 16:24) suggests that it was fairly exorbitant.

By now, Abraham cannot withdraw from the transaction without losing face. Not that he wants to. He "agreed with Ephron". The distinctive idiom of legal vocabulary dominates verses 16 to 18. We are being assured that this purchase will be unquestionably legal. Similar vocabulary is found in Jeremiah 32:6–15 when Jeremiah purchases a plot of land at Anathoth which had once belonged to his family. Jeremiah's action is a statement of confidence in the eventual future of his people in the land even on the eve of the Babylonian exile. Similarly here, Abraham's purchase of the tomb is both fulfilment and promise. For the patriarchs and matriarchs themselves, it meant that the promise was coming to fruition, since in death at least they were "no longer strangers", but really belonged in the land. For their descendants in Canaan, Palestine or exile, it was a pledge, as Jeremiah eloquently puts it, that "houses and fields and vineyards shall again be bought in this land" (Jeremiah 32:15).

24:1–67 We are going on a long and dreamy journey. The tempo of this leisurely chapter reflects the swaying pace of the camel caravan with which Abraham's servant journeys to Aram-naharaim (literally Aram-between-the-rivers, i.e. Mesopotamia) to find a bride for his master's son.

This is the longest narrative in Genesis 12–36. Its style of narration, by which in verses 34–49 the servant repeats to Rebekah's family virtually the whole of what we have already read in verses 1–27, deliberately slows the story down. It is as though the writer is telling us that what is happening now is make-or-break time for God's promise to Abraham—if the right wife cannot be found for Isaac, everything could still ultimately fail. We need to be assured that Rebekah is the correct choice, and it is worth taking the time to do so, although we are kept in suspense until the story nears its conclusion.

It is Rebekah's story. She is exceptionally proactive (certainly for an Ancient Middle Eastern girl!). By contrast, Isaac, her future husband, feels strangely passive in his own betrothal sequence. Note that he is not mentioned by name anywhere between verses 14 and 62, he is simply referred to by the servant as "my master's son". There may well be good reasons why Isaac should not go back himself to his father's earlier home to find his own bride, but this surrogate wooing for a man of forty effectively prepares the way for the quiescent and almost supine Isaac we will meet again in Genesis 25:28; 27:1–46.

Abraham was old, well advanced in years. If there is to be a future, it will be with a new generation. Sarah is already dead, but before she died, we heard of the birth of another woman (22:23) who may be her substitute and successor as matriarch. That hint is now to become actuality.

The Lord had blessed Abraham. During the course of this story, we will discover that this includes economic prosperity (24:35), as well as the birth of the sons about which we knew already. God's blessing, as expressed by the theology of this chapter, does not involve clear and direct intervention by the divine, but is rather the undergirding by God of basic aspects of human life, nudging it in the direction of wellbeing. Similarly God is present in the actions of this story, but not as obviously as in Genesis 12–22. We are invited to regard the eventual success of the servant's mission as being due to the overarching providence of God, but are not forced to see it in these terms.

Abraham said to his servant who ... had charge of all that he had. The status of the servant is an indication of the importance of this mission. However, it is remarkable that the servant remains anonymous throughout this lengthy narrative. (We perhaps assume he is to be identified with Eliezer of Damascus, 15:2, but this is nowhere stated.) The effect is to accentuate the role and guiding hand of Abraham himself in the journey and the negotiations which follow: the servant is not acting as an independent entity.

The LORD, the God of heaven and earth. The designation of God in the oath sworn by the servant to Abraham recalls the blessing formula used by Melchizedek (14:19). Abraham's vision of God is growing steadily wider: such a designation is appropriate for a deity who will accompany his servant on a journey that will take him far from the promised land. The assurance of the story that YHWH can be prayed to and worshipped (24:12,26–27) in a foreign land contrasts with the picture given in 2 Kings 5:17, where YHWH's presence seems to be linked to the very soil of the land of Israel.

You ... will go to my country and to my kindred and get a wife for my son Isaac. Abraham's anxiety over possible intermarriage between his family and native Canaanites undergirds the story. The same concern is raised in relation to Jacob (27:46–28:5). The situation of the Babylonian exiles (who would have lived not far from the hypothetical site of Aram-naharaim) and concerns about intermarriage in the early post-exilic period may be reflected here. Is the story implicitly criticizing those who were prepared to intermarry with non-Israelites living in or near Canaan? (See also comments on Genesis 28 on p. 226)

The phrase used to describe the servant's destination is striking: "my country ... my kindred". Similar phrases are used at two further points in the story (24:38,40). They are reminiscent of the expression used in YHWH's original call of Abraham (12:1), and in case we fail to notice the parallel, Abraham conveniently repeats it in 24:7: "The LORD the God of heaven, who took me from my father's house and from the land of my birth." For the woman whom the servant selects will need to make a similar leap of faith to that made once by Abraham himself, agreeing to travel with this anonymous servant to meet an unseen and apparently anonymous bridegroom in a land far from her own family. Yet only such a woman would be suitable for the role of matriarch of God's people.

The LORD ... will send his angel before you. The angelic messenger has a different role in this story as compared for instance with Genesis 16 or 22. There he spoke or was seen directly: here he is the personification of a more vague guiding presence who will accompany the servant on his journey. When the servant "bowed his head and worshipped the LORD" (24:26), it is presumably before the accompanying angel. It is, however, notable that the only time the angel is mentioned again in the story is when the servant is recounting his mission to Rebekah's family, so is the eventual success of the mission due to angelic guidance, or human intuition, or is there a relationship between the two? A similar expression is used several times in the Exodus account of the wilderness wandering (Exodus 23:20). There too a divine presence watches over a difficult journey.

You must not take my son back there. This strong statement seems to be linked to God's promise of the land which Abraham has just reiterated (24:7). For Abraham or his descendants to return to Mesopotamia might undo this promise. And yet eventually one—Jacob—would have to. And what about Abraham's later descendants who had been taken to Mesopotamia as exiles? Had this invalidated the promise?

The servant put his hand under the thigh of Abraham his master and swore to him. The intimate touching of Abraham's genitals that this implies reminds us of the connection between the servant's mission and the destiny of Abraham's progeny. The servant's own future is being vowed as well—if he breaks his oath, he too will lack descendants.

Taking all kinds of choice gifts ... [the servant] went to Aram-naharaim. These helped to establish his credentials as the servant of a wealthy man, which might well make his mission easier to accomplish. They would also be used to pay the formal bride-price which was customary.

To the city of Nahor   Nahor, Abraham's brother, is suddenly mentioned in the story. We are aware of who Nahor is through the references to him in 11:26–29 and 22:20.

By the well   So far in Genesis a well has been a place where God has been seen (16:7–14), where an angel has saved the lives of Hagar and Ishmael (21:19), where a covenant has been made (21:25–30) leading to the name of Yhwh being invoked there. What will happen at this well? On the surface it is something more secular—finding a bride—but will God be present at this well too?

For the first time in Genesis, we listen to the actual words of a human being praying. Cain (4:13–14) and later Abram (15:2–3) perhaps called out to God in an agony of spirit, but these words and the later prayer of the servant in 24:27 are the first formal prayers in the Bible. In those earlier instances it may also be that God was regarded as being visibly present with the speaker, whereas now it is a petition to an unseen God. That prayer is an important part of the story is made clear by the way it is twice emphasized (24:42,48) when the servant recounts his experiences to Rebekah's family. From now on prayer will be an important way for human beings to relate to God; it will bridge the gap between the earthly and divine worlds: "Through prayer, this little part of worldly life is made into a part of the ongoing and providential purposes of God."[38]

Although the condition the servant imposed upon himself (24:14) for selecting the "right" bride might seem arbitrary, it actually shows a good deal of worldly wisdom. The test he has devised will reveal clearly whether the girl has generosity of spirit.

Rebekah is on the move! She suddenly appears in a hurry: "before he had finished speaking", and throughout her story she moves and speaks fast and decisively (24:20,28,58). The swiftness of Rebekah seems like the ideal response to the servant's prayer. She has some obvious attributes (her beauty) which both we and the servant can see, and others (her virginity and genealogy) to which at the moment we alone are privy. But what about her inner beauty? How will she fare in the servant's test?

Once before generous human hospitality had proved decisive in God's plans (Genesis 18); Rebekah's response reminds us of Abraham's on that earlier occasion. And as then, there is a touch of comedy around. In both instances what is described as a little (18:5; 24:17) quickly becomes a lot! We fail to realize what a massive operation watering ten thirsty camels would have been; Rebekah must have been going up and down to the well like a yo-yo for an hour or more! No wonder she, and the story pauses (24:19a) after the servant himself drinks, before she eventually makes the offer on which her future will, unbeknown to her, rest. It must have been a long pause—especially for the servant.

Robert Alter's work on "type-scenes" has made us aware of how certain typical literary scenarios can be repeated with subtle differences.[39] One of these "type-scenes" is the betrothal. In such stories a hero journeys to a foreign land, meets a young and beautiful maiden at a well, water is drawn, the hero meets the girl's family, and then she eventually becomes his bride. This "type-scene" is reflected here, in Genesis 29:1–10; Exodus 2:15–20; Ruth 2:9, and even John 4:4–30, when Jesus meets the woman of Samaria at a well. It then becomes significant to note where a particular story deviates from the standard type. There are two points where Rebekah's does so. First Isaac, "the hero" and potential bridegroom is not present in person; secondly it is often the man that does the water-drawing, particularly if it involves the large-scale watering of animals. Viewed in this light Rebekah's actions become even more remarkable. She will be a worthy daughter-in-law for Abraham.

The man gazed at her in silence to learn whether or not the LORD had made his journey successful. YHWH clearly had done exactly this, but not by the kind of direct intervention we had seen earlier in the story of Abraham but working through a human heart and mind. In fact, YHWH helps the servant out on his mission even further. In his eagerness for his "test", the servant had temporarily forgotten an important element of

Abraham's original criteria, that the bride should be from "my kindred" (24:4). And now the servant gives away weighty jewellery, presumably intended as part of the bride-price, without first enquiring who this girl is. It is somewhat forward on his part: it could even be disastrous!

It is indeed fortunate that the servant eventually discovers she is from the ideal family—there are no closer kin to Abraham. Is this mere coincidence, or does God's providence work like that? The servant's prayer in response gives us his view. In speaking of how YHWH "has not forsaken his steadfast love and his faithfulness" he uses language that is rooted in Israel's covenant traditions: the words *hesed* (steadfast love) and *'emet* (faithfulness) that are paired here are also paired in God's own self-designation to Moses at Sinai ("The LORD, a God ... abounding in steadfast love and faithfulness", Exodus 34:6). God is fulfilling his covenant with Abraham by using the common sense of the prudent servant to ensure that the right woman is discovered. It is more than chance.

The girl ran and told her mother's household. Note that the subject of marriage has not yet been broached; it would be unthinkable to raise it directly with the girl herself, in an era of arranged marriages. Yet we already have a sense that Rebekah will be no passive object in the decisions of others. It is her "mother's household" to which she runs—an unusual expression. It fits with the way that her descent from a woman, Milcah, has been stressed (24:15,24). By contrast, her father Bethuel plays less of a role in the marriage discussions than might be expected (24:55): Laban, Rebekah's brother, plays a paternal role, perhaps a sign that it is time for the new generation to assume prominence.

Rebekah had a brother whose name was Laban. Our first meeting with Laban raises our suspicions. On the surface, he is exceedingly hospitable, but we cannot help wondering whether the warmth of his welcome has been coloured by the expensive jewellery that his sister has been given. Would he have run "out ... to the spring" unless he had first seen the "nose-ring, and ... bracelets"? When we meet him again in his dealings with his nephew Jacob our original suspicions will be more than confirmed.

However, the servant insisted "I will not eat until I have told my errand." The sharing of food helps to ratify relationships. It is only appropriate to delay eating until the business has been done. The speech of the servant recapitulates what we have already learned from the narrator, and by listening to the servant's conversation with Rebekah. But there are some subtle differences, which reinforce our impression that this servant is a man who is worldly-wise. He emphasizes the great wealth of Abraham (24:34) and the fact that Isaac is the heir to "all that he has". It is from Abraham's "father's house" rather than simply his wider kindred (24:4) that the bride is to be found. The servant does not explicitly mention God's promise (24:7). Intriguingly, in his speech he changes the order of his dealings with Rebekah: now he states that he discovered that she was Bethuel's daughter before giving her the presents, whereas we know this discovery was only made afterwards. This alteration clears the servant from having made what would have been a social faux pas—it also helps to put the pressure on Rebekah's family to agree to the match! His final words veer somewhat towards moral blackmail: "if you will deal loyally and truly with my master, tell me". The servant repeats the same Hebrew words *hesed* and *'emet* with which he had thanked YHWH (24:27 see above). It reinforces the impression that the choice of Rebekah is providential, and that God has had a hand in it, working through the anonymous servant. His words have the desired effect.

Throughout the chapter, the name YHWH has been used by both the servant and by the members of Rebekah's family: sometimes it appears in association with God (*'elohim*). The choice of this "particular" name for the deity helps to remind us that Rebekah's family are an intrinsic part of Abraham's kin. Although they reside far away, they are in effect closer to him than either Abimelech or Hagar, both of whom ultimately relate to God only as *'elohim*. The bride for Isaac has to come from a family where YHWH is already known as YHWH.

Were Rebekah's family having second thoughts by the next morning? We probably should not read a great deal into their delaying tactics: it is rather that the servant sounds abnormally anxious to depart. Now that his mission is accomplished, the pace of the story speeds up. But the exchange allows Rebekah a voice to participate in the decision about her future. We suggested above how it is important for the wider story of Genesis that a woman should make the same "leap of faith" that once Abraham himself had made. But how is this to be made clear in this culture of arranged marriages where women, especially, had little choice over their potential marriage partners? In the earlier discussions with Rebekah's family, she did not speak; she was simply an object to be passed over: "Rebekah is before you, take her and go." Now she has the opportunity to imprint her own assent. Her stark response "I will" (one short word in Hebrew) reprises the verb with which Yhwh had commanded her future father-in-law to leave Haran sixty-five years before. Though God might be speaking to her through the promise of a new human relationship rather than the challenge of the totally unknown, she has proved herself a worthy matriarch of the family of faith. It is right that the blessing her family speak over her as she departs deliberately recalls the words of the blessing spoken to Abraham by the angel of the Lord after the near-sacrifice of Isaac.

It is intriguing that Isaac should have moved to Beer-lahai-roi, the very place to which Hagar, his father's concubine, fled while pregnant with his half-brother Ishmael. Does one detect in this a need on Isaac's part to distance himself now from Abraham, to find his own relationships and to discover his own future? The text gives us an impression of a reflective and perhaps solitary Isaac.

But what happens at this place of seeing is now very different from that which Hagar had experienced. Instead of divinity Isaac and Rebekah now catch sight of each other: and the loneliness of Isaac's existence after the death of his mother is apparently to be cured by their mutual love. This is only the second time the verb for love has been used in Genesis (cf. 22:2), and the first time it has described the relationship between a man and a woman. Since Isaac and Rebekah are apparently the only absolutely lifelong monogamous couple with a major role in Genesis 12–50, it is appropriate that it should be spoken of them. There are echoes of Genesis 2 around: for Isaac has now emotionally left his father and his mother (24:67) and attached himself to his wife. True there are differences: for the nakedness of the garden has been replaced by the reticence and veiling of Rebekah, but the link is made again through the comment that Isaac was "comforted" by Rebekah. It is the same vocabulary as was used of Noah, who brought relief (5:29) from the curse of the ground. The mutual love between this couple may help to unravel the breakdown of relationships into which Genesis 3 dissolved. Westermann puts it well: "The story of love is also part of the history of God's dealing with his people."[40] There are no parts of human experience outside the purposes of Yhwh.

25:1-11 After the agonies of the intricate interrelationships between Abraham, Sarah and Hagar, Abraham's concluding years seem all so simple. He marries again, a wife whose name, Keturah, may link her to the "incense trade" that originated from western Arabia. Some of their sons bear names (e.g. Midian) that associate them geographically with the tribes that peopled north-west Arabia and southern Transjordan. The names of some of Midian's sons (e.g. Eldaah, Abida, Hanoch) also seem to hint at the reputation of this region for wisdom (e.g. 1 Kings 4:30).

In contrast with his indecisiveness in dealing with Hagar and Ishmael, Abraham takes firm action to ensure that these sons do not threaten the position of Isaac. He sends them away, though this time provided for, "eastward to the east country". As well as being far out of Isaac's way, the "east" is also, in the theological geography of Genesis, out of Yhwh's sight (e.g. 4:16; 11:2): they will not be sons of the promise, although the history of their descendants would interweave with that of Israel.

But it is not quite so simple as it first seems. What is the relationship between Ishmael and these other sons? Intriguingly, rabbinic tradition actually suggests that Keturah was another name for Hagar! And why does Ishmael suddenly reappear in the story (25:9), when he had been so conclusively dismissed by Abraham in Genesis 21. There also appears to be some overlap between the list of the sons of Keturah and those of Ishmael (25:13-15); although the names may be different, they are linked to the same geographical area. Similarly there is also an overlap between these genealogies and the genealogy of the descendants of Joktan given in 10:26-31.

It is probable that 25:1-11 was composed quite late in the development of Genesis and drew upon several different and sometimes conflicting earlier sources. But it is too simplistic to suggest that the writer was simply careless in his editorial work. On the one hand, the presence of these various genealogical lists which have strong links with north-west Arabia helps to reinforce the sense of close ethnic ties between Abraham's family and those whom later history would call the "Arabs". On the other hand, the apparent discrepancies provide a theological statement that the history of salvation is never neat and tidy, however much humans might like it to be so!

God fulfils his promises: Abraham died "in a good old age, an old man and full of years" just as Yhwh had promised (15:15). He is buried alongside Sarah, and the detail about his burial place clearly recalls the account of its purchase in Genesis 23 and reminds us that in his death he too becomes an actual inheritor of the promise of the land.

And yet those outside the covenant are not simply forgotten. Perhaps Ishmael logically shouldn't be there at his father's burial, but he is, acting in harmony with his brother Isaac.

25:12-18 The special *toledot* formula used to introduce a genealogy is now employed to list the descendants of Ishmael (see p. 6). As suggested above, there seem to be links between this list and that of the descendants of Abraham and Keturah. Again the names seem to be connected with north Arabia: the name of Nebaioth, the eldest son, may possibly be associated with the Nabateans; Massa is referred to in Proverbs 30:1; Kedar is a location mentioned in Psalm 120:5 and Jeremiah 49:28. The specific mention of twelve sons is clearly intended as a fulfilment of the promise made in 17:20. Ishmael, like Isaac, will be fruitful (indeed, even more so!).

The concluding words about Ishmael remind us of the previous episodes in his life. Shur is mentioned, to which Hagar had fled while pregnant with him (16:7); so is Egypt, Hagar's own native land and the country from which Ishmael's wife had come (21:21). The NRSV translation of the final comment on Ishmael conceals the fact that it virtually mimics the language used about him in the angelic birth oracle ("and he shall live at odds with all his kin", 16:12). Although it is read by the NRSV as a geographical statement, "he settled down alongside of all his people", it may in fact be a statement of relationship—and just as when the words first appeared in 16:12, it was ambiguous as to whether hostility was implied, so too the ambiguity may linger here (see further Theological reflections on p. 200).

With the genealogy of Ishmael, the story of Abraham is finally completed. 25:19 will open the story of Jacob. To focus on the unfavoured son who is—just—outside the covenant is perhaps an unexpected way to conclude this great saga of promise, but it is deliberate. In a similar fashion, the story of Jacob will conclude with the genealogy of his unfavoured brother, Esau. Both examples are salutary reminders that God will not be bound by any human desire for theological tidiness. Alongside "the scandal of particularity", universality refuses to be forgotten.

Theological reflections

1. Context and promise

In his deceptively simple yet profoundly influential work *The Theme of the Pentateuch*, David Clines has suggested that one reason that the Pentateuch still fascinates and challenges us today is because it is presented as a "travel story".[41] People in it are always on the move. That is especially true of Abraham. He starts in Ur, and travels via Haran in Upper Mesopotamia to Canaan. Even when he arrives in Canaan, he doesn't stay in one place; in Chapters 12–22, we have followed him down to Egypt (12:10), going through the length and breadth of the land (13:17), journeying to Mamre, Beer-sheba and then Moriah. The verbs chosen seem to emphasize his restlessness. And if he seems to settle somewhere it is made clear that this is only provisional—Abraham is always and everywhere a *ger*, and this fact dominates his story from beginning to end (e.g. 12:10; 20:1; 21:34; 23:4).

Who constructed this "travel story" of Abraham and why did they do so? The short answer seems to be that it assumed its present structure, certainly with its distinctive focus on movement, in the exilic or early postexilic period, and that it did so because of spiritual, emotional, political and existential needs in the exilic community, either in Mesopotamia or during this community's partial return to Palestine.

It may well be that the figure of Abraham was celebrated in some circles prior to the seventh/sixth centuries BC, although intriguingly the name of Abraham (unlike that of Jacob or Isaac) does not crop up in the prophetic literature which can be clearly dated to the pre-exilic era. It is also fascinating that when references to Abraham do appear in prophetic literature, they suggest that the figure of Abraham was not uncontroversial (see e.g. Ezekiel 33:24–25; Isaiah 63:16). One possibility is that Abraham may have originally been the founder (whether historical or legendary) of the sanctuary at Mamre near Hebron, and that the stories told about him there included a celebration of his overcoming infertility. Since the Davidic monarchy in Jerusalem had close and long-lasting links with the Hebron area, they may have regarded him as a patron. This would help explain Abraham's eventual paramount position in the triad of patriarchs, Abraham, Isaac and Jacob, which is puzzling in view of the fact that the figure of Jacob in particular seems to have been much more widely known in the pre-exilic period. Abraham's name presumably facilitated this: *'ab* (= father), suggesting that it was appropriate to consider him as the ultimate ancestor, the epitomy of the "fathers" (Hebrew: *'abot*), a term which begins to be used in the Deuteronomic and prophetic literature in the late seventh century. *'ab* is also a royal title (see Isaiah 9:6), since the king was considered the "father" of his people, so between his name and his Davidic connections Abraham was well placed to become a powerful emblem of the nation during the exile.

He was probably particularly important to the leading groups of society, those who were actually transported to Babylon and some of whom later returned to Judah after the Persian conquest of Babylon. Indeed those who remained in Palestine seem to have objected to the way that Abraham was "adopted" by these royal and priestly classes and used as a tool to reinforce their specific political and economic ends (as in Ezekiel 33:24–25 and Isaiah 63:16).

Yet those who took the raw tales of Abraham and constructed the narrative that we now have in this section of Genesis did so in a way that not only spoke profoundly to their own situation but has also carried on responding to the needs of generations since. Many even today have seen in Abraham their own longing for "roots" and for a "home", and with him have celebrated a promise that seems to go beyond hope.

It is possible that there was a connected story of Abraham's adventures composed during the monarchy. Traditionally this has been linked to a figure referred to as the Yahwist, though many today would date this hypothetical Yahwist to the later monarchic period (during the time of Josiah c. 625 BC) rather than, as was once popular, during the time of David and Solomon. Such a story would have been concerned to show how God's promises to Abraham were fulfilled, responding to the anxiety of the immediate pre-exilic period when the tension between Josiah's expansionist hopes and the harsh reality of Mesopotamian imperial rule created insecurity. There are apparent connections with Deuteronomic theology (Genesis 18:19; 22:18) which argue for links at some point during the composition of the Abraham cycle. The concept of God's promise of the land given in Deuteronomy to those who had fled from Egypt was now transposed back into a greater antiquity to give it additional authority.

Others would suggest that this Yahwist was himself an exilic writer. What we can say with more certainty is that if there was such a "first edition" of the Abraham cycle, it then provided the framework for an expansion of the story later in the exile or post-exilic period. This expansion (which may have happened over several stages) probably drew in the story of the destruction of Sodom and led to the deliberate construction of a number of the "doublet" stories. Further on still the Priestly writers added their distinctive touches (e.g. in Genesis 17) and the shape of the cycle took on its present form.

As it developed the story of Abraham acted as both reassurance and challenge to the Jewish community living in the Babylonian diaspora. It is not now a tale of fulfilment so much as one of promise. Abraham is an example of a person who is called by God to journey from Ur of the Chaldees (an appropriate starting point if the story is directed towards those themselves living in Mesopotamia) to a land which he had been promised. His journey will not be problem-free, and he may not be able fully to possess the land to which he is journeying, but he will be bearing with him the threefold promise of God: a promise of progeny, a promise of relationship with God, and an eventual promise of land. Abraham is being presented as an example for those who were in Babylon to encourage them to return to their homeland and help remake their nation.

A major theological impetus during the exile was the use of the traditional memory of an Exodus from Egypt to anticipate the hope of a new Exodus from Babylon (see e.g. Isaiah 51:9–11; Ezekiel 20:34–44). The Abraham cycle is itself drawn into this trajectory, so that the stories are presented as a kind of proleptic foreshadowing, an Exodus before the Exodus. This is very clear in the account of Abraham's expulsion from Egypt (Genesis 12:10–20), the reference to the enslaving and oppression of Abraham's descendants (Genesis 15:13–14), and in the intricate interplay of the stories of Hagar the Egyptian, whose treatment at the hands of Abraham and Sarah is used as a hinted rationale for the later slavery of Israel. Similarly the experiences of Abraham anticipate the giving of the law at Sinai. Although Abraham lived before the giving of the law the behaviour demanded of him is analogous to that found in the law (see e.g. Genesis 18:19; 22:1,18; 26:5, cf. Deuteronomy 4:1). The restlessness of Abraham points us forward to the Exodus, but beyond that to the conquest of Canaan. Yet this telescoping of the past is not simply an antiquarian exercise; it is concerned with the present and the future:

- This is "not only a narrative written in retrospect about an ancient 'once upon a time'. Where God . . . condescends to his people and promises himself to this people, we are not dealing with an aorist tense, but rather with a perfect, yes, even with a future perfect."[42]
- "The theme of the Pentateuch is entirely concerned with a future bound to a past out of which the present lives."[43]

As Jürgen Moltmann has commented so eloquently in his *Theology of Hope*, the nature of promise, a motif which is so dominant in the Abraham cycle, is that it binds human beings to the future.

Other specific issues that concerned the exilic community can be seen represented in these stories. There was the problem of justice with which the exilic literature wrestles (see e.g. Isaiah 40:2; Jeremiah 31:29; Ezekiel 18:1–32). What is the relationship between individuals and their community? Does God punish a righteous individual because of the corporate wickedness of their social group? Conversely, can a righteous person prevent punishment falling on the unjust? Genesis 18:23 addresses these questions which were a topic of lively debate among the exiles.

The extensive description of the destruction of Sodom and Gomorrah also reflects an issue which concerned those who lived through the destruction of Jerusalem. It is likely that the story of the downfall of Sodom and Gomorrah was a well-known "myth" which circulated widely in Canaan in the pre-exilic period. But already in the writings of pre-exilic prophets, parallels were drawn between the fate of these cities and the destruction of Israel (Hosea 11:8) and later Jerusalem (see Isaiah

1:10–17). According to Isaiah Jerusalem is to be punished because she is "unrighteous", as were Sodom and Gomorrah. After the destruction of Jerusalem in 586 BC the parallels were emphasized even more strongly (Ezekiel 16:46–58). It is wearing these exilic spectacles that we need to read Genesis 19.

Similarly, the account of the birth of Moab and Ammon in Genesis 19:33–38 reflects the tensions during the exile or perhaps in the period of resettlement afterwards. We know that the shift in the balance of power in Canaan/Transjordan when Jerusalem was destroyed allowed a surge in Moabite and Ammonite power, at least for a brief interval of time. This was bitterly resented by all Judaeans whether in exile or remaining in Judah. After the exile, the ambiguity of the relationship between the Moabites, Ammonites and the Jews is a topic that is specifically highlighted in, for example, Ezra 9:1 and Nehemiah 13:23–27. Either or both of these situations could be reflected in the account of the unorthodox birth of the eponymous founders of these nations. The story of Ishmael may similarly reflect the strains of Judaean relationships with the developing power of the Arabs and Nabateans (see below).

If there are features of the Abraham cycle that show a wariness towards foreign nations, there are also incidents that suggest a positive relationship is possible. The story of Abimelech stands out. So too does the third clause of the original blessing of Abraham in Genesis 12:3, whatever its precise meaning (see p. 107). There are nuances here of the language of Deutero-Isaiah, who of course drew on the figures of Abraham and Sarah (Isaiah 41:8; 51:2). Along with the importance given to circumcision (Genesis 17:9–14), such examples reflect the situation of the diaspora Jewish community, faced with the tension of remaining distinctive and yet relating more immediately to the non-Jews amongst whom they were living.

The topic that dominates the Abraham cycle from beginning to end, that of the barrenness of Sarah, reflects a major social question for those living in Babylonia during the exilic and Persian periods. They were comparatively few in number and were surrounded by the seductive glamour and might of Babylonian culture and religion. They needed to know that they were not the last generation, that their faith would have children, despite all appearances. The traditions of Abraham and the poetry of Isaiah 40–55 (Isaiah 54:1–3) laugh and sing their message of hope down the centuries, perhaps even to our own time when the alienation of children and young people from the churches seems to some to threaten a barren future. To all of us who want to have faith in the future, the stories of Abraham offer their challenge and consolation: "Anyone who knows of promise and fulfilment is responsible to a yesterday about which he has heard something, and he walks toward a tomorrow."[44]

2. Abraham, the figure of faith

One of the most attractive descriptions of Abraham occurs in Isaiah 41:8. Abraham, says God, is "My friend". This is alluded to in the New Testament by James 2:23 in a discussion about faith and works. As well as mentioning that "Abraham believed God, and it was reckoned to him as righteousness", James goes on to note he was called, "the friend of God". In Islam too the same description of Abraham is found: "God took Abraham for a friend" (Qur'an, *Sūra* 4), and of all the titles that Muslim tradition could give him, its preferred one is "Khalil Allah" (= the friend of God). For Abraham is not only a figure of faith for the Old Testament, but also for the three great religions Judaism, Christianity and Islam, which have their roots in the Old Testament tradition, and which are often jointly called the "Abrahamic faiths". We have all claimed Abraham for ourselves, and sometimes we have demanded exclusive possession of him. And yet perhaps it is the restlessness of Abraham the *ger* which means he refuses to allow himself to be held captive by any one religion. Significantly in all three religious traditions, Jewish, Christian and Muslim, Abraham is honoured as someone who practiced monotheism before the time of any special revelation, whether Law, Gospel or Qur'an, and his life therefore shows that it is possible to be a true believer without being governed by the distinctiveness of these later religions.

I write from within the Christian tradition, although appreciative of the wisdom of both Judaism and Islam. It is appropriate to consider in particular the way Abraham is used in the New Testament, the foundation document of my faith.

The name of Abraham appears extensively in the New Testament, beginning with the very first verse, where it helps to shape the genealogy of Jesus in Matthew's Gospel (Matthew 1:1-2). In Luke's Gospel, Abraham appears as a father-figure of suffering (13:16), repentant (19:9), or even condemned (16:24) members of the Jewish nation. The figure of Abraham is used extensively in John 8:31-59, where the debate between Judaism and Christianity assumes a polemical form, as the author of John's Gospel challenges the claim of the Jewish community of his day to call themselves Abraham's children. That debate is continued, though in a more positive spirit and without John's particular "edge", in the Pauline literature (Romans 4:1-25; 9:6-9; 11:1, Galatians 3:6-29; 4:22-5:1). Here Paul is not so much denying the claim of contemporary Jews to call themselves children of Abraham as claiming that right for Gentile Christians. He also wrestles at length with the question of what is meant by Abraham's righteousness: a key text for him is Genesis 15:6. Paul's views on this have influenced the way that Abraham has been perceived in Christian tradition ever since. Then, of course, Abraham is the great hero of the galaxy of Old Testament saints in the Epistle to the Hebrews. His willingness to travel and then to offer Isaac in sacrifice seems to epitomize what the writer of Hebrews means by faith (Hebrews 11:8-19).

Yet because he has been so appropriated by the New Testament as this figure of faith it is difficult sometimes for Christians to read the Old Testament account of Abraham without their New Testament spectacles filtering out the real humanity that is apparent in these Abraham stories. We have been so impressed with Abraham as a figure who is "justified by faith" that we find it almost scandalous to contemplate him as a person who has "warts and all". It may be significant that the only New Testament writing which dares to describe Abraham with that exquisite yet humane phrase "friend of God", is the Epistle of James, one of the most Jewish of New Testament books.

Commenting on Hebrews 11, Gabriel Josipovici suggests that despite its "rousing call" it still leaves anyone who has read the stories for themselves in the Old Testament a "little uneasy":

> As we read this chapter, we inevitably ask ourselves whether it corresponds to our own memory of the text. Is this all there is

to say about these people? We remember Sarah laughing when God tells Abraham in her hearing that she will bear a son, a scene important enough to be commemorated in the very name of the child, Yitzhak; we remember the early life of Moses; we remember the enormously complex and ambiguous relation of David to God—and we wonder: can all this be summed up under the single rubric of faith?

Quoting words of Mary Douglas, Josipovici goes on to suggest that our New Testament vision of Abraham is a little "thin".[45] One of the benefits of a narrative approach to the Old Testament is that it enables us to see how Abraham develops through the fourteen chapters under discussion. It allows us to admit that he isn't perfect, he is someone who makes mistakes and takes false trails, and that his dealings with both Sarah and Hagar leave something to be desired! Looking at the stories from a feminist perspective can be a refreshing and important tool in this exercise. There are important questions to be asked by feminist scholars: why is it, for example, that Abraham, so brave in the defence of Lot, is so cowardly when it comes to Sarah that he lies about their relationship and puts her at risk by his deceit? Some may respond that these are "modern questions", but in fact they are posed by the text itself. (It is clear, for example, that the ancient commentaries on Genesis such as the Genesis Apocryphon feel a need to rewrite the story of Genesis at this point to present Abraham in a less unfavourable light!)

To point up the humanity of Abraham in this way does not lead to "debunking" him, but rather can help us discover in him more easily a real rather than ideal model for our faith. Karl-Josef Kuschel, whose book *Abraham: A Symbol of Hope for Jews, Christians and Muslims* makes clear the relevance of the figure of Abraham in interfaith issues, comments as follows:

> If we look closely at Abraham's way we discover that his faith is quite a complex one. There is no trace of blind readiness to follow, of an irrational act of the will, of the obedience of an automaton. Abraham's faith is tested by a long experience of life. And because this is the case, this faith is made up of quite different

ingredients: there is a touch of doubt and a touch of cunning, a touch of anxiety and a touch of risk-taking with his God; a touch of wordless obedience and a touch of canny haggling. This faith includes humble sacrifice to this God and bold negotiations to spare innocent human beings. Here is a unique profile: faith as a process of setting out despite everything: despite all reservations, despite all gnashing of the teeth, despite all anxiety.[46]

At the heart of the Abraham story lies the man we meet in Genesis 18: the exuberant giver of hospitality who "entertained angels without knowing it" (Hebrews 13:2). Even though he may be a bit "over the top", even though he still leaves us with questions over his attitude to Sarah, he helps us in this encounter to discover God through his sheer humanity. It is therefore highly appropriate that this story of the hospitality of Abraham has provided the basis for the Orthodox Christian icons of the Holy Trinity. The hospitality that Abraham showed to these unexpected visitors reflects the mutual and overflowing hospitality that is at the heart of the life of the divine. A quotation from a twentieth-century Jewish source sums it up:

> Abraham's house was open to all the children of men,
> those going past and those returning,
> and day by day they came
> to eat and drink with Abraham.
> To those who were hungry he gave bread,
> and the guests ate and drank and were filled.
> Those who came naked to his house
> he clothed,
> and helped them to experience God,
> the creator of all things.[47]

Abraham is a man of contrasts. As we commented on 17:17, there is something extraordinary in the scene when he lies prostrate before God, laughing to himself. Is it an accident that laughter is such a strong verbal motif in the Abraham cycle? Not if you believe the following words of Harvey Cox:

> Laughter is hope's last weapon. Crowded on all sides with idiocy and ugliness, pushed to concede that the final apocalypse seems to be upon us, we seem nonetheless to nourish laughter as our only remaining defence. In the presence of disaster and death we laugh instead of crossing ourselves. Or perhaps better stated, our laughter is our way of crossing ourselves. It shows that despite the disappearance of any empirical basis for hope, we have not stopped hoping ... It could conceivably disappear, and where laughter and hope have disappeared, man has ceased to be man.[48]

Abraham never ceases to be man.

3. The *Aqedah*

The story of the near sacrifice of Isaac is often referred to in Jewish and Christian theology as the *Aqedah* ("Binding") which describes what Abraham did to Isaac as he prepared for the sacrifice (22:9). It is, as the writer to the Hebrews was aware (Hebrews 11:17), a major example of what we mean when we call Abraham a "figure of faith", but this episode in the life of Abraham has been so influential in later religious history that it seems right to treat it separately. Søren Kierkegaard, for example, in his classic work *Fear and Trembling*, exploring the story from a Lutheran perspective, believed that it expressed the essence of what "faith" means.

But is it really an example of Abraham's faith? What about Isaac, the intended sacrificial victim? Although Genesis clearly presents the story as a test of Abraham, the father, later Jewish tradition (and in a different way, Christianity) developed it as the self-sacrifice of Isaac.

For a start, how old was Isaac supposed to be when he was so nearly sacrificed? Our mental picture is probably of a young boy, not more than six or seven: such a child is pictured in the depiction of the scene by the famous Beth Alpha synagogue mosaic (sixth century AD). But rabbinic commentaries on the passage measured Isaac's age quite variably—up even to thirty-seven years old! (on the basis that the next incident referred to in Genesis is the death of Sarah, aged 127). Obviously a thirty-seven-year-old's perception of what is going on differs radically from that of a six-year-old. Isaac therefore becomes a willing participant in, rather than an unwitting victim of, the sacrifice. Indeed in several rabbinic texts Isaac actually sets in train the process that leads to the sacrifice, by offering himself to God during the course of a debate with his brother Ishmael. (In the process, of course, God is thereby let off the hook and declared innocent of any unreasonable divine demands!) If then this is a voluntary sacrifice of Isaac, it bestows upon him a particular merit. In turn this merit can be called upon by Isaac's own heirs, the Jewish community of a later period. There are many examples of this viewpoint; the following from the *Pesikta de-Rav Kahana* is particularly striking: "By the merit of Isaac, who offered himself upon the altar, the Holy One (blessed be He) will in the future resurrect the dead."[49]

Another development in the Jewish understanding of the offering of Isaac was to gradually link it to the sacrifice of the Passover lamb. It becomes a kind of prototype of the Passover sacrifice by the blood of which Isaac's descendants in Egypt escaped into freedom. This development has already taken place by the time the Book of Jubilees was written in the second century BC.

The link that was made between the sacrifice of Isaac and Passover was in turn to prepare the way for the Christian use of the Isaac tradition. For though Christians did on the one hand continue to see the sacrifice of Isaac as an example of the faith of Abraham, a more radical development of the *Aqedah* tradition quickly took root. Jesus Christ had died at Passover, possibly at the very time that the Passover lambs were being slain (John 19:14). The link between Passover and the *Aqedah* had already been made. Therefore, reflected Jesus' first followers, there must be a close connection between the near death of Isaac and the actual death of Christ. Christ was a "new Isaac", and his death was the sacrifice that went one stage further than Abraham and Isaac had been required to go. The link was facilitated by parallels that could be drawn out of the respective stories of Jesus and Isaac. There was in both cases the "wood"—of the cross, and on which Isaac had been bound. There was the close connection with the temple in Jerusalem, hinted at in Genesis 22:14, and which played a dominant role in the events leading to Jesus' crucifixion. And there was the terrible three-day journey that both Isaac and Jesus undertook.

It is clear that the link between Christ and the Isaac tradition was firmly established by the time Paul wrote his letters to the Galatians and Romans. Not only does he refer to Christ as Abraham's issue (Galatians 3:16), an epithet that originally belonged to Isaac, but in a meditation on the love of God in Romans 8:32 he reflects how [God] "did not withhold his own Son, but gave him up for all of us". The verb "withhold" here is based on a comparatively rare Greek word, which also appears in the Septuagint translation of Genesis 22:16 ("you have not withheld your son").

Once this link was made, it influenced the development of New Testament Christology. It is likely that the description of Christ as the beloved son in the synoptic narratives of the baptism (Mark 1:11), the transfiguration (Mark 9:7) and the Parable of the Wicked Tenants (Mark 12:6) is owed partly to the description of Isaac as the beloved son. The association is still more pronounced in John's Gospel, where the link with Isaac not only seems to underlie the description of Christ as God's "only son" (John 1:14,18), but also to be interwoven with the title "Lamb of God" given him by John the Baptist (John 1:29,36), and indeed with the language of God's love as it is expressed in John 3:16. There are those who would suggest that the Christian doctrine of atonement owes much in its formulation to the fact that the Jewish *Aqedah* tradition had already treated Isaac's suffering as atoning for the sins of his descendants. What is certainly true is that to speak thus of Christ is also to "re-vision" God. For if Jesus represents Isaac, then God must be Abraham, and the cost to God of the death of the beloved son takes on a pathos that far removes it from the juridical language of the courthouse in which Christians have often verbalized their faith. Rather than omnipotent judge of innocent and guilty, God becomes the agonized and vulnerable father.

There is no doubt that the *Aqedah* tradition has enriched Jewish and Christian literature and theology down to the present time. It has been drawn on by Jewish writers and artists trying to make theological sense of the non-sense of the Holocaust (Shoah). Israel itself is become Isaac, sacrificed now even to death. Among many possible examples, the following passage by Elie Wiesel (himself a former inmate of a concentration camp) is particularly striking:

We have known Jews who, like Abraham, witnessed the death of their children; who, like Isaac, lived the *Akeda* in their flesh; and some who went mad when they saw their father disappear on the altar, with the altar, in a blazing fire whose flames reached into the highest of heavens...

Isaac survived; he had no choice. He had to make something of his memories, his experience in order to force us to hope. For our survival is bound up with his survival... Why was the most tragic of our ancestors named Isaac, a name which evokes and signifies laughter? Here is why. As the first survivor, he had to teach us, the future survivors of Jewish history, that it is possible to suffer and despair an entire lifetime and still not give up the art of laughter.

Isaac, of couse, never freed himself from the traumatizing scenes that violated his youth; the holocaust had marked him and continued to haunt him forever. Yet he remained capable of laughter. And in spite of everything, he did laugh.[50]

And yet? In recent years there are those who would argue that the story of the sacrifice of Isaac has seduced us by the exquisite beauty of its telling, so that we have forgotten to ask the questions we should have demanded of it. Perhaps the remarkable poem by the British war poet Wilfred Owen offers a salutary warning of how dangerous a story it could be:

Parable of the Old Man and the Young

> So Abram rose, and clave the wood, and went,
> And took the fire with him, and a knife.
> And as they sojourned both of them together,
> Isaac the firstborn spake and said, "My Father,
> Behold the preparations, fire and iron,
> But where the lamb for this burnt offering?"
> Then Abram bound the youth with belts and straps,
> And builded parapets and trenches there,
> And stretchèd forth the knife to slay his son.
> When lo! an angel called him out of heaven,

> Saying, Lay not thy hand upon the lad,
> Neither do anything to him. Behold,
> A ram, caught in a thicket by its horns;
> Offer the Ram of Pride instead of him.
> But the old man would not so, but slew his son,
> And half the seed of Europe, one by one.

A Jewish rabbi in Canada has dared to remark: "Avraham failed the test. He chose God over his son. He chose being God's servant over being his son's father. He loved God more than he loved his own son, and he made the wrong choice."[51] Feminist commentators on this story have pointed out how it reinforces a model of patriarchy in which a father has the power of life or death over his children. It begs some difficult questions: "Why is the willingness to sacrifice the child at God's command the model of faith, rather than the passionate protection of the child? What would be the shape of our society had that been the model of faith?"[52]

And what of Sarah, so entirely absent from the story: her voice surely deserves to be heard. In the fourth century, St Ephraem, the voice of Syriac-speaking Christianity, did explore the biblical story from Sarah's point of view, but by and large Sarah's silence has echoed down the centuries. More recently, Phyllis Trible has reflected on Genesis 22 in an article entitled "The Sacrifice of Sarah", a telling title in view of the way she has indeed been sacrificed in Bible and church tradition.[53] But a meditation by Trevor Dennis entitled "The Other Women (at the Cross)" offers us the opportunity finally to listen to Sarah:

> Sarah was there also [at the cross]. Isaac had never come home. He had gone off one morning with his father, and she had never seen him again. Abraham had talked wild talk of a three-day journey, of fire and a knife and the building of an altar and the binding of her son, of how he had stopped and sacrificed a ram instead, and all she had asked was where Isaac was. He had not been able to tell her, so she had left and gone hunting for him. She had gone back to Ur, from where they had come originally, but Isaac was not there. She had gone down to Egypt, where once Abraham had so humiliated her, but they had heard nothing of

her son. Christ had first discovered her among some tombs above the Sea of Galilee, where she had gone to see if Isaac's name was on any of the graves. Wild with grief, she had called Christ all the names under the sun and beaten his chest with her fists, and he had waited till she was done and could accept his embrace. She had kept him company ever since.

So she came to Golgotha, and waited till he died. And when they came to take his body down, she sat on the ground and asked them to lay his body in her lap. And so they did, and she bent her face to his, and said over and over again, 'My son, my son, my son, my son.'[54]

4. Isaac and Ishmael: Palestine— the much promised land

Nobody today can read the stories of the Abraham cycle (or the stories of the other ancestors) without being aware of their impact on modern Middle Eastern politics. There is no tenser tinderbox in the Holy Land than the traditional site of the Cave of Machpelah in Hebron, bought by Abraham as a burial place for Sarah (Genesis 23), and where he, Isaac and Jacob, as well as Rebekah and Leah are supposedly buried. It, like Abraham, is claimed by both Judaism and Islam: often the claims have been made with violence. Ironically the Arabic name for the city of Hebron is "Al Khalil" (= the friend), recalling the title first given to Abraham.

It might be more comfortable for Christians if they could totally dismiss modern Israel as a completely secular state, with no relationship to a biblical past, or at least reject the territorial dimension of the promise to Abraham ("And I will give to you, and to your offspring after you, the land where you are now an alien ... for a perpetual holding." Genesis 17:8) as a pledge which has been superseded by the coming of Christ. But it is not that easy. When I lived in Beirut in 1982 throughout the Israeli invasion of Lebanon and siege of that city, I might have laughed at the way the Israeli advance up the Lebanese coast was sometimes referred to on Israeli radio as the repossession of the territory of Asher and Naphtali—for, like Sarah, laughter in such a situation was the alternative to succumbing to terror. But intellectual integrity compelled me to acknowledge that within its own theological framework the ongoing doctrine of a promised land may well be a part of Judaism. It was not a theoretical question for me: as it certainly was not either for the Palestinian Christian students in Beirut to whom I taught Old Testament. Naim Ateek, a Palestinian Christian theologian puts it thus:

> In Israel-Palestine today, the Bible is being quoted to give the primary claim over the land to Jews. In the mind of many religious Jews and fundamentalist Christians the solution to the conflict lies in Palestinian recognition that God has given the Jews the land of Palestine forever. Palestinians are asked to accept this as a basic truth ... Palestinian Christians must tackle the land from a biblical perspective, not because I believe that the religious argument over the land is of the *bene esse* of the conflict, but because we are driven to it as a result of the religious-political abuse of biblical interpretation.[55]

What can we say about this question, on the basis of our exploration so far of the stories of Abraham? There are three points I would like to offer for reflection:

1. The first is the suggestion made by David Clines in his study of the theme of the Pentateuch that the promises in the Pentateuch exist in a tension between expectation and fulfilment.[56] They were offered in a historical context when they could not immediately become fully operative. The promises therefore accompany Israel through its historical development and struggle as goals to be aimed for; sometimes these goals seem an unrealistic burden, a mirage; sometimes challenging and attainable. But is their physical attainment perhaps to destroy the nature of the promise itself? Like the ancestors themselves there is the need to live today in the interval between yesterday's promise and tomorrow's redemption.
2. In an interesting study entitled *The Land is Mine*, Norman Habel has drawn attention to the fact that the land-theology of the Old

Testament is not monolithic. Several different ideologies are given space. Habel suggests that the ideology of the ancestral stories speaks of "land as host country", and he explores how in the Abraham cycle the land is offered and received within stories of mutual hospitality, between Abraham the *ger* and the inhabitants of Canaan.[57] In other words, we can argue that unless land is lived in and shared in a hospitable spirit, the promises to Abraham cannot be used as sanction for ownership of such land. Such a viewpoint would have clear implications for any who choose to claim land as "promised".

3. The crucial role that Hagar and Ishmael play in the Abraham cycle is also relevant. Did their stories originate and first circulate among the Arab and proto-Nabatean tribes of the Negev and southern Transjordan, before they were adopted by those who composed the Abraham cycle and incorporated into their larger framework? The vividness of the language suggests that they may originally have been told among those who venerated Ishmael as their ancestor, or Hagar as the Madonna of a desert shrine at Beer-lahai-roi. Certainly both figures were later to have a life outside the pages of Genesis in the foundation stories of Islam. Hagar's name may be included in the Syriac word *Mahgraye* and the Arabic *muhajirun* by which the earliest followers of Muhammad were known.[58] The name referred to the flight, or *Hijra*, that took them from Mecca to Medina, marking the beginning of the Muslim era, and for which the flight and banishment of Hagar (Genesis 16:21) provided a sort of prototype. Ishmael was viewed among early Muslims as the favoured son of Abraham, and stories told in Genesis of Isaac are then recounted of him. In Islamic tradition it is usually understood to be Ishmael who was nearly sacrificed by his father at a shrine at Mecca, visited by those who go to the city on pilgrimage.

If Jews count Isaac as their ancestor in the faith, then Arabs reserve that honour for his brother Ishmael. Is it possible to use the stories of Genesis that deal with Hagar and Ishmael to suggest a model of co-existence that can be emulated by their descendants? I believe that read sensitively the stories can be used to challenge any who seek to use the promises to Abraham to sustain a glib particularity.

In the comments on Genesis 16, we noted that "Hagar is the woman who complicated the history of salvation". We also suggested that many of us find it easier to identify with Sarah than with Hagar. But that reflects the bias of white First World commentators—Elsa Tamez observes how women from the Third World would naturally identify with Hagar. The analysis that we have suggested for the Abraham cycle, with the story of the birth of Ishmael taking centre stage in the cycle, leads us to ask whether this identification with Hagar is what the writers of Genesis actually intended all along, so that particularity is not allowed totally to displace universality, and so that Ishmael retains a place in the continuing story along with his brother Isaac. The comments made on Genesis 15–16 (see p. 123 and p. 125) suggested that a hint was being offered that the very reason for the later slavery of Abraham's descendants in Egypt is the mistreatment that was once meted out to a woman of Egypt at the hands of Israel's founding father and mother. Somehow a demand for justice and compassion for all "aliens", of whom Hagar is being presented as an archetype, is being written into the very fabric of the covenant.[59]

The implication is being made that the healthy continuance of this covenant relationship depends at least in part on the willingness of Abraham and his family to offer justice to others, so that the eventual destiny of Isaac's descendants is affected by how Ishmael and his mother are treated. Certainly his role is completely different to the other half-brothers, who are born to Abraham after the death of Sarah (Genesis 25:1–6). Alongside his brother Isaac, Ishmael alone shares in burying their father at Hebron, the two brothers standing alongside each other in a way that would be unthinkable to many of their present-day spiritual descendants. There are, as we commented on p. 154 also remarkable parallels between the trials both Ishmael and Isaac suffer—in each case almost to death. In the birth oracle of Ishmael (16:12), the angel had predicted to Hagar that Ishmael would "live at odds with all his kin". That is one possible translation, and it is the one adopted by the NRSV. But in fact the Hebrew words are more ambiguous and may not include a sense of hostility at all: some other versions tell us that Ishmael will live "alongside his brothers". The destiny of the Holy Land perhaps lies held between these two possibilities. There is a powerful poem by the Israeli poet Shin Shalom included in the liturgy for the New Year Festival in Reform synagogues in the United Kingdom. It expresses just how much Isaac and Ishmael, and their respective descendants, still need each other. If there is to be a future, it will—and must—include them both:

Ishmael, my brother,
How long shall we fight each other?

My brother from times bygone,
My brother, Hagar's son,
My brother, the wandering one.
One angel was sent to us both,
One angel watched over our growth—
There in the wilderness, death threatening through thirst,
I a sacrifice on the altar, Sarah's first.

Ishmael, my brother, hear my plea:
It was the angel who tied thee to me . . .

Time is running out, put hatred to sleep.
Shoulder to shoulder, let's water our sheep.
(Shin Shalom)[60]

The story of Jacob

25:19–36:43

Titling this section "The story of Jacob" begs the question: what about Isaac, where is his story? In fact, there really is no separate "Isaac" cycle in Genesis; such episodes as feature him are woven into one of the two major sequences of stories about Abraham and Jacob. Isaac figures almost as a tool to knit together the episodes relating to the other two patriarchs. It is interesting to note the effect created by the placing of the references to Isaac. Locating the only chapter in which Isaac is the major figure (26) after the account of the birth of the next generation helps to suggest that past, present and future depend upon and inform each other (see further comments on Genesis 26 on p. 210).

The Abraham cycle began in spectacular and optimistic mode: "a New Start", a divine command and very shortly afterwards a divine appearance (12:7). By contrast, the Jacob cycle commences in a much more gritty fashion: a difficult conception, a dangerous pregnancy, and two brothers who squabble from birth. It is not another "new start" but God continuing to work with and through the raw human material that is available. The opening of the cycle prepares us for what lies ahead: these will be stories in which the horizontal (human-human) relationships will assume as much prominence as vertical (divine-human) ones. God will appear in these stories, in spectacular and numinous form. But God will not appear so often—and he will not assume the role of *deus ex machina*, which he seemed to play on occasion during the life of Abraham. God will also increasingly use dreams as a means of communicating with humanity and will encourage human beings to work out their own salvation among themselves, albeit with fear and trembling.

The Jacob cycle seems, like the Abraham cycle, to fall into a concentric or chiastic pattern—not perhaps as tightly knit, but still effective.

> **The literary structure of the story of Jacob**
>
> **A1** Birth of Jacob. Struggle of Esau and Jacob
>   **B1** Isaac and Abimelech (Relations with non-Israelites)
>   **C1** Theft of Esau's blessing
>   **D1** Jacob meets God at Bethel
>   **E1** Jacob and the well-stone
>   **F1** Laban tricks Jacob (about his bride)
>   **G** Birth of Jacob's sons (culminating in birth of Joseph)
>   **F2** Jacob tricks Laban (over his herds)
>   **E2** Jacob and the stones of the covenant with Laban
>   **D2** Jacob meets God at Penuel
>   **C2** Offer of restitution of Esau's blessing
>   **B2** The rape of Dinah and destruction of Shechem (relations with non-Israelites)
> **A2** Birth of Benjamin, Death of Rachel and Isaac. Joint burial of Isaac by Esau and Jacob

This means that the birth of the next generation lies at the heart of the story. "Genesis" lives up to its name.

Double trouble
25:19–34

As we suggested above, placing this introduction to Jacob's sons, which takes them in a few verses from conception to active adult protagonists in the story, before the incidents in which their father appears, will encourage us to read Chapter 26 as a kind of interlude, almost a byway, in the ongoing narrative.

25:19–26 *These are the descendants of Isaac, Abraham's son.* The language in Hebrew is exactly and deliberately parallel to that with which

Ishmael's genealogy had been introduced (25:12). But what follows is entirely different. Not a simple list, but a complicated story, in which once again the very existence of these descendants is only possible because of YHWH's direct intervention.

Note how Isaac is referred to: he is "Abraham's son". The information is then immediately repeated. "Abraham was the father of Isaac." Throughout most of the events of his life, particularly in Genesis 26, that is how Isaac will appear. He will be presented as a reflection of his father, rather than as a fully independent agent.

Isaac... married Rebekah... of Paddan-aram. The reference back to Isaac's marriage provides a perspective from which to view the episode of Rebekah's childlessness. Twenty years pass before the children are eventually born (25:20,26), a bitterly long time: yet in contrast with the childlessness of Sarah the years are subsumed in only a few verses. It is an indication that in the life story of Isaac and Jacob the topic of progeny, so prominent in the Abraham cycle, will yield to that of the possession and use of the land and the meaning of nationhood. But nonetheless the fragility of the family of promise is emphasised by the positioning of this episode after the account of the death of Abraham. According to the chronology Rebekah's childlessness must have been resolved before Abraham died (Isaac was sixty when Esau and Jacob were born, seventy-five at the death of his father). To locate the issue here reinforces the sense that once again the future hangs by a thread, and that YHWH will need to intervene directly in the lives of his chosen instruments.

Paddan-aram is an alternative name for Aram-naharaim (24:10) and is the term preferred in this section. "Paddan" is probably a word loaned from Aramaic (the language used in northern Mesopotamia). It is likely to mean something like "Field of Aram". It may indicate the Mesopotamian background of those who were responsible for creating the consecutive narrative of Jacob out of a number of diverse threads.

Isaac prayed to the LORD. The technical vocabulary of prayer and worship is employed here, as also when Rebekah "went to seek guidance of the LORD". Relationships between humanity and divinity are still possible, but they begin to assume a formality that is qualitatively different from the unfettered conversation between YHWH and Abraham.

[The LORD] said to her ...   Remarkably Rebekah alone is the recipient of this oracle, and there is no suggestion that she shared the information with Isaac. It grounds her preference for Jacob (25:28) in God's purposes: by contrast Isaac's predilection for Esau is linked to his own stomach! Partly on the basis of her role here it has been suggested that Rebekah (rather than Isaac) is the key ancestor of this generation.

Two nations ...   The binary thrust and repeated sense of doubling which runs through the entire story of Jacob and Esau is grounded in this key poetic oracle which both introduces it and seems to control the later narrative. Although there are other pairs of brothers in Genesis who are contrasted with each other, especially Cain and Abel, who provide perhaps the closest parallel to Jacob and Esau, nowhere else is the contrast taken back to the moment of birth—or even into the womb—and nowhere else is it delineated in such a wholehearted fashion, incorporating physical appearance, moral attributes and the love of their parents.

A comparison between two brothers

Jacob	Esau
Stronger	Weaker
Younger	Elder
Master	Servant
Smooth	Hairy
Stayed in tents	Outdoor man
Loved by Rebekah	Loved by Isaac
Cooks vegetables	Hunts and prepares meat
Lives for the future	Lives for the present
Scheming	Sensual
"Female"	"Male"
Israel	Edom

As we move into the story of Jacob, it becomes increasingly clear that we are travelling into the story of two nations, Israel and Edom. In the development of the story, the individuals eventually become their eponymous peoples, in a fashion that goes well beyond anything in the earlier story of Abraham. This crucial oracle alerts us to what lies ahead and how we should read what is, on the surface, simply an account of bitter family rivalry.

There were twins in her womb. The relationship between Jacob and Esau is thus as close as is biologically possible. This reflects an awareness that there was a close ethnic (and possibly religious) relationship between the Edomites and Israelites, of a different order to that between Israelites and other nations. Texts such as Deuteronomy 23:7, for example, treat Edomites as a "special case". This did not rule out intense hostility between the Edomites and Israelites/Judaeans which had ancient roots. The Edomites resented the vassal status to which they were consigned by David and Solomon (1 Kings 11:14–25); in turn, they took the opportunity provided by the Babylonian conquest of Judah to invade Judaean territory, an action regarded by several Old Testament prophets as "back-stabbing". In the early post-exilic period, Edomite control spread over much of the Negev. It is no accident that the description of how the twins "struggled together" in Rebekah's womb employs a verb that could equally be translated "oppressed". The Old Testament prophetic oracles about Edom are particularly vitriolic, but the hatred contained in them seems partly due to the supposed relationship between the nations—Edom should have behaved differently, precisely because it was Jacob's brother (see Obadiah 10; Malachi 1:2).

There is some evidence that the roots of Yahwism are linked with the region of Edom. The original homeland of the god Yhwh may have been Mount Seir (Judges 5:4; Isaiah 63:1), before the worship of Yhwh was adopted by the Israelites. This would accentuate Israelite closeness to the Edomites—but also explain the bitter rivalry for birthright and blessing which is the central motif of the Jacob story. In reality, once upon a time, Esau's descendants may have been the primeval people of Yhwh, and it was not a position that they would willingly concede.

From the Israelite perspective, the words of the oracle that predict how Esau will "serve" Jacob are both reminiscence and aspiration—there was a time when this might have been true, but by the time the final form of Genesis was written it was far from the case.

The first came out red, all his body like a hairy mantle. This initial description of Esau makes clear his links with Edom. The name "Edom" is related to the word for "red" (Hebrew: *'adom* or *'admoni*)—because of the remarkably red sandstone rocks of the region, most famously at Petra, that "rose-red city—half as old as Time". "Hairy" (*se'ar*) alludes to Seir, the mountainous heartland of the country. The writer allows us to make the connection for ourselves rather than spelling it out at this point—saving up his punchline for 25:30, when the birthright is sold off so cheaply.

His brother came out, with his hand gripping Esau's heel. Jacob's name is transparently related to the word for "heel" (Hebrew: *'aqeb*). It not only pictured his action during his actual birth, but also his behaviour throughout his life: he was a "heel" or fraudster—a description that is as disparaging in Hebrew as it is in English! The punning will continue in 27:36 where we will discover how Jacob *supplanted* (a word from the linked Hebrew root *'aqab*) his brother.

It is extraordinary how the Old Testament is so willing to be ruthlessly honest about the moral nature of the figure who became the eponymous ancestor of Israel. Nor is this honesty restricted to Genesis. Besides the reference to Jacob in Hosea 12:3, the identical pun on "supplant" occurs in Jeremiah 9:4, while in Malachi 3:6-9 a similar sounding, though unrelated, verb meaning "to defraud" (Hebrew root: *qaba'*) is used several times in a way that suggests it is being connected to the name of Jacob.

25:27-34 *Jacob was a quiet man, living in tents.* The tents were the province of the women—he is definitely a "mummy's boy"! The NRSV's "quiet" contrasts with the unrestrained and violent temperament needed by hunters like Esau. However, it is a slightly unexpected translation for the Hebrew word *tam*, which normally means something like "wholesome", or "morally innocent". A closely related word appears in

20:5, where it forms part of an expression translated "integrity of my heart". It is tempting to wonder if its use here for Jacob is ironic.

Isaac loved Esau ... Rebekah loved Jacob. Now that love has been let loose in the world (see comments on 22:2), it is a dangerous and powerful phenomenon and must not be abused—or cheapened. By not telling us the rationale for Rebekah's fondness for Jacob, the writer encourages us to connect it to the providential oracle she received earlier. By contrast the stated reason for Isaac's partiality for Esau, "he was fond of game", hardly portrays either father or son in a good light.

Once when Jacob was cooking a stew. The flair of the writer of this story is evident in this choice of words which deliberately use a verb that hints that what Jacob "cooked up" was not only a pot, but a plot!

The brief description of Esau's actions is also a brilliant character sketch! "Let me eat some of that red stuff." In reality, Esau can't even remember the name of the food; he is so anxious to stuff himself that he actually calls it "that red, red ... !" (Hebrew: *'adom*) It is now, significantly, that the writer makes explicit the connection with Edom. Therefore "he was called Edom". For our mental picture of Edom is thus coloured (literally!) not so much by Esau's physical circumstances at birth but rather by his adult behaviour: Edom comes across as a greedy, inarticulate nation with no interest in the higher aspects of life. (A slander, incidentally, upon the Edomites, who were well known for their expertise in "wisdom", e.g. Jeremiah 49:7.) The rapid-fire series of verbs with which Esau leaves the scene "he ate and drank, and rose and went his way" reinforces this portrayal of an almost animal being, who lives only for the present.

Jacob, by contrast, plans for the future! Perhaps that is what the bearer of the promise needs to do. The birthright of the eldest was a very concrete package. Deuteronomy 21:15–17 makes it clear that he inherited the lion's share of his father's property. Ancient law codes are even more specific than this. Esau presumably assumed that this positive bias in the inheritance was what he was relinquishing. We know, and we may wonder whether Jacob was aware, that the birthright in this case means much more and it included inheriting the covenantal promises made to Abraham. In this episode of wordplays one final one is left hanging over—by spurning the *bekorah* (birthright) in this private conversation with his brother, Esau effectively sets in train the process that will lead him shortly to be deprived of the *berakah* (blessing).

His father's son
26:1–35

"There is nothing new under the sun" (Ecclesiastes 1:9). It is striking how, with the possible exception of the sowing of seed in 26:12–13, all the incidents in Genesis 26:1–33 mirror or allude to previous events in the life of Isaac's father Abraham. The chapter has been constructed by a writer who was aware of the content of Genesis 12–22, and clearly drew upon it, at the same time making subtle but important changes.

Why are these incidents related at this juncture in Genesis? What we have reads like an interruption in the story of Jacob and Esau which has just begun and which is going to continue so explosively in the following chapter. Yet it also feels "out of time" because of the continual harking back to parallel events in the life of Abraham. It both breaks into the future and reminds us of a mixed bag of incidents from the past.

That is exactly the point:

> The perceived repetitions begin to create a sense of design to what otherwise might be considered random, indeed rambling stories. Each generation, at least to some extent, relives the plot of its predecessor. The larger story of the family is not simply linear, but frequently coils around to pick up bits of the past—failures as well as successes. Every generation essentially provides the same kind of "stuff" from which God is to build a "great nation".[61]

It is striking that the most lengthy parallel is the attempt by Isaac to pass off Rebekah as his sister. For this shows him in precisely the same unsavoury light as the earlier examples of the genre/incident did his father. It is as if all the hopes for a "new start" that we have invested in Isaac, the long-awaited child of the promise, are being brought down to earth. He is made of the same old all-too-human stuff as Abraham. And by locating this chapter after the rivalry between Jacob and Esau has been made apparent, the broad hint is being offered that future generations of this family will not be problem-free either.

And yet ... this is not a replay of Genesis 1–5, when the story of humanity went so far downhill that it ended in cataclysm. This time God will stick with these people, instead of bitterly regretting (see 6:6) his choice to deal with them. It will be a choice that will prove costly to God, even before the end of the story of Jacob (32:26).

26:1–5 The undercurrent of famine pervades the whole chapter. It also takes us straight back to Abraham's story with its reference to the famine that had taken Abraham down to Egypt (12:10–20). That had been a false step in Abraham's life and so many complications had resulted from it. Isaac must not make the same mistake: "Do not go down to Egypt." Unlike his father Abraham, Isaac is not summoned by Yhwh to go anywhere, but rather to stay. It is in living in this country, Canaan, as an alien, that blessing will be found.

The words Yhwh addresses to Isaac allude both to the original command of Yhwh to Abraham in Genesis 12:1–3, and also quite strongly to the words spoken after the near-sacrifice of Isaac. The motif of obedience in particular connects it to Genesis 22:18. The whole story of Abraham seems to float before our eyes as we listen to these words: "because Abraham obeyed my voice". Underlying this translation are the words "heard my voice". We might ruefully reflect that eventually Abraham did, with the willingness to sacrifice his son being the supreme example, but it took a long time, and that first he listened to Sarah.

Note how everything that is offered to Isaac is grounded in God's relationship with Abraham: "I will fulfil the oath that I swore to your father Abraham". In Genesis 22, we saw how Abraham and Isaac became "one"—this is the theological consequence. Effectively God relates to Isaac through and because of Abraham: this will not be the case with Isaac's own son, Jacob whose relationship with God will be intensely personal and travel as yet untrodden paths. The one crucial additional promise that God makes to Isaac is "I will be with you" (26:3; cf. 26:24). It is strange that these words, central to God's self-revelation throughout the

Bible, were never precisely said to Abraham. Perhaps because God was with Abraham so often, it didn't really need to be stated. But their explicit statement now is an assurance that even if God withdraws from such overt contact with human beings as Abraham experienced, humanity will not be abandoned. God has become Immanuel.

On the whole, Isaac is a conservator, an inheritor rather than an innovator. His role in the story includes reopening "the wells of water that had been dug in the days of his father Abraham" (26:18), and that feels like a metaphorical symbol for his life, as well as comment on a specific action. But does this mean that Isaac can use the point Abraham reached in the journey of faith as his starting point—so that we don't have to work through the chapters of mistakes to get there?

26:6–11 Or do we? Isaac may not have gone down to Egypt, but he immediately makes a similar false move to his father—attempting to pass off his wife as his sister. It is striking how this third example of the wife-sister motif in Genesis draws from, and needs to be read in the light of, both the previous two examples of the genre. (Instead of supporting the hypothesis of separate Yahwist and Elohist sources a careful scrutiny of these three incidents undermines it.)

We already know from the previous incident that Abimelech is a godfearing king and Gerar is a godfearing place, so Isaac's deception is totally unnecessary. Although chronologically one might wonder whether the person named Abimelech in Genesis 26 could be the person of the same name in Genesis 20 it seems clear we are intended to identify them. Isaac's deception is also incompetently executed—this time the king does not need either divinely sent plagues or a dream to discover the truth; he can use the evidence of his own eyes, since Isaac cannot sustain his hoax. He fully lives up to his name: Isaac is discovered "Isaacing"—or "fondling" (Hebrew: *metsaheq*) his wife. Note the pun once again (see p. 134). Is Isaac a person gripped by sensual pleasures—sexual and of the gullet? By contrast, Rebekah's role in the trickery seems completely passive, even more so than Sarah in the earlier incidents: a striking feature in view of her proactive role in other episodes. Perhaps it encourages our sympathy for her and our sense that when, in the next chapter, she in turn conspires to deceive Isaac, it is no more than his due!

26:12-18 *Isaac sowed seed ... and in the same year reaped a hundredfold.* Given that this was during a time of famine (26:1), the miraculous fertility of the land is a clear sign of Yhwh's blessing. There is no indication that Abraham planted crops: he was a pastoralist. Isaac's actions constitute an important development—gradually the patriarchs are becoming rooted in the land where they are residing as aliens (see 26:2-3). God's blessing is steadily coming to fruition. Isaac's agricultural success is carefully linked to the original blessing of Abraham by the threefold repetition of the word for "great" which is present in 26:13 (though concealed by the English translation), recalling its appearance in the original blessing of Abraham (12:2). A literal translation of 26:13 might be "The man became great, and went on growing great until he was very great". The connection is also hinted at by the verb "sow" itself (Hebrew: *zaraʿ*). As we pointed out in the comments on 4:25 (see p. 50), one of the features of many modern translations, including the NRSV, is that they choose not to preserve the fact that when the ancestors are promised "descendants", the Hebrew word used (*zeraʿ*) is one that can also be translated "seed". Isaac's success with seeds in the ground acts as a sign that the "seed" of Abraham and his family will be equally fruitful.

Isaac's blessing is dependent on that which had been promised previously to Abraham. It is symptomatic that when he reopened those wells of his father which had been stopped up "he gave them the names that his father had given them".

26:19-33 The quarrel with the Philistines also reflects an earlier story, that of Abraham's dealing with Abimelech (21:25-34), but it takes on a different hue. Then the relationship between Philistines and Abraham's people had been resolved without major confrontation. Now, however, the quarrel over the meagre resources that the land can provide assumes a bitterness that reflects Israel's long-term hostility to the Philistines as well as foreshadowing the breakdown of relationships which will be the theme of the next chapter and dog the whole story of Jacob. Eventually the conciliatory attitude of Isaac helps to mend the breach. So too does Yhwh's transparent blessing of Isaac, and Abimelech's refreshing willingness to acknowledge this. He eventually shows the same open spirit as he had displayed when he encountered Abraham.

This only transpires after disputes over specific wells—whose names are intended to reflect their role in the conflict ("contention", "enmity", see NRSV footnotes). It is no accident that the conflicts cease once Isaac has dug the well at Rehoboth (= room): its very name evokes the promises to Abraham; when Abraham was told to "walk through the length and the breadth of the land" (13:17) that instruction included a word linked to Rehoboth. This name Rehoboth seems to register an awareness that all too easily one people's promised land can become another people's dispossession, and hint that this is not God's intended way forward. There can be room for all: only then will the final clause of the Abrahamic blessing be fulfilled (12:3). It is therefore appropriate that at this point God appears directly to renew once again the promise and blessing to Isaac. But even now this is for "my servant Abraham's sake". Isaac remains overshadowed by his father.

The final episode of the dealings between Isaac and Abimelech clearly reflects the earlier account of the covenant made between Abraham and Abimelech, and makes the same pun on the name Beer-sheba (see comments on Genesis 21:22–34 on p. 158). As he had done previously with Abraham, Abimelech acknowledges that "the LORD has been with you", so God's promise to Isaac ("I am with you") of a few verses earlier is already being visibly fulfilled. However, Abimelech's retinue has now increased in size—this time with the addition of "Ahuzzath his adviser". The name Ahuzzath means "Possession"; it is identical to the Hebrew word used in 17:8 and 23:9 to refer to Abraham's possession of the land. What are we to make of this? Is the involvement of a person of this name in this covenant made with Isaac a visible symbol that God's promise of possession (17:8) is coming to fruition? Or is it rather that Abimelech is determined to hold on to possession of his lands in the face of the threat posed by Isaac? Perhaps the ambiguity is deliberate. There is clearly tension around: the very rationale for the covenant is expressed negatively rather than positively. There is also self-interest on Abimelech's part, but this is appropriate given that the original words to Abraham spoke of blessing those who blessed him and cursed those who cursed. It is in Abimelech's vested interests to discover a modus vivendi with this disturbing *ger*. It is a modus vivendi, not more: after the covenant Isaac and Abimelech part company. They have found a way of living nearby each other, although not together. Genesis is realistic in its expectations. The model of breach and rapprochement offered by this chapter is a pattern for a similar exploration in the coming story of Jacob and Esau, though there the story will unfold with greater passion given that it is a quarrel between brothers.

We have found water are the last words addressed to Isaac in this chapter. Isaac's adventures here began with famine but end with a life-giving discovery. To this day the scarcity of water resources is a major underlying cause of conflict in the Middle East. Isaac may be (literally) a laughable figure, but the laughter associated with him can perhaps, as in Psalm 126, be linked to the discovery of water in the arid Negev Desert (Psalm 126:4) and become a source for the renewal of life.

26:34-35 *When Esau was forty years old*—the same age as Isaac was when he married Rebekah (25:20). Is Esau thereby hoping that he will please his father? Is he going to be a chip off the old block in his turn? If so, he goes about it the wrong way. The verses introduce the topic of marriage/intermarriage which will be a major concern throughout the Jacob story. The Hittites are the same people elsewhere referred to as Canaanites (see notes on Genesis 23:3 on p. 170). At one level these verses feel misplaced and as though they should be located at the beginning of Genesis 28. However, their placement at this point seems deliberate. Esau's behaviour provides an apparent justification for the actions of Rebekah and Jacob in Genesis 27.

In fact, Esau's choice of brides must indeed have "made life bitter for Isaac and Rebekah". One of his new fathers-in-law was named "Beeri" (which means "My well")—not a tactful choice in view of the dissension over wells which has dominated the second half of this chapter!

The stolen blessing
27:1–28:9

Now we will discover how the hasty and private transaction over the birthright (Hebrew: *bekorah*) between Jacob and Esau in Genesis 25:33 is to result in an objective and semi-public consequence: not only the *bekorah* but also the *berakah* (blessing) is passed to the younger brother. Note the pun on the two words in 27:36. But does Jacob ultimately receive this blessing because of his own deviousness, both then and now, or because throughout Genesis God chooses younger sons? The question remains tantalizingly open.

The structure of the story emphasizes how Jacob's blessing is almost "torn" out of Isaac, for whom Esau is the favourite son: willy-nilly he is forced to reverse Esau's position and bless the son who deceives him. In 27:1–4, he expresses his intention to bless Esau, but the sequence concludes in 28:1–4 with him blessing Jacob yet one more time.

It is telling that nowhere in this episode do Jacob and Esau appear "on stage" together: a narrative demonstration that their relationship has already been fractured—by Jacob's acquisition of the birthright, or perhaps even from the time of their prenatal quarrels.

At the heart of the story are the two poems in 27:28–29 and 27:39–40, which like poetry elsewhere in Genesis (see p. 28) help to set the prose narrative in which they appear within the context of God's grand design.

27:1–4 Once before in his life Isaac had heard the reply "Here I am" (Hebrew: *hinneni*) in response to his exclamation of 22:7. Back then he had called out, "My father": here he cries out "My son". Is this a hint that we need to read this story, set in the twilight of Isaac's life, in the context of that earlier experience? In both cases, he seems to be ignorant, even deceived. At Mount Moriah, his father Abraham had come to a new insight, literally and symbolically (note the play on "seeing" throughout Genesis 22 on p. 164). Abraham seems to have been a person of vision throughout his life. Yet now when we meet his son Isaac "his eyes were dim so that he could not see". Does Isaac's blindness epitomize his blinkered view, skewed by his attachment to sensual pleasures? Or, as in the case of Oedipus in the Greek dramas, does this physical blindness now facilitate spiritual sight? After all, if Isaac had now been able to see, Jacob would never have been blessed, and YHWH's oracle to Rebekah (25:23) would never have been fulfilled.

The physical senses will play an important role in this story. Again and again, Isaac is guided—and misled—by his senses of taste, touch and smell (27:4,9,12,14,21,22,26,27). It is because he "likes" the taste of Esau's "savoury food" that Esau is his favoured son (25:28). Three times Isaac's liking for this dish is stressed (27:4,9,14), a sign of its importance to the storyteller. In fact, the verb "like" here is the same Hebrew word elsewhere translated "love". Somehow "love" has been cheapened by this use for the word. Love had only entered human history when it was employed to emphasize the exquisite pain that Abraham experienced when summoned to sacrifice his son (22:2). It had then been used appropriately to describe the love of Isaac for Rebekah, a man for a woman (24:67), yoking them together to become bearers of God's promise, and afterwards for the parents' love for the two children of that union (25:28). But now to employ it of mere food: it seems almost promiscuous! From the moment that love has been let loose in the world we will discover that it can be dangerous (37:3). It must not be abused, yet that is exactly what Isaac now appears to be doing.

Perhaps it is not Isaac's fault. Has he been irreparably scarred by that experience of his youth, which will echo again in this story (27:18)? Is it easier simply to restrict oneself to the practical and overtly physical? If we care too much for someone or something, will it eventually be taken from us?

Robert Alter also suggests a connection between Genesis 22 and this scene. Isaac is "the most passive of the patriarchs. We have already seen him as a bound victim for whose life a ram is substituted; later as a father, he will prefer the son who can go out to the field and bring him back provender, and his one extended scene will be lying in bed, weak and blind, while others act on him."[62]

27:5-17 If Isaac is controlled by his senses of taste, touch and smell, Rebekah, by contrast, is someone for whom hearing is central. "Rebekah was listening" (27:5) . . . "I heard your father say" (27:6) . . . "Obey (literally "listen to") my word" (27:8); ... "Obey my word" (27:13). "Now ... my son, obey my voice" (27:43).

She was the one who had originally heard the oracle of Yhwh regarding the eventual destiny of the sons in her womb. She already knows the importance to the divine schema of being willing to listen. As the story of Genesis develops, hearing becomes a key physical sense. Even now at key moments in the story, women, in particular, have listened (e.g. Eve, Hagar, Sarah) and helped to change the course of history. Rebekah's listening to Isaac's conversation with Esau stands in the tradition of Sarah who listened behind the tent-flaps, and it is equally momentous.

Yet who you listen to is critical. When women themselves are heard, complications invariably seem to ensue. Once again (see comments on Genesis 16:2 on p. 125) the dangerous phrase "Listen to the voice of ... " makes its appearance. Although partly concealed by the English translation it comes three times in this story (27:8,13,43) as Rebekah demands that Jacob should listen to her. What will happen to Jacob as a result of his willingness to listen to his mother's plan may ultimately be part of God's intentions, but it will involve pain, exile and separation (as did the story of Hagar and Sarah). When Jacob is forced from home as a result of their mutual deviousness, Rebekah will apparently never see this beloved son again.

Bring me game ... that I may bless you before the Lord before I die. In retelling the words of Isaac to Jacob, Rebekah subtly embroiders them. There had been no mention of Yhwh's involvement in Isaac's actual speech. What he had been proposing was perhaps simply a familial rite of inheritance for the eldest son: how interested was Isaac really in Yhwh's "big picture"?

Rebekah, however, knows that the consequences of her family history reach well beyond the interests of this unit of four people. It embraces the destiny of nations, and perhaps even of humanity. "Before the Lord" (literally "to the face of the Lord") was a phrase used to describe the way Abraham himself was called to live (17:1; 24:40); significantly it was a phrase that Abraham had begged for Ishmael but which was withheld from him (17:18, same idiom in Hebrew, though NRSV translates "might live in your sight"). Rebekah knew, perhaps more than Isaac himself realized, that to be "before the LORD" was the foundation of her family's role in YHWH's promises.

Go to the flock, and get me two choice kids. This will not be the only time that goats assist with deception in the story of Jacob—and his sons (see 37:31; 38:17).

Esau is a hairy man ... I am a man of smooth skin. The connection with Mount Seir in Edom that had been made at Esau's birth is reinforced (see p. 208). Jacob's contrasting smoothness extends to more than his skin! In Hebrew, as in English, the word "smooth" has a wider negative ring such as "smooth talker" (see e.g. Psalm 12:2–3; Proverbs 26:28).

Perhaps my father will feel me, and I shall seem to be mocking him, and bring a curse on myself and not a blessing. There is irony in Jacob's words, even if he doesn't realize it. Literally the words are "I shall be in his eyes as one playing a trick", yet he knows full well that those eyes cannot see anything. As Jacob worries about being cursed rather than blessed, our thoughts are taken back to the original blessing of Abraham which mentioned both possibilities (12:3). Those words of 12:3 will shortly be explicitly repeated for the first time when Isaac does bless Jacob (27:29). But for all Rebekah's protestations we may wonder whether Jacob does bring a curse upon himself—as well as the blessing—and perhaps upon his mother too. The aftermath of their deception will be bitter for them both.

Then Rebekah took the best garments of her elder son Esau, which were with her in the house, and put them on her younger son Jacob. From the beginning of human history clothes have been used to conceal reality (3:7). As the story of Genesis continues, they will increasingly be used as instruments of deception (e.g. 37:31–33; 38:14; 39:15). "In the house" is a reminder that the lifestyle of Isaac's family has become more sedentary than that of his father who lived in tents (18:1).

27:18–29 *He went in to his father and said, "My father"; and he said, "Here I am; who are you, my son?"* In Hebrew, the first word of Jacob in this scene and the first word of Isaac's response are identical to the words which Isaac and his father spoke as they travelled to Moriah (22:7). In both cases, the exchange is followed by a sentence through which Isaac is deceived—in the past by Abraham about the identity of the proposed sacrifice, now by Jacob about his own identity. The parallel intensifies the sense of Isaac's passivity and vulnerability here. There is something almost obscene about this trick played here upon a helpless old man. However, in the previous chapter Isaac falsified his own identity (26:7), so perhaps it is little more than he deserves. Those who deceive will be deceived in their turn, as Jacob will, in the future, discover to his cost.

And yet, that parallel with the journey to Moriah somehow helps to relieve the guilt of Jacob's deception. If we were willing to forgive Abraham's earlier misleading answer to Isaac, because we believed it to be part of God's plan, should we not do the same for Abraham's grandson, since the primacy he is now seeking has been so clearly proclaimed even before his birth (25:23)?

Jacob's answer is clearly false—he is not Esau: yet there is more truth about it than appears at first sight. For here the description "firstborn" (Hebrew: *bekor*) that he claims is a word closely related to that for "birthright" (*bekorah*) that he has purchased from Esau. The link is reinforced by Jacob's request for the blessing (*berakah*) in the same verse.

However, his response to his father's query about the speed with which the dish has been prepared is breathtaking in its cynicism: "Because the Lord your God granted me success." Whatever "taking the name of the Lord in vain" (Exodus 20:7) may have originally meant, to use the divine name to reinforce such deception surely comes close to it! It is of a piece with Rebekah's deliberate addition of Yhwh's name (27:7) when she retells the conversation between Isaac and Esau.

It is no accident that Jacob speaks of "the Lord your God". Yhwh is Isaac's God, but not so far Jacob's! Even when the longed-for blessing is bestowed on Jacob in 27:28 it is given in the name of God (*'elohim*) rather than that of the more particular and relational Yhwh. Jacob will not begin to know Yhwh as his own God until his vision at Bethel (28:13), but even then something of the closeness which is associated with knowing God as Yhwh will elude him (32:29): the rejected Leah will use this name more readily (29:32–35) than Jacob himself will do.

Isaac's suspicions are clear and are hinted at several times throughout the sequence. From his initial question, "Who are you?" (27:18), through his concern about apparent speed (27:20), his puzzlement over Jacob's voice (27:22), his repeated query about identity (27:24), and even his request to be kissed (27:26) which allows him to smell his son, one senses that Isaac is aware that something is not right. Is it possible that Isaac deliberately allowed himself to be deceived? It would have been the easiest way of allowing his natural inclination for Esau to be overruled by what he had perceived to be the intention of Yhwh.

Yet the writer nowhere suggests that this is what happened. Rather, a contrast is made between his sense of hearing which, like his wife Rebekah, Isaac should have trusted, "The voice is Jacob's voice", and his other senses, on which he erringly depends. Rebekah has done her work well: it might have seemed unnecessary to dress up Jacob in Esau's clothes since Isaac will not be able to see them, but it is the smell of these clothes that finally convinces the father. Perhaps a father who makes the bestowal of his blessing contingent upon his sense of taste—"Bring it to me, that I may eat of my son's game and bless you."—deserves no less than to be misled by his sense of smell.

For the first time, we meet the word "recognize" (27:23). It is a link word which will draw together what is now taking place with Rachel's deception of her father Laban (31:32), the robe of Joseph dipped in goat's blood to deceive Jacob himself (37:32), Tamar's deception of Judah (38:25), and eventually Joseph's own unrevealed recognition of his brothers (42:7–8). Each time it is used it is with a twist which points up discrepancy between what is being recognized and the underlying or present reality. As the first of this long list, it suggests that the consequences of Isaac's lack of recognition will be far reaching.

Throughout this chapter when Isaac's blessing of his son has been referred to, it is literally said that it is Isaac's *nephesh* which will transmit the blessing. *Nephesh*, the same Hebrew word used when Yhwh first made humanity in 2:7 emphasizes the way the total personality of Isaac is bound up with this action. Karen Armstrong puts it like this:

> When clerics bless their congregation today, it can be a rather impersonal gesture ... This is very different from the biblical

> notion of blessing. [Isaac] was communicating his life essence to his son, breathing his very soul into the other. To do this, he had to get close to Jacob. He asked him to approach, kissed him, felt his body, and smelled his clothes. Blessing involved the body as well as the spirit. Only when this degree of intimacy had been created could he pass the power to his son.[63]

Equally a blessing should be appropriate for the person to whom it was delivered. In this instance the "smell" of Esau's clothes reminds Isaac of "the smell of a field", which epitomizes Esau who was a "man of the field" (25:27). In turn, this dictates the content of the first part of the blessing, which seems ironically more appropriate for Esau for whom it was intended than Jacob to whom it was actually given. The agricultural prosperity, "plenty of grain and wine", alluded to hints at the changes that have taken place in the lifestyle of Abraham's family since he first travelled to Canaan as a pastoralist with herds.

Then the blessing moves onto a different plane, reminiscent of the earlier oracle to Rebekah (25:23). Is the reference to "mother's sons" (27:29) intended to draw our attention to this link? Now it is not so much Jacob, or Esau, the individual who is being addressed, but the relative destinies of the nations of which they will become the progenitors.

The poetic form of the blessing helps to make clear its fundamental character: it is one of the defining moments of Genesis. Blessings can never be withdrawn, even if they are bestowed upon the wrong person. But words spoken as poetry have greater significance still—for in these moments the human beings that speak them tap in to the very structure of creation:

> Cursed be everyone that curses you,
> And blessed be everyone who blesses you!

The explicit verbal link between these lines and the original blessing of Abram (12:3) is striking. But their irony is also powerful. Isaac believes that he is cursing the enemies of Esau, though it is actually Jacob, Esau's "enemy" who hears them spoken. So are they for Jacob blessing or curse? Perhaps they are both: as the next chapters of Jacob's story make clear, to steal the blessing brings difficulties and dangers in its train.

THE STOLEN BLESSING (27:1–28:9)

27:30–40 There is a farcical quality to what happens next—beginning even with Esau's entrance. The analogy is appropriate. One could imagine a dramatization of the story with Jacob going off stage left just as Esau enters stage right!

The dialogue between Esau and Isaac reflects the earlier exchange between Isaac and Jacob. But subtle differences emphasize the closer relationship between Isaac and Esau. Throughout the whole episode it is notable that Isaac has nowhere called Jacob "my son" except when he believes that he is Esau.

Your brother came deceitfully. Significantly the Hebrew word translated "deceitfully", used of Jacob's actions, reminds us of the adjective "cunning", which described the serpent in Genesis 3:1. Jacob has been a real "snake in the grass" in this family, and like Adam and Eve before him, Isaac has allowed his senses to control him—with unwanted results.

Esau said, "Is he not rightly named Jacob? For he has supplanted me these two times. He took away my birthright; and look, now he has taken away my blessing." The puns both on the name of Jacob, and on birthright (*bekorah*) and blessing (*berakah*) are here revisited. The concrete nature of the Hebrew language means that the verb "supplant" (Hebrew: *'aqab*) derives from the noun "heel" (Hebrew: *'aqeb*)—with the literal sense of "coming up on one's heel", i.e. overtaking someone. Jacob has really lived up to his epithet of heel! A similar link between Jacob's name and his action of supplanting is made in Jeremiah 9:4 and Hosea 12:3 (see also comments on p. 208).

Esau lifted up his voice and wept. Esau comes over as pathetic in his despair. Three times he beseeches his father for any "left over" blessing (27:34,36,38). It is a dangerous request, for when Isaac finally responds to it, he does so with words that sound more like curse than blessing, but which, because they have now been uttered will inevitably come to pass.

It is the mirror image of Jacob's blessing. Servitude rather than lordship, and aridity rather than plenty. Once again, the destiny of a nation is referred to: both in terms of Edom's status as vassal of Israel, from the time of David and throughout much of the monarchy, and also in terms of its geographical situation in southern Transjordan ekeing out an existence in terrain that is often indistinguishable from desert. Those who wrote this story knew of the perennial conflict between the desert and the sown which has so dominated the history of the region:

> But when you break loose,
> you shall break his yoke from your neck.

The one meagre hope offered to Esau is that one day this servitude will be ended, a presumed reference to the time of the Babylonian destruction of Jerusalem when the Edomites took the opportunity not only to throw off any remnants of Judaean/Israelite lordship, but also participated in looting Jerusalem and southern Judaean towns.

27:41–45 *Esau hated Jacob.* We fear a rerun of the saga of Cain and Abel: that it is avoided seems to be due to Rebekah's adroitness.

The days of mourning for my father are approaching. In fact, Isaac lasts at least another twenty years—all of the period of Jacob's "exile" in Mesopotamia. He is still alive when Jacob returns (35:27). Our awareness of this length of time he spends in a supine state reinforces how passive this patriarch is.

[Rebekah] called her younger son Jacob . . . Now therefore, my son, obey my voice. Unlike Isaac, Rebekah knowingly addresses Jacob as "my son". The expression "listen to me" repeats the same Hebrew words as were used in verses 8 and 13. Because Jacob listened to his mother on that earlier occasion and participated in the deception of his father, he must now listen to her again and accept a future of exile. (A similar pattern occurred in the Abraham cycle, see p. 125)

I will send, and bring you back. In fact, after this chapter Rebekah completely disappears from the story. She never sees her son Jacob again. The banishment forced upon Jacob because of the imminent expectation of his father's death is ultimately unnecessary, but results in permanent separation between a mother and her beloved son. Is a moral price being paid for their mutual plotting? As a result of listening in, Rebekah has secured the blessing for Jacob: now she listens in again (27:42) and believes that she is securing his life—but this time the listening ultimately proves unnecessary. She has listened once too often.

The story of Abraham climaxed with the near death of his beloved son; now the story of Rebekah and Isaac comes to an end with a different kind of "death" for her much-loved child. Will it also be a pattern repeated in the next generation?

27:46–28:9 At first sight, these verses tell a very different story to that portrayed in the previous family quarrel. The rationale for Jacob's journey to Mesopotamia is now to avoid intermarriage and preserve the purity of his family lineage. The verses come from a different hand to that of the original author of 27:1–45. But this new reason for Jacob's departure is clearly composed in awareness of the earlier story, with 27:46 as a seam which joins the two. The narrative appears to come from a period in Jewish history when the issue of intermarriage was particularly pressing, with opposing views being expressed by different sections of the Jewish community (see also comments on Genesis 24 on p. 173).

Rebekah said to Isaac, "I am weary of my life because of the Hittite women!" Rebekah is determined to keep Jacob safe, but needs to get Isaac on her side to permit him to travel to Mesopotamia, particularly in view of the fact that Isaac before his marriage had been prevented by his father from travelling there. She skilfully uses this ruse of the need to avoid contact with the local "Hittite" women. The verse should be read alongside 26:34–35, which at one time it may have directly followed, where Esau's marriage to such women has been reported. As an additional bonus, Rebekah now cleverly manages to damn Esau without even mentioning him by name!

The final editor of this section of Genesis has been as adroit as Rebekah: two different reasons for Jacob's departure have been seamed together!

To describe Canaanite women as "Hittite" suggests that these verses come from the same hand as the author of Genesis 23.

Then Isaac called Jacob, and blessed him   This additional blessing for Jacob reinforces the sense of exclusion for Esau. It seems that Isaac did have more than one blessing to give, but they are both for Jacob!

Go at once to Paddan-aram to the house of Bethuel.   Although there are connections between the account of Jacob's journey to meet his Mesopotamian kin and the earlier journey there of Abraham's servant, the two episodes seem to originate from different hands. One clue is the different name for their destination: in Genesis 24:10 Aram-naharaim, here Paddan-aram (see comments on 25:20 on p. 205).

May God Almighty bless you and make you fruitful.   This is only the second time that the title God Almighty *(El Shaddai)* has been used in Genesis. The first occurrence was in 17:1. As there, it appears now alongside a promise of fruitfulness and fertility and is also linked to possession of the land (see notes on 17:1 on p. 131). Here it is remarkable how the promise of the land is made to Jacob just as he is forced to leave it. Promise therefore assumes the character of reassurance.

The blessing builds on, yet also corrects, the impression given by the account of Isaac's marriage in Genesis 24. As in that earlier story, the land of Mesopotamia is viewed positively; it is a place which facilitates the preservation of the purity of genealogical lineage. But Genesis 24 was adamant that Abraham's descendant must not himself return there: did this therefore blight those from Judah and Jerusalem who had been taken to Babylon by force? So now a later descendant of Abraham does go there himself and will discover that God does not abandon him through his years of servitude.

Esau went to Ishmael, and took Mahalath daughter of Abraham's son Ishmael.   Even now Esau can't quite get it right. In attempting to please his parents, he ends up reinforcing his status as an outsider. In linking himself with Ishmael through marriage to his daughter, he seems to be edged out one stage further from the blessing, promise and covenant. The geographical territory of the Edomites and that of Ishmael's Arab descendants overlapped. The apparent familial connection probably reflects a recognized historical reality.

Visions of the night
28:10–22

Jacob's numinous experience at Bethel is one of the two major theological pillars in the construction of the Jacob cycle. It seams together the stories of Jacob and Esau and those of Jacob and Laban. It resonates against the other seam and pillar, Genesis 32:22–32: the two episodes complement each other.

28:10–15 *Jacob left Beer-sheba and went towards Haran.* He is beginning Abraham's journey in reverse; it is appropriate that this is the moment when the voice that once spoke to Abraham will finally speak to him. Up till now God has never related to him directly: as he had rightly said to his father Yhwh was "the Lord your God" (27:20) not Jacob's own. Perhaps Jacob even hoped to leave Yhwh behind in Canaan, along with all his family troubles. All that will now change, as for the first time Yhwh confirms to Jacob that he is indeed the bearer of the promise, even if it was apparently gained by trickery.

He came to a certain place. The word *maqom* (= place) has more resonance in Hebrew than "place" does in English and may suggest that there was already a sanctuary at Bethel before Jacob's visit. However, whatever the actuality, the story seems to suggest that Bethel became a sacred site precisely because of Jacob's experiences there.

[He] stayed there for the night, because the sun had set. We will not read of the sun rising again until after Jacob's fight at Penuel on his return to the land (32:31). A powerful symbolic darkness pervades the whole period of time Jacob spends in a strange land.

One of the stones of the place Stones feature significantly from now on in Jacob's story (28:18,22; 29:10; 31:45–47; 35:14). They reflect his changed situation—no longer is he a "mummy's boy" but becomes capable of Herculean feats of strength, hard himself, like stone. The last time that "stone" was mentioned in Genesis was when people attempted to use bricks for stone to build the Tower of Babel, the falsity of this action reflecting their false move. Jacob's vision at Bethel is now presented as a contrast with that earlier attempt to link heaven and earth.

And he dreamed This is the first time a member of Abraham's own family has explicitly encountered God by this method. Previously the relationship had been more informal. Jacob's experience at Bethel has a numinous quality that probably exceeds anything we have encountered up till now (Genesis 15:17 may be the exception), but the corollary of this will be that interchange between human and divine will never be so "normal" or easy again. Dreams will be increasingly used by God to communicate with human beings—perhaps a reflection of increasing distance between the two worlds.

There was a ladder We are probably intended to think of this as a kind of ramped tower, like a Babylonian *ziggurat*, which symbolically connected earth and heaven. *The top of it reaching to heaven* closely parallels the description of the Tower of Babel, "with its top in the heavens" (11:4). The difference is that this structure is clearly sanctioned by God, reaching down from heaven to earth, rather than that vain attempt of the human builders to reach up from earth to heaven.

The angels of God were ascending and descending on it. The heavenly traffic indicates that this place is a "boundary" on Jacob's journey away from Canaan. Is one way that God can be present with people when they are away from this land via an angel (cf. Genesis 24:7; 31:11, cf. Exodus 23:23)? The angels may be descending to earth in order to accompany Jacob on his journey, although they will then be invisible (see further on New Testament links to this passage on p. 277).

And the LORD stood beside him and said, "I am the LORD". God finally reveals himself as YHWH to Jacob, as he had previously done to Abraham, and more ambiguously to Isaac. The relationship between YHWH and Jacob has at last been established, although it will never be a totally easy one, and for long years Jacob will apparently have to survive by his wits, rather than by YHWH's ready intervention.

The God of Abraham your father and the God of Isaac   The language recalls the earlier oracle to Isaac (26:4–5,24–25) and before that the promises to Abraham (13:14–16; 17:7–8; 22:17–18). The continuity is itself a form of reassurance in view of Jacob's desperate plight. But the words to Jacob go beyond even the extravagance of these earlier assurances. "You shall spread abroad." Is the implication that the "spread" of Jacob's descendants will extend even further than the land of Canaan, to include the diaspora? That would be appropriate in view of Jacob's intended destination and would resonate with any early readers of this passage who happened to be in Babylon. It would suggest that even there they were not outside the limits of God's promise! In Hebrew, the verb translated as "spread" sounds similar (though is not related) to the word "scattered" which described God's response to the builders of the Tower of Babel (11:8). It is a positive echo of that earlier action: to be spread is now clearly stated to be a means of blessing, rather than a form of punishment.

I am with you and will keep you wherever you go.   Although Yhwh had previously promised to be "with" Isaac (26:3,24), these words assume an even deeper significance here, as Jacob prepares to depart from Yhwh's own land. Other Old Testament texts hint at the perplexity people felt as they wrestled with the issue of whether Yhwh's presence could be effective away from Canaan (2 Kings 5:17–18; Psalm 137). Yet as Exodus 33:16 makes clear, if people were without God's assurance of presence any promise that Yhwh was their God and that they were Yhwh's people was ultimately meaningless. During Jacob's stay with Laban, God will not feature frequently, but Jacob seems to be confident that despite contrary appearances God is with him (31:5).

I ... will bring you back to this land.   Abraham's journey required him to turn his back on the past and his homeland. Not so, this time with Jacob. That is important; otherwise the future that began with Abraham would be soon aborted.

But the words also bear another significance. Unlike Abraham where wrong paths that have been trodden seem to be eventually banished from the story, in the story of Jacob mistakes have to be revisited and redeemed. In the time of Abraham, Hagar and Ishmael were expelled; but for Jacob one day peace and reconciliation in "this land" will have to be sought from his brother Esau.

28:16-22 *Surely the LORD is in this place—and I did not know it ... This is ... the house of God ... the gate of heaven.* In the ancient world, what gave a sacred building its meaning was the belief that a god was present there. A temple was the dwelling place or "house" of the deity. Among other purposes, the episode therefore seeks to explain why the important Israelite sanctuary of Bethel gained its special character. The very name Bethel (= House of God) that Jacob now gives to the place is a pun on the function that it will have (see 28:17,19,22). In view of the extremely negative portrayal of Bethel in several parts of the Old Testament (e.g. 1 Kings 12:28-13:34), it is striking that Bethel should be presented so positively here, with its name suggesting that it was the archetypal temple, or house of God (see comments on p. 277).

Temples were regarded as locations where heaven and earth could meet, hence Jacob's words "a gate of heaven". But there may be another reason for the choice of this phrase. The real meaning of the name Bab-el (Babylon) is "gate of God", although in 11:9 the name is deliberately misconstrued as "babble". Could the writer of Genesis 28 be challenging Babylon's claim to this epithet by claiming it for this site in Canaan? The other resonances between 11:1-9 and 28:10-19 make this feasible.

He was afraid, and said, "How awesome is this place!" Jacob has learned "fear" of God, a quality for which Abraham was praised at the time of his great test (22:12). He is already a different personality from the son who uses YHWH's name to deceive his father (27:20).

He took the stone ... and set it up for a pillar. Stone pillars or *matsebot* are common features of Canaanite sanctuaries and can be seen today at many archaeological sites in the Holy Land. Originally, they may have symbolized a "male" deity, but, gradually, as here, they came simply to represent the divine. The hostility of certain parts of the Old Testament to such cult symbols is quite marked (e.g. 2 Kings 23:14). Perhaps the careful way in which the writer here links the "pillar", with the ladder which was "set up" (28:12) on the ground and the fact that YHWH "stood" by it (28:13) (all three words are connected, in Hebrew, to the root *natsab*) is due to the need he felt to justify Jacob's setting up of this object. It is also remarkable how intricately Jacob himself is linked with the divine message: the wordplays associate his own head (28:11), the head ("top") of the ladder (28:12) and the head ("top") of the stone (28:18). Perhaps at the end of the day Jacob has become part of this open portal to heaven (see further on p. 278).

Poured oil on the top of it. Anointing with oil was the normal way an object (or person) was "consecrated" for divine service.

Jacob made a vow, saying, "If God will be with me..." Jacob's words remind us of his desperate plight. Despite two extravagant blessings from his father which promised "the fatness of the earth" (27:28), he had arrived at Bethel uncertain even of the basics of food and clothing. God had come to him when he was at his lowest ebb. And for the first time in his life, he wants to give something rather than take it! But the words also remind us that Jacob was a perennial bargainer: with Esau (25:31), Laban (29:18, 30:31–33), and here even with God!

Tricksters tricked
29:1–31:5

At first sight what we now have is a "pastoral symphony"—an interlude with plenty of folklore and comic touches, to encourage readers to laugh at their ancient enemies the Aramaeans. But the experience of Jacob during his stay with Laban is deliberately placed at the heart of the Jacob cycle, the "trickery" which is a motif dominating these three chapters acting as a counterpoint to Jacob's earlier deception of his father and his brother. Within the chapters, the account of the birth of Jacob's children forms an inner core, highlighted by the wordplays that greet their birth. Born away from the land of promise they may be, but their existence and their number constitute the guarantee that God's extravagant promise of 28:14 was not an empty word.

29:1-14 *Jacob went on his journey.* The literal meaning of the Hebrew words that underlie this translation is "Jacob lifted up his feet and went". This unusual expression suggests that after his dream at Bethel there is now a new spring in Jacob's step!

The land of the people of the east First Adam and Eve, then Cain, and later Ishmael had all settled in the east. People who live in the east appear to be on the edge of God's purposes.

He saw a well. Momentous events have previously transpired at wells. Our appetite is whetted: what is going to happen this time?

The stone on the well's mouth was large. A good omen? Jacob's last encounter with a stone provided salvation.

When all the flocks were gathered Words derived from the Hebrew verb *'asap* will run like a thread through the story, in 29:3,7,8 translated as "gathered" and in 29:22 "gathered ... together". Finally, in 30:23, the identical verb (translated there as "taken away") will be used to explain the name of Joseph, Jacob and Rachel's son. It is as though we are being alerted in advance to the climax of these chapters, the birth of offspring to this shepherdess (29:9) and this super-shepherd (29:7; 30:29).

My brothers, where do you come from? Before now Jacob's appreciation of the requirements of brotherhood has been singularly lacking. Is this story going to provide him with an opportunity to redeem his understanding of brotherhood?

Laban son of Nahor Although strictly speaking Laban was Nahor's grandson this description of Laban as Nahor's son, rather than the son of Bethuel helps take us back to the time of Abraham and sets what is to follow within the wider framework of the whole story of Abraham's descendants.

Here is his daughter Rachel, coming with the sheep. Rachel's name means "Ewe", a pointed link both to her own profession and to her later role as a matriarch of Israel, YHWH's own "flock" that he has promised to watch over (28:15; 49:24).

It is still broad daylight ... Water the sheep, and go, pasture them. In contrast to the shepherds, apparently lazy and not wanting to exert themselves with the heavy stone, Jacob is now prepared to give lessons in basic husbandry! His skill at shepherding seems to have developed considerably since the days when he was "living in tents" (25:27).

Now Jacob saw Rachel ... Jacob went up and rolled the stone from the well's mouth, and watered the flock of his mother's brother Laban. The contrast now is not only with the indolent shepherds, but also with Jacob's own father Isaac, whose vicarious wooing of Jacob's mother, Rebekah, these actions now recall.

A generation ago another well nearby was the scene for the meeting of Abraham's servant with Rebekah. Now this "type-scene" which leads us to expect matrimony is repeated. Once again, a "hero" from a foreign land meets a virgin by a well. But unlike Isaac, Jacob does his own wooing—he needs no substitute—and this time the water is drawn by the man for the woman after performing a super-human feat of single-handedly removing the stone over the mouth of the well. Jacob's virility here compares with the passivity with which Isaac is portrayed. For Isaac it was so easy: the bride was his simply for the servant's asking. It seems that it may be as simple for Jacob: before the next verse is through "Jacob kissed Rachel", a brazen gesture that scandalized Calvin when he commented on this passage! But in fact, the stone that Jacob needed to remove symbolizes the obstacles that will be put in his way before he is able to consummate this relationship with Rachel.

He was her father's kinsman. As elsewhere, the Hebrew word underlying kinsman is *'ah*, literally "brother", which is often employed to describe a blood relationship that is more distant than sibling. But its use here encourages us to read the story of Jacob's dealings with Laban in the light of his earlier exchange with Esau, his actual brother. Will Laban be any better "brother" to Jacob than Jacob had been to Esau?

Laban ... ran to meet him ... and brought him to his house. On the surface, Laban's actions signal generous hospitality, but we cannot forget that we first met Laban when Rebekah was wooed—and then he seemed far too interested in the apparent wealth of the visitor who came from the west (24:30). Will Laban be disappointed when he discovers that this visitor has arrived as a fugitive rather than with a camel train of jewels? He certainly sets Jacob to work very quickly and gets a month's free labour out of him.

Jacob told Laban all these things, and Laban said to him, "Surely you are my bone and my flesh." What was it that Jacob confessed to Laban— how he had stolen what had belonged to his brother? If so, there is irony in Laban's response. At first reading, it sounds as though Laban's exclamation is returning us to Eden; for his literal words "You are my bone and my flesh" echo Adam's cry of joy there at meeting Eve. Has Jacob truly found a "brother", is Cain's conflict with Abel undone and paradise restored? That must have been what Jacob was longing for! And yet Laban's answer can also suggest that he was recognizing in Jacob a kindred spirit, a fellow-trickster—on whom the tables will soon be turned.

29:15-28 At first, Laban seems more than reasonable. "Because you are my kinsman [brother], should you therefore serve me for nothing?" It is only when we look a little closer that we discover that Jacob has already been labouring for Laban for a month presumably without payment, and it is only when we read on that we discover that, because of Laban's later trick, Jacob will in reality labour for Laban "for nothing" for seven whole years!

Now Laban had two daughters. The last time the word "two" appeared it described the prenatal hostility between Jacob and Esau. Trouble surely lies ahead, especially as the two sisters are then contrasted, as were Jacob and Esau in 25:23.

Rachel was graceful and beautiful. The identical description is given of Rachel's son, Joseph, in 39:6. Beauty, as we already discovered in 12:14, can cause problems!

Jacob loved Rachel. Three times Jacob's love for Rachel is mentioned (29:18,20,30); it is a powerful force. But as with the love of Isaac and Rebekah, each for their favoured son, love is dangerous and can cause strife.

Jacob served seven years for Rachel, and they seemed to him but a few days. A "few days" was literally the expression Rebekah used in 27:44 (translated there as "for a while") when she encouraged Jacob's "temporary" departure. Those few days have become years of exile. But it is symptomatic that finally Jacob has to remind Laban that his time is up.

Laban ... made a feast. There would have been lots of wine to drink. Was it a drunken Jacob on whom Laban passed off the deception, and his elder daughter?

When morning came, it was Leah! Jacob's comeuppance is well and truly executed! As the darkness of his father's blindness had helped his own deception of his father Isaac, so in turn the darkness of night facilitates Laban's deception of him.

Jacob said to Laban, "What is this you have done to me?" The screws of nemesis are further tightened as Jacob refers to how Laban has "deceived" him? Did he not know that his own trickery was described by the cognate word "deceit" when he cheated his brother out of their father's blessing? There is a snake in the grass in Paddan-aram, just as there was in Canaan, and as there had once been in Eden (see notes on 27:35, p. 223).

Laban said, "This is not done in our country— giving the younger before the firstborn." The slap in the face for Jacob is brutally ironic. His own trick had involved a younger sibling taking the rightful place of the elder. Now Laban's trick on him has resulted in an elder sister taking the place intended for the younger. The words are carefully chosen: "firstborn" had been used to describe Esau and is closely linked to birthright. Laban's self-justification acts as a clear rebuke to Jacob for the way he had seized the place that belonged to his elder!

Then Laban gave him his daughter Rachel as a wife. On the surface, it looks as though the deception is quickly resolved in a way that meets the needs of everybody, certainly with far less grief than Jacob's deception of Esau. But appearances are themselves deceptive: the emotions that have been stirred by these actions will have consequences that will reverberate throughout the rest of Genesis.

29:29-35 *When the LORD saw that Leah was unloved, he opened her womb.* The translation is euphemistic. Leah is positively "hated", partly because of her complicity in her father's deception of Jacob. However, the language also recalls the lawcode of Deuteronomy 21:15-17, which reads almost like a commentary on the later story of Jacob and his sons:

> If a man has two wives, one of them loved and the other disliked, and if both the loved and the disliked have borne him sons, the firstborn being the son of the one who is disliked, then on the day when he wills his possessions to his sons, he is not permitted to treat the son of the loved as the firstborn in preference to the son of the disliked ...

If only Jacob had adhered strictly to this law, how much less grief would there have been later on!

God's bias towards the unfavoured is evident here in the story, in the lawcode, and in the rest of Genesis. It is fascinating that the naming of at least one of Leah's sons, Simeon, recalls the name given to Hagar's son Ishmael, as does the rationale for the giving of that name (see 16:11; 29:33). And when Leah speaks of her "affliction" as her first son is born, she uses the same word (*'oni*) that the angel applied to Hagar (16:11). It seems that Hagars can exist within the community of promise as well as outside it. That same word *'oni* will also be used when the last son of Jacob is born, Benjamin, whom Rachel sought to name Ben-oni as she died giving birth to him. Leah had the fertility, and Rachel the love. Is the story suggesting that one without the other is dangerous and can be the cause of humiliation and grief?

Leah conceived and bore a son. In apparently rapid succession, Leah has four sons. She names each, explaining her choice of name, with an explanation linked to it by sound.

In each case, Leah associates YHWH with the giving of the son. The names of the first three all reflect her despair, as well her desire to be loved by Jacob. But with the fourth son, Judah, she apparently manages to overcome her pain, and his birth is an occasion of fulfilment: "This time I will praise the LORD."

Does this reflect Judah's special place among Leah's children, both in terms of the story (he figures prominently in the story of Joseph) and as the eponymous ancestor of the tribe and kingdom of Judah? In a book, Genesis, in which younger sons assume particular prominence, Judah, the youngest among this initial quartet of Leah's sons, may be specially marked out by God, particularly because his eldest brother Reuben appears to lose his birthright (35:22; 49:4), and the next brothers Simeon and Levi are condemned by their father for their violence (34:30; 49:5).

30:1–24 *Give me children, or I shall die!* This is actually the first time we have heard Rachel speak, and these impetuous words seem to define her character. She even makes it clear both now, and after Joseph is born, that she is not content with one son. Does her outburst paradoxically presage her early death, while giving birth to Benjamin?

Jacob became very angry with Rachel, ... "Am I in the place of God?" Robert Alter has pointed out how often the biblical narrative responds to the situation of a barren but favoured wife by offering an "annunciation" in which the woman prays to God, and the deity promises the wife a child.[64] But in the case of Rachel, we have to wait till 30:22 for this to happen. Quite literally Rachel seeks to make Jacob "take the place of God"—and it is telling that the name YHWH does not appear again in the story until Joseph is eventually born.

Here is my maid Bilhah.   We seem to have returned to the story of Abraham and Sarah, as Rachel offers her slave-girl as a substitute wife. She even uses the same phrase, punning on the sound link between "build" (*banah*) and "son" (*ben*) as did Sarai: "I too may have children through her." Rachel almost seems to be playing Sarai to Bilhah's Hagar! And as with Sarai the apparent successful outcome will really be no solution.

She may bear upon my knees.   The placing of the newborn child of her slave-girl upon Rachel's knees was a recognized gesture of adoption.

Jacob went in to her [Bilhah]. And Bilhah conceived.   It is notable that the naming of the two sons of Bilhah does not bring Y<small>HWH</small> into the frame.

The rivalry between the two sisters now begins to take on the character of a bedroom farce as Leah, not to be outdone, offers her slave-girl Zilpah as a surrogate for Jacob. Although Leah has no problem with fertility, she seems to be denied sexual access to her husband. Y<small>HWH</small> is being further and further excluded from these human machinations: note that in the case of these sons, Gad and Asher, neither God nor Y<small>HWH</small> is associated with their naming. Indeed, both these names may well be linked to the titles of pagan gods.

Reuben ... found mandrakes.   These plants, with oddly shaped roots, which are native to Palestine and neighbouring countries, were long held to have magical properties, both as an aphrodisiac and as an aid to fertility. Leah apparently could do with assistance in one respect, and Rachel in the other! But the Old Testament is consistently hostile to such magical attempts to manipulate God. Is it accidental then that though it is Rachel who makes use of the mandrakes, having "hired" them off Leah, it should be Leah rather than Rachel who then bears another son? God (not mandrakes!) is the giver of new life: the next son is borne because "God heeded Leah".

Leah said, "God has endowed me ... "   At first sight, the sequence seems confused. Shortly after Leah sleeps with her husband, having hired (Hebrew: *sakar*) him by giving the mandrakes to Rachel, she bears a son named Issachar (Hebrew: *yissakar*). However, she links this name not with the episode of the mandrakes, but to the fact that she had previously "hired out" her slave-girl to Jacob. Perhaps the narrator is trying to establish that employing mandrakes or other magical means is absolutely not God's way; even the use of a surrogate is preferable!

Afterwards she bore a daughter, and named her Dinah. Dinah is quite literally an afterthought! Apparently not even her name merits attention, or a pun. The sad story of her life (see Genesis 34) is being foreshadowed.

Then God remembered Rachel, and God heeded her and opened her womb. Finally the longed-for child is born; not via mandrakes, nor a substitute slave-girl, nor even Rachel's desperate cry to Jacob. The child is born through God's initiative, and because of God's relationship with this woman. For the first time since 29:35, the name of Yhwh now appears in the story: "She named him Joseph, saying, 'May the Lord add to me another son!'"

Two completely different reasons are given for the naming of Joseph. Not only is it linked to the root *yasap* (= add), but in the previous verse it has been connected to *'asap* (= take away). It is strange to link this one child to two words that have almost opposite meanings. Is it a signal that Joseph was supposed to achieve in his life a balancing of opposites—a kind of equilibrium that might bring harmony to this unruly family?

Note how the link with *'asap* "catches up" and reiterates a word which was used several times as the story of Jacob and Rachel opened (see p. 232). It perhaps hints that the purpose of Jacob's time in Laban's land is now drawing to its close.

30:25-43 *Jacob said to Laban, "Send me away".* Certainly, that is Jacob's view. It is time to return to Canaan—and not empty-handed! "Now when shall I provide for my household also?"

At the beginning of the negotiations, Jacob and Laban agree on one salient factor. Laban states: "the Lord has blessed me because of you". Jacob agrees: "the Lord has blessed you wherever I turned".

Despite the apparent secularity, and some unsavoury features, of Jacob's interlude in Paddan-aram, Yhwh has been working through him, to bless others. The promise that Abraham and his descendants would be a channel of blessing for others is being fulfilled; and this blessing of Yhwh extends to the realms of everyday life and economic prosperity.

Laban's remark, "I have learned by divination", may feel rather jarring to the modern reader. But it preserves a link to a theme which will become important in the story of Joseph (44:5), and in the context of Chapter 30 it offers a reminder that Yhwh's power to bless is apparent even to those, such as Laban, whose religious practice (i.e. divination, presumably linked with foreign deities, see 31:19) locates them outside the immediate community of faith.

The negotiations between Jacob and Laban begin politely, in a way that is reminiscent of the occasion when Abraham bargained over a tomb for Sarah. But two consummate bargainers and tricksters are at work here, each flexing their skills against the other. And as with Abraham and Ephron even if little is being ostensibly requested, much is in reality being demanded—by both parties.

It is not in fact clear whether Laban is prepared to let Jacob go at all. Is his offer to Jacob to "name your wages" a device to persuade him to stay? In his opening gambit to Laban, Jacob had used the words "served" and "service". They are loaded words, used also of the later Israelite slavery in Egypt. There too people had come as guests, and eventually found that they had become slaves and were unable to leave. Is that what is transpiring here? One reading of 31:41 might suggest that between the time of these negotiations and Jacob's eventual departure, six whole years elapse.

At any rate, by verse 31, Jacob agrees to "keep" [Laban's flocks] once again, and makes the seemingly generous proposal that for his wages "you shall not give me anything". But as with Ephron's apparent generosity in the earlier negotiations with Abraham he is actually asking for quite a lot. He requests the unusually marked sheep and goats from Laban's flock for himself.

Although Laban ostensibly agrees to the suggestion, he then immediately takes steps to ensure that the sheep and goats in this category will be as few as possible. At one level it is appropriate that Laban should specifically remove every goat "that had white on it", since they have an intrinsic connection to his very name, Laban, which means "white". But the assumption that Laban is also making is that by removing animals in this category, any offspring produced among Jacob's flock will not be the sort which Jacob can claim. Was Jacob expecting this trick? It seems likely, since he then has one of his own up his sleeve.

Behind Jacob's actions seems to be the traditional belief, popular in the days before the science of genetics, that the sight of a particular object at the moment of conception influenced the appearance of what was conceived. In other words, animals seeing stripy rods produced stripy offspring. In describing Jacob's actions, the narrator includes another subtle pun on Laban's name—for the word for the "poplar" tree (*libne*) also comes from the Hebrew root *laban* (= white), and we are further reminded of this through Jacob's action in "exposing the white of the rods". With a chuckle we are being told how Jacob is managing to out-Laban Laban! Last time there was a discussion about wages (29:15–28) Laban had outmanoeuvred Jacob, but now the tables are turned. Scientifically (and perhaps morally) dubious all this may be, but like both his forbears Abraham (24:1) and Isaac (26:13), Jacob simply cannot help prospering: so Jacob "grew exceedingly rich", a clear clue that God's blessing is with him as much as it was with his perhaps more conventional ancestors.

31:1–18 However, just as one deceit leads to another, once ill-feeling has set in, it spawns further bad relationships. Jacob's outwitting of Laban's attempts literally to "fleece" him, simply exacerbates the tension with Laban and his family. "And Jacob saw that Laban did not regard him as favourably as he did before." In the concrete and vivid idiom of the Hebrew language, the words here are "Jacob saw Laban's face, and behold it was not with him ... " Over the next two chapters, the language of "face" will become a central motif as Jacob journeys back to Canaan to encounter Esau once more. The appearance of the word just at this point, as Jacob receives YHWH's command to begin the journey, is a foreshadowing of what is to come.

The LORD said to Jacob, "Return to the land of your ancestors and to your kindred." The vocabulary deliberately echoes the original command to Abraham. Once again, a patriarch is directed in the direction of Canaan: but this time it is to return to his kindred, rather than to leave them. Yet in view of the hostility surrounding Jacob as he left his home twenty years ago, to return may be for him the more difficult option.

I will be with you.   The identical phrase spoken by God at Bethel had pointed Jacob into exile. As Jacob is shortly to affirm to his wives (31:5), it had been amply fulfilled. Now the phrase points him home again. In 28:15, a promise of protection was explicitly added: here it is included implicitly.

Jacob sent and called Rachel and Leah into the field where his flock was. This instruction suggests that Jacob is aware that his projected return is rapidly turning into a flight. He needs to have a conversation with his wives without the danger of being overheard.

The repetition of the comment about Laban in 31:5, first made in 31:2, intensifies the focus on "face" (see comment above).

Your father ... has changed my wages ten times.   The number "ten" here probably means "a lot"; it does not need to be understood literally. However, Jacob's further complaint (31:8) suggests that the wheeling and dealing between him and Laban was even more complicated than it appeared in 30:32–42.

Thus God has taken away the livestock of your father, and given them to me.   Jacob seems to suggest to Rachel and Leah that his success in outmanoeuvring Laban is due to God's direct intervention. This is the first we had heard of that; in 30:37–40 it seems to be simply a question of Jacob's own native cunning! The reference to God's role in this, as well as the detailed description of Jacob's divine dream, seems designed to help persuade Rachel and Leah to take the momentous step that Jacob is asking of them. He succeeds!

He has sold us, and he has been using up the money given for us. Normally, the bride-price, which a bridegroom offered for his wife, would be channelled by her family at least in part to the married woman. Rachel and Leah complain that Laban has appropriated their bride-prices (namely Jacob's seven years of labour for each of them) solely for his own benefit.

All the property . . . belongs to us and to our children. Gradually, Jacob's departure from Laban is taking on the hues of the later Exodus of Jacob's descendants from Egypt. And as that escape included plundering the wealth of the Egyptians (Exodus 12:36), Laban's wealth (and even his household gods) are now apparently the booty of Jacob and his wives (see also comments on 12:16,20).

To go to his father Isaac in the land of Canaan. This is the first indication we have that Isaac might still be alive, twenty years after we last met him on his apparent deathbed!

31:19-55 *Rachel stole her father's household gods.* The household gods were small terracotta figurines which, in pagan culture, represented the gods responsible for the well-being of a family or household. Their loss would have been felt keenly. What was the motivation for this theft? Perhaps Rachel was concerned lest they might bequeath Laban power over the fugitives, or perhaps she was unable to leave her past behind as she fled into an unknown future.

The hill-country of Gilead, east of the Jordan, where Laban caught up with Jacob, was frontier territory for the later Israelite tribes. It marked a boundary with the Aramaeans of Damascus. The description here of Laban as "the Aramaean" hints at this later political division, and also distances Laban from the intimate family of Jacob.

Take heed that you say not a word to Jacob, either good or bad. This injunction, apparently spoken to Laban by God in a dream, and repeated as Laban recounts the dream in 31:29 echoes the words used by Laban and Bethuel as they permit Rebekah's departure in 24:50. It suggests that the departure of Laban's daughters, Rachel and Leah, is following the pattern established first by Laban's sister, Rebekah, which was clearly intentioned by God.

You have deceived me, and carried away my daughters like captives of the sword. Laban's words of complaint to Jacob accentuate the motif of "plunder". The "carrying off" of his daughters is described in terms that suggest the "driving off" of cattle seized as war booty. The Hebrew root *ganab* resonates throughout 31:19-30. With its underlying meaning of "steal", it is used to describe both Rachel's theft of the *teraphim* (31:19,30,32) and Jacob's duping of Laban with his surreptious departure (31:20,26,27).

Why did you steal my gods? At the end of a lengthy tirade in which Laban's remarks are either unbelievable (can we really believe that he would have thrown a party to celebrate Jacob's departure?) or unjustifiable (as in his description of his daughters being herded like cattle, although they had gone from their own free will), his final complaint of theft has validity.

But anyone with whom you find your gods shall not live. Rachel, the thief of her father's gods, is not in fact found—as a result of her own "trick". She hides the figurines under where she is sitting and announces that she is menstruating (31:35), which means that both she and her seat are made "unclean", and Laban is thus prevented from a close search. Menstruation, the visible sign of her difficulties in bearing a child, now becomes the means of her successful deception of her father. But do Jacob's words unintentionally condemn Rachel to the early death that she will suffer when later she bears her second son in Canaan? Perhaps they seem to hint at this. Throughout the story of Jacob trick has been piled upon trick, first Jacob, then Laban, now Rachel. In fact, this trick of Rachel mirrored the "trick" of Jacob with which Jacob's story had opened: both, younger siblings, deceive their father in order to obtain a blessing, Jacob from Isaac's lips, Rachel via the household gods which were believed to bless those who possessed them. Does all this deceit finally somehow have to be brought to an end and Rachel pay the ultimate price for them with her own life?

There is, of course, another issue. The veneration of household gods was a pagan practice—clearly Rachel despite her marriage to Jacob had not fully understood what it meant to be a worshipper of Yhwh. Will her desire to hold on to the ancient religious practices of her ancestral home ultimately disqualify her from participation in the community of Israel? At the very least, Rachel's actions suggest that she is no Rebekah willing to set out in blind faith for a strange land.

Point out what I have that is yours. As the theme of trickery draws to a close, another motif has begun to be explored. Rightful and wrongful identification or recognition of people or objects will dominate the story of Jacob's sons. The Hebrew word *nakar* meaning "identify" or "recognize" and here (31:32) translated as "point out" has already been used when Isaac failed to recognize Jacob because he was dressed up in Esau's clothes. But soon Jacob himself will be on the receiving end of the verb (see comments on 27:23).

Jacob became angry, and upbraided Laban. Jacob's pent-up anger, which festered under the surface during his twenty years of near servitude, suddenly explodes with a verbal violence using language that is reminiscent of the law court. He throws a series of accusations at Laban, which are intended to make it clear that he had acted above and beyond the normal call of duties of a shepherd. He rounds off the speech with another legal idiom, although this is not as clear in the NRSV's comment that God "rebuked you last night" as in some other translations which render the verb as "delivered his verdict" or "gave judgement", presumably via the dream that Laban had experienced.

During the speech Jacob refers to the help he had received from "the God of my father, the God of Abraham and the Fear of Isaac". One suggested way of looking at the relationship between Jacob and Laban (at least from 30:25 onwards) is to view it as a "contest" between the gods of both parties: YHWH on the one hand, and the household gods of Laban on the other. If so, it is no contest! The power of YHWH, who can impose his will upon opponents (e.g. Laban, via the dream) is contrasted with the impotence of Laban's gods who have to be protected—by an unclean woman! The same kind of contrast is made in literature from the exilic period, e.g. Isaiah 46:1-4 and Psalm 96. The Exodus events are also presented in a similar fashion, as a contest between YHWH and Pharaoh (e.g. Exodus 7:8-25). It is interesting therefore how Jacob notes "God saw my affliction and the labour of my hands", a description which parallels God's observation of the suffering of his people in Egypt (Exodus 3:7). See also the comments on *'oni* on p.**.

The unusual title of "the Fear of Isaac" given to the God of Jacob occurs only here and in verse 53. The meaning of the Hebrew has been disputed: an alternative translation of "Kinsman of Isaac" has been proposed, which would emphasize the close relationship between God and Jacob's family. However, the NRSV translation may well be correct: God has been fearsome in the life of Isaac (Genesis 22), and he will soon be fearsome in the life of Isaac's son. In fact, does the introduction of the title here and in verse 53 suggest that Jacob's psyche is beginning to anticipate the dangers that lie ahead and the anxiety that he has about his homecoming, and meeting with Esau once more? However, the title probably also includes the sense of "the Fearsome one who protects Isaac", with the incident in Genesis 35:5 almost acting as a commentary on this meaning. Similar epithets suggesting protection are linked to the other patriarchs: Shield of Abraham (15:1), and Strong One (Bull) of Jacob (49:24). In both cases, as also here, the titles appear at crisis moments in the ancestral story (see also comments on "covenant" on p.**).

The juridical nature of Jacob's complaints is appropriately addressed by the making of a pact or covenant, which itself has a legal status.

As with the earlier pact that Isaac made, it is the other party (26:28) who proposes making the agreement and who thus implicitly acknowledges the power of YHWH: "The LORD watch between you and me, when we are absent one from the other." The traditional features of a covenant-making ceremony, the oath (31:53) and the feast (31:54) are represented in both covenants. But unique to this pact is its visible reminder, the setting up of a stone pillar (31:45,51) and a stone cairn (31:46,51–52). Once again stones figure prominently at key moments of Jacob's life, indeed the pillar here recalls the stone pillar Jacob had erected twenty years previously at Bethel (28:18), which was also highlighted in a dream (31:13) as a symbol of God's protection. In this case, the stones also function as a boundary marker, designating a political division, between the territory belonging to Jacob's descendants (the Israelites) and that belonging to the descendants of Laban (the Aramaeans). For as the story of Jacob unfolds, the individual person is gradually taking on the features of a nation. The international character of what is transpiring is emphasized by one of the names given to the site of the covenant: "Laban called it Jegar-sahadutha; but Jacob called it Galeed." The two names have an identical meaning, "Cairn of Witness", but Laban has used Aramaic, the "international" language of the Ancient Middle East, which originated with his putative descendants, the Aramaeans, while Jacob has employed Hebrew.

The previous pacts in the Old Testament made between human beings, between Abraham and Abimelech (21:27) and Isaac and Abimelech (26:31) were both made with people that were unrelated by blood to the patriarchs. They created a reasonably civilized relationship where none had previously existed. By contrast, Laban is Jacob's uncle, cousin and father-in-law! The family links are emphasized in his words: "The daughters are my daughters, the children are my children." Yet the effect of covenant-making on this occasion is to create a formality and a distance, emotional as well as physical, so that Laban's position becomes parallel to that of Abimelech, a person with whom Jacob's descendants might have civilized and non-aggressive dealings, but no longer part of the family. Too much mutual hostility has happened to expect more than that. In making the covenant, Laban is, as he acknowledges, giving up the rights of control over his daughters and their children.

Does the reference in Laban's final words to "the God of Abraham and the God of Nahor", the grandfathers respectively of Jacob and Laban, indicate for one final time that Laban is striving for a parity between their gods and reminding Jacob of their relationship? And if so, is Jacob's oath taken only in the name of "the Fear of Isaac" a deliberate omission: a refusal to grant equal status to a foreign deity? Or does the title hint once more at what lies ahead: for the next chapter contains possibly the most numinous episode in the entire Book of Genesis?

Laban's final actions, which mirror his opening gestures (29:13), signify the closure of this long section as well as his role within the story. He will not appear directly again: not even in a genealogy.

Touching God
32:1–33:20

One can meet God in a variety of ways, but the two different means by which Jacob will now meet God approach the profoundest insights of biblical spirituality. These chapters have the quality, and the mystery, of some of the resurrection stories of Jesus. Indeed, we are about to read a story of death and resurrection: in which symbolically Jacob dies and Israel is reborn. They are not comfortable chapters, indeed that is their power. We, like Jacob, need to wrestle through them. But, as Jacob himself ultimately discovered, it is only by struggle that the blessing comes, and the people of God is brought to birth.

Intriguingly, these chapters fall about as far from the end of the book of Genesis as the mysterious encounters of Abraham with God in Genesis 18 do from the beginning of the book. There too the interweaving of the vertical and horizontal dimension of faith was prominent, there too the ambiguities of the relationship between God and humanity was explored. It may be more comfortable to meet God in the noonday of a lunch party, as Abraham did, than in the dark night by a lonely river, but there is a sense that Jacob's experience is the one that many of us can identify with and make our own.

One of the particular features of this section is the extensive use of wordplay. Indeed, "wordplay" seems a superficial term for what is happening here. "It seems . . . to be an attempt to bed down the meaning of the story, right into the roots of the words actually used to tell the story. [The writer] is not tinkering with the narrative to produce a clever effect but is deeply structuring his writings to create a climate for the acceptance of particular theological concepts."[65]

32:1–8 The angels of God at Bethel had bidden Jacob farewell for his journey to Mesopotamia; now angels, almost like divine border-guards greet him on his return to the land of promise. An easy symmetry—but a deceptive one. For in these chapters, it is God's turn to play the trickster, and the true parallel with Jacob's experience at Bethel will not be these welcoming angels, but the mysterious antagonist that still lurks for him near the fords of Jabbok. In the depths of Jacob's despair at Bethel,

God had lifted him up. Now he is returning, replete with family and possessions: flushed with his victory over Laban. Jan Fokkelman has commented that when Jacob leaves Laban: "As God's protege, [he] goes away a victor; he is unassailable, and he knows it."[66] But the God who lifts up the broken in spirit is the same as the one who brings low the proud; theology and theodicy demand that Jacob does not have it too easy on the road ahead. Before God is through with him the unassailable must be made vulnerable.

Punning on his meeting with the divine "company" or "camp" Jacob names the place Mahanaim (= Two Companies/Camps). The duality explicit in this name will quickly write itself into the story. "Jacob ... divided the people that were with him, and the flocks and herds and camels, into two companies" (32:7, see also 32:8). Duality has been a striking feature of the Jacob stories so far: two brothers who were twins (see comments on p.**), two sisters, two locations, home and exile, even the division of the flocks that Jacob was guarding for Laban into two distinct sections. Now this sense of duality comes to dominate the narrative, giving everything that happens its own mysterious undercurrent or consequence. Though it even threatens to overwhelm Jacob, tearing him apart to the core of his very being, it is, as he discovers, ultimately cathartic, giving him the integration, at least for a short space of time, for which he had yearned for so many years.

Jacob sent messengers. These are human messengers, but the Hebrew word used is identical to that translated "angels", i.e. messengers of God, in 32:1. The encounter with the divine messengers seems to have prompted Jacob to take the initiative in seeking a way forward in his relationship with his brother Esau.

To his brother Esau in the land of Seir, the country of Edom. We last met Esau at the family home in Beer-sheba, but while Jacob has "stayed" (literally "lingered") with his uncle Laban Esau has migrated to Edom and already become the kingdom that was associated with him from birth. Jacob has a lot of catching up to do!

Thus you shall say to my lord Esau: "Thus says your servant Jacob." The language used is courtly and deferential, such as a vassal might use in correspondence with his overlord. Is this the way that one brother should greet another? It is ironic that Jacob has to adopt this tone: for it inverts the vocabulary used in his blessing and Esau's anti-blessing, which spoke specifically of Jacob as lord (27:29) and Esau as servant (27:40). That stolen blessing is haunting the story and demanding its retribution.

I have oxen . . . Jacob is superficially self-confident. His omission of any direct offering of a gift is striking, but does the reference to his desire to "find favour in your sight" (an aim that is picked up and explored more extensively in 33:5–11) suggest that he is attempting to restore the fruits of the stolen blessing? Though they are worlds apart in meaning, and in the English language, the consonants used in the words for "company/camp" (*mahaneh*) and "favour" (*hen*) are very similar in Hebrew. Is the link intended to suggest that it is the appearance of this divine company sent by God (32:2) that has prompted Jacob to seek Esau's "favour"? Grace received leads on to grace offered (see further on 33:5–11, p. 259).

Esau . . . and four hundred men The number suggests a reasonably sized raiding party: potentially made even more terrifying in view of the promise given to Esau in 27:40 that "by your sword you shall live".

32:9–12 *And Jacob said* Jacob's shattered confidence leads him swiftly to prayer. This is the longest formal prayer in Genesis. It alludes both to Yhwh's command to Jacob to return to the land (31:3), and to the earlier encounter Jacob had with God at Bethel (28:13–15). But it reaches back beyond both of these experiences of Jacob to link with God's original call to Abraham. As in 31:3, the language used deliberately recalls Abraham's summons of 12:1–3. We are also pointed in that direction by Jacob's expansive opening "God of my father Abraham and God of my father Isaac". In the later pages of the Old Testament, there would be other occasions when people would ground their prayers in the assurance of God's love for Abraham and the other patriarchs (e.g. Deuteronomy 26:5–11). Jacob is the first of many, and his words implicitly suggest that by facilitating his own homecoming God is also bringing his ancestor Abraham "home" at last.

I am not worthy of the least of all the steadfast love and all the faithfulness. True enough, yet is Jacob aware, as the first readers of Genesis certainly were, that the God of the Bible is one who almost extravagantly expresses a bias towards the "unworthy"? And with the vivid concreteness of Hebrew idiom Jacob is actually saying, "I am too small", using a verb from the identical root as the adjective "younger", which has been used twice before to describe him vis-à-vis Esau. We know that the God of Genesis consistently seems to display partiality towards younger brothers: is Jacob, even in his fear and contrition, subtly reminding God of this?

Steadfast love ... and faithfulness. If any words can sum up God's "character profile" in the Bible, it is these. "Steadfast love" conveys the quality of God's constancy, "faithfulness" God's reliability, particularly linked with covenant promises and relationship. They appear again when YHWH introduces himself to Moses on Mount Sinai, after the episode of the golden calf (Exodus 34:6).

I crossed this Jordan. The Jordan marked the eastern boundary of the land of promise (Deuteronomy 3:27) and to cross it was to leave or enter the land. The reference apparently contradicts Jacob's presumed actual location, near the River Jabbok. It may suggest some Deuteronomic editing of this passage (see further on Jabbok below).

Deliver me, please, from the hand of my brother, from the hand of Esau. This is the heart of the prayer, to which Jacob has been building up.

You have said, "I will surely do you good". This phrase, which echoes the words Jacob used in 32:9, may be an example of him gilding the lily. Although 28:14–15 does refer to Jacob being blessed, the explicit promise God makes there is to be with Jacob, rather than to make him prosper. Is the inveterate bargainer of the previous chapters still up to his old tricks?

The prayer of Jacob clearly marks a significant shift in Jacob's relationship with God, with his brother Esau, and with himself. But even as it is prayed—heartfelt though it may be—it still leaves questions in the reader's mind. Is the link between Jacob's self-interest and his new-found religiosity too close? Back in Genesis 21, we wondered whether Abraham was using God a bit too conveniently, to sort out domestic difficulties. But he was then confronted by a trial of faith (Genesis 22), which cut to the quick of his being; will a similar trial await this patriarch?

32:13–21 *[Jacob] took a present.* The sound-plays of verses 1–8 still seem to continue with the deliberate choice of the word *minhah* for "gift". It too contains the letters *hn* (albeit in a different order). The "company" (*mahaneh*) of angels has encouraged Jacob to seek Esau's favour (*hen*) by offering him a gift (*minhah*). However, *minhah* is used especially to describe either an offering made to a god or a tribute given to a political superior. The word itself, as well as the size of Jacob's gift, reinforce the sense of Esau's powerful superiority.

We may well wonder, however, whether the complicated organization of the gift is a device to mislead Esau into believing that Jacob is more powerful than he actually is.

Your servant Jacob ... my lord Esau   As with 32:4, the terminology inverts the language used in Isaac's blessing of Jacob.

And moreover he is behind us   Jacob has always been a "behind" (*'ahar*) or "afterwards" person, from the very moment of his birth (25:26). He had "stayed" (32:4) for a long time with Laban, a verb which is related to the preposition *'ahar*. The preposition itself is repeated twice in 32:20. To understand the role of the concept in this story it helps to realize that it is probably linked to a word for the physical "back" or "hinder parts" of a human being or animal (in the same way as the preposition "before" derives from the word for "face", see below.) "Behind" accurately defines Jacob— the "heel" who came up on people from the rear and overtook/ supplanted them (27:36). Very shortly Jacob himself is forcibly going to be turned right round and compelled to look others in the face!

I may appease him with the present that goes ahead of me and afterwards I shall see his face, perhaps he will accept me.   There is an extraordinary quality to the story here, which can only be conveyed by giving a very literal translation of the Hebrew: "I shall appease his face with the gift going to my face, and afterwards I may see his face. Perhaps he will lift up my face!"

The words themselves begin to sing the story, as the concept of "face" (Hebrew: *panim*), which will interpret Jacob's next two encounters: with God (32:30–31) and with his brother Esau (33:10), is now introduced almost as a chorus. (See comment above on the link between "before" and "face".) Jacob has never found it easy to look his brother in the face. It is remarkable how the lengthy episode in which Jacob steals Esau's blessing keeps the two brothers apart, so that they are never in each other's presence, and Jacob steals Esau's blessing from behind his back (see e.g. 27:30). He needs this gift to act as a precursor, before he can attempt a face-to-face meeting.

Appease suggests both Jacob's awe of Esau—and his sense of guilt. It is a technical word from the vocabulary of sacrifice, used particularly to describe an offering to an angry deity. Its connection with sin and atonement indicates that Jacob has a guilty conscience for what he has previously done to his brother.

He himself spent that night in the camp. The word *mahaneh* ("camp") appears again and continues the verbal jousting which has been prominent in this chapter.

32:22–32 Literary critics have tried to analyse what makes this brief (less than 200 words) narrative so compelling. There seem to be two complementary features.

First, it is a story in which layer is built imperceptibly on layer. There is a hint that this was originally a tale about a river demon, who controlled a ford, whose power was only operative at night and who could not tolerate the daylight: a sort of Ancient Middle Eastern "Billy Goats Gruff". On top of this was etched an ancient traditional story of how the Israelite patriarch Jacob wrestled with an angel which dates back at least to the time of the prophet Hosea (see Hosea 12:3–4). It may be that during the exile was added another layer, which drew upon a reflection in Jeremiah 30:5–17, in which Jacob comes to personify the exiles, as hope is expressed for their return to the land. Finally, those who drew the account into the wider story of creation and the ancestral history created a new layer, with cross-references to the extended story. Gerhard von Rad's comment cannot be bettered:

> [The narrative] contains experiences of faith that extend from the most ancient period down to the time of the narrator; there is charged to it something of the entire divine history into which Israel was drawn. This event did not simply occur at a definite biographical point in Jacob's life, but as it is now related it is clearly transparent as a type of that which Israel experienced from time to time with God. Israel has here presented its entire history with God almost prophetically as such a struggle until the breaking of the day. The narrative itself makes this extended interpretation probable by equating the names Jacob and Israel.[67]

Another aspect of the story—which has been illuminated by an influential essay by the French structuralist critic Roland Barthes—helps to explain its peculiar frisson.[68] Barthes noted that traditional (folk) tales like this one normally operate on a standard format. There is a Hero, who is sent on a Quest by an Originator, and who, before the Quest can be fulfilled has to confront and defeat an Opponent. The story of Jacob at the Jabbok contains all these features. Jacob is the Hero (albeit a dubious one!) who is sent on a Quest (to return to the land) by an Originator (God). But then dramatically the form is subverted as at its denouement we realize that God the Originator is also the Opponent. The ordered world of the folk tale has been turned upside down—and that can be terrifying, for the reader who reflects on the story as much as for the Hero who participates in it.

The same night "Night" here is not simply a chronological reference, but as in John's Gospel (e.g. John 3:1; 13:30), it vividly intensifies the precariousness and uncertainties of the situation. In the dark night, Jacob—and we—cannot easily see whether his antagonist is God or Esau.

He took... his eleven children At this point in the story, Jacob apparently had twelve children—eleven sons and a daughter. It is interesting that among the family sent across the ford there is no mention of Jacob's daughter Dinah: a telling omission.

The ford of the Jabbok ... a man wrestled with him. The name "Jabbok" sounds very similar to the verb "wrestled" (Hebrew: *'abaq*) which appears in both verses 25 and 26. A wordplay is clearly intended. The name "Jacob" also contains the identical letters (in a different order) as "Jabbok", a point of which the storyteller was well aware. The double wordplay helps to reinforce the sense that this is Jacob's defining moment: his destiny from the moment he was named was to arrive at this place and consummate there the "wrestling" that had been part of him ever since he was in the womb.

This may lie behind a puzzling feature of the story. A careful plotting of the place names given in the course of Jacob's journey from Paddan-aram (i.e. Gilead, Mizpah and Mahanaim) reveals that at this point Jacob was apparently south of the river Jabbok, and that he had just sent his family across the river from south to north (which might suggest that he was sending them out of Esau's power). In that case, the man who wrestled with him was preventing Jacob himself from retreating to the safety he sought, a safety which would mean refusing God's command to return to the land of promise. However, normally the story is read rather differently, with the struggle to cross the river in some way marking Jacob's entry to Canaan. It is just possible that at some point in the story's history, it was the Jordan, rather than the river Jabbok that was the scene of the contest (see 32:10), and that the location was later transferred to the Jabbok (perhaps by those who were not personally acquainted with the geography of the region) because of the close bond the name expressed both with the name of Jacob and the action of wrestling.

Rembrandt painted a picture of the scene. In it, Jacob is held by the wrestler in such a way that his head is gradually being forced round so that he is compelled to look his opponent in the face. He will not be allowed to avoid confronting his past, his present and his future.

He struck him ... and Jacob's hip was put out of joint. Jacob was called Jacob because of the link made to the word "heel" (25:26), but if one delves deeper in the Hebrew language, the word "heel" itself may derive from a root that means "curved" or "not straight". Is that what is happening here? In dislocating Jacob's hip, is the night wrestler making visible what Jacob really always has been—crooked, rather than straight?

Touch had been the primary means by which Jacob had deceived his father Isaac. So it is appropriate that his wounding comes by this stranger's touch.

"I will not let you go, unless you bless me".   The night wrestler's anxiety to disappear before daybreak is the point where this story comes closest to the world of fairy tales. It is reminiscent of the traditional troll who will be changed into stone by sunlight. Jacob's response reminds us how his desire to be blessed had governed his whole life. But unlike the blessing which he had obtained from Isaac by trickery, this blessing will be legitimately won by arduous struggle. But before the blessing can be bestowed there is a question ...

"What is your name?" And he said, "Jacob".   As with other significant narratives in Genesis the episode appears to be structured so that it pulls the reader into its centre, in other words, to this question and answer and the night wrestler's further response. The whole of Jacob's past life has been leading up to this question—once before, years ago, he had been asked a very similar one by his father Isaac, and he had given a fraudulent response, claiming to be his brother Esau (27:18-19). The last twenty years of his life have been shadowed by that lie. This time the truth is dragged out of him. As Fokkelman points out, in acknowledging that he is called Jacob, he is effectively making a confession of guilt, for he has named himself as "Fraud", the intrinsic meaning of the word Jacob (27:36).[69] It is only when this has been publicly stated that his healing and blessing can begin.

You shall no longer be called Jacob, but Israel.   Like Abraham, Jacob's name is to be changed as a sign of his new relationship with God. But this name change means both more—and less—than the earlier one. It is more because the new name and the circumstances in which it came about somehow describe not only an individual, but a whole people and the history of their struggling relationship with God. It is less because Jacob cannot entirely leave his old name behind: in both the later chapters of Genesis and in the history of the people for whom he will be the eponymous ancestor, this name Jacob will continue to be used alongside that of Israel. As Paul was to observe centuries later, the "old man" can never be wholly vanquished (Romans 7:15-20).

The name "Israel" is interpreted by the text itself as meaning "the one who strives (Hebrew: *sarah*) with God (*'el*)", although originally the name probably meant rather "God strives". Perhaps there is a deliberate ambiguity: for the story suggests that now the destinies of God and his people are inextricably interwoven. The fact that the name also contains within it the consonants of the word *sar* ("prince") offers an additional resonance.

Is this renaming the blessing that Jacob has sought? This may be what we are supposed to assume. For the content of the bald statement "And there he blessed him" is not otherwise spelt out. To become Israel rather than Jacob is a blessing, albeit a hazardous one. It means that Jacob is now expressing, in his very name, God's promise "I will be with you", but, as he has just discovered, that too can be a dangerous promise. The moment of his life when God is most with him is this wounding and lengthy struggle.

Why is it that you ask my name? Ultimately, the relationship between Jacob and the divine wrestler is not and cannot be a completely equal one, despite Jacob's prodigious strength. The divine wrestler preserves a difference and distinction: Jacob does not learn the name of his opponent despite being forced to reveal his own. God will not be revealed as YHWH, until he himself chooses to make that revelation (Exodus 3:14); see further comments in Theological reflections on p. 281.

I have seen God face to face. Jacob's exclamation echoes the earlier relief of Hagar (16:13). A few others in Israel's later history will "see" God, but they will always be aware it is a dangerous favour (Exodus 33:20; Judges 13:22; Isaiah 6:5). The "seeing" that had once seemed so natural to Abraham will become an exceptional privilege, until it is re-gifted in the pages of the New Testament (John 1:14,18). It is no accident that when God is seen by a Moses or Isaiah, he is closely associated with fire: "God has a terrible double aspect, a sea of grace is met by a seething lake of fire."[70] Jacob is the first person in biblical spirituality to discover God as a "fearful yet fascinating mystery".

My life is preserved   Earlier in the chapter (32:12), Jacob had prayed "Deliver me". The storyteller suggests that now his prayer has been answered. But this has happened by his willingness to participate in a dangerous struggle with God, for the word "preserved" comes from the same Hebrew verb that was earlier translated as "deliver". The struggle had spared—and saved—him.

The sun rose upon him as he passed Penuel, limping because of his hip.   The sun that set upon Jacob all those years before at Bethel as he journeyed towards exile has now finally risen upon him again as he becomes a new person, with a new name and a new life. With his limp he now walks "crookedly" but is able to look his brother Esau straight in the eye as he meets him at last.

The Israelites do not eat the thigh muscle that is on the hip socket.   This is one of the few occasions when the author of Genesis steps back from the story to address his readers directly, here linking a common practice to these shattering events at Penuel. It is also the first time "Israelites" have ever been mentioned, an appropriate point to introduce them just after their eponymous ancestor has himself been named Israel.

33:1-11   *Jacob looked up and saw Esau coming.*   Whenever the Hebrew expression underlying "looked up" has been used before, the sight to be seen has always been important, sometimes miraculous, or at least directly prompted by God (e.g. 13:14; 22:13; 31:10). No less is true here. Jacob had not seen his brother for two decades, but now he was going to be enabled to see him in a new light.

He divided the children.   By placing Joseph and Rachel at the rear he was offering them the place of greatest safety. The favouritism which will divide his family during the story of Joseph is being foreshadowed.

He himself went on ahead ... bowing himself to the ground seven times. Having seen the "face of God", Jacob has ceased to be a "behind" person (see comments on p. 252). He now goes "ahead" or "before" to see and greet Esau. In the blessing that had been stolen from Esau, Jacob had been promised that his "mother's sons would bow down" to him. That he himself, as well as his descendants (33:6,7), should now bow down to Esau not once, but seven times, is ironic retribution being exacted from him.

Esau ran to meet him. The spontaneity of Esau's generous welcome still contrasts with Jacob's more formal responses. Throughout the episode, it is Esau alone who addresses Jacob as "my brother" (33:9). That intimate endearment is never reciprocated by Jacob, who insists, even after their reconciliation, on addressing Esau as "my lord". The depiction of Esau's generosity is reminiscent of the father's welcome to the younger son in the Parable of the Prodigal Son (Luke 15:20). This is hardly surprising, for the parable itself seems to draw on the story of Jacob and Esau for its colouring. But in terms of that parable Esau is playing a double role—he is both the elder brother and the father. Jacob's words in 33:10 will express this "dual" significance of Esau's position.

After the violent wrestling of the previous incident, as well as the "sparring match" Jacob and Esau have experienced since their shared days in the womb, this loving, rather than brutal, embrace is all the more unexpected.

The verbal playing on the Hebrew letters *hn* that dominated the previous chapter now suddenly sparkles into life again, almost like a firework display.

It includes:

- The children whom God has graciously (*hanan*) given (v. 5)
- This company (*mahaneh*) that I met (v. 8)
- To find favour (*hen*) with my lord (v. 8)
- If I find favour (*hen*) with you (v. 10)
- Please accept my gift (*minhah*) (v. 11)
- God has dealt graciously with me (*hanan*) (v. 11)

A clear connection is being made between the graciousness Jacob now perceives he has received from God's hand, and his desire to show graciousness to and receive it from Esau.

Truly to see your face is like seeing the face of God. The connection is made even more explicit as the writer digs deep into the word *panim* once more, to express the profound climax of these two chapters. Now we glimpse another meaning of that dangerous divine encounter: there was indeed a connection between that strange wrestler and Esau. There are rabbinic legends that suggest the wrestler was the guardian angel of Esau, and those legends contain an implicit truth. At the very least, Jacob's experience has changed the way that he looks at Esau, perhaps he has even begun to understand the truth that it is only by loving our brothers and sisters that we can begin to see and love God (1 John 4:12). In overcoming, for a brief moment, the duality between God and humanity, the division between human beings themselves is also overcome. And in becoming one with his brother, perhaps at last Jacob has become whole. Has he finally earned the epithet *tam* with which he was credited in 25:27 (see p. 208)?

Please accept my gift. The NRSV, like other English translations, inevitably has to conceal the way Jacob's vocabulary has shifted between verse 10 and verse 11. Up till now, the word "gift" has been translating *minhah*, which, as we suggested (see notes on 32:13, p. 252), conveys the notion of tribute or an offering for a god. It is an appropriate present therefore for Jacob to proffer as he suggests that seeing Esau is like seeing the face of a god. But when "gift" reappears in 33:11, it is now translating *berakah*, more usually translated as "blessing", that word which Jacob stole from Esau twenty years before (27:35). Its use at this point seems to suggest that at last Jacob is restoring the cheated blessing to his brother. He now had no need of it, for he now possessed another blessing that he had won for himself by struggle rather than deceit. Yet by this time we have known Jacob too long not to wonder even here at possible duplicity. To shift from *minhah* to *berakah* is also to shift the power relations, for the one is offered by inferior to superior, the other by superior to inferior. No longer is Jacob's language awestruck by terror of Esau: if he can stand as equal with God, he can stand at least as equal with this brother who has received him in God's own way. And though he may offer to return the blessing to Esau, it is noticeable that he never explicitly restores the birthright.

33:12–20 *Esau said ... but Jacob said to him.* The brief moment of complete unity soon passes, even though a real reconciliation has been accomplished. It is clear that Jacob never intended to follow Esau to Seir; his destination was always going to be the land of promise. Was the reason for his polite dissembling to preserve face for Esau, or was he still afraid of him and the military escort that his brother was proposing? There is quite a lot of the "behind" Jacob still around in his suggestion! And as Robert Alter points out, in Hebrew, the very last word Jacob addresses to his brother is "my lord"![71]

That day The phrase is employed to suggest a key moment in the history of God's dealing with his people. It is a time when Esau makes his choice—and so does Jacob.

[At Succoth, Jacob] built himself a house, and made booths for his cattle. This is a signal that the long period of wandering for Jacob, and his ancestors before him, has come to an end. God's promise of permanence is finally coming to fruition. This is the first time one of the patriarchs explicitly builds a house (though see 27:15). Now even the cattle get "booths" (Hebrew: *sukkot*) constructed for them!

Jacob came safely to the city of Shechem, which is in the land of Canaan. The comment sits uneasily with what has just gone before it. It suggests that having built his house at Succoth, Jacob immediately ups sticks and travels to Shechem. In doing so, he crosses the important theological boundary of the River Jordan; Succoth is to the east of the river, Shechem to the west. His purchase of land here for the price of "one hundred pieces of money" is another important signal (cf. Genesis 23) that he and his family are now being rooted in the land of promise. But in view of what will shortly happen, for how long?

Jacob came safely.   The word translated "safely" comes from the same Hebrew root as "shalom". Its use here suggests that this arrival fulfils the promise of a return "in peace" expressly desired by Jacob in 28:21. Ironically, however, it is also related to a word that will appear in 34:21. "These people are friendly (*shelemim*)". As it turns out, that will be far from the case! Yet the word *shalom* stems from a root whose basic meaning is "whole", and perhaps its use here also hints at the way that the sense of "duality", which has been so dominant in the story of Jacob has finally been replaced by wholeness.

There he erected an altar and called it El-Elohe-Israel.   The name of this altar "God, the god of Israel" sums up both Jacob's own experience at Penuel, and what his father and grandfather have been moving towards.

A troublesome brood
34:1–31

With Genesis 34, we have reached an uncomfortable chapter, both theologically and in terms of its position within Genesis. The young children who need protection in Genesis 32–33 have suddenly grown up and start taking the law into their own hands. Is Genesis 34 a later addition to the body of the book, perhaps partly prompted by the need to explain Jacob's words to Simeon and Levi in 49:5? On the other hand, it does seem to reflect ancient traditions about Shechem, which consistently portray the city both as a key location for the establishment of Israel as a political and national entity (Joshua 24) and also as the site of attempts by groups of Israelites and Canaanites to unite together in marriage and in covenant (see Joshua 24 and Judges 9).

It is, however, also worth noting that the issue of intermarriage between Jews and others also arose in the region of Shechem during the post-exilic period and is one factor behind the rise of the Samaritans. It is intriguing that the writer of Ben Sira refers to "the foolish people that live in Shechem" (Sirach 50:26), since foolishness is a motif that runs through Genesis 34. Jewish attitudes to the Samaritans may be reflected in this story.

It is notable that God does not appear in this chapter at all, despite the brothers' apparent concern for the religious nicety of circumcision (34:14).

34:1–12 *Now Dinah the daughter of Leah, whom she had borne to Jacob* In this description Dinah is not only separated from Jacob by nine words, but also by an emotional gulf. She is the daughter of his less favoured wife; whose name had no explanation attached to it at birth, and who didn't count when the family crossed the river (32:22). She had apparently received no paternal concern up till now, and she will receive none in this story.

Shechem son of Hamor the Hivite, prince of the region, saw her. The use of the name Shechem, identical to the name of the city, at this point is a clue that we have here a tale that is as much about the political and social relationships between two peoples as it is about Jacob's own family. From the point when Jacob is named Israel (32:28), the story of Genesis begins to shift its focus towards the national history of the people Israel, as tribes and as a nation.

As for Shechem's father, his name Hamor means "ass" or "donkey", and it was as uncomplimentary a label then as it is now. As the episode develops, it is clear that he is a bit of one!

Hivite is one of the terms used to describe the original Canaanite inhabitants of the land (see Genesis 10:17).

He seized her. Apparently, he then raped her, although the Hebrew is more ambiguous than the translation suggests. But it is immediately made clear that he had a real affection for Dinah: the Hebrew verb *dbq* used in the phrase "his soul was drawn" recalls the language used of husband and wife in 2:24; "loved" had previously described the relationship between Isaac and Rebekah, and Jacob and Rachel.

The phrase translated "by force" is actually the verb *'anah*, which is elsewhere used when for example Sarah ill-treated Hagar (16:6). Clearly it does have a wider range of meaning than "rape". Lyn Bechtel, in a provocative article entitled "What if Dinah is not raped?", argues that in 34:2 it should be translated "humiliated", not necessarily implying that she was forced to have a sexual relationship with Shechem, but that by choosing to have such a relationship with someone outside her clan/family she was humiliated and defiled in the eyes of her brothers.[72] I well remember a railway journey in 1979 along the banks of the river Euphrates in Syria. Travelling with my husband (an Anglican priest), we met and started talking to an Assyrian Christian from north-east Syria. On discovering that we were fellow-Christians, he started confiding his family problems to us. Apparently, he had had a sister who had chosen to marry a Muslim. In the eyes of her birth family, this had brought shame upon her and her kin. So, our travelling companion proudly informed us, he himself took a gun and shot both his sister and her husband dead. For this double murder, he was put in prison, but fortunately (from his perspective) his religious community considered that he had performed an honourable deed, so they paid money and he was soon released. The story of Dinah sprang to mind as he related this. Certainly Dinah's tale focuses more on her family's sense of defilement than it does upon Dinah's personal feelings.

Jacob held his peace. Clearly inertia had its advantages, in view of Jacob's precarious situation with his sons away from home, but his lack of concern for his daughter is hardly impressive. It is notable that Jacob does not speak at all throughout the episode until 34:30.

The sons of Jacob ... were indignant. Jacob's response contrasts with that of his sons. The same verb was used in 6:6 to picture God's indignation and grief before the flood. Something cataclysmic may happen here too!

He [Shechem] had committed an outrage in Israel. Here the narrator is clearly stepping back and giving us a later perspective on the story. The fact that the words echo those used by Tamar, daughter of David, as she is raped by her brother Amnon (2 Samuel 13:12) may suggest a literary link between the two incidents.

Make marriages with us. The eagerness of both Hamor and Shechem to resolve the issue with appropriate decorum is emphasized as well as Shechem's continuing affection for Dinah. On the face of it the suggestion is very conciliatory, and advantageous to Jacob's family. An opportunity is being offered to this group of semi-nomadic travellers to become part of a settled society, with the economic and security advantages that would bring. Is this even perhaps the way that God's promise of land to Jacob can be fulfilled? The only problem is that Deuteronomy 7:3–6 forcefully prohibits exactly what Hamor suggests!

34:13–31 *The sons of Jacob answered Shechem ... deceitfully.* Like father, like sons. The identical word was used to describe Jacob's own earlier deception of Isaac. Like him these sons are now going to act like snakes in the grass! (See comments on 27:35 on p. 223)

We cannot ... give our sister to one who is uncircumcised. Although no direct reference is made to the command to Abraham in 17:10–14, the assumption that circumcision is the sign of God's covenant with Abraham's descendants seems to underlie the brothers' demand. If the Shechemites agree to be circumcised "and become one people" with Jacob's descendants, effectively becoming one religious as well as ethnic community, then God's promises of land and descendants will no longer be threatened. The situation presupposed by Deuteronomy 7 would no longer apply. Awareness that circumcision was originally a ritual of puberty and marriage (rather than infancy) seems to be indicated here.

The young man ... was the most honoured of all his family. The good qualities of Shechem are emphasized at several points in the story.

These people are friendly with us. How far can one be deceived! The sentence reuses a Hebrew root *shalam*, here translated "friendly", which appeared earlier when Jacob arrived "safely" at Shechem (33:18). A related word was employed to describe how Jacob's father Isaac lived peaceably (26:29,31) with other non-Israelites. So up till now the stories of the patriarchs have stressed how they sought to live in harmony with the peoples of the land: Hamor's confidence is not unreasonable, even if naïve. In "selling" the potentially uncomfortable proposal to their people Hamor and Shechem inevitably emphasize the eventual benefit: "will not their livestock, their property ... be ours?" That does not speak of an equal future between the two parties. Perhaps neither side in this discussion is being totally honest.

The attack which follows, instigated by Simeon and Levi, is portrayed in terms that accentuate its treachery and totality. Hoped-for ethnic unity swiftly becomes the Bible's first example of ethnic cleansing. It is also the first time in Genesis that the prohibition of murder after the flood (9:6) has been contravened.

Jacob said to Simeon and Levi, "You have brought trouble on me." Finally, Jacob speaks, but words that smack of cowardice and self-interest. This is a break between two epochs, not simply two generations. During this episode, the balance of power has shifted: Jacob is no longer pictured as devious son, clever nephew, wily brother, fought-over husband, but as a father, and a not very competent one at that! The time of patriarchal coexistence is drawing to a close; the days of nationalist conquest are dawning.

This story has been frustrating to read because the narrator never quite allows us to decide where our sympathies should lie; yet this moral ambiguity is also its strength. The story goes out of its way to elicit some understanding for Shechem despite the apparent brutal action with which he set events in motion. It allows us to feel that Simeon and Levi's response is disproportionate, even if, at first sight, it tallies with the viewpoint regarding non-Israelites enjoined by Deuteronomy 7. Surely, shouldn't the willingness of Hamor and his family to undergo circumcision have counted for something, so that the demands of Deuteronomy no longer apply to the situation? And as for Jacob, is he to be praised for his seeming desire for moderation, or damned for his uncaring insouciance regarding his daughter? Dinah, alone, is unambiguously a victim, a voiceless one, and after this story she will undoubtedly remain alone for the rest of her life. The family honour may have been restored by her brothers' action but her defilement—"like a whore"—will endure in the eyes of her family.

Deaths and births
35:1–36:43

35:1-29 We now move into a series of short episodes, probably originating from a variety of hands, which seem to be drawn together to round off the story of Jacob. They remind us of the transitoriness of human life and death, set against the eternal nature of the promises of God.

God said to Jacob, "Arise, go up to Bethel". The comparative importance of Bethel as Jacob's religious goal is indicated by the expression "go up", which we see frequently in the Bible in relation to Jerusalem. These verses allude back at several points to God's earlier appearance to Jacob at Bethel (28:10-22), and Jacob's actions are an acknowledgement that God had carried out the promises he made then.

To mark this important religious moment a ritual of purification is introduced. The motif of purification in these verses contrasts with the theme of defilement which had pervaded the previous chapter. There are two aspects to this purification: "change your clothes"—the change of garments is a ritual used in several religions to suggest a decisive break with the past and to mark a new beginning (e.g. primitive Christian baptismal practice)—and "put away the foreign gods". The idols referred to would presumably include the household gods brought by Rachel from her father's house, as well perhaps as the gods of the Shechemites which Jacob's family might have been attracted to during their stay there. Earrings were also buried: these were shaped as small figures of the gods. Joshua 24:14 also associates the site of Shechem with a decisive rejection of other gods. It is a symbolic statement that the family of Jacob are in the land, but not of it. Such ritual actions prepare the way for the new stage (with a new name) that is going to be offered at Bethel.

What has happened in the last chapter and now here reads almost like a commentary on Deuteronomy 7:21-26.

There he built an altar. This is the first time that a patriarch has built an altar in response to a direct demand from God (35:1). Does God's next appearance to Jacob depend on the fact that he has followed this instruction?

Deborah, Rebekah's nurse, died. It is strange to learn of the death of a person whose name we previously did not know. It is also strange that Rebekah's nurse was travelling with Jacob! Probably Deborah's grave was a well-known site near Bethel, and the mention of Bethel has prompted this notice. However, by referring to her burial the writer has framed the remaining incidents in this chapter within an awareness of human mortality: they begin with the death of Deborah and end with the death of Isaac.

In view of the desperate struggle through which Jacob acquired the name Israel in 32:22–32, it is strange and rather jarring to read in verses 9–15 a repetition of the granting of this name, reported seemingly without any awareness of the previous occasion. These verses actually seem to conflate Jacob's earlier experiences at both Bethel (28:10–19) and Penuel (32:22–32). Presumably, different literary sources play a part: but the presence of divergent accounts within Genesis reinforces the ambiguity of what it means to be Israel; it is both struggle (32:22–32) and also, as here, freely given gift. It may also remind us, after Jacob's less than impressive performance at Shechem, that Israel needs to be reborn as Israel, again and again!

Despite its not particularly dramatic context, the oracle that follows delineates a key juncture in the structural progression of Genesis. Its language of fruitfulness marks it out as one of a sequence of oracles or blessings that reach back to creation (1:28) and the new world after the deluge (9:1). Its closest affinity is the promise given when God's covenant is made with Abraham (17:6). It finally fulfils the hopes expressed when Isaac blessed Jacob in 28:1–5, echoing the language found there: "God Almighty" (28:3), fruitfulness (28:3), a host of nations (28:3), the gift of land (28:4), as well as the reference to Paddan-aram (28:5). It is telling that Isaac himself may have been blessed, but he did not directly receive a blessing by God named as God Almighty. Such a privilege is given only to the patriarchs who themselves have just been renamed (17:5; 35:10), and each time it marks a distinctive stage in God's relationship with this family. As with Abraham, the blessing of Jacob promises kingly offspring and also extends the promise of the land beyond Jacob into the future time of his descendants. It is against these words that we need to measure the rest of this chapter.

Jacob set up a pillar. The detailed description of Jacob's cultic actions makes it clear that he is seeking to carry out scrupulously the promises he made at Bethel more than twenty years before (28:20–22).

Over the course of this chapter, the relationship between God and humanity has subtly shifted. We are not told the context in which Abraham received the blessing of God Almighty, unless perhaps it was a lunch party (see comments on 17:1–22). But Jacob's blessing had apparently happened at a place already sacred, and after he and his family had undertaken a ritual act of purification. In Israel's future, holy places and holy things will increasingly become the channel for divine-human association.

Rachel was in childbirth The midwife's words during this labour, "now you will have another son" echo Rachel's own earlier hopes when Joseph was born (30:24). But with ironic tragedy the birth also recalls Rachel's angry cry from the time of her infertility: "Give me children, or I shall die!" (30:1) At last, she has indeed been given more than one son by Jacob, but it is also the last moment of her life. Rachel, who could not bear to leave her ancient gods behind in Mesopotamia is herself buried, just after these gods have been buried by Jacob in order to begin his new life in Canaan.

So, Benjamin is born in pain and grief, and from that originates the name Ben-oni, "Son of My Sorrow", that Rachel sought to give him. Intriguingly years earlier her sister Leah had used the same word *'oni*, there translated "affliction", when she celebrated the birth of her first son, Reuben: "The LORD has looked on my affliction" (29:32). So the births of Jacob's children, the children of Israel, are encircled by pain and suffering: an apparent foreshadowing, for the word *'oni* will be used many times during their slavery in Egypt.

But his father called him Benjamin. For all his love for Rachel Jacob would not fulfil her dying wish. To do so would have condemned this youngest child to an "unlucky" future. He tried to avert this by renaming the boy. *Yamin* means "right (hand)", and as in many cultures the "right" is associated with prosperity. But it also suggested the special place Benjamin held in his father's affections: he was his "right hand boy"!

Rachel died, and she was buried on the way to Ephrathah, (that is Bethlehem). There is geographical confusion apparent. Ephrathah was a small town in the territory later linked with the tribe of Benjamin, a few miles north of Jerusalem, not far from Bethel and Ramah. According to 1 Samuel 10:2, this was where Rachel's tomb was to be found. However, possibly under Judaean pressure, a competing site for Rachel's tomb, near Bethlehem, grew up (multiple and competing sites for "holy places" is a feature not restricted to the *modern* Holy Land!), and at some point, a gloss associating Bethlehem and Ephrathah was added to the text.

Originally and appropriately, it seems that Benjamin was born and Rachel died in the territory of the tribe of Benjamin. In Israelite history, Benjaminite territory was to be the buffer between the northern tribes and Judah, and therefore perhaps the "heart" of Israel.

And in view of its place within Christian tradition as the birthplace of Jesus Christ, it is also telling that the first time Bethlehem is mentioned in the Bible it is as a place of birth—and death.

Reuben went and lay ... with his father's concubine. This is an action that is explicitly prohibited by Deuteronomy 22:30. As a result of it, Reuben lost the prerogatives of the firstborn (49:3-4). Why did Reuben do this? Was it the birth of Benjamin, named as his father's "right-hand" boy, a position that Reuben as the eldest would have considered his by right, that finally provoked him to take revenge for the humiliation of his mother Leah over decades? Or perhaps it is an attempt to seize power in the family from his ageing father: in the story of David the seizure of power by Absalom is accompanied by his expropriation of his father's concubines (2 Samuel 16:20-22).

The sons of Jacob were twelve. The "fruitfulness" promised in 35:11 is now becoming an actuality, after two generations in which family survival seemed tenuous. The tradition preserved in these verses (which come from the same hand as 35:9-12) seems to conflict with 35:16-18 by suggesting that Benjamin too was born in Paddan-aram.

Jacob came to his father Isaac at Mamre. Finally, Jacob has come home to his "father's house" as he had prayed to do in 28:21.

Isaac ... died ... and his sons Esau and Jacob buried him. Isaac's age when he died as the oldest of the patriarchs suggests the blessed equilibrium that marked out his life. That his burial was organized by his two sons acting as one, reinforces a sense of peace and reconciliation. Esau is even listed first: a sign that despite Jacob's purchase of Esau's firstborn rights, Esau still has a valued place in the family.

36:1–43 *These are the descendants of Esau (that is, Edom).* The impression given by 35:29 is reinforced by this whole chapter. Introduced by the ninth example in Genesis of the *toledot* formula (36:1, repeated 36:9), it is the longest unbroken section containing genealogical information in the entire book.

There are four distinct sections:

1. A list of Esau's wives and sons, to which is appended a notice about Esau's migration to Seir (36:1–8).
2. A list giving details about the families of Esau's sons, in two parallel forms (36:10–14,15–19).
3. A list giving the genealogy of Seir the Horite, "the [original] inhabitants of the land", i.e. before Esau moved there (36:20–30).
4. An ancient king-list of Edom, which shows an awareness that the institution of kingship developed in Edom centuries before it arose among the Israelites (36:31–43).

Taken as a whole they suggest considerable interest by the writers of Genesis in the situation of the Edomites, as well as a willingness to make use of Edomite sources, which must have helped in garnering at least some of the information. The "untidiness" of the lists is suggestive of authenticity. At points, there are discrepancies, e.g. the names and parentage of Esau's wives and the overlap with the family of Ishmael. There are a number of names listed which appear elsewhere in the Old Testament, for example there is an Eliphaz who is a friend of Job (Job 2:11) and a Reuel who is described as the father-in-law of Moses (Exodus 2:18). Though we cannot be sure that Genesis 36 is identifying the two sons of Esau mentioned in 36:10 with these figures, the commonality of names reminds us that there were a number of different tribes and nations (e.g. Edomites, Midianites, Ishmaelites, etc.), broadly speaking all linked to the geographical area of north-west Arabia, who seem to have overlapped in the Old Testament retelling of history.

In 36:12, "Amalek" is almost certainly intended to be seen as the eponymous ancestor of the Amalekites. The Old Testament reserves a special vitriol for the Amalekites (e.g. 1 Samuel 15:18).

Seir the Horite (36:20)   Horite probably means "cave-dweller". A careful reading of the lists indicates that this family, the indigenous people of Edom, intermarried at several points with Esau's descendants.

The particular information that "Anah ... found the springs in the wilderness" (36:24), reminds us how important water resources were in a region as arid as Edom.

Taken as a whole, the lists of names suggests an awareness of an ongoing relationship between the Edomites and the descendants of Jacob throughout different epochs of history. At times, there was rapprochement, at other moments, vicious hostility. In part, this would have been dictated by the political currents that eddied round the Ancient Middle East, and also by internal power politics in the Judaean capital of Jerusalem or the Edomite capital of Diban.

Esau's departure from Jacob and migration to Edom is, in this chapter, portrayed in terms that are amicable. The brothers may not be able to live close together, but this is because of their mutual prosperity, and they finally part fraternally on good terms. The Old Testament is aware that there is a "special relationship" with Edom: "You shall not abhor any of the Edomites, for they are your kin" (Deuteronomy 23:7).

That there were kings in Edom "before any king reigned over the Israelites" (36:31) is perhaps a sharp reminder that, blessing or no blessing, the family of Esau has prospered more speedily than the family of his brother Jacob. But the fact that, in this chapter, Esau has so clearly become the nation Edom, prepares us for Genesis 37–50, during which the sons of Jacob will overtly become the nation Israel.

Theological reflections

1. The setting

If the Abraham cycle appears to have its geographical centre in the south of Canaan, around Hebron and Mamre, the Jacob stories appear to originate in the north, with their focus on Bethel and Shechem. Unlike the figure of Abraham, who does not figure prominently in texts which are clearly pre-exilic, the name of Jacob appears in prophetic materials that stem from the time of the monarchy. A particularly interesting example comes in Hosea 12:2–4, which appears to suggest that several of the tales about Jacob circulated widely for some centuries before they evolved into the connected narrative we find in Genesis 25–35. A tradition about Jacob also surfaces in Jeremiah 9:4, while Jeremiah 31:15 apparently knows of a tragic event associated with Rachel. There are also texts from pre-exilic (as well as later) times that seem to be fully aware of Jacob's traditional hostility with Esau, e.g. Obadiah. In these passages, the name "Jacob" is sometimes used to refer to the patriarch himself, and sometimes to the people and nation Israel. For example, "Jacob" appears frequently in poetic texts in parallelism to "Israel" (e.g. Isaiah 43:1; Jeremiah 31:7). The two different usages inform and explicate each other, so that the people called "Jacob" are frequently painted with the character traits of their ancestor, while the stories of the ancestor clearly reflect the historical experience the nation Jacob/Israel is going through. Israelites in exile, as well as more recent readers, could readily identify with Jacob, whose exile and restoration mirrored their own. It is what gives these stories their particular compelling quality: however unattractive Jacob may be as a person, we can discover through him what it means for us too to wrestle with God and to rediscover our brothers and sisters with new eyes.

The northern geographical references in these stories suggest that the figure of Jacob was particularly associated with the northern kingdom during the period of the divided monarchy. This fits with the reality that "Israel" was primarily a designation adopted by the Northern Kingdom. The major shrine of the northern kingdom was Bethel (1 Kings 12:32), while Penuel (1 Kings 12:25) and Shechem (1 Kings 12:25) both had strategic roles in the history of this kingdom. All three sites figure prominently in the stories of Jacob. After the fall of the northern kingdom in 722 BC, it is likely that the Jacob traditions became the common heritage of the community centred on Jerusalem, which regarded itself as the heir of "Israel".

The positive role allotted in Genesis to these northern locations, particularly Bethel, contrasts with its consistently negative presentation in 1–2 Kings, and in various prophetic texts. Perhaps it suggests that although the Jacob cycle has reached us via post-exilic Judaean spectacles, the traditional tales of Jacob, firmly rooted in oral tradition over several centuries, had for so long associated his name with Bethel that not to link Jacob's experience with this particular sanctuary was unthinkable.

It may also be that despite the destruction of the sanctuary at Bethel by King Josiah of Judah (2 Kings 23:15–18), Bethel remained more important in the post-exilic period than the traditional "history" of Israel allowed for and actually continued as an important religious site for several further centuries. This tallies with the current reanalysis of the history of the region. Certainly, though Genesis in its final form is a post-exilic production it is less dominated by a pro-Jerusalem bias than some other parts of the Old Testament.

2. An immoral God?

One of the striking, and refreshing, features of the Old Testament tradition is the willingness of "Israel" to identify itself with an ancestor whose morality seems, to our eyes at least, distinctly dubious. Those prophets, and others, who spoke to the Israel of their day had no illusions about the human frailties of their audience. Even though they regarded Israel/Jacob as having a particular role to play within God's purposes, it was a task that had to be undertaken by fallible human beings (see e.g. Isaiah 42:19). For such a "chosen people", Jacob was the ideal chosen ancestor.

Jacob's devious character was an inheritance for his descendants, just as much as the blessing he had been granted by God (e.g. Malachi 3:6–7).

Clearly, it would be inappropriate to try and use (as some Christian traditions are inclined to attempt) Jacob as a moral exemplar. This stricture applies to all the patriarchs. They are not role models for behaviour in the twenty-first century. But at the same time the Jacob stories do raise, in a different form from that of the book of Job, the question of the morality or immorality of God. Does God reward trickery and deception? Is this how God wants his people to operate—"smoothly", just as Jacob did?

One of the valuable aspects of the Jacob cycle is the way it subtly addresses questions about morality without labouring the point. Jacob's deception of his father, and his claim of the right that belonged to the firstborn, is matched by a similar deception that he himself experiences at the hands of Laban, when Laban insists on the rights of his firstborn daughter. It is a form of just retribution. Indeed, in the section that explores the relationship of Jacob and Laban, one trick is piled on top of another—until finally Jacob unwittingly invokes a death sentence on the then unknown thief of Laban's household gods—and Rachel's premature death seems to be an exacting of the penalty, in part vicariously, for the whole cycle of deception into which she has been caught up. The irony of the stories is a powerful moral tool: we feel a sense of satisfaction that Jacob who, as a result of the theft of the blessing, has been promised that his brother would "bow down" (27:29) to him, should before his story is through end up bowing low to his brother—not once but seven times! (33:3)

This intricate and sometimes humorous interweaving that melds the cycle together creates the impression that wrongdoing does not remain unpunished. Justice may be slow, but its day will come. But conversely, God continues to work with and through imperfect human beings and imperfection is not a pre-emptive disqualification for having a starring role in the working out of God's purposes. Such a message was critically important to those in Babylonian exile, battered by the condemnations issued by the pre-exilic prophets, and having come to understand their exile as divine punishment. God could still work with them, as he had worked with their ancestor Jacob, and their ongoing struggle for life and faith in the middle of adversity is not only retribution but also an opportunity for growth, since in the struggle is also the blessing (32:29).

3. An elusive God-with-us

Just as interaction on the human plane between Jacob, Esau and Laban helps to foster a process of moral development in Genesis 25–36, so also the relationship between human beings and God is matured.

God does not appear or speak directly in every chapter. But new ways for relating to him begin to be explored. A family plagued by infertility can "inquire" of him through an oracle (25:22); God speaks in dreams to both Jacob and Laban (31:11,24); God can be accessed via religious and ritual actions, such as tithing (28:22), anointing (28:18; 35:14), formal prayer (32:9-12), the erection of sacred pillars (28:22; 35:14) and an offering (35:14). There are the beginnings of formality in relating to God. One might say that God spoke with Abraham as a man to his friend. That does not quite happen in the stories of Jacob. Was it on Mount Moriah that fear first became a necessary element of the divine-human relationship (22:12)? If so, Jacob now lives at a time when God's gracious friendship with the family of Abraham has begun to be tinted with an element of fear.

It is interesting to notice how reticent the Jacob stories are about using the name "Yhwh", which has previously expressed an intimacy between God and human beings. In fact, the final time it appears in this cycle is in Jacob's prayer in 32:9, when Yhwh seems to be linked specifically with the land of Canaan and with the command to Jacob to return to it. The refusal of the night wrestler to disclose his name (32:29) seems to deny Jacob the right to use the name Yhwh during the rest of his life. Before Jacob dies in 49:33, the word Yhwh will only pass his lips once more, in his final blessing of his sons (49:18). And even here, it expresses future hope as much as a present relationship. Jacob's wives, particularly Leah, used the name more freely in naming their sons. Perhaps this reflects a powerful link between Yhwh and creativity. Jacob's own preferred description for God seems to be "the God of my father". Does this title bring God near, within "the family" or distance him—at one generation, so to speak? The ambiguity remains.

However, the Jacob cycle also speaks of two major encounters with the divine, at Bethel and at Penuel, and these two passages, which stand like two matching structural pillars, holding together the stories of Jacob, have had an immense impact in developing our comprehension of God, both within the biblical tradition and more widely.

The ladder at Bethel
When we read of Jacob's experience at Bethel (28:10–22), we both enter and subvert a world in which temples provided a meeting point for humanity and divinity. The Ancient Middle Eastern understanding of a temple was that it was the "house" of a god. The god dwelt there in order to be accessible to his human worshippers, although he also had an abode in the heavens. The heavenly and the earthly dwelling were symbolically connected in as visible a form as was possible. Perhaps the temple was on the highest hill in an area; perhaps it was designed in the form of a *ziggurat* as a human-made ramp between earth and heaven.

Jacob's experience at Bethel reflects this understanding. The ladder links the heavenly and earthly dwelling place of Yhwh. Significantly the place is actually called Bethel, i.e. "House of God", the very name suggesting that it is the archetype of a temple. The presence of Yhwh standing by Jacob fulfils the purpose for which temples were built: so that worshippers could "see" their deity and sense his protection.

Yet at the same time the words spoken by Yhwh challenge the *raison d'être* of a holy place. Yhwh promises to be with Jacob "wherever you go". Normally worshippers had to come to a specific holy building, a temple, to find their god: but this God assures Jacob that he can find him anywhere. This is a God who is not confined by a building or even a holy land. He will not be a god who is carried along in a caravan like a household idol. He will be Jacob's travelling companion—but on his own terms. Even here in this holy place Yhwh has come to Jacob before he is invoked.

Centuries later, resonances of Jacob's vision are found in the Gospel of John. In John 1:51, after meeting Nathanael, whom he describes as "an Israelite in whom there is no deceit" (an oblique allusion to Jacob),

Jesus affirms that his disciple will see "heaven opened and the angels of God ascending and descending upon the Son of Man" (John 1:51). As elsewhere in this Gospel (e.g. John 2:12–22), a holy place is apparently being declared redundant, because Jesus Christ fulfils in his own person the reason for its original existence, to be a meeting-place for God and human beings. It is on the Son of Man, rather than on the ground of Bethel that the ladder is to be set up. Yet the subversiveness of the author of John's Gospel may have been anticipated by those who composed Genesis 28, for even as the story of Jacob's ladder provides us with an aetiology for the well-known temple at Bethel, at the same moment it inspires us to leave that temple behind.

Though we may be able to discern this, it is doubtful that Jacob could, at least if we go by his actions on awakening. He behaves rather like the disciples who witnessed the transfiguration of Jesus. After seeing Jesus in this new light, their response was to seek to build three shelters on the mountain (Mark 9:5). They had failed to comprehend that the divine light could not be held captive in a place—however awesome—but could only be refracted via a person. Similarly Jacob after his dream seems unaware that the key to unlock the "gate of heaven" that suddenly opened the previous night, may be found in himself rather than at the portals of Bethel's temple. But to become the gateway to heaven for others, their means of access to the divine, is a fearful vocation. It is more comfortable to tuck such a challenge safely away in a place that you will hope one day to come back to: to consecrate a shrine at Bethel (28:18), rather than yourself. There will come a day when Jacob will be ready to become the Israel of God, but that will only happen when another human person, his brother Esau, can become in turn for him a gateway to God (33:10).

It is interesting how Jacob's experience at Bethel accords with that of Moses in Exodus 33–34. There is a similar anxiety expressed about the need for God to accompany his people on their travels; indeed, it is actually spelt out by Moses that unless God goes with them, they cannot fully be his people (Exodus 33:16). And startlingly, Moses himself provides a dramatic illustration of what it might mean for a human being to become a gateway to heaven. He so loses himself in his concern for his people that he becomes the answer to his own prayer, his shining face as he comes down the mountain reflecting the glory of God to them. Perhaps it is not surprising that there should be this thematic link between the story of Jacob and the narrative of Exodus, for both probably assumed their basic shape in response to exilic anxieties about the possibility of presence in a strange land.

The wrestler at Penuel

Perhaps, however, the story of Jacob's divine encounter at Penuel is the one which speaks more directly to people today. Martin Buber perceived the episode of wrestling Jacob as a metaphor for a wrestling with life's existential questions by all of humanity. Our age has had to struggle with questions of God's goodness and the problem of evil on a massive scale, none more so than Jacob's spiritual heirs, adherents of the Jewish faith, as they have tried to respond to the challenge to faith thrown up by the Shoah or Holocaust. What does it mean for Israel, God's people, to be honoured with the name Israel—the one that strives with God, and will not let God go despite the wounds inflicted by the lengthy struggle? Elie Wiesel, a great interpreter of his people's suffering during the Nazi era, puts it like this:

> Both were wounded: Jacob at the hip, the angel in his vanity. Yet they parted friends, or was it accomplices? Jacob accepted his aggressor's departure willingly; the latter, as if to thank him, made him a gift: a new name which for generations to come would symbolize eternal struggle and endurance, in more than one land, during more than one night.[73]

The episode by the river has had a profound effect also on Christian spirituality. The tradition of mystical theology expressed by the phrase "the dark night of the soul" draws on this biblical episode for one of its roots. So too does the willingness of spiritual writers to recognize that when we engage in prayer we are entering into dangerous territory. Prayer is not always an entering into stillness; it can involve us in arguing with God, as Job did, or even, like Jacob, in wrestling with God and suffering life-changing wounds. Gerard Manley Hopkins summed it up by saying, "battling with God is now my prayer", while John Donne asked God to "[b]atter my heart, three-person'd God".

The story has also been viewed as a statement of our ambivalent attitude towards the presence of God: terrifying yet life-giving. This is expressed in the great Charles Wesley hymn: "Come, O Thou Traveller unknown", which exults in the moment when Jacob is blessed by his adversary and is left to discover his new self:

> 'Tis Love! 'Tis Love! Thou diedst for me!
> I hear thy whisper in my heart;
> The morning breaks, the shadows flee,
> Pure universal love thou art;
> To me, to all, thy mercies move:
> Thy nature and thy name is Love.

Alluding to this hymn, the Methodist writer J. Neville Ward concluded his classic book *The Use of Praying* as follows:

> Sometimes faith confidently and easily interprets experience as from God; sometimes only slowly and after much argument with itself and life. And sometimes it simply has to hold on, like the troubled wrestler by the dark river, trusting that when the light breaks it will appear that the imagined enemy was Love all the time.[74]

When we meet Aslan in C. S. Lewis' *The Lion, the Witch and the Wardrobe*, we discover that he is definitely not a tame lion: "Who said anything about safe?" "Course he isn't safe. But he's good. He's the King."[75] Jacob makes a similar discovery about his divine opponent, as the story draws our attention to the untameability and elusiveness of God. That is a motif that permeates the Old Testament, and this episode is one of its foundation stones.

In looking for a theological centre to the Old Testament, Walther Zimmerli has drawn attention to the importance of the name of God, Yhwh, both in terms of its meaning, and a reticence to disclose and use it at all. Zimmerli suggests that these two features help to emphasize the sovereign freedom of God, who refuses to be the puppet or plaything of humanity. In the culture of the Ancient Middle East, the knowledge of someone's name granted power over them. It is notable that though Jacob is forced to reveal his name, and is rewarded with a new one, his opponent deflects Jacob's request for a similar revelation with the question "Why is it that you ask my name?" Though the antagonist may be held by Jacob he still refuses to surrender himself into Jacob's power. When the day finally arrives that Yhwh will disclose his name, to Moses during the Exodus, the explanation associated with it, "I AM WHO I AM" (Exodus 3:14), will confer upon this God a quality of hiddenness, one who is known as unknown, and who chooses to be what he will be.

So, ironically, though Jacob was not granted knowledge of the name, he did indeed experience the reality of Yhwh, as the elusive one, through this night encounter. By his refusal to be controlled, the divine opponent is giving expression to what his name actually signifies. It is interesting how, from this point in Genesis the actual name Yhwh is used only rarely in the text, yet at the same time the "hidden" quality of God and his activity will become more apparent, particularly in the story of Joseph and his brothers. It seems that in this episode with Jacob God has been made known as Yhwh in a fashion that is even more profound than his name.

Conversely, Jacob is granted a privilege that will be withheld from Moses. The literary tradition which emphasized how God's name was revealed to Moses, also suggests that Moses could not see God's face (Exodus 33:20). By contrast Genesis 32 suggests that Jacob did so (verse 30). Perhaps the dual grace of sight and name is too extravagant, and dangerous, to confer upon any one human being. It is dangerous for God as well as human beings. For the God who Jacob meets on that dark night is not only elusive but one who risks intimacy. Trevor Dennis has commented:

> It gives us a picture of an extraordinarily intimate God. This God has his hands on Jacob! The two of them are locked in struggle for hours on end! We have not seen God at such close quarters with a human being since the creation of the man and the woman in Eden. We will not see God at such very close quarters again in scripture. It tells of a God incarnate, for he meets with Jacob in the form of a "man".[76]

Speaking from within the Christian tradition one can suggest that this intimate God of Jacob foreshadows the intimate relationship which God will have with his prophets and his people, par excellence in Jeremiah. But as Jeremiah knows only too well (Jeremiah 8:21), intimacy leads to vulnerability and perhaps ultimately to suffering. For God to be with us costs God. There is a path that can be traced from Penuel to Golgotha. It is not only a Christian insight. Once again, Elie Wiesel has dug deep into the meaning of this story:

> Jacob has just understood a fundamental truth: God is in man, even in suffering, even in misfortune, even in evil. God is everywhere. In every being, not only in the victim. God does not wait for man at the end of the road, the termination of exile; he accompanies him there. More than that: He is the road, He is the exile. God holds both ends of the rope, He is present in every extremity, He is every limit. He is part of Jacob as He is part of Esau.[77]

4. A vision of brotherhood

From the time that human beings left Eden, what it is to be a brother has been a topic that Genesis has revisited again and again. It is almost as if the writers are aware that if this could be got right, then the primal relationship between human beings and God can become what it was always intended to be. The theme has been explored through the stories of Cain and Abel, Ham and his brothers, Isaac and Ishmael. It also surfaces in the dealings between Abraham and Lot, and Jacob and Laban, for the Hebrew word *'ah*, which is normally translated as "brother", is often used, as with Lot and Abraham, to define a looser relationship than that of siblings. It will, of course, be a motif that will dominate the story of Joseph and his brothers, and the briefer account of the sons of Judah. But nowhere in Genesis does "brotherhood" get explored as seriously as in the story of Jacob. In part, this is a reflection of the intimacy of the relationship between Jacob and Esau, not merely even full brothers, but actually twins sharing the same womb. The intensity of their relationship is what makes it particularly dangerous—as well as offering unparalleled opportunity. That this topic is a dominant motif in Genesis 25-36 is stressed by the way Chapters 29-30 focus on the relationship of the two sisters, Rachel and Leah, almost as a counterpoint to that of Jacob and Esau.

The topic attains its zenith in Genesis 32-33 in the interplay between Jacob's encounter with a divine antagonist, and his meeting the next morning with Esau, the brother, whom he expects to meet as an antagonist, but whose graciousness surprises him. The wordplays make the connection crystal clear. "'Truly to see your face is like seeing the face of God—since you have received me with such favour'" (33:10). It is only if we are prepared to continue our struggle with God that we can see our "brothers" in their true light, as God sees them. Conversely, it is when we wrestle for a more authentic relationship with our brothers and sisters that we discover that we are given God's blessing. Our relationship with God and that with our brothers belong together and woe betide us if we try to separate them. If we do, our faith has ceased to be biblical. The icon "Christ is our reconciliation" was created for Pax Christi International as a Millennium project.[78] The central scene of the icon shows the reconciliation of Jacob and Esau as described in Genesis 33, yet with a gesture that somehow speaks both of embracing but also wrestling. However, a ladder—clearly recalling the events at Bethel twenty years earlier—is also pictured in the scene. Anomalous it might be, but it conveys the deep truth that it is only when brothers are reconciled that the ladder really can bridge the gap between earth and heaven.

The author of 1 John expresses a similar vision in a vivid passage that may actually be alluding to the story of Jacob and Esau: "Those who do not love a brother or sister whom they have seen, cannot love God whom they have not seen" (1 John 4:20). Does not Jesus' parable of the Elder and Younger Brother (Luke 15:10-32), which has probably been coloured by the Old Testament traditions of Jacob and Esau, express something of this in pictorial form?

There is a wonderful tale from Jewish tradition that exemplifies this:

> Two brothers worked together on a family farm. One was unmarried and the other married with children. They shared what they grew equally as they always did, produce and profit. But one day the single brother said to himself, "You know, it's not right that we should share the produce equally, and the profit too. After all I'm all alone, just by myself and my needs are simple. But there is my poor brother with a wife and all those children."
>
> So in the middle of the night, he took a sack of grain from his bin, crept over the field between their houses and dumped it in his brother's bin. Meanwhile, unknown to him, his brother had the same thought. He said to himself, "It is not right that we should share produce and profit equally. After all, I am married, and I have my wife to look after me and my children for years to come. But my brother has no one to take care of his future." So he too, in the middle of the night, took to taking a sack of grain from his bin and sneaking across the field to deposit it in his brother's. And both were puzzled for years as to why their supply did not dwindle.
>
> Well, one night it just so happened that they both set out for each other's house at the same time. In the dark they bumped into each other carrying their sacks. Each was startled, but then it slowly dawned on them what was happening. They dropped their sacks and embraced one another. Suddenly the dark sky lit up and a voice from heaven spoke, "Here at last is the place where I will build my Temple. For where brothers meet in love, there my Presence shall dwell."[79]

But Jacob's dealings with Esau also impinge on relationships other than those of blood kin, or even (as with 1 John) of members of the same close knit religious community. Genesis itself encourages us to realize this by the clear link made between Esau and the nation of Edom.

The triangle of relationships between Jacob/Israel, the divine wrestler and Esau/Edom appears to suggest that the vocation of Israel is to wrestle both with God and with the world of national and political reality in which God's people found themselves. If Israel turns its back on either a relationship with God or a relationship with the "foreign nations" (symbolized by Esau/Edom) then it becomes less than Israel. It is both a challenge to a glib secularism, and a statement that biblical faith must be worked out in the world, rather than become a flight from it. It is, and will be, a struggle. But only in the struggle will be the blessing. That is the mystery of Israel.

Rabbinic tradition suggested that the divine figure with whom Jacob wrestled was the guardian angel of the Edomite nation. It states an important truth. Our enemies, such as Edom historically became in the history of Israel, have their place in God's scheme, and their divine protectors: and we cannot deal with God without also dealing with them.

The question Jesus asked in Mark 3:33, "Who is my brother?", was explored centuries earlier in Genesis 32–33, and a radical, almost shocking, answer was given to it.

It may well be that these reflections have some relevance to the current world of Middle Eastern politics and religion and complement the earlier observations on Isaac and Ishmael (see p. 197). But if Christians choose to refer to themselves as "a New Israel" (see Galatians 6:16), then the vocation of struggling both with God and God's world belongs no less to them. The story of struggling Jacob then stands in theological continuity with the great Parable of the Sheep and the Goats (Matthew 25:31–46), which makes it clear that the face of God's Christ is to be seen in the hungry and the alien. Genesis' great themes of human beings as the image (icon) of God and the struggle for brotherhood also come together in the moving words of the Arab Christian Palestinian writer Elias Chacour:

> The true icon is your neighbour, the human being who has been created in the image and with the likeness of God. How beautiful it is when our eyes are transfigured and we see that our neighbour is the icon of God, and that you, and you, and I—we are all the icons of God. How serious it is when we hate the image of God, whoever that may be, whether a Jew or a Palestinian. How serious it is when we cannot go and say, "I am sorry about the icon of God who was hurt by my behaviour." We all need to be transfigured so we can recognize the glory of God in one another.[80]

The Old Testament will never again wrestle quite so powerfully with this topic of brotherhood. It is as though it is too painful to do so. Human beings cannot bear so much reality. It is easier for Jacob to travel to Canaan and Esau to Edom, rather than live together face to face. But once on a dark night and a sunlit morning we were given a glimpse that we cannot ignore. This blessing will not be taken from us.

The story of Joseph and his brothers

37:1–50:26

If people know only one story from the Old Testament, it is likely either to be Noah's flood—or the tale of Joseph and his brothers, which is going to unfold between Chapters 37 and 50. This tale catches up and reworks into a larger canvas the topic of family conflict and fraternal strife that was first introduced in the primeval account of Cain and Abel and has been revisited several times since. In the story, there are woven together several of the perspectives that have appeared in previous sagas: brotherly jealousy, fatherly favouritism, the elevation of the younger, the almost-lost beloved son.

And yet this section of Genesis also has a character distinct from any other in the book. It is a more cohesive and sustained narrative, punctured only by a few episodes (e.g. Judah and Tamar in 38:1–30; the vision of Jacob and the list of his descendants in 46:1–27; the Blessing of Jacob in 49:1–27) which feel as though they have stepped out of Chapters 12–36. The bulk of the material in Genesis 37–50 has an urbanity, and an urban perspective, which marks it out from the earlier narrative of Genesis. Its writer was a consummate storyteller, who employed subtle literary and psychological techniques. The description of it as a "novella" is apt. The chapters are certainly composed in an awareness of what has gone before, and detailed cross-references are made to earlier stories, vocabulary and themes. But there is substantial involvement of different, and probably later, hands from those responsible for 12–36. It may be that those episodes (examples given above) which currently "jar" in 37–50 were part of an original ending which has now been displaced by the lengthy tale we now have which so overtly focuses on Joseph.

Although Joseph is a name known in pre-exilic Israel as a designation for a group of the northern tribes, "the house of Joseph", including

Manasseh and Ephraim, there is little evidence (Psalm 105:16–22 is an exception) in the rest of the Old Testament outside Genesis that a story of Joseph's rise to power in Egypt was well known. In fact, the interest in Joseph seems often to have centred on his bones! It raises the question as to whether the development of the story of Joseph in the form in which we now have it in Genesis happened after most of the rest of Genesis was already composed—perhaps in the period when the Ptolemies of Egypt ruled Palestine (323–200 BC). It is interesting that there was an infamous Jewish tax-gatherer called "Joseph the Tobiad" who rose high in the administration in Egypt during this period, and it is tempting to wonder if there could be some link. The main body of the "Praise of the Ancestors" given in Sirach 44:1–49:13 does not include Joseph and moves straight from Jacob to Moses (Sirach 45:1). Joseph does appear in Ben Sira's final summary (Sirach 49:15), but the Hebrew version of this verse significantly omits the words "the ruler of his brothers and the support of the people" which were added in the Greek translation, and therefore merely states of Joseph, "even his bones were cared for". There was a large Jewish community in Egypt in the third century BC who would have known of Egyptian court "wisdom" traditions which play a part in the Joseph saga, as well as traditional Egyptian folk tales ("The Tale of the Two Brothers") which may also have influenced its development. Is the story of Joseph therefore constructed out of an amalgam of Egyptian practices and folklore married with long-standing Israelite traditions (particularly concerning those "dem bones"!) about Joseph, one of the eponymous ancestors of the Israelites? Its purpose would be to explain how the family of Jacob had come to live in Egypt, and to help provide an appropriate prologue for the Exodus. It would thus act as a bridge between the traditions about the ancestors and those about the deliverance from Egypt, which had originally been distinct and separate.

That is of course necessarily speculation—and other suggestions would include relating the story of Joseph to incidents during the early period of the monarchy when northern Israelite leaders such as Jeroboam I had close links with the Egyptian court (see 1 Kings 11:40). Although it is not laboured in what initially reads like the story of a quarrelsome family, there are interesting issues implicit in the narrative about the relationship of the northern tribes (linked to Joseph) with their southern counterparts (linked to Judah), and the relative importance of these two tribes in the history of biblical Israel and Judah.

Our view of the date of the Joseph saga may be affected by our perception of Joseph himself. Is he a "hero"—or the opposite? The fact that it is so difficult to decide the answer to that question is perhaps a reflection of the subtlety with which the authors of this saga have told their tale.

The structure of this section reflects its role within the wider book of Genesis. Like the Abraham and Jacob sagas it has a broadly chiastic structure, with elements at the end of the story responding to those highlighted at its outset. (For example, the seventeen years that Jacob resides in Egypt corresponds to the fact that Joseph is seventeen years old when the story begins; Joseph's dreams in Chapter 37 are fulfilled—or not—by his brothers' clear subservience in Chapter 50.) The centre of the narrative seems to be Chapters 45 and 46 which describe the reconciliation of the family and their descent into Egypt. However, it has been plausibly suggested that Chapters 37–50 may also act as a foil to the opening chapters of Genesis itself. The preservation of life with which God is so concerned (50:20) is an appropriate ending for a book which has begun with life's very explosion into being (see further on p. 26).

Going down ... and up
37:1–41:57

The coming chapters will be marked by a series of sharp reversals of fortune, particularly for Joseph, but also for the other players in the drama which is to unfold. Although Chapter 38 appears at first sight to be very different from the surrounding story, there are verbal and thematic links which connect it to the chapters which precede and follow it.

Taking these chapters as a whole, one of the fascinating issues that they raise is the varied modes of God's presence, or lack of it, in the story. This ranges from an apparent total absence of God in Chapter 37 to "direct action" from YHWH in Chapter 38, to the "frame" which YHWH provides for Chapter 39, and eventually to a link between God and the dream interpretation of Chapters 40–41.

37:1–2a *Jacob settled in the land.* The opening phrases suggest a permanence, of finally belonging in a place, after the wandering and alienation that had marked most of Jacob's life in Chapters 25–35. It is also contrasted with the experience of his own father, who "had lived [there]as an alien". But, as so often, appearances can be deceptive, and Jacob will end his life not settled in Canaan, but in the foreign land of Egypt.

This is the story of the family of Jacob. For the last time, the *toledot* formula appears in Genesis. It is paired with the example in 36:1. There it was used to introduce a genealogy, now it introduces a story. A similar pairing occurred in 25:12 and 25:19, where the expression was first used to introduce the genealogy of Ishmael, and then the lengthy story of Isaac and his sons. What follows is the story of Jacob's descendants, not specifically Joseph, although that is how the following chapters are often read. But the story which unfolds will have roles for Reuben, Judah, Simeon and Benjamin as well as Joseph himself, and it is arguable that it is Judah rather than Joseph who is the real hero of the tale.

37:2b–11 *Joseph, being seventeen years old* The introduction is innocent: but much can be read into it. He was shepherding—apparently a pastoral idyll. But rulers in the ancient world were often called shepherds (Jeremiah 23:1–6; Ezekiel 34), and both Moses and David began their rise to leadership while working as shepherds. Yet his role is as "a helper to the sons of Bilhah and Zilpah". These were the two slave-wives of Jacob, so Joseph, son of beloved and free-born Rachel, begins in the lowliest of all positions. It is clearly not a position he relished.

[He] brought a bad report of them. Straightaway he is presented as impossibly tactless. Already we sense that Joseph needs to be refined and tested before he can meet his destiny.

Israel loved Joseph more than any other of his children. Love, as we have already discovered in Genesis, can be a dangerous emotion. The last time a younger son had been loved, it had almost resulted in his death (22:2). The last person that Jacob himself loved (29:18), Rachel, had met an early death. Our expectation is heightened: what will happen to this beloved one?

The use of Jacob's "new" name, Israel, at this point hints poignantly that the story that will unfold is part of the greater story of the people of God, of Israel, the people that is God's own beloved son (Hosea 11:1–3), so often lost and with so far to travel.

A long robe with sleeves   It is a "royal" garment, suggesting great status: Tamar, daughter of David, wears one described in the same terms (2 Samuel 13:18). Hardly a "tactful" present, since it makes transparently visible Jacob's favouritism for Joseph.

Clothing will be a powerful symbolic motif throughout the following chapters: its introduction here reminds us of the first gift of clothing, by YHWH to man and woman as they left the garden (3:21). Does this hint at good or ill lying ahead?

Joseph had a dream.   Both dreams clearly reflect Joseph's vision—hope?—boast?—of his future lordship. The symbols they employ are not haphazard—the sheaves of grain link to the later famine. We have met dreams before in Genesis, but then it was made explicitly clear that God was using them as a reliable medium of communication (see e.g. 20:3). That is not so now; there is no mention of God—indeed Genesis 37 is one of the very few chapters of Genesis from which God appears entirely absent. Joseph's universe seems at the moment to be entirely centred upon himself. Are these "real" dreams, that will predict Joseph's future? Or is he simply engaging in wish-fulfilment? It is notable that it is not actually Joseph himself who interprets the dreams here. For the first dream it is his brothers (37:8), and for the second his father (37:10). Does this mean that the dreams are more—or less—likely to be authentic? We are left in carefully crafted suspense.

They hated him even more. Both here and in the repeated expression "even more" in verse 8, the Hebrew contains the root *yasap* (= add) — from which Joseph's own name is also derived (30:24). It emphasizes how visceral the brothers' hatred for Joseph runs; it is bound up with the very essence of his being.

Your mother The implication is that Rachel is still alive, which conflicts with 35:19. Does this, however, hint that Joseph's dreams may not be entirely fulfilled, since Rachel will clearly not be around at the denouement of the story?

His father kept the matter in mind. But his response was hardly wise. Jacob bears considerable responsibility for what will happen to Joseph, as he also bore much of the responsibility for the disaster which surrounded his daughter Dinah. Apart from exacerbating his elder sons' jealousy, his action in sending Joseph to "see if all was well with his brothers" (especially wearing *that* robe!) was naïve in the extreme. The Hebrew text makes it crystal clear: in 37:4, "The brothers ... had harsh words for him" (literally they were not able to speak to him with *shalom*). So is it likely that they will welcome Joseph when he now goes to "see the *shalom* of his brothers and the *shalom* of the flock" (a literal translation of 37:14)?

37:12–30 *Israel said to Joseph, "Are not your brothers pasturing the flock at Shechem".* Once again, the use of the name "Israel" alerts us to the father's role and responsibility for the destiny of his descendants. He sends Joseph on the long journey from Hebron to Shechem because this is the place where Israel will become Israel (see, e.g. Joshua 24). However, given what happened when the family of Jacob were last located at Shechem (34:1–31), when the brothers' potential for violence was all too apparent, it is perhaps also a dangerous place to be sending Joseph.

He answered "Here I am". Two previous protagonists in the story of Genesis have indicated their willingness to hear a command with this expression — in Hebrew *hinneni*. The first one was Abraham (22:1), and it led to him being summoned to sacrifice his son: the next was Esau

(27:1) and it resulted in him being deprived of his blessing. What will this response mean for Joseph?

A man found him wandering in the fields. Who is this mysterious man who directs Joseph to his brothers at Dothan? In doing so he leads him still further away from Jacob and presumable safety. The previous anonymous "man" we met in Genesis was the apparently divine figure with whom Jacob wrestled at Penuel (32:24). Is this a similarly perilous—and divine—encounter? The ambiguity of the figure whom Joseph meets is noted especially by Jewish commentators; in the context of the story of Joseph, this "man" may perhaps be both human being and also divine messenger. If Joseph had not had this encounter, he would have returned to Jacob without meeting his brothers, and the whole of later history would have been different: no descent into Egypt, no Exodus ... no biblical future for Israel and Israel's children. As the tale of Joseph's experiences in Egypt unfolds, we will notice how God is understood to "nudge" the story along not by direct divine intervention but by working through human interaction (see e.g. p. 352). Is it not appropriate therefore that God may be working here at the beginning of Joseph's tale in a similar fashion through this "chance" meeting? Indeed, the rest of the book of Genesis will depend on it.

However, for the careful reader the expression "in the fields" is also reminiscent of the time that Cain led Abel out into the field—with sinister intent.

They saw him from a distance Did the long robe with sleeves make him particularly distinctive—and somehow seal his fate? Even to wear such a costume on the journey hinted at Joseph's dreams of lordliness, which would have infuriated his brothers. It was not a working man's garment. This robe will have further important roles to play in the story.

In the brothers' scornful words "Here comes this dreamer", the Hebrew expression underlying the word "dreamer" means literally "master of dreams". The phrase emphasizes Joseph's egocentrism and the brothers' anger and fear that his dreams might actually come true. It also prefaces, with a nice touch of irony, their determination to try and frustrate Joseph's ideas of grandeur through a deed which will turn him into the opposite of a "master".

They conspired to kill him.   The text seems confused. Two different versions may have been conflated. The basic version appears to be one in which Reuben acts as the responsible eldest brother, seeking to prevent the murder of Joseph by suggesting that he is taught a lesson by a cooling off period in an empty cistern (37:21–24,28a,29–30). But while Reuben is absent, Midianite traders come upon Joseph and kidnap him (with or without the other brothers' knowledge). Into this first scenario has been inserted a variant in which Judah comes up with an alternative plan—to sell Joseph to Ishmaelite traders who arrive on the scene (25b–27,28b).

Although the interweaving of the two versions creates confusion, it also heightens Judah's culpability. For as the text now stands it means that, despite his fine words, Judah's suggestion to sell his brother to slavers cannot be understood primarily as a means of at least preserving Joseph's life. Reuben had already resolved that issue. Instead, he is presented as sickeningly specious: "What profit is there if we kill our brother and conceal his blood?" Although it meant that they were absolved of blood-guilt (cf. Genesis 9:6), the earliest readers of Genesis would have been well aware that selling a person into slavery in Egypt was, in normal circumstances, condemning him to a lingering death. Did Judah have a particular animus against Joseph? After all Reuben, Simeon and Levi had all, in various ways, incurred their father's displeasure. Judah was now the oldest of the remaining sons of Leah, who might feel more acutely than any other the competition that Joseph posed in their father's affections.

Two actions heighten the awfulness of what the brothers do to Joseph. "They stripped him", and "they sat down to eat". The first is deliberately humiliating, but understandable in view of the symbolic weight Joseph's robe carried in their family. It was a focus for their anger. The second is a cruel inversion of the way that meals often provide the setting for reconciliation or covenant-making.

[They] sold him to the Ishmaelites   So the family of Ishmael have not entirely departed the story of Abraham's descendants. We had heard of their Egyptian connection (21:21; 25:18); now we see that it facilitates

the role they are to have in working out a larger providence. It is ironically appropriate that the offspring of Ishmael, a less favoured son, should work together with another generation of less favoured brothers, to despatch the favoured one to the kind of fate which had once seemed to be Ishmael's own.

37:31–36 The robe itself now takes centre stage. It is dipped in the blood of a goat. Goats have played a significant role in Jacob's life up till now: it was by the skin of a goat that he had deceived his own father (27:16), as his sons will now deceive him. Jacob "recognized it". Again a word that resonates with Jacob's own deception (2:23): Isaac had not recognized him, but now he, Jacob, recognizes the robe—yet is deceived as to its meaning.

Tellingly, as the brothers present the garment to Jacob they asked: "See now whether it is your son's robe or not?" For Joseph may be Jacob's son, but he is in no way their brother, nor are they his keeper. Jacob's extravagant, possibly even overextravagant, grief alienates them from proper family relationships still more: Joseph, he says, is "my son"—so what place remains for the others?

Jacob tore his garments; and put sackcloth on his loins. The importance of the motif of clothing is further accentuated by Jacob's own change of garment.

All ... sought to comfort him ... he refused to be comforted. The repetition of the Hebrew root *naham* (= comfort) emphasizes the grief that Jacob wallows in. But the appearance of the root at key moments within Genesis (5:29; 6:6; 50:21) may suggest that it reflects more than personal grief. A very similar expression is used in Jeremiah 31:15 to describe Rachel's grief for her lost children (including, presumably, Joseph). There it relates to the historical fate of the tribes associated with the "house of Joseph".

No, I shall go down to Sheol to my son mourning Sheol is the underworld, the place of the dead. Jacob actually speaks of "going down" to Sheol, a phrase which parallels the verb used when Joseph goes down first into the cistern, and later into Egypt. There are several psalms (e.g. Psalm

30:3; 88:3–4) which speak of going down to Sheol, in terms of going down into a pit or cistern. For us who know of Joseph's near death in the cistern, there is a hidden appropriateness to Jacob's choice of words: the near death of Joseph in the cistern, creating "death" for his father. Jacob's life is bound up—too bound up?—with the life of his son (cf. 44:30).

38:1–26 The chapter that follows has puzzled, and irritated, generations of commentators on Genesis. It seems to interrupt the flow of Chapters 37 and 39. 39:1 reiterates and resumes where 37:36 left off. At first sight, the story it tells has little to do with the major focus of Chapters 37–50, and apparently ignores the chronology of the surrounding chapters. The events it describes must elapse over a period of twenty years or so and can barely have been completed before the brothers travel to Egypt in search of food—but 39:1 reverts to the point in time of Joseph's kidnapping. So Genesis 38 is a jarring insertion of a possibly already existing story about Judah. Yet the insertion is there for a purpose. The chapter has significant verbal and thematic links with Genesis 37 and 39. It not only counterbalances the focus on the "northern" ancestor Joseph in the rest of 37–50 by providing a narrative about the "southern" ancestor Judah, but also offers an interlude which helps us to understand the development of the character of Judah between Chapter 37 (when he is the "bad guy"!) and 44:18–34, when his offer of self-sacrifice facilitates the reconciliation of Joseph and the other brothers.

Judah went down from his brothers The parting is not simply a geographical one. The expression "went down" seems to have moral undertones. Judah's subsequent actions, becoming close friends with an Adullamite, and marrying a Canaanite woman, distance him emotionally and perhaps religiously from his family (cf. 28:8) as well. Is it his bad conscience over his leading role in Joseph's disappearance that is driving him away?

The various places referred to in this chapter appropriately seem to fall within the later territory of the tribe of Judah. Both the barrage of actions and the names that follow are ominous. Judah "saw … married … went in to … ". It is a swift and brutal mating, with no sense of tenderness about it. Their eldest son is called Er: "he was wicked in the sight of the

Lord". He was at least named appropriately—the letters Er spell "wicked" backwards in Hebrew! The name of Onan, the second son, signified "vigorous", even though his vigour was to be inappropriately applied. The place where the third son, Shelah, was born was called Chezib, which means falsehood! An unsavoury family. By contrast Tamar, Judah's presumably Canaanite daughter-in-law, bears a name that speaks of both beauty and fertility—a "palm tree".

The Lord put him to death. The evil that Er did is not specified. But it is notable that the only two points where Yhwh is involved in direct action during this chapter is in a retributive taking away of the life of Judah's two sons. In Genesis 37, we might have thought that Yhwh was now "out of the picture" and the brothers' violence towards Joseph would go unpunished. The present verse is a sharp reminder to us that this is not the case. Yhwh is still active in the history of this family. And what about Judah—did he see any connection between what happened to his own sons, and his leading role in depriving his father of Joseph, his beloved son?

Then Judah said to Onan ... perform the duty of a brother-in-law to her. Onan was being required to fulfil the law of the Levirate (Deuteronomy 25:5–10). This stated that if a man died without leaving a son, the next eldest brother was required to marry the widow, and the first son to be born of that union would be counted as the offspring of the deceased brother, so that his name "may not be blotted out of Israel". In view of biblical laws of inheritance, making such a marriage could often be to the financial disadvantage of the second brother. Clearly that was Onan's view, and his deliberate practice of *coitus interruptus* was intended to frustrate any possibility of a son being produced for the deceased Er. The law of the Levirate is a major theme of the book of Ruth (which is aware of the parallel with this story of Tamar, see Ruth 4:12).

Judah's efforts to dominate the lives of his sons seem to be highlighted, and to contrast with his own freedom to choose his own wife. But ultimately his efforts at control are all in vain—we quickly discover that it is Yhwh, not Judah, who orders events.

After the death of both Er and Onan Judah clearly regarded his daughter-in-law as "unlucky". His efforts to prevent the death of his youngest son Shelah may be understandable, but they are unfair to Tamar: to return her as a widow to her father's house is anomalous; such an action consigns her to social limbo—and deprives her of any status at all.

In course of time   A reminder that Tamar's purdah had gone on a long time and that Judah had no real intention of fulfilling the requirement to give her in marriage to Shelah, his youngest son.

The wife of Judah, Shua's daughter, died.   The death of Judah's wife bestowed a special preciousness on Shelah, the one remaining son. There would be no more after him, so risking his life becomes even more unthinkable. It also "explains" Judah's desire to use a prostitute.

When Judah's time of mourning was over   The same root, *naham*, which described the grief of Jacob in the previous chapter (37:35) is used again. The contrasting speedy "consolation" of Judah gives us the impression of someone who is infinitely more hard-headed than his father.

[She] sat down at the entrance to Enaim.   The place name, Enaim, has a connection to the Hebrew word for "eye". Sight is clearly a key motif in this story. (Note that the name is repeated in verse 21.)

When Judah saw her, he thought her to be a prostitute, for she had covered her face.   A veil was probably part of the traditional dress of a prostitute. But there is an irony about this "veiling", for it actually conceals Tamar's true identity. As in the previous chapter (37:32) and in 27:15–16, clothing becomes a means of deception.

What will you give me, that you may come in to me?   Tamar's question echoes the brusqueness of Judah's demand. "Come in to me" accurately conveys the impersonality of the words used in Hebrew. It is significant that the normal Hebrew idiom for sexual intercourse—know—is not used here. Transparently Judah does not know Tamar in any meaningful sense.

A kid   Tamar's wages for her services again echo Judah's own deception of Jacob, who had done so by dipping Joseph's robe in the blood of a goat. This parallel was noticed in rabbinic times: "The Holy One, praised be he, said to Judah, 'You deceived your father with a kid. By your life, Tamar will deceive you with a kid.'" (*Bereshit Rabbah* 84)

Give me a pledge, until you send it.   Tamar is "savvy" enough not simply to trust the word of this man. The tokens of pledge she demands, "your signet and your cord, and the staff that is in your hand", amount to the Ancient Middle Eastern equivalent of Judah's identity document and are unique to him; without them Judah could not properly function in society. But Tamar may also be using a double entendre at Judah's expense. The word translated "staff" (*matteh*) also means "tribe" and can refer to the "tribes" of Israel. Is Tamar effectively telling Judah (though he doesn't realize it!), "Give me a tribe of descendants, which will establish us as part of Israel"?

Judah sent the kid.   Judah's next actions suggest that he was embarrassed by what he had done. He uses Hirah the Adullamite as an emissary to try to recover his tokens of pledge, rather than seeking Tamar out again himself. He also suggests to Hirah that he had visited a "temple prostitute", which is one notch up the social ladder from a common whore.

Tamar has played the whore ... she is pregnant.   The double standards are apparent. What is acceptable behaviour for Judah is prohibited for his daughter-in-law. The double standard operates in another dimension as well. Having neglected to take any responsibility for Tamar in the past, sending her back to her father's house, he now assumes the role of paterfamilias and insists on his rights over Tamar's life—and death.

Tamar's moment of triumph is all the greater—coming in the nick of time to save her. She said, "Take note" ... Judah acknowledged them. Both "take note" and "acknowledge" are in Hebrew forms of the same verbal root *nakar* whose core meaning is "recognize". The identical root has also previously appeared in the similar sequence when the brothers had confronted their father with the deceptive robe after the disappearance of

Joseph, and in his response (37:32–33). Once again *Bereshit Rabbah* notes the parallel: "The Holy One, blessed be he, said to Judah, 'You said to your father "Recognize". By your life Tamar will say to you, "Recognize"'".

She is more in the right than I. Finally, Judah acknowledges Tamar's "rights" under the religious code of the time, and that she has taken steps to ensure them, for the well-being of the community. The previous person to be called *tsaddiq* (= in the right) in Genesis was the Gentile Abimelech. Once again, an outsider, Tamar (probably a Canaanite) has been a teacher of righteousness to members of Abraham's family. The acknowledgement of guilt that Judah has made here acts as a precursor to the repentance that he will demonstrate when he and his brothers fall foul of a powerful and mysterious official in Egypt (42:21; 44:18ff.).

38:27-30 The birth of Tamar's twins echoes the birth of their grandfather Jacob and his twin Esau (25:24–26), particularly in view of the mention of "crimson thread" (cf. 25:25) and the fact that the name Zerah (38:30) is also given to one of Esau's grandsons (36:13). The link is a hint that this unorthodox birth to an unorthodox woman is going to be particularly significant in the fulfilment of God's promises to Abraham and his family—even though it is beyond the scope of Genesis to spell this out in full.

The focus of the birth story is clearly on Perez, named after his "Breach". It is Perez who will become the ancestor of the great King David and who will appear in the genealogy at the end of the book of Ruth (Ruth 4:12,18) and at the beginning of the Gospel of Matthew (Matthew 1:3). Once again, a younger son (though this time ambiguously so) will have the major role to play. And the mention of the birth of Perez at just this point in the story, before we hear about the "bondage" of Joseph in Egypt, is probably a hint that there will be a future for Jacob's family beyond Egyptian slavery—but it may not be associated with Joseph.

39:1-39 We move back to focus on Joseph and pick up exactly where we left off in 37:36. And now, for the first time, God and Yhwh seem to make their mark in the life of Joseph. In fact, the six times the name Yhwh comes in this chapter, framing it at the beginning and the end, are almost the only times that it appears in the entire Joseph saga (see comment on 49:18 on p. 337). The name seems to be used by the narrator of the story to highlight his own theological convictions: that Yhwh was working through the ups and downs of Joseph's life to fulfil his purposes and promises to the ancestors. We are told four times that the Lord was with him (39:2,3,21,23), a reflection of Yhwh's promise first to Isaac (26:3) and later to Joseph's father, Jacob (28:15), and twice that Yhwh blessed the household of Potiphar because of Joseph (39:5-6), recalling Yhwh's commitment to Abraham (12:3). In the previous chapter, the activity of Yhwh had been jarringly brutal, suddenly terminating the lives of Judah's wicked sons. What we have now provides a contrast: Yhwh's activity can be beneficial, and part of an ongoing and almost imperceptible process. The comments on Yhwh's activity set the scene for the whole of Joseph's experiences in Egypt—even though Yhwh will not appear by name, he is apparently there in the background bringing about a providential outcome.

Potiphar, an officer of Pharaoh   The word translated "officer" can elsewhere mean "eunuch". A number of interpreters of this passage in antiquity understood this to be Potiphar's situation. In ancient cultures, eunuchs were often preferred for leading political roles. If Potiphar was a eunuch, it might mean that the behaviour of his wife towards Joseph was more understandable!

The Lord blessed the Egyptian's house for Joseph's sake.   As elsewhere in the ancestral stories (e.g. 26:28), a descendant of Abraham becomes a means of blessing for others.

He [Potiphar] left all that he had in Joseph's charge.   Several times in this chapter, it is stated that first Potiphar, and later the prison governor give everything into Joseph's capable charge—or literally "into his hand" (39:4,6,8,22,23). Even in situations of apparent weakness, as a slave or a prisoner, his controlling power quickly becomes apparent. This accentuates the contrast with the situation Joseph will find himself in when he rebuffs Potiphar's wife: he is forced to leave his intimate garment and his fate behind—"in her hand" (39:13). The powerful one is made powerless in the hand of another.

Now Joseph was handsome and good-looking. When an episode is introduced with a line like this we can be sure that trouble lies ahead! What is more, the identical description, in its feminine form, had been used of his mother Rachel (29:17), and that had provoked the bitter love triangle of Jacob, Leah and Rachel. Indeed, one could say that it was Rachel's beauty that had landed Joseph in this predicament in Egypt. It was because of Jacob's love for his mother that Joseph had become the spoilt son, disliked by his half-brothers.

His master's wife cast her eyes on Joseph. The book of Proverbs knows of women like Potiphar's wife, the wily foreign woman out to seduce innocent young men, and warns them to beware (Proverbs 7:1–27). Joseph's response is the "wise" one that Proverbs enjoins on its readers—even though, for the moment, it appears to lead him to disaster. Is a contrast being drawn between Potiphar's wife, who by attempting to lead Joseph astray threatens the existence of his people, and Tamar, another foreign woman, whose actions in the previous chapter had helped to ensure their future?

Lie with me. It is a bald request, (or is it command?) that Potiphar's wife makes to Joseph. The one other person in the Old Testament who is addressed in the same way is Tamar, daughter of David, before she is raped by her brother Amnon (2 Samuel 13:11). Given the fact that this Tamar is also the only other person to own "a long robe with sleeves" the coincidence is intriguing, especially since another Tamar, daughter-in-law of Judah, has just featured in the previous chapter of Genesis. Whatever their literary and historical relationship may be, there do seem to be interesting resonances between family quarrels of David's sons (2 Samuel 13–1 Kings 2) and the stories of the unruly sons of Jacob.

But he refused. In the Hebrew Bible, over the word translated "refused" there is the rare *shalshelet* sign (see comment on 19:16 on p. 144). Here it suggests that Joseph may have considerably wavered before making up his mind.

"How then could I do this great wickedness, and sin against God?" This is the first time the word "God" has passed Joseph's lips. He is no longer the centre of his own universe. God (rather than YHWH) is appropriate here since Joseph is speaking to an Egyptian (see also 40:8; 41:16, etc.). The moral code by which Joseph is operating would have been accepted by both Israelites and Egyptians, for both of whom adultery was a serious offence. The Egyptian "Tale of the Two Brothers" in which the wife of the elder brother attempts to seduce his younger sibling provides a close parallel to this incident.[81] But Joseph also refuses the advances of the woman because it would have betrayed his master's trust. The inference of the passage is that the tenets of prudence and human decency are a good guide to the will of God: such a view is characteristic of the wisdom tradition in both Israel and Egypt.

My husband has brought among us a Hebrew to insult us. Hell hath no fury like a woman scorned. She tries to get the rest of the household on her side and distance Joseph from them by choosing to describe him as a "Hebrew". The word takes us "fast forward" to the time of Israel's slavery in Egypt when it will be used frequently in Exodus 1–3. Joseph's descent into Egypt may save his family's life, but it will also ultimately lead to their servitude. Her cry of "insult", repeated by the woman to her husband in verse 17, comes from the root *tsahaq*, which has appeared at various key points in Genesis, variously translated as laugh, jest, play, fondle, or indeed "Isaac" (see p. 134). Its use here may reinforce the sexual undercurrents of its other appearances, but also helps to draw connections between this chapter in the life of Joseph and the story of Isaac, when YHWH had first explicitly promised to be "with" Abraham's family.

She kept his garment by her until his master came home. This is the second time in the life of Joseph that an article of his clothing has been used by others as an instrument of deception. The reference to Potiphar as "his master" instead of by his name reinforces the precariousness of Joseph's situation.

When his master heard the words that his wife spoke to him ... he became enraged. But with whom? Did he have a shrewd idea of his wife's complicity? If he had really been convinced of Joseph's guilt it is likely that he would have fed him to the Nile crocodiles! Slaves were executed for less. Instead, he seeks to solve the conundrum by ridding himself of Joseph in a way that may be unpleasant but is at least not inevitably terminal.

The LORD was with Joseph. Not only does the writer remind us again of Yhwh's presence with Joseph in the guardhouse, but his comment that Yhwh "showed him steadfast love" draws on the word *hesed* from covenant vocabulary. Joseph is the great grandson of Abraham. Joseph has gone down into the pit, down into Egypt, down into slavery, and now down even further into prison, and apparently forgotten. But Yhwh will not forget his promises—or Joseph.

40:1–23 *Some time after this, the cupbearer of the king of Egypt and his baker offended their lord the king of Egypt.* We are not told how these royal officials had erred or whether their imprisonment was justified. But the arbitrary nature of their eventual contrasting fates perhaps hints that their initial imprisonment was itself due simply to the capriciousness of Pharaoh—an implicit reminder that others, as well as Joseph, could experience a miscarriage of justice.

They both dreamed. The story of Joseph—and his descent into the "pit"—had begun with a pair of dreams—does this next pair of dreams now indicate that we have reached another point of transition in Joseph's life?

Do not interpretations belong to God? Please tell them to me! Joseph's remarks are ambiguous—probably deliberately so. Is he contrasting an "Israelite" view with the traditional Egyptian one which held that dream interpretation was a science that could be mastered by study? On the surface, he sounds like a very different figure to the arrogant "master of dreams" (37:19), whose own dreams placed himself at the centre and allowed no space at all for God. Yet read carefully, the juxtaposition of the two sentences results in Joseph making a significant claim for himself—interpretation may belong to God, but he, Joseph, is implicitly setting himself up as God's interpreter. He may be appearing to efface himself, yet at the same time he is claiming special access to divine wisdom. From this point on, Joseph will appear increasingly "god-like"; possessing a hidden knowledge about events and people that is concealed from other participants in the story.

But remember me when it is well with you. After assuring the cupbearer that he will be restored to favour and "raised up" once again, Joseph asks for a favour in return—that of being remembered.

Make mention of me to Pharaoh. Underlying this phrase is a verb (*zakar*) that also comes from the same verbal root as "remember", which Joseph has used in the first half of his request: "remembering" will become increasingly important in the following chapters as Joseph encounters his brothers once again.

I was stolen ... I have done nothing that they should have put me into the dungeon. This is actually the first time since his troubles started that Joseph has been allowed to express his feelings about the injustice of his situation. Stripped of his garments (twice), he is now also metaphorically unmasked. Soon he will be reclothed in glory—once again with a mask to hide his emotions behind. The passion of these words is accentuated by Joseph's choice of vocabulary. The emphatic repetition in Hebrew of the verb "stolen" gives a glimpse into Joseph's sense of pain which so far has been concealed by the narrator, while the word he has used for "dungeon" was that previously used for the "cistern" into which his brothers had thrown him. He has sunk down—and down again. The treachery he experienced in Potiphar's house has resonated in his mind with the betrayal by his brothers.

When the chief baker Rabbinic comments on the differing fates of the two officials tried to maintain that the arrangement of the loaves and baskets in the baker's dream suggested that he was less conscientious than his cupbearing contemporary and thus deserved his punishment. Joseph's interpretative skills are employed here with at least a hint of sadism. He uses the identical expression, "lift up your head", as had previously depicted the cupbearer's restoration to favour—but then shatters the baker's hopes. In this case the head will be up—and off!

The chief cupbearer did not remember Joseph, but forgot him. These verbs of remembering and forgetting here accentuate this moment as the nadir of Joseph's life. He has, quite literally, reached the pits! The previous chapter, although it moved Joseph from being house slave to prisoner, at least ended with a positive note that recapitulated the chapter's introduction. Not so here. We had hoped that the dreams might indeed indicate a change of fortune for Joseph, but it is not to be. He is not only imprisoned; he is also now totally alone.

41:1–57 *After two whole years Pharaoh dreamed.* This third set of dreams, again a pair, finally fulfil our hopes—and ultimately the hopes of Joseph's own dreams—while the dreams of the previous chapter had only tantalized us. The Hebrew idiom emphasizes the passing of time—Joseph remained forgotten in the dungeon for a long time.

He was standing by the Nile. The story begins to take on particular local colour—as well as using a number of words borrowed from the Egyptian language, e.g. "reed grass" (41:2). Since the prosperity of Egypt always depended on the annual flood of the Nile, the fact that in his dream Pharaoh is standing on the riverbank is appropriate and symbolic. And the number seven plays a key role, acting as a clear link between Pharaoh's two dreams.

Blighted by the east wind This too is a note of geographical realism. The *khamsin* wind that blows from the eastern desert in Palestine and Egypt as winter moves into summer is notorious for its fierceness and ability to shrivel vegetation overnight.

I remember my faults today.   An ambiguous comment. Is the cupbearer referring to his earlier "offence" against Pharaoh, or his omission in forgetting to mention Joseph's name to him earlier? The ambiguity probably hints at the embarrassment the cupbearer felt at "reminding" (the Hebrew root *zakar* ["remember"] is used again) Pharaoh of how he had once fallen so catastrophically out of favour. Memories are not always pleasant—and can be difficult to acknowledge.

When he had shaved himself and changed his clothes   Once again leaving his clothes behind marks a change of status for Joseph—only this time for the better.

It is not I; God will give Pharaoh a favourable answer.   Joseph seems to have learned humility and "erases" himself to allow God to take centre stage. But as with 40:8 we might question how real this self-effacement actually is, since he immediately assumes for himself the role of God's mouthpiece. Indeed, since on the surface the dreams seem to presage disaster—rather than prosperity—it is a strange assurance that Joseph feels able to offer. Perhaps indeed that is why Pharaoh's own wise men had felt it wiser not to interpret the dreams! Joseph's assurance is one that cannot be fulfilled simply by his interpretation of the dreams, but only by the advice he himself then goes on to offer.

The doubling of Pharaoh's dream   Repetition is often used in the biblical tradition to underscore the importance of an event. But, if Pharaoh's dreams are more sure because of their repetition, is not this also a hint that Joseph's own doubled dreams, experienced all those years ago, will very shortly—and surely—be fulfilled?

Let Pharaoh select a man who is discerning and wise.   Joseph now takes the opportunity to extend his advice beyond bare dream-interpretation, making practical suggestions as to how Pharaoh should respond to the events predicted by the dreams.

The Hebrew root *hakam* ("wise") only appears in Genesis in Chapter 41. In 41:8, it describes the "wise men" of Pharaoh's court, whose wisdom had failed them when they had been asked to interpret Pharaoh's dream.

Is Joseph's remark a pointed one—pointing in his own direction? Certainly, Pharaoh picks up this hint when he repeats the expression in 41:39. The suggestion that Pharaoh "should set [someone] over the land of Egypt" echoes the situation Joseph had found himself in as overseer, in both Potiphar's house (39:4) and the prison (39:22).

Can we find anyone else like this—one in whom is the spirit of God? Back at humanity's beginning, there had been a close connection between God's spirit, creativity and planning, and the task and boundaries assigned to humanity (e.g. 1:2; 6:3). Are we to see Joseph as fulfilling at last the role that was intended for human beings—finding through God the wisdom that the man and woman had sought illicitly (3:6)? And will Joseph's viceregency in Egypt correspond in some ways to the position of viceroy of creation which God had hoped to bestow on humanity? Joseph is virtually portrayed here as a royal figure: wearing a royal ring, with royal garments (note the change of attire once more!) and ornaments (41:42). The connection with the "spirit of God" observed by Pharaoh further confirms this royal status: for the "spirit of wisdom" was par excellence a gift bestowed on kings (Isaiah 11:2). Joseph's own past dreams of grandeur are now well on the way to being fulfilled.

Pharaoh gave Joseph the name Zaphenath-paneah. Joseph is being thoroughly Egyptianized. He is given an Egyptian name, which seems to mean "God speaks and he lives". It is worth remembering that Joseph's father Jacob had also been renamed: by his divine assailant at Penuel (32:28). It was then that Israel had become Israel. What therefore does it imply when Israel's son is renamed by a foreign ruler, especially one who claimed to be a god? The ambiguity in this name change is reinforced by its meaning. The connection with "life" is appropriate for the story of Joseph, but the name could be interpreted to mean that either Pharaoh, or even Joseph himself, was the giver of this life. He is also given an Egyptian wife, who seems to have an intriguing possible connection with the family of Potiphar, the household where Joseph was a slave. Both Abraham and Isaac had been concerned to ensure that their sons should marry within the family, preserving the purity of their lineage. Joseph's situation provides a sharp contrast: accentuated even more since his wife has important links with Egyptian religion. "On" (modern Heliopolis) was the major sanctuary of the Egyptian sun-god, Ra.

Joseph gained authority over the land of Egypt. Walter Brueggemann points out how many times the word "all" (variously translated into English) occurs between 41:45–57. The effect is to emphasize the total control that Joseph exercises—not only over the Egyptians, but ultimately over the destiny of the world. "Either he [Joseph] acts for God or he usurps the life-giving function of God. Either way, he is the immediate source of life and well-being."[82] Perhaps this apparent ambiguity with which the narrator presents us is deliberate. How far does this "new Adam" avoid Adam's mistakes, even while fulfilling Adam's destiny?

Two sons ... Joseph named the firstborn Manasseh By naming his first son "Causing to forget" Joseph seems to be turning his back on his past, and committing himself and his family to a totally Egyptian future. To forget all his troubles—his past servitude and imprisonment—he needs also to forget his father's family whose antipathy to him had been their cause. But in a narrative in which remembrance has such a pivotal role to play can forgetfulness be a solution? Will not memories, both good and bad, be forced upon him?

The second he named Ephraim. If the name of the elder boy marked an attempt to reject the past, the name of the younger clearly points to a fruitful future. It is not a fruitfulness that is to be restricted to Joseph alone—it is what he was also offering to the Egyptians. It was, moreover, what God had commanded human beings to do at the point of their creation (1:28) and a promise that he had reiterated when he made a covenant with Abraham (17:6) and pledged to Joseph's own father Jacob when he had travelled to a foreign land (28:14). Despite all his attempts at "forgetting", it seems that Joseph is a descendant of Abraham in spite of himself.

Lives bound together
42:1–45:28

Chapters 42–45 form a parallel to 37 and 39–41. In the earlier chapters, we experienced the passion and resurrection of Joseph; now we are going to share in a passion and resurrection of Jacob and his other sons. There are a number of verbal hints that make this connection clear. Both sequences are recounted in detail and with no attempt at an economy of words. And in both cases, there are one, or possibly more, false climaxes—when we expect a denouement or resolution, but we are forced to wait for it. There is, however, one important difference: in the earlier chapters Joseph is one participant among several in the story, and sometimes its victim. Now the "voices" of Joseph and the narrator of the story seem to coalesce, and the direction of the story is quite clearly controlled by Joseph, who is privileged to have information concealed from the other characters in the plot.

42:1-38 *"Why do you keep looking at one another?"* The hesitation of the brothers is pointed up by the harsh words Jacob uses to them. Despite the gap of space and time (twenty years!) provided by Chapters 39–41, we seem to be back to the old story of intra-family hostility. The last occasions on which the verb "look" was used with Jacob's sons as its subject it described how they saw with envy that Joseph was their father's favourite (37:4)—and how they saw an Ishmaelite caravan of slave traders bound for Egypt (37:25) to which they then had consigned Joseph. No wonder that they are now paralysed by inaction. Is it their guilty consciences, or an innate Israelite hostility to Egypt that deters them from making a move in the direction of the one country which could offer food to its neighbours in times of shortage?

Jacob did not send Joseph's brother Benjamin with his brothers The old cycle of "favouritism", which has plagued family relationships since Cain and Abel, begins again. This time can there be a more positive outcome?

The sons of Israel ... came to buy grain Imperceptibly Joseph's brothers (42:3) have become the sons of Israel—not merely the sons of Jacob. It is as the sons of Israel that they will grow to the size of a nation in Egypt, and under that name that their descendants will experience the Exodus.

Joseph's brothers came and bowed themselves before him. The old dream in which Joseph saw his brothers prostrating themselves before him is now being fulfilled—even if Joseph's brothers are oblivious of this.

When Joseph saw his brothers, he recognized them, but he treated them like strangers. A deep sense of split runs through these chapters—and the story will not be able to come to its end until this has been healed. It is a division that reaches back into earlier sections of Genesis. The word "recognize" (Hebrew: *nakar*) has a key function in helping to create this "splitness". It has been used at several significant moments in the past when people have tried to deceive each other. Isaac did not "recognize" Jacob because of his deceptive garb (27:23); Jacob invites Laban to "point out" (same Hebrew verb) his household gods—a task that is made impossible because of Rachel's deceptive actions (31:32); Joseph's brothers invite Jacob to "recognize" their brother's robe deceptively dipped in the blood of a goat (37:33); and Tamar also uses the word when she invites Judah to reclaim the objects that she had previously taken from him while playing her assumed role of harlot (38:25). Here, by contrast, the fact that Joseph recognizes his brothers is a statement of truth: they really are his brothers, and he really does recognize them. The falsity is not now in the recognition, but what comes afterwards. For instead of acting as one might when recognizing long-lost relatives, Joseph pretended not to know them. Ironically, and punningly, the phrase "treated them like strangers" comes from the same Hebrew verb as does the verb "recognize"—even though its meaning in translation is so very different. It is the writer's way of suggesting to us that Joseph is for the moment internally "split". He cannot bring himself to be "whole", and so the truth cannot yet be visible.

The point is underscored by the laboured repetition in the next verse: "Although Joseph had recognized his brothers, they did not recognize him." Full and mutual recognition cannot take place until the brothers are capable of recognizing their own guilt.

Joseph also remembered the dreams that he had dreamed about them. Recognition (Hebrew: *nakar*) and remembrance (Hebrew: *zakar*) belong together, and indeed in Hebrew the verbs have a similarity of sound. For Joseph who had called his first son "Causing to forget", remembering is a painful process, and provokes him to anger. Memories have still much healing to go through. It is interesting to note precisely what Joseph remembers—the dreams in which his family lay prostrate before him—a memory triggered by the fact that this is what his brothers have just done. But as the dreams led ultimately to his servitude, his memories lead him swiftly to recall his brothers' treachery. The narrator encourages us to enter Joseph's thought processes without precisely spelling them out. "You are spies" might sound like an illogical accusation, but it makes sense in view of Joseph's sense of betrayal.

No my lord; your servants The expression "your servant/servants" will be repeated more than twenty times in the coming three chapters. Though its use is due to the "courtly" context in which the action is taking place, the frequent repetition acts as an implicit reminder that Joseph's dreams of grandeur vis-à-vis the rest of his family have clearly been fulfilled.

We are all sons of one man. The brothers say more than they realize, as they unwittingly seem to include Joseph among their number.

We, your servants, are twelve brothers. Once again, using the present tense, the brothers inadvertently group Joseph with themselves.

The irony continues as they claim "And one is no more" precisely as they are talking to that very "one". The same Hebrew idiom appeared in Reuben's anguished cry when he discovered Joseph's disappearance from the pit (37:30). Throughout these verses the emphasis on unity as "sons of one man" adds to the pathos of the fractured family.

Here is how you shall be tested. The test that Joseph proposes would not check whether or not the brothers are "spies"—indeed if they had been it would have facilitated the successful completion of their spying mission. It does, however, begin to put them to the real test Joseph is setting before them—to uncover their attitude to Benjamin, Joseph's full brother, currently kept safe by his father's side, who had apparently replaced Joseph as family favourite.

As Pharaoh lives   This is the only instance in the Old Testament when an "Israelite" takes an oath by a foreign god or royal figure. Joseph's apparent assimilation is very thoroughgoing! It also begs the question when, in his next sentence, he offers the reassurance "for I fear God", as to which God or god he fears.

If you are honest men   The mitigation of Joseph's original command that all except one should remain prisoner, into the alternative suggestion that all except one might return, is still for the moment conditional. How will Joseph decide if they are honest men? Is it as a result of the conversation between the brothers which Joseph then overhears?

For the first time, we hear of Joseph's distress in the pit. "He pleaded with us." That agony of Joseph had not been mentioned previously. Fittingly the brothers themselves have just had to plead for their own lives—even though they did not realize to whom they were doing so. This beginning of the brothers' repentance seems to convince Joseph that they are honest men, and to ameliorate his sentence even though the brothers themselves must have been puzzled as to why this has happened—especially since they do not know that Joseph can listen to them. As in 37:22, Reuben seems to act as the conscience of the brothers.

There comes a reckoning for his blood.   Judah had implied (37:26–27) that a reason for the selling of Joseph had been to avoid bloodguilt. Are the brothers' guilty consciences now prompting them to admit to themselves that they had effectively been consigning their brother to a death-sentence?

They did not know that Joseph understood.   If they had refused to listen when Joseph had pleaded with them in the past, it is a fine touch that Joseph should now be listening to them with an unnecessary interpreter acting as a decoy. Joseph had never really heard his brothers in his past life either—being all too full of his own importance. Is there also a significance that it should be Simeon—with "hearing" in his name (see 29:33)—whom he selects as his hostage?

He turned away from them and wept. The three times that Joseph weeps as his reconciliation with his brothers progresses mount towards an emotional crescendo. Little by little Joseph himself seems to change to match the alteration in his brothers.

Joseph ... gave orders ... to return every man's money to his sack. The word translated as "money" is the same word as appears in Chapter 37 as "silver". After their "sale" of Joseph the sons of Jacob had then returned to their father with silver instead of one of their number (37:28). This action on Joseph's part seems intended to "spook" the brothers into remembering more deeply that earlier "trade" of a brother for silver.

What is this that God has done to us? Here and in 44:16, where the brothers see God's hand in their predicament, they ironically speak more than they know. Corresponding to the "split" within Joseph, the brothers too find themselves operating, albeit unwillingly, on two levels. On the one hand, they are involved in and punished for a series of incidents for which they are genuinely innocent, which lead, however, to the uncovering of their long-suppressed guilt relating to Joseph. We, the readers, know that the brothers' cry of anguish here relates, even if unconsciously, to God's retribution for their earlier apparent fratricide. But perhaps even we do not yet know the whole story: if we accept Joseph's "reading" of events, as will be suggested in 45:5 and 50:20, "what God has done to them" is ultimately to preserve the family of Jacob at a time of famine. Over the next two chapters, these two sets of "splits", in Joseph and the brothers, will gradually collide together. Will integration or fragmentation be the result?

The man, the lord of the land The description of Joseph as lord of the country is repeated in 42:33. Even in their self-selected turn of speech the brothers find themselves putting into effect Joseph's earlier dreams of grandeur.

You may trade in the land The brothers subtly "edit" their conversation with Joseph when they report it to their father. Not surprisingly they omit the discussion they had concerning their involvement in Joseph's disappearance. But they add this comment—which was not in Joseph's original words. The verb "trade" is closely related to the noun "traders" (37:28). Are their guilty consciences prompting them to remember aloud the previous occasion when they "traded" with Egypt—their own brother? And although Joseph had never mentioned "trading" with the sons of Jacob, another "foreigner" had once done so—Hamor, the prince of Shechem (34:10), and he had been treated with a duplicity that had disgusted even Jacob. Might not this mention of "trading" start to trigger memories in Jacob's mind of just how violent and deceitful his sons could be?

In each one's sack was his bag of money ... they were dismayed. It is far from clear that the brothers had yet mentioned to their father the one lot of silver that they had discovered on the journey. Now they are in no position to conceal from him this far greater quantity. Who are they afraid of? At this distance it is surely not Joseph. Is it God? Or their father? The last thing they wanted to do was to remind him of a former occasion when they had returned home minus one of their brothers, and with a mysterious quantity of silver.

I am the one you have bereaved of children. This apparent accusation is the closest Jacob gets to suggesting that the brothers had complicity in the loss of Joseph. Is it simply an extravagant figure of speech? Or has Jacob really suspected the true story all these years?

Reuben said to his father In these verses, the characters of both Reuben and Jacob are delineated. Reuben makes a suggestion which is well-meaning but feels as ineffectual as when he had once tried to assist Joseph. Just as then he had not succeeded in restoring Joseph to his father (37:22), so now his extravagant offer does not give Jacob the confidence that he will be able to "restore" Benjamin. Similarly, Jacob remains self-centred in his grief, in a way that parallels the end of Chapter 37.

My son shall not go down with you. The comment illustrates the sharp disparity between the comparative worth of Benjamin and Simeon in Jacob's eyes. To state "he [Benjamin] alone is left" in front of nine of his other sons is a sharp reminder of the favouritism that had caused the problem in the first place.

43:1–34 The pace of the story now seems to slow down—at times almost unbearably so. How long will Joseph be able to maintain his charade, or will his feelings at last overwhelm him?

The language of the story shifts as well: it takes on both a new formality and a pathos. Throughout this chapter the brothers' father is referred to consistently as "Israel" rather than Jacob. The brothers refer to Joseph as "the man" (43:3,5), and in turn are called by him "the men" (43:16). Yet we also meet for the first time in Genesis expressions such as "grant ... mercy" and "overcome with affection", both of which contain the Hebrew root *raham*, that is connected with the word for "womb" and is often used when powerful emotions are at stake. It is used to describe God's parental feelings for Israel in Jeremiah 31:20. Indeed, the exquisite passage Jeremiah 31:15–22 has a number of interesting links with Genesis 43. Both are concerned with Rachel's children; in both weeping is prominent. Is it possible that in Genesis 43 we have in story form something of the grief and pain experienced by the nation "Israel" and its lost tribes (see e.g. Jeremiah 31:7–8) throughout its history? The note in 43:32 is possible confirmation of this. It reads not simply as a comment about social behaviour on a particular occasion but reflects on the ongoing relationship with Egypt throughout centuries of history.

If you will send our brother with us Jacob may have refused to "trade" Benjamin to save the life of one of his other brothers, but with the continuation of the famine it is Benjamin's own life, as well as that of the rest of the family, which is at stake, and this forces a change of mind on Jacob's part. His complaint to his sons that they had admitted that they had another brother is somewhat incongruous. Was he asking his sons to be deceptive? It is as incongruous as the brothers' protestation, both directly to Joseph (42:11) and repeated in their report to their father (42:31), that "[w]e are honest men". A strange twist coming from men who have lived a lie for a whole generation, and who even now slightly "doctor" the report they present to their father of the conversation they had in Egypt (43:7).

Judah said... "I myself shall be surety for him" The interplay between the "effective" Judah and the "ineffective" Reuben (42:37) parallels their roles in Chapter 37. But the word "surety" also recapitulates Judah's experiences in Chapter 38, when he had offered a "pledge" (a word that comes from the same Hebrew root), to Tamar. The inner growth of Judah through that experience will become obvious in the course of the next two chapters.

Carry... down as a present to the man. Once before Jacob/Israel had sought to propitiate a wrong by offering an expensive gift (to his brother Esau). Now even though the "wrong" is not his own he tries the same tack. Inadvertently, he suggests a gift that links us back to the moment when Joseph was abducted to Egypt—via a camel caravan carrying many of the same items (37:25).

Take double the money. Suddenly a sense of "doubling" pervades the narratives: the money, and the journey that could have been made twice (43:10). Perhaps it reinforces the hint that in some senses Benjamin is the "double" of Joseph. Certainly, Jacob's comments about the grave or Sheol (42:38) as he expresses his potential grief for Benjamin recall the similar words he used when he actually grieved for Joseph (37:35). So are the brothers going to commit the "double" of their first crime? It will not be difficult to "lose" Benjamin on this hazardous journey.

May God Almighty grant you mercy before the man. "God Almighty" is a title reserved for use at significant moments in the ancestral story (17:1; 28:3; 35:11). Its association with blessing and fruitfulness makes it appropriate at this time of famine, and its link with the patriarchal promise of descendants means that it is telling that Israel should use it as he fears for the loss of further sons. "Grant you mercy" is echoed in the way that Joseph responds to Benjamin (see above and notes on 43:30 below). Jacob is presumably hoping that the powerful Egyptian will not maltreat a group of defenceless strangers. However, we, the readers, are wondering at the same time if Joseph is eventually going to be merciful to his brothers.

The men are to dine with me at noon. Is it significant that it is noted twice that this meal is at midday? (See also 43:25.) Presumably the meal that the brothers ate while Joseph was in the pit (37:25) was also a midday meal. The fear that the invitation to share in this meal engendered in the brothers (43:18) suggests that if the invitation was a deliberate attempt to prod guilty consciences, it was succeeding.

Your God and the God of your father must have put treasure ... for you. The steward's comment verbalizes many of the ironies of this narrative. Although he must have known that it was people acting at Joseph's behest who had replaced the silver in the sacks, he is in one sense telling the truth: for the implied premise is that God's will is activated via the deeds of the human protagonists in this story. And although the silver in the sacks might have seemed a threat to the brothers it was in reality treasure—a symbol of God's efforts to fulfil his promises to Abraham and his family. The phrase "God of your father" further hints at the patriarchal promises (e.g. 26:24).

There is, however, perhaps another irony: are we meant to think that Joseph is acting as though he believes he is God?

They brought him the present ... and bowed to the ground before him. The story is "closing in" on its protagonists with the presentation of the gifts that would have reminded Joseph of his brothers' treachery, accompanied by a gesture of subservience which again recalled his own dreams.

Your servant our father is well. By their turn of phrase, the brothers now further fulfil Joseph's dreams, this time including their father (at least by proxy) in their language of subservience. The word "well" translates the Hebrew *shalom* which appears three times in 43:27–28. We are swiftly rewound to the opening verses of the entire story when we had been explicitly told that Joseph had been sent by his father to Shechem to enquire about the *shalom* of his brothers (37:14; cf. 37:4).

His mother's son   As well as helping us to identify Benjamin, the only full brother of Joseph, this phrase accentuates the pathos. The Rachel who wept for her children (Jeremiah 31:15) and died tragically young in giving birth to Benjamin echoes through this phrase. Joseph's yearning for Benjamin verbally parallels the grief that Rachel and even God feel for their children: it is symptomatic that Joseph's first words to his brother are "God be gracious to you, my son!" Surely concealed behind this familial phrase seems to be Joseph's desire to recognize Benjamin as his brother—and his agony that this is a step he is still psychologically unable to take.

Joseph ... was about to weep   The pressure is building up. But wise men were proud of being able to control their emotions. So Joseph ensures that his weeping is done privately.

They served him by himself.   Just as he had been kept separate when his brothers ate that other meal years before (37:24–25).

The Egyptians could not eat with the Hebrews, for that is an abomination. We suddenly stand outside the story for a moment and hear of centuries of alienation. The term "Hebrews" immediately identifies the brothers as outsiders, part of a group distrusted by "settled society" whether in Egypt or elsewhere. But the complicated eating arrangements also highlight the fact that even Joseph himself was not fully accepted by the Egyptians (43:32). For all his apparent power he too still remained a "Hebrew" outsider.

The firstborn according to his birthright and the youngest according to his youth.   The mysterious knowledge that is being indicated about the family age order might well cause the brothers to look "at one another in amazement". It was accentuated by the special honour shown to Benjamin, since normally the eldest in a family would receive this position. In several ways, this meal functions like a "rerun" of the day when the brothers had sold the "favourite", Joseph.

So they drank and were merry with him. So often in stories recognition takes place while people are eating and drinking together—remember the road to Emmaus?—that we are primed to expect Joseph's revelation of himself to his brothers to take place—now. The further delay is almost painful for the reader.

44:1-34 The story now progresses to its denouement, catching up not only events in the earlier history of Joseph and the brothers, but even incidents that date back to the adventures of Jacob himself.

Put my cup, the silver cup, in the top of the sack of the youngest. Benjamin is the deliberate target for Joseph's actions—it is only by framing him that Joseph will be able to measure how far his other brothers have changed.

Does he not indeed use it for divination? That the cup is ostensibly used for divination is clearly a significant feature of the narrative. The link is reiterated in 44:15. The reference to the divining cup helps to preserve Joseph's cover as an Egyptian: divination was a popular skill in Egypt. At the same time, it would have uncomfortably reminded the brothers that Joseph was likely to be able to "see through" them, even their previous misdeeds that they hoped were safely buried deep in the past. The use of the Hebrew root *nahash* to refer both to the divining cup and to Joseph himself as diviner suggests a further possibility. There seems to be a connection intended between this incident and Jacob and Rachel's earlier dealings with Laban. Laban (30:27) uses the identical Hebrew root when he comments in 30:27 "I have learned by divination" (see comments on 30:27 on p. 240). And what is the connection between this ability of Laban to "divine", and the household gods that Rachel then stole from her father? Were they Laban's divining tools, the equivalent of Joseph's cup?

Should it be found with any one of your servants, let him die. Once before, similar rash words had been uttered. That time it had been Jacob who pronounced a death sentence on the one who had "stolen" Laban's household gods, without realizing that it was his beloved Rachel who had done so (31:32). When later Rachel died in childbirth it seemed in effect the working out of Jacob's curse. Now a similar death sentence is being uttered over the one who has stolen this religious object. It will soon turn out that Benjamin is the thief, albeit unwittingly. Will he have a similar penalty to pay to that exacted from Rachel? The association becomes sharper because it was the very act of giving birth to Benjamin himself that had been the immediate cause of Rachel's death. Are all the lies and trickery that have plagued this family for generations now going to land on Benjamin's innocent head—for him to pay the penalty?

The cup was found in Benjamin's sack   By the time the discovery is made, the penalty that is to be exacted has been lightened. It is agreed that the culprit will be enslaved, not killed, and that he alone will be liable. This would allow the brothers, if they chose, to abandon Benjamin to his fate with a reasonable conscience—only slavery, not death—exactly as they had once abandoned Joseph decades previously. The fact that they all choose to return to the city is an indication that they have radically changed.

God has found out the guilt of your servants   Which crime is Judah talking about? The "innocent" theft of the cup of which they are publicly being charged, or the long-hidden guilty "theft" of their brother whom they had allowed to be "stolen" (40:15) from his native land? It is as though the two events are coalescing in Judah's mind. The divining cup, hidden in a sack of grain, has almost become a visible symbol for Joseph the diviner, "hidden" for so many years in Egypt, land of grain.

Only the one ... shall be my slave.   Joseph gives them yet another opportunity to abandon Benjamin. After all, by now, the brothers must have got quite used to explaining to Jacob how they had come to return home with one of their number missing!

Then Judah   What follows is the longest speech by a human being in the whole of Genesis. In it, the book seems to come full circle, at least in some measure "healing" the hurts that have plagued human beings since Cain's jealousy of his brother Abel erupted into violence. Judah can finally accept the unfair and arbitrary nature of parental love, however personally painful to him it is.

His father loves him. What has brought about this sea change in Judah—the brother who in Chapter 37 took the lead in seeking to be rid of a favoured brother (37:26) by selling him as a slave? Perhaps it is his experiences with his own sons, the loss of two and the desire to keep hold of the remaining one, about which we heard so much in Chapter 38, that has led him to be more understanding of the passion of parental love.

His life is bound up in the boy's life. The way that one human life interweaves with and affects the lives of others is a key theme of the saga of Joseph, and the whole of Genesis.

It is debatable whether the NRSV translation of the word *naar* as "boy" is most appropriate here. Perhaps "young man" would be better. The same word *naar* also described Ishmael (21:17) and Isaac (22:5). Its use here reminds us of the preciousness of Benjamin: is he to be lost to his father, like those earlier two boys/young men almost were to theirs?

Let your servant remain as a slave ... in place of the boy. With this offer to act as a substitute Judah atones for the crime of Chapter 37 in which he played a leading role. His acceptance of servitude for himself is appropriate retribution for his involvement in the enslavement of another. The expression "your servant became surety", which is in origin a legal term, helps to underline the formal seriousness of what Judah is offering, as well as the links back to Judah's experiences in Chapter 38 (see also comments on 43:9, above). Jon Levenson comments:

> The enormous power behind Judah's offer derives from the complicated set of substitutions that it articulates. Judah will be the substitute for Benjamin, accepting upon himself the slavery to which Joseph has sentenced his younger brother. But Benjamin is himself a substitute, standing in for that other beloved son and child of Rachel and Jacob's old age, Joseph. And Joseph and

Benjamin are both, in some deeper sense, substitutes for their father and thus paradigms for the people Israel.[83]

45:1-28 *Joseph could no longer control himself.* As a result of the words of Judah, the impasse is finally broken and the convoluted layers of mutual deceit fall away.

Joseph made himself known to his brothers. Finally too, knowledge, sight, recognition and hearing all coincide, and all are true—instead of as previously, so often playing off against each other as instruments of deceit.

He wept so loudly The motif of Joseph's weeping also reaches its climax. He has now become almost the antithesis of the traditional picture of a "wise man", who prized themselves on their composure. Weeping is a stage on the road to healing and reconciliation, as elsewhere in the Bible it sows the seeds of transformation and resurrection. A Jewish midrash on this passage aptly puts it, "Tears extinguish the coals of the heart" (*Midrash Lekah Tov Gen* 43:30).

I am Joseph. Is my father still alive? The words of Joseph are even simpler in the Hebrew than English. It is significant that Joseph's first thought after his self-disclosure is for his father. In view of his brothers' earlier remarks (e.g. 43:28; 44:20) it was not a question he really needed to ask. That he does so now further hints at the way that the lives of Joseph and his father are bound so closely together. Just as the apparent death of Joseph had provoked Jacob to speak of going down to Sheol (37:35), so the "resurrection" of Joseph will bring new life to his father.

His brothers could not answer him Though the brothers are formally in "his presence", they cannot yet emotionally "face" Joseph or speak to him. Echoes of humanity's discomfiture before YHWH in Genesis 3, and perhaps the reconciliation of Jacob and Esau, are present.

God sent me before you to preserve life... It was not you who sent me here, but God. Joseph is very sure of himself. Certainly, the God of Genesis is a God who grants and seeks life, despite the flood. But just as we might remember that Joseph's dreams of greatness in Chapter 37 were Joseph's own and God did not feature in them, so we might also wonder whether, now that they have been apparently fulfilled, God was quite so involved in the process that led to this as Joseph might like to believe. Are human beings quite such passive pawns in a grand schema as Joseph implies? The stories of his father (Genesis 27:1–33:17) suggest that human beings need to bear responsibility for their actions, even if they are also part of a greater providence. And by letting his brothers off the hook, Joseph is conveniently also side-stepping the fact that his own behaviour may have contributed to their hostility.

To keep alive for you many survivors   The language used echoes the motif of the "remnant" which is a significant theme in prophetic literature, particularly in relation to the exile (see e.g. Isaiah 10:21–22). It is also a term used in Sirach 44:17 to describe the role of Noah. There are subtle hints that link this famine "throughout the world" (41:57) to the flood. Joseph's brothers are being told that they are fortunate to escape such a calamity.

God has made me lord of all Egypt.   In 41:41, we were explicitly told that it was Pharaoh who established Joseph in this position. What does this imply for the relationship between God, Pharaoh and Joseph? One reading would be that Joseph was somehow "identifying" God's will with Pharaoh's: a dubious proposition in a country such as Egypt notorious for regarding its ruler as divine.

The "land of Goshen" was a fertile area near the Nile delta, close to Sinai. Historically nomads were often allowed to settle there by the rulers of Egypt.

Tell my father how greatly I am honoured in Egypt.   It is difficult to like Joseph even at this moment of apparent reconciliation. He still remains the "spoilt" son who wants his father to realize how much he has "made good". And he seems very much determined to stay in control of his brothers' and his father's lives.

He kissed all his brothers. They are only able to "talk with" Joseph when they have been individually greeted by him. They, no less than Joseph himself, need to be treated as unique individuals.

I may give you the best of the land of Egypt. Pharaoh is almost excessively generous. But the relationship between Egyptians and Joseph's family will go through an almost imperceptible shift even before the end of Genesis.

Joseph's provisions and instructions for his brothers' journey are telling. There is still the same favouritism for Benjamin. The extra sets of garments for him recall Joseph's own special robe, and perhaps how he was stripped of it (37:23). The "pieces of silver" remind us, and presumably the brothers too, of the silver for which they sold him. And the command not to "quarrel along the way" offers a nice sense of pragmatic realism.

[Jacob] was stunned ... the spirit of their father Jacob revived. Jacob's heart literally missed a beat when they told him Joseph was alive—ironic in view of his earlier protestations. The vivid language of his spirit reviving again emphasizes the interweaving of the lives of father and son.

Hints of the future
46:1–50:26

In these chapters, Jacob and Joseph seem to jostle for control of the narrative. Unlike Chapters 42–45 where events are largely orchestrated by Joseph, here Jacob (or perhaps rather "Israel") seeks the opportunity to offer a different perspective which may at times conflict with Joseph's priorities. Some of these chapters (e.g. 46:1–27 and 47:27–48:22) remind us of earlier sections of Genesis. Their style, and particularly their view of God's way of working with human beings, contrast with perceptions in other parts of Chapters 37–50. Perhaps they originally provided a conclusion to an earlier edition of Genesis which did not include the story of Joseph in its present form.

46:1-27 *Israel... came to Beer-sheba.* It is an appropriate location for Israel to offer these sacrifices to "the God of his father" (46:1,3), both because Beer-sheba was important in the life of Isaac, his father (26:1-33) and because it marked a traditional boundary of the land of Canaan. Israel needs divine reassurance as he leaves the land once again, particularly as he is going down to Egypt, a place which Isaac had been specifically prohibited from travelling to (26:2). But it is intriguing that the first mention of Beer-sheba in Genesis (21:14) is associated with Hagar. It was the place to which she and her son had been sent out to die. Perhaps the interweaving of Abraham's story with that of Hagar and her descendants is still continuing (see comments on 15:13 and 16:1-15 on p. 127).

This is the first time since 35:11-12 that God has spoken directly to anyone. It takes place "in visions of the night". The phrase reminds us of two of Jacob/Israel's earlier numinous experiences which had taken place at night (28:11; 32:22). Appropriately for this time of famine, the promise does not focus on land (that was mentioned previously in 35:12) but on the fact that Israel's descendants will become a "great nation". The doubled "Jacob, Jacob" reflects the solemnity of the occasion, and recalls the previous time the angel of God had repeated the name of a patriarch in such a way (22:11). Jacob's response also echoes that of Abraham in the earlier story. "Here I am" (Hebrew: *hinneni*). That willingness to be at a deity's or a father's beck and call has led the ancestors on some uncomfortable pathways in the past—what will it lead to on this occasion and in the future?

Israel goes down into Egypt. The person, the ancestor, now begins imperceptibly to shade into the nation, his descendants. The genealogy given at this point hints at this. The promise is made by God, "I will also bring you up again" (46:4). Perhaps this refers in part to the return of Jacob's body, after his death, to Canaan. But the writer's eyes are already set on a greater return, at the time of the Exodus, when the whole nation of Israel is brought out of Egypt.

The genealogical list of Jacob's descendants numbering seventy (46:27) echoes the list of the "Table of the Nations" (10:1-32), which also seems to be intended to include seventy names. Israel had not been named among the other nations in that earlier list—and a key theme of the rest of Genesis has been about how that omission will be corrected.

It is intriguing that the Canaanite woman who bore a son to Simeon should be specifically mentioned (46:10), particularly in view of Simeon's violent objection to his sister's involvement with a Canaanite (34:25).

Other than Dinah (46:15), the only female descendant of Jacob mentioned is Serah, the daughter of Asher (46:17). She will also be one of the few female figures listed in the census in the wilderness in Numbers 26:46, where a literal reading might suggest that she was still alive centuries later. Rabbinic writers wove fascinating legends around Serah—suggesting that she was the one individual who spanned the period between the entry into Egypt and the Exodus, and as a result she was able to tell Moses where Joseph's bones were buried. The tradition further developed that Serah, like Enoch and Elijah, escaped death and was granted immortality. It is intriguing to wonder whether even in the biblical text there could be the foreshadowing of such later developments: is Serah mentioned here as a sign of hope—a pledge being offered at this moment of uncertainty that there is a future for Jacob and his descendants?

46:28-30 Judah's role (46:28) in organizing the reunion between Joseph and their father balances the roles he plays earlier in the story (37:26; 44:18-34) and foreshadows the fact that he will not be forgotten when the time for final blessings arrives (49:8-12).

Although this reunion itself is clearly a defining moment in the lives of both Jacob and Joseph, there is an imbalance in the emotion expressed by the two participants. Rabbinic tradition suggested that Jacob/Israel's comparative restraint was due to his belated realization that his unhealthy favouritism for Joseph was a form of idolatry. If he was to fulfil his role as the father of the entire nation, he needed to embody all, not simply one son, within himself.

46:31-47:12 Still Joseph has not lost his astuteness. He wants his family to settle in the land of Goshen, the eastern part of the delta, nearest to Canaan—and renowned for its fertility. But this might have been regarded as a security risk by the Egyptians. So Joseph advises his family to admit that they were shepherds, people who (according to the story) were held in horror by the Egyptians. Then Pharaoh would insist that they should settle in Goshen—as far away from the cities as possible. Joseph's ploy works —even though the brothers nearly spoil it by blurting out too much—their desire to settle in Goshen! Yet we have already quietly shifted from the situation that applied in 45:18–20 when Pharaoh's words were almost embarrassingly welcoming. The precise expression "holding" (*'ahuzzah*) recalls the previous times the same word was used—as property in Canaan (23:4,9,20) and as fulfilment of God's promise to give land there for a "perpetual holding" (17:8). Is there something jarring about the fact that this land has been given in Egypt? The mention of the "land of Rameses", which would have been anachronistic to the story, seems like a hint of the slave labour that awaits the Israelites as they are set to build the city of that name (Exodus 1:11). All in all, the episode is a quiet reminder that however powerful Joseph may be, or think he is, he (like everyone else) lives precariously in Egypt at the whim of the Pharaoh.

Jacob blessed Pharaoh.   In the course of this negotiation, there is an unexpected—at least from the perspective of Pharaoh—inversion of the normal social order. In fact, Jacob is the first of the ancestors to utter a blessing on anyone other than a member of his family. In embryo, the promise that Abraham's family would be a means of blessing for others is now being fulfilled.

The years of my earthly sojourn are one hundred and thirty.   Underlying the expression "earthly sojourn" is the Hebrew root which appeared first in 15:13 as *ger* (= alien, see comments on p. 122). It also appeared in the brothers' request "to reside as aliens" (47:4) in Egypt. As Genesis is drawing to its close, we are being reminded that this is a family who up till now has had "no abiding city". They will not ultimately find it in Egypt either: threats as well as promises are beginning to come to fulfilment, including Yhwh's covenantal comment (15:13) of the 400 years to be spent as aliens and slaves in Egypt.

47:13-26 Most modern readers feel a sense of distaste as they come across these verses. Are we really meant to approve of Joseph's cleverness as Pharaoh's administrator—a cleverness which finally results in virtually all of Egypt belonging to Pharaoh? Is the famine relief operation really only a gigantic manoeuvre enabling Pharaoh to reduce people to the status of landless serfs? Only the priests remain owners of their lands. In spite of various attempts to justify Joseph's behaviour (e.g. "at least the people survived"), it is highly questionable whether the author of Genesis viewed these actions of Joseph in a positive light.

As for the people, he [Joseph] made slaves of them from one end of Egypt to the other. In this translation, the NRSV is following the Septuagint and the Samaritan versions of Genesis. This reference to enslaving is probably the original reading in the Hebrew as well—but this was just too much to stomach for the revisers of the Massoretic text (the Hebrew version of which our English translations are based on), who offer a reading "He (Joseph) removed them to the cities", which appears as a footnote in the NRSV. (It only requires the amendment of a few Hebrew letters to move from one alternative to the other.) And if Joseph did indeed "enslave the Egyptians as slaves", his callous ruthlessness provided ample reasons, both practically and theologically, for the later enslavement by the Egyptians of Joseph's own descendants.

The comment that the priests alone remain owners of their lands contrasts with the Israelite tradition that the priests were the one group who did not own land. It is perhaps telling that Joseph himself had married into an Egyptian priestly family! In a few short verses the writer of Genesis has drawn a picture which reads like the reverse of the Old Testament ideal, with its sabbatical and Jubilee traditions of freeing slaves, remitting debts and serving God, in whom alone perfect freedom can be found.

The language with which Joseph is addressed, "May it please my lord" (47:25), echoes the kind of language used for a god. Aaron Wildavsky's comment is justified: "If Joseph does have a moral blind spot it is that from beginning to end he does not recognize the potential of abuse of power without limits. Joseph's Egyptianization reflects his identification with power."[84] The next book of the Pentateuch will introduce another

"Hebrew", Moses, who will also have close connections with Pharaoh's court (Exodus 2:10). Moses, however, will break free of Pharaoh's control in order to free others who are slaves. Joseph was "freed" from prison and slavery into Pharaoh's power in order to enslave those previously free. It is hard to avoid the suspicion that the two figures are being deliberately contrasted. The readers of Genesis are being invited to reflect on alternative models of leadership. Choose this day which path you will take!

47:27-31 *Israel settled in the land of Egypt ... and were fruitful.* Here for the first time in Genesis we have the name "Israel" (not simply "sons of Israel") used with a plural verb. Israel has now become a nation, at least in essence. We have heard the language of fruitfulness in Genesis several times before, but up till now it has usually been spoken as a promise or blessing (Joseph's words after the birth of his son Ephraim in 41:52 provide the exception). A strange place and a strange time therefore for the blessing of creation and the promise to Abraham to receive its fulfilment: a foreign land and a time of scarcity and famine. It does, however, also beg the question as to how far Joseph's own kin suffered the same economic hardships that the Egyptians experienced, or whether perhaps they even indirectly benefited from their plight. Is this, along with Abraham and Sarah's treatment of Hagar (see p. 123), possibly the reason that Jacob and Joseph's descendants must become slaves in Egypt (15:13)?

Jacob lived in the land of Egypt for seventeen years; so ... the years of his life were one hundred and forty-seven years. The mathematics of the patriarchs' ages is fascinating: Abraham lived 175 years, i.e. $5 \times 5 \times 7$; Isaac 180 years, i.e. $6 \times 6 \times 5$, and Jacob 147 years, i.e. $7 \times 7 \times 3$. In each case, the squared number increases by one, and the other number decreases by two. Furthermore, the sum of the three numbers in each case adds up to seventeen—which is also the number of years that Jacob lived in Egypt (as well as being the number of years that Joseph spent in Canaan in his youth). The effect is to suggest that events in the ancestral story did not happen at random: their lives have been lived under God's precise and providential care, and form part of a greater design.

Put your hand under my thigh. This was an action that indicated the solemnity of the oath that Jacob is demanding from Joseph. Presumably, he therefore touched his father's genital organs. It repeats the gesture that Abraham demanded of his servant before sending him back to Haran to find a wife for Isaac (24:2). In both cases, the oath that is sworn seems intended to preserve the distinctiveness of the family. There is an obvious connection with the covenant (of circumcision) offered to Abraham, as well, perhaps, as with Jacob/Israel's own experience of wounding at Penuel (32:25). The covenant connections are reinforced by the idiom "loyally and truly", vocabulary which is used elsewhere to express fidelity to a covenant (see Exodus 34:6; cf. 32:10). It may be that Joseph, because of his sale into slavery, was legally no longer Jacob's son, and this ceremony was a form of reintegration into the family and covenant community. It is associated with the request "Do not bury me in Egypt", since it was important for Jacob, as for his ancestors Abraham and Sarah (see 23:4), that God's covenant promise of land should become a personal reality, even if only to provide the grave for his burial.

Israel bowed himself on the head of his bed. Is it a gesture towards Joseph, the fulfilment of Joseph's dream of grandeur (37:9), or of thanksgiving towards God?

48:1-22 The account of the adoption and then blessing by Jacob of Ephraim and Manasseh seems to weave together threads from both the family saga and the story of the nation. If it was indeed the case that Joseph, through his sale into slavery, had, at least temporarily, legally lost his position within the family this might put any sons born to him during this period in an anomalous position which Jacob feels a need to rectify. But it is also interesting to note that 1 Chronincles 9:2-3 could be read as suggesting that in the post-exilic period the core of Israel was constituted by Judah, Benjamin, Ephraim and Manasseh. It is possible that some of the storyline of Genesis 37-50 (perhaps particularly this chapter) reflects this development.

Jacob said to Joseph, "God Almighty appeared to me". Jacob's speech seems to recapitulate the words he had directly heard from God Almighty

(Genesis 35:11–12). Once again, "God Almighty" is linked with fertility and fruitfulness. It is only those who themselves have been direct recipients of God's blessing who can legitimately impart it to others: Joseph, for all his greatness, has never received a direct revelation, and so if his sons are to be included within the community of promise the words will need to be uttered by Jacob his father. The vision at Luz (identified with Bethel in 35:6) is recalled as Jacob's authority for what he is about to do.

I ... will give this land ... for a perpetual holding. The significant word *'ahuzzah* which first appeared in 17:8 (see p. 131) reappears again. It had, however, also been used in 47:11 to describe Joseph's—or Pharaoh's—allocation of land to Jacob's family. Its use here is perhaps pointed: God's promise of land in Canaan is "for all time" over against the temporary "loan" of territory in Egypt.

Ephraim and Manasseh shall be mine, just as Reuben and Simeon are. It is not quite clear whether this comparison with the two oldest sons of Jacob by Leah means that Ephraim and Manasseh will supersede Reuben and Simeon by holding the privilege of the birthright due to the firstborn. 1 Chronicles 5:1 seems to suggest this was the case.

The sudden and slightly surprising mention of Rachel (48:7) may be due to the fact that in Chapter 35 (with which the present chapter seems to be closely linked) her death is recorded just after the divine appearance to Jacob at Bethel/Luz. Yet it is also a reminder that that early dream of Joseph (37:10) in which (apparently) he saw his mother bowing down to him, along with the rest of his family, can never completely be fulfilled. On the emotional level, Rachel's early death (after only producing two sons) helps to explain Jacob's desire to adopt "Ephraim and Manasseh" (notice the order).

Now the eyes of Israel were dim with age. Once before an aged patriarch with failing eyesight had had to bless male heirs (27:7). Then Isaac had been deceived and had (at least from his own perspective) blessed the wrong/younger son. We remember that story as we read of how the original deceiver will now choose deliberately to bestow a special blessing on a younger son.

God has let me see your children also. Literally the Hebrew speaks of "seeing your seed". Though obscured by the variety of ways it has been translated (e.g. "descendants", "sons"), the word has appeared throughout Genesis. Here it suggests that Joseph's sons, as "seed" will stand in a line which will link back to the promises made to Abraham (12:7), yet also reach into the future.

Joseph removed them from his father's knees. Placing a child between the knees of a person was a formal gesture that signified an act of adoption.

He bowed himself with his face to the earth. At the last it is Joseph who bows before his father—despite the message of his dreams which suggested the reverse.

Though introduced by the comment "he blessed Joseph", this oracle of blessing is focused more on Joseph's sons. It recapitulates the past in order to point towards the future. It echoes phrases and incidents that come from the life of Jacob/Israel and from the lives of his own forefathers. "The God before whom my ancestors Abraham and Isaac walked" recalls the demand made of Abram in 17:1; the image of shepherd has featured at key moments in Jacob's story (29:1–10) and will be referred to again in Jacob's blessing of Joseph (49:24); the "angel who has redeemed me" alludes to episodes such as 28:12; 32:1 and 32:22–32. However, the choice of the word translated "redeemed" (Hebrew: *ga'al*) surely also points forward towards and hints at the Exodus, with which it is characteristically associated (Exodus 6:6). As God has redeemed in Israel's own past, so he will also redeem in Israel's future. Finally, the repeated reference to "name" takes us right back to the initial call of Abram, and the pledge then to make his name great (12:2). Yet the very act of calling the two boys by Israel's name is an indication that Israel himself has now become more than a person. He is being transformed into "a multitude".

This one is the firstborn; put your right hand on his head. Although (unlike the time when Jacob himself had seized Esau's blessing) both brothers will be blessed, a blessing bestowed by their grandfather's right hand would indicate Manasseh's pre-eminence. But that is not how it is going to be—indeed it never has been throughout the whole book of Genesis. Instead, Ephraim will receive the greater blessing.

I know, my son, I know. The emphatic repetition of "know" suggests that more may be meant than simply an old man insisting that he is in full possession of his faculties. Is Jacob claiming for himself the knowledge and wisdom that have been sought by humanity throughout Genesis— part of which seems to be expressed in God's mysterious preference for a younger son?

His descendants will be a whole nation in themselves. Although Manasseh's name was given to one of the clans (e.g. Numbers 26:29–34) Ephraim was to become a synonym used frequently for the whole people of Israel (e.g. Jeremiah 31:8; Hosea 11:1–3). Significantly it is often employed in passages which speak of God's tender, paternal love.

I now give to you one portion [of land] more than to your brothers. The old favouritism still comes to the fore. As the NRSV notes, underlying "portion" is the word *shekem*, which can mean a "shoulder" of land, but is also an oblique allusion to the city of Shechem, which has played a significant part in both the ancestral story (12:6) and that of Joseph himself (37:13). It will become part of the territory allotted to the house of Joseph in the division made in Joshua 16–17, and it will be where Joseph is eventually buried after the Exodus from Egypt (Joshua 24:32).

I took from the hand of the Amorites with my sword and with my bow. Is this an ironic reference to the pillage of Shechem in Genesis 34 (in which Jacob actually plays a passive role), or does it relate to another story circulating about Jacob which has not been incorporated in Genesis?

49:1–28 The range of blessings which Jacob offers at the end of his story (to Pharaoh, to Ephraim and Manasseh and now to his twelve sons) seem to parallel his hunger to be blessed (by his father and Yhwh) near his story's beginning. And just as earlier there was considerable ambiguity about the blessings Jacob received—so now his own blessings have a questionable character. As one writer puts it, "If these are Jacob's blessings, what would his curses be like?"[85] At the end of the sequence, 49:28 will be the final occasion in Genesis that the verb "bless" and the noun "blessing" are used—the motif that has dominated the entire book of Genesis and especially the story of the ancestors. Rereading the original blessing and promise given to Abraham (12:2–3) alongside this chapter is instructive: it suggests that there is still some way to go, both now, and even in the kind of future presupposed by Jacob's words, before the divine words to Abraham can be said to have come to fruition. We are being pointed into a future beyond Genesis itself, and perhaps even beyond the present of the writer. The explicit words "I may tell you what will happen to you in days to come" with which the "blessings" are introduced are a reminder that Genesis is ultimately a book of promise rather than fulfilment.

It used to be thought that the "Blessings of Jacob" might have been an originally separate and archaic poem inserted at this point into the story of Jacob's family. That seems unlikely, at least in its present form. Several of the blessings allude with verbal puns to incidents which are recounted earlier in Genesis. Perhaps rather we should think of this as an earlier poem which has been edited and adapted to fit its present context. It is interesting to compare this passage with the corresponding Blessing of Moses in Deuteronomy 33:1–29.

The six sons of Jacob by Leah are listed first.

Reuben Though given prime position, as the firstborn, Jacob's words remind us of the incident (35:22) in which Reuben committed incest with his father's concubine and suggest that as a result of this Reuben lost the "primacy".

Simeon and Levi Similarly harsh words are addressed to Simeon and Levi, in their case probably recalling the murderous attack on Shechem which they led (34:25–31). Unlike the "Blessing of Moses" (Deuteronomy 33:8–11), there is no particular awareness here of Levi as a "priestly" tribe. However, Levi's "fervency for YHWH" expressed in the Shechem incident, may also be reflected in the violent enthusiasm Levi elsewhere shows for his priestly role (Exodus 32:28; Deuteronomy 33:9). The text reflects the fact that in later history none of the tribes of Simeon, Levi or Reuben were significant politically or numerically.

Judah With his three older brothers disposed of, the text then concentrates on Judah, reflecting both his significant position within the story of 37–50, and the importance of the tribe of Judah. It opens with a ringing pun on Judah's name, "your brothers shall praise [*yodu*] you". Then the terms "sceptre" and "staff" are used to highlight Judah's later strength—and to remind us that David's family sprang from this tribe. Not surprisingly this passage has been interpreted both in Judaism and Christianity as a messianic prophecy. Matthew 21:7 seems to allude to it as he describes Jesus' triumphal entry into Jerusalem. The text also probably hints at the story of Judah and Tamar in Genesis 38. Some of the words in 49:10–12 could be explained as (fairly obscure) puns on the vocabulary and incidents in that story, for example, "his eyes" which may be a reference to Enaim, where Judah met Tamar in her prostitute's garb (see p. 298).

The mysterious reference to "Shiloh", relegated by the NRSV to a footnote because it was considered too difficult to translate, may refer to the fact that the town of Shiloh seems to have had at one point an important role as a religious and political centre of Israel (Joshua 18:10; Judges 21:19; 1 Samuel 1:3). The town's own history is also something of a mystery. Although we assume from the narrative of 1 Samuel 1–4 and references in Psalm 78:60, and Jeremiah 7:12–15 that the sanctuary at Shiloh, in Ephraimite territory north of Jerusalem, was destroyed in the premonarchic period, figures associated with Shiloh (e.g. Ahijah, 1 Kings 11:29–39) seem to play an ongoing part in the nation's history, in Ahijah's case associated with the split between northern and southern kingdoms. One possible understanding of the NRSV footnote readings, "Until he comes to Shiloh/until Shiloh comes", is that Judah's hegemony among the brothers would endure until the time when the prophet Ahijah of Shiloh encouraged Jeroboam to rebel against the Judaean monarchy at the time of Solomon. Alternatively, the reference to Shiloh in Genesis 49:10 may be intended as a promise of the time when this division between south and north, Judah and Israel, which the brothers Judah and Joseph personify, is healed. Additionally, several Jewish targums (Aramaic paraphrases of the Hebrew text) identify Shiloh directly as a reference to the Messiah, and this interpretation has also been adopted in some Christian circles. Joanna Southcott, an eighteenth- and nineteenth-century English prophetess, believed that she was going to give birth to "the Shiloh".

Whatever the meaning of the precise details of the oracle about Judah may be, it is certainly striking that it is Judah, rather than Joseph, who is promised "your father's sons shall bow down before you" (49:8).

With *Zebulun* and *Issachar*, the references in the "blessings" are largely geographical, loosely alluding to the regions elsewhere associated with these tribes. The pun linking Issachar's name to "hire" (*sakar*) which was made at his birth (30:16-18), is also apparent here.

The next four sons are born from the slave-wives.

A pun on *Dan's* name introduces the words about him. The Hebrew root *din*, normally meaning "to execute judgement", is reflected in the epithet of "judge". His description as a "viper" who "brings down" a stronger foe has led some to see in this passage an allusion to the violent story of Samson the judge, from the tribe of Dan and his victory in death over the Philistines, pulling down the temple of Dagon upon himself and a crowd of Philistines.

This is followed by the enigmatic outburst "I wait for your salvation, O Lord". This is the first time that Yhwh has been named since 39:23. And it is the first time that Jacob himself has called upon Yhwh since 32:9-11 when he prayed "Deliver me". Perhaps this utterance suggests that Jacob is still waiting for Yhwh's full deliverance, promised in those encounters in his earlier life, which in 28:13-15 had included a promise of return to the land of Canaan.

The words about the following three sons again seem to allude to the geographical location of the tribes linked to these names. The punning on *Gad's* name is powerful: "Gad shall be raided by raiders, but he shall raid" (*gad gedud yegudenu, wehu' yagud*). There is probably a connection between the prosperity predicted for Asher and the fact that the word *'ashrey* means "fortunate".

Then come the two sons of Rachel—first *Joseph*, whose blessing is as long as that assigned to Judah. The fertile territory of the area linked with the "house of Joseph", around Shechem and Samaria, is clearly alluded to (as also in the corresponding passage in the Blessing of Moses, Deuteronomy 33:13-17, on which the present verses may be based). The word "blessing", which actually had not been used by Jacob in his words to his sons up till this point, now appears five times, and along with the hint about Joseph's fruitfulness (49:22) perhaps reminds us of the beginning of Genesis—as does the references to heaven (49:25; cf. 1:1) and the deep (49:25; cf. 1:2). But there are apparent links to other biblical texts as well, Psalm 80:1,12 for example, and possible intricate intertextual allusions to earlier parts of the story of the ancestors. Nahum Sarna notes how the Hebrew of 49:22 may conceal a cryptic reference to "the spring on the way to Shur" (16:7), where Hagar saw the angel.[86] In fact, 49:22-26 is very obscure—what NRSV translates as "fruitful bough" is in some other biblical versions rendered as "wild ass". Sarna sees here an allusion to Ishmael who is described as a "wild ass" (16:12) and an "expert with the bow" (21:20; cf. 49:23). Remembering the role of the Ishmaelites in the sale of Joseph into slavery (37:25), the oracle may be reminding us how the destinies of the actions of the ancestors, for good or ill, influence the lives of their descendants. It is only when the suffering has been spent that the blessing can be gained.

And finally, *Benjamin*—what a contrast with the way Benjamin has been portrayed in Genesis 42-44! There are tales in Judges which associate the tribe of Benjamin with acts of ferocity (Judges 19-21), which perhaps lie behind this description of Benjamin as a tribe of particular savagery. Intriguingly, the description of Benjamin in the Blessing of Moses (Deuteronomy 33:1-29), where he is given the epithet "beloved" (Deuteronomy 33:12), fits much more closely with the portrayal of Benjamin in Genesis.

These are the twelve tribes of Israel. At last, Israel has moved from being a family to being a nation. The implication of the entry of the seventy names into Egypt is actualized—even if only as a promise for the future.

49:29-33 Jacob reaches his final moments. He has taken a long time getting there, having in effect been "dying" since he reached Egypt (47:9,29-31). The importance that Jacob attaches to being buried in Canaan is emphasized by the repetition here of his earlier demand to Joseph (47:29-30). It is now spelt out in more detail: he is to be taken to the tomb at Machpelah where his ancestors were also buried. In death, Leah will have to herself the husband she had to share in life, since Rachel is buried elsewhere (see 48:7), though it is also notable that, unlike Sarah and Rebekah whom he describes as the wives of their respective husbands, Jacob does not call Leah "my wife". That title is reserved for Rachel, and Rachel alone (see 44:27).

50:1-14 The aftermath of Jacob's death highlights the many ambiguities that Joseph and his family are now facing in Egypt, and in Canaan. All may not be quite as it seems. The post-death rituals offered to Jacob, including embalming, seemingly emphasize the honour in which Joseph's father is held by the Egyptians, as does the mourning period of 110 days (40+70)—since this was probably a significant number (see notes on 50:22). Yet when Joseph comes to fulfil his pledge to bury his father in Canaan the care with which he has to tread suggests the vulnerability of his family. Joseph requests members of Pharaoh's household, "If now I have found favour with you, please speak to Pharaoh as follows". Is this the same Joseph who once proudly boasted to his brothers "God ... has made me a father to Pharaoh, and lord of all his house" (45:8)? And his choice of words sanitizes his father's instructions to him. Admittedly it might not be tactful to mention that Jacob had bluntly stated "do not bury me in Egypt" (47:29), but Joseph's comment that Jacob wished to be buried "in the tomb that I hewed out for myself in the land of Canaan" is a subtle distortion of the truth (it wasn't Jacob who bought that grave!)—but one made presumably to put emotional pressure on Pharaoh. The pledge with which the permission is sought "Let me go up, so that I may bury my father; then I will return" suggests that Joseph and his family may rapidly be becoming not so much guests as prisoners, albeit in a gilded cage.

That impression is reinforced by the description of those who accompany Jacob's funeral cortege in Canaan—and those who do not.

Do "all the servants of Pharaoh ... and all the elders of the land of Egypt" (50:7) participate as a guard of honour, or simply as a guard? And though it might have been realistic to leave behind the flocks and herds while on this journey, the children who remained in Goshen acted conveniently as hostages ensuring the family's return.

Yet perversely when the funeral cortege reaches the boundary of Canaan, the Canaanites mistake the family for Egyptians (50:11). What an unfortunate fate for a grandson of Abraham, even though he is eventually buried in his grandfather's tomb. The ancestral promise of the land seems further away from being fulfilled than it has ever been. Neither in Egypt nor in Canaan can Jacob and his family be comfortably at home.

50:15–26 A different set of ambiguities then arise. The brothers fear that the day of reckoning has at last arrived for their original act of betrayal, and that Joseph's earlier reconciliation with them had been feigned—due to his desire to see his father again. The deception that has played such a large part in this family's story makes its reappearance: the purported message from their father to Joseph is highly suspicious. Did Jacob really say that, or is not more likely the brothers' own fabrication? Truth breaks through, however, when the brothers address Joseph directly in their own right. "Forgive the crime of the servants of the God of your father." In the "false" message from their father to Joseph, they described themselves as "your brothers", but now speaking directly they recognize that they forfeited the right to call and be called "brother", that day when they speciously did "not lay our hands" (37:27) on their brother but rather sold him as a slave. They can only plead the bonds of shared familial faith. Their desperation is made more transparent as they finally acknowledge "We are here as your slaves", accompanying their words with a grovelling gesture which fulfils the old dream that had originally angered them so bitterly (37:6–10). By selling Joseph as a slave, they had set in train a process that had both led to his dream's fulfilment and had resulted in this metaphorical "slavery" for themselves.

In turn, Joseph's reaction and response can be understood in a number of different ways. The uncertainty is probably deliberate. It reminds us that forgiveness and healing is complex. Why did Joseph weep when confronted with his brothers' devious words? Was it sorrow that he was still misunderstood? Or is it relief that the unexpressed bitterness of the years is now out in the open? It was notable that when the apparent reconciliation with his brothers had taken place in Chapter 45 the initiative had been totally Joseph's own. His brothers had found it difficult to talk to him then. Now it is their turn to do the talking.

But there are then two comments Joseph makes in return, alongside insisting that his brothers have no reason to fear him. The first is a question "Am I in the place of God?" The second is a longer comment in which the "meaning" of what has happened over the last fourteen chapters of Genesis is explained. Yet both remarks may be more equivocal than is apparent at first sight. Our immediate reaction to Joseph's enigmatic question "Am I in the place of God?" is to dismiss it as merely rhetorical. We are relieved that at last the self-centred youth of Chapter 37 has learned enough to place God rather than himself at the centre. But does this question also mean he is not qualified to judge his brothers—or not qualified to forgive them? And if we reflect a bit more deeply, we might even begin to wonder whether our immediate instinct was right after all. Once before the identical phrase was used—by Joseph's own father to Joseph's mother as she demanded a child from him (30:2). As we suggested there, Jacob did in some senses "take the place of God"—at least until Joseph himself was born. There is indeed a sense that Joseph has been "playing God" in the last few chapters, with the cat-and-mouse game he played with his family, with the oppression that he has meted out to the Egyptians, with his absolute certainty that he knows the mind of God (41:16,25; 45:8). That perhaps makes us a little suspicious as to how we should interpret Joseph's next words in which he offers his explanation for the events he and his family have experienced. It is comforting to think of what has happened as the work of an overarching providence. Joseph's comment about "good" (50:20) also provides appropriate closure for a book which had begun with God's pronouncement of creation as "very good" (1:31), and his view about the working of providence was, broadly speaking, characteristic of Israel's wisdom tradition. Joseph was, as we know, a "wise" man (41:33). Psalm 33:10–11 provides another example of such theology—of how the evil plans of human beings can be enfolded in the ultimate purposes of God. There are pointers in earlier parts of the saga of Joseph that this is how it is here too. In Chapter 39, for example, we have been told at both the beginning and end of the chapter how Yhwh was operating, there in the background nudging the human actors along even when they didn't always realize it.

But we last met that deity when Joseph was in the prison, and he seems to have disappeared from the picture since Joseph rose to glory and control of the destinies of others. So is it through Joseph's eyes alone that we should seek to read and understand the story? If Joseph is right God has, in withdrawing from the scene, succeeded in controlling it more absolutely. Karen Armstrong has commented that Genesis as a whole does not accept Joseph's "theological view of a wholly omnipotent and irresistible God, in whose grand designs human beings are mere pawns".[87] Should not the brothers be allowed to own their own guilt, however painful it might be? (see further in Theological reflections on p. 351).

In this way he reassured them, speaking kindly to them.   Perhaps these words of the narrator hint at an alternative theological explanation which we are being reminded of. The verb *nhm* is here translated as "reassured" but often appears as "comforted". Along with "speaking kindly" (literally "speak to the heart"), it appears in Isaiah 40:1-2 to introduce Chapters 40-55, a part of the Bible that contains, in passages like Isaiah 52:13-53:12, some of the most profound reflections on guilt and suffering in the entire Bible. Are we meant to hold the exquisite struggle of Isaiah 40-55 to *our* hearts to help us balance Joseph's perhaps too easy theodicy?

Nhm (comfort) is a word that has appeared at key moments in Genesis. It was what Noah was born for (5:29) and what Jacob refused (37:35) after Joseph's own disappearance. In the apparent rapprochement of this divided family have we finally reached what humanity has yearned for through so many generations? Or do the ambiguities that we have detected even in this episode "hint" at the later alienation between the brothers' descendants in the divided kingdoms that will emerge after the era of David and Solomon?

One hundred and ten years old   The repetition of Joseph's age at his death (50:22,26) suggests that it is important. There is some evidence that 110 years was considered the "perfect" age in Egypt. It also has a mathematical relationship to the ages of his ancestors, Abraham, Isaac and Jacob. Each of their ages contains a square number (see comments on p. 330), in Abraham's case 5^2, in Isaac's 6^2, and in Jacob's 7^2. Joseph's age is the sum of these squares, i.e. 25+36+49. It provides a way of suggesting that he is the "completion" of the patriarchs, as well as once again indicating God's oversight of history. 110 years was also the lifespan of Joseph's descendant Joshua, from the tribe of Ephraim (Joshua 24:29). There are various links between the two figures—one of whom "oversaw" the entry of the Israelites into Egypt, and the other their return to Canaan. They both also have connections with Shechem (Joshua 24:1-32).

So the age of Joseph at the end of Genesis symbolically looks both back to the ancestors, but also forward to Moses, Joshua and an Exodus from the land to which Joseph had brought his family.

The future Exodus and return to the place from where Joseph came is also the subject of Joseph's last words, "God will surely come to you". It is fascinating, however, that the theological view this statement implies, of a God acting directly in history, does not exactly equate with Joseph's understanding of the workings of God as it has been expressed by him up to this point. Nor does the fragility of this paragraph quite tally with the picture of the man who has, for the last few chapters, been omnipotent in relation to his own family. Joseph's bones and his future will be in the hands of his brothers and their descendants: he will depend upon them to return him to the land from which they had banished him (Exodus 13:19). Joseph will finally get to Shechem again (Joshua 24:32), the place where he had gone to meet his brothers all those years ago (37:14), due only to the cooperation of those self-same brothers.

The final sentence of Genesis is extraordinarily "low key" given the vast scope of this book. Read against the first verse of the story of Joseph and his brothers which had emphasized how Jacob had "settled" (37:1) in Canaan, the comment that Joseph was placed in a "coffin in Egypt" suggests that God's promises to this family are now no nearer to—and possibly even further away from—being realized than they were almost a hundred years previously. But there is in this sentence one tantalizing pointer to the future. The word translated "coffin" (Hebrew: *'aron*) is the identical word which will appear elsewhere (e.g. Exodus 25:10) to describe the Ark (of the covenant). When the sons of Israel eventually return to Canaan, they will be carrying both Joseph's coffin and this Ark. Two boxes, one with the "bones" of the past, the other with tablets containing guidance for the future. Yet perhaps the vitality of the future will depend on the remembering of the past. In his eulogy of the ancestors, Ben Sira comments about the judges: "May their memory be blessed! May their bones send forth new life from where they lie, and may the names of those who have been honoured live again in their children!" (Sirach 46:11–12). Might a similar epitaph be applied to Joseph, certainly in his own eyes? In this book of Genesis or "beginnings", which has, from its start to its finish focused on the importance of life, does this box of bones constitute not an end, but the "seed" for the future?

Theological reflections

1. Joseph, caution and paragon

The wealth of traces of the story of Joseph in extra-biblical religious texts and world literature offers a startling contrast to the comparative absence of the story in the rest of the Old Testament.

As regards the Old Testament, the relatively late date of Genesis 37–50 may partly explain the absence. So too may the association of Joseph with the northern tribes, in view of the southern ("Judaean") bias of most of the Old Testament. But these factors are unlikely to be the whole picture. The ambiguities that we can discover by a careful reading of the story might prompt us to ask the question whether the ultimate purpose of the story of Joseph in Genesis is as a cautionary tale: that it ought to be the path *less* travelled by his descendants. It is a false trail, a dead end, which is only righted when Joseph's descendants eventually leave Egypt, and can pick up the story of Abraham, Isaac and Jacob again (Exodus 3:6,15). Joseph goes wrong through his overwillingness to assimilate to the life and mores of Egypt. Remember how he named his first son "Manasseh" with the intention that he would forget his father's house (41:51). But it is not simply his understandable desire to forget the painful memories associated with his family which is the problem; it is rather the very nature of the society to which he has nailed his colours. He has bought into a world where royal power is absolute, reinforced by being equated with divinity. He has become part of that ideology. He suggests as much in his words to his brothers during their apparent reconciliation. His elevation to power, previously explicitly stated as being due to Pharaoh (41:41) is now credited by Joseph to God (45:8). Implicitly Pharaoh is God. And this in turn, of course, has implications for how Joseph feels that he can behave towards those for whom he is responsible, the citizens of Egypt. He represents "God" to them. His absolute power over their lives deprives them of their human dignity (47:18–25). It is a totalitarian vision of the state.

It is interesting to note that the story of the Tower of Babel has been interpreted as the first totalitarianism.[88] It may be significant therefore that just as the primeval story ended with the failed attempt to build Babel, so the ancestral story ends with this other, not dissimilar, failure linked to Joseph. Not that it seemed like failure at the time, at least to Joseph himself: but perhaps the reason that Joseph was so easily forgotten (Exodus 1:8) was that the memories associated with his name were not pleasant. Joseph's vision fostered an idolatry of unity. It did not allow for "the dignity of difference", that phrase made famous by Rabbi Jonathan Sacks. Rabbi Sacks suggests that the concept of covenant, fundamental to the biblical tradition, is marked specifically by a respect for the difference and dignity of the partners involved. As Exodus will follow Genesis, the covenant at Sinai with its model for organization of community will follow the autocracy of Egypt.

Comparisons and contrasts have often been drawn between Joseph and various other personalities who appear in the biblical literature. He has been compared with both Solomon and Ezra, and contrasted with Moses and Daniel. None of these comparisons are explicit within the biblical text but they are not unreasonable. Like Joseph they are all portrayed as figures of state who are confronted with "realpolitik", and in particular with the need to define the relationship between "Israel" and the powerful empires that dominated the Ancient Middle East, such as Egypt, Babylon and Persia. It is interesting to reflect that the story of Joseph may well have been incorporated into Genesis at a point in history when Jewish identity vis-à-vis the Hellenistic world, particularly in Egypt, was a live issue on the theological agenda. How far is assimilation possible, or desirable? How far does it need to be resisted, and at what potential cost to an individual or the community? Should Judaism be following the path of Joseph, or of Moses, or even Joseph's own brother Judah whose story in Genesis 38 and 44 may be designed to provide another counterpoint to him? Joseph may indeed be cast into a pit and a dungeon, but unlike Daniel it is not one that is full of lions, and he does not get thrown into it for refusing to participate in idolatry.

Yet despite his absence from other Old Testament books, there are few other biblical characters who have featured so extensively in extra-biblical religious writings and world literature as has Joseph. It starts already in the Apocrypha; although Joseph is only briefly referred to in Ecclesiasticus, he is clearly a hero to the author of the Wisdom of Solomon. "When a righteous man was sold, wisdom did not desert him, but delivered him from sin. She descended with him into the dungeon, and when he was in prison, she did not leave him, until she brought him the sceptre of a kingdom and authority over his masters. Those who accused him she showed to be false, and she gave him everlasting honour" (Wisdom 10:13–14). It is interesting that Joseph's deliverance from sin seems to be linked to his refusal of the charms of Potiphar's wife. His self-control in this incident becomes an increasingly important dimension in the retellings of his story, and he is seen as an ethical model, keeping "[God's] commandment" (1 Maccabees 2:53).

Not surprisingly, Joseph was a popular figure among the Hellenistic Jewish community living in Egypt. As well as the Wisdom of Solomon, he appears in several of the writings of Philo, who is ambiguous about him—on the one hand admiring his chastity and temperance, but on the other suggesting that he was not oblivious to some of the temptations of power. One of the best known extra-biblical retellings linked to the name of Joseph is the romance of *Joseph and Aseneth*, probably dating from slightly before the New Testament period and written in Egypt, in which Joseph is responsible for the conversion to Judaism of Aseneth, the daughter of the Egyptian priest of Heliopolis, before he marries her (cf. Genesis 41:50).

Joseph, as the ancestor of the northern tribes, was also an obvious hero for the Samaritan community, although it is difficult to date precisely the Samaritan sources in which he features. It is interesting, however, in this connection, to note Joseph's appearance, along with Abraham and Moses, in Stephen's speech (Acts 7:9–16). His story becomes an example of God's ability to be present with people away from the Temple, and outside the Holy Land. A number of New Testament scholars have seen "Samaritan influence" on the traditions expressed in this speech, for example the fact that, according to Acts 7:16, all the patriarchs, rather than simply Joseph, are buried at Shechem rather than Hebron.

But it is in the Qur'an and Muslim sources that the figure of Joseph receives some of its most extensive development. Joseph is the one biblical patriarch who has a lengthy connected narrative and complete *sūra* of the Qur'an devoted to him, Sūra 12, titled *Yusuf* ("Of Joseph"), which refers to his adventures as "the finest of stories" (Sūra 12:3). The outline of the tale of Joseph in Genesis is retold up to the point where Joseph's family come to settle in Egypt, though particular attention is paid to the episode with Potiphar's wife, which is considerably developed, with an "assembly of ladies" involved all of whom vouch for Joseph's extraordinary beauty. The key to the Qur'an's interest in Joseph is given early in the Sūra: there are "many significant things in the story of Joseph and his brothers for those who are of enquiring mind".[89] Perhaps part of the reason for this interest in Joseph is precisely the theological viewpoint which is implied in Genesis itself by Joseph's comments in 45:7–8 and 50:20, namely the sense of an overarching providence, and of God's sure guidance in human affairs. Joseph's final words in the Qur'anic version of his story include this comment: "My Lord deals graciously according to His will: for He is ever wise and knowing ... My Lord, you have brought me to power and made me learned in interpretation of storied things."[90]

And what of the Christian tradition, and its reflection on the figure of Joseph? Early on in Christian history Joseph became viewed not simply as a model of right behaviour to follow, but also a "type" of Christ. In the second century AD, Melito of Sardis in the hymn "On Pascha" spoke of how Christ was prefigured "in Joseph sold". The fact that both Jesus and Joseph were traded for silver facilitated this comparison, as did the way Joseph spent time in the "pit", particularly in view of the number of psalms which use the "pit" as a metaphor of death.

In modern times, the most extended comparison between Joseph and Christ was that made by Thomas Mann in his novel *Joseph and His Brothers*. This great novel, which covers the life of Jacob as well as Joseph himself, was produced in several parts between 1934 and 1945, a period when Mann was exiled from Germany and when Germany itself was undergoing a sort of passion. One of the features of the novel is that the association between Joseph and Christ broadens out to encompass the entirety of human suffering. In the process, resonances of the ancient and archetypal myth of a dying and rising god are incorporated into the story. A mysterious figure (the man whom Joseph meets near Dothan) speaks to Reuben over the empty pit from which Joseph has disappeared and puts it as follows:

> I know not what thou understandest by dead and what by living. Thou hast laughed at the childish elements of things, but yet I may remind thee of the grain of corn when it lieth in the grave, and ask thee how thou thinkest of it in reference to life and death ... For it is so that the corn falling into the earth and dying bringeth forth much fruit... I saw a youth descend into the grave in garland and festal garment, and above him they slaughtered a beast of the flock, whose blood they let run down, so that it ran all over him and he received it with all his limbs and senses. So that when he ascended again he was divine and had won life—at least for some time to come.[91]

Mann is here reading far more into the story than the bare narrative of Genesis seems to allow, but he has tapped into themes that are embedded deep in the human psyche, and which are hinted at by the biblical writer. The recurrent motif of weeping which accompanies the gradual reconciliation between Joseph and the brothers, 42:24; 43:30; 45:2 is a reminder of how often, and how powerfully, tears can be the seed of transformation—and even resurrection. In a book which suggests that life is all important (50:20) weeping is an essential part. "May those who sow in tears reap with shouts of joy." (Psalm 126:5) We are being told that laughter demands weeping, reaping requires sowing, fertility seems often to be prefaced with sterility, and death is part of the cycle of life.

2. A technicolor dreamcoat

Thomas Mann is not the only modern writer to draw creatively on the story of Joseph. In a completely different vein is the musical *Joseph and the Amazing Technicolor Dreamcoat* by Tim Rice and Andrew Lloyd Webber. Its very lightheartedness offers some unexpectedly helpful insights. The delightful cynicism of the brothers' chorus to Jacob after their sale of Joseph:

> There's one more angel in Heaven
> There's one more star in the sky
> Joseph, we'll never forget you
> It's tough but we're gonna get by.[92]

enables us to cut through the overfamiliarity of the biblical text to an appreciation of the outrageous way in which they seek to deceive their father at this point.

Nor is it an accident that the musical has a reference to the "dreamcoat" in its title. "This coat", as the brothers say, "has got our goat". For the story of the family of Jacob could be said to be dominated by the motif of clothing. It "carries" the tale, and in this respect Genesis 37–50 is simply making more explicit a motif which has been in evidence since the man and the woman encountered each other in the garden, firstly naked (2:25), then with loincloths stitched from fig leaves (3:7), and finally with coverings of skins given as a gift by Yhwh (3:21). Clothing is a symbol of status (24:53; 37:3; 41:42; 45:22), of transformation (35:2; 37:23; 38:19; 41:14), of deception (27:15; 37:32–33; 38:14; 39:12,15,18). Deprived of our clothing we are made vulnerable, and yet our clothing is curse as well as blessing, because it facilitates duplicity. It protects us from a too-painful integrity, from our real selves. Some years ago, I designed creative worship for Holy Week which focused around the theme of clothing. It was a powerful experience, and given the traditional linkage made between the story of Joseph and the passion of Christ (see above), could also be said to act as commentary on this part of Genesis. Think about the wealth of images: the garments strewed on Palm Sunday, the robe divested and the towel on Maundy Thursday, the purple cloak and crown of thorns at the trial on Good Friday, the discarded grave clothes on Easter Sunday. But think too about what happened later on Good Friday—how the soldiers took the clothes of Jesus, divided them among themselves, and left him to hang on the cross completely naked. Our sanitized representations of the crucifixion (even according to Mel Gibson!) do not allow us to see this. Yet there is deep meaning in that aweful nakedness. The God whom the psalmist had celebrated as "clothed with honour and majesty, wrapped in light as with a garment" (Psalm 104:1-2) had first of all divested himself of his heavenly mantle to make it safe for humanity to see him once again (cf. Genesis 3:10). But that was not enough. We humans next sought to clothe him with our desires and passions, and veil him again from our sight. The naked power of the cross was God's response. It is then that we are able to see God face to face in all his terrible glory—and live.

Read against this parallel, we can see that as the story of Joseph draws to its conclusion, we are being told about a modus vivendi for humanity rather than an ideal. Nakedness has to be concealed, whether it is physical or emotional or spiritual. Even Jacob's and Joseph's dead bodies have to be protected by embalming and their coffins. Do Janet Morley's words written for a Good Friday litany read as a judgement on the power and prestige of Joseph, as God laments:

> 'I abandoned my power like a garment,
> choosing your unprotected flesh:
> but you have robed yourselves in privilege,
> and chosen to despise the abandoned'?[93]

3. The ambiguity remains

At the start of this section of Genesis, the brief encounter that Joseph has with "a man ... in the fields" (37:15-17) introduces the motif of ambiguity. What is the relationship between divine involvement in and control of the narrative and apparently autonomous human actions? It is a motif that will recur throughout the remainder of the story of Joseph.

In the comments on 45:7-8 and 50:20, we raised the question as to whether Joseph's "reading" of his and his brothers' experience was the correct one, whether it was true that God was making use of his brothers' malice towards him for a "higher purpose"? It is a dangerous assumption: think only of some of the more grotesque evils of the last hundred years. To suggest that they somehow happened as a working out of a divine "greater plan" feels like a mocking blasphemy.

Yet it is also a strangely comforting viewpoint. "Everything works together for good" is a thought that has given meaning to many human lives. It is not an accident that Islamic tradition has viewed the story of Joseph so favourably: Joseph's own view, taken at face value about what happened and why, resonates strongly with a Muslim theology of history. Certainly, one of the developmental threads we have seen running through Genesis has been a sense of trial and error as God experiments with ways of relating to humanity, and Joseph's comments seem to reflect a particular stage on that journey—perhaps not the ultimate stage, but at least the last word as far as the writer of Genesis was concerned. Robert Cohn puts it like this: "In stages, the divine director retreats from the scene permitting the actors to shape their own world. Finally, equilibrium is achieved as Joseph and his brothers, acting on their own initiative, unwittingly and ironically become the agents of providence."[94]

Possibly we can allow that thought to stand, but with one caveat. Joseph thinks that he understands God's way of working, and he is keen to tell his brothers so. He may indeed think that he does so, but the problem may be that even if his vision is larger than theirs it is still not large enough. Joseph's god is too small. The God who is YHWH is marked by a refusal to be confined by the boxes that human beings seek to make for him, whether physical, spiritual or intellectual. The particular box which Joseph has constructed for him was too focused on Joseph's own family and his own immediate situation. The ultimate irony of Joseph's remark may be that even while he is right about God's ability to accomplish his purposes, he has failed to realize quite how generous and broad those purposes are. Perhaps Thomas Mann caught something of this, when, on the last page of his novel, his "Joseph" admits: "One can easily be in a story and not understand it. Perhaps that is the way it ought to be and I am to blame myself for always knowing far too well what was being played."[95]

Notes

1. R. N. Whybray, *The Making of the Pentateuch: A Methodological Study*, JSOTSup 53 (Sheffield: JSOT Press, 1987).
2. Gerhard Larsson, "Ancient Calendars Indicated in the OT", *Journal for the Study of the Old Testament* 54 (1992), pp. 61–76, 68.
3. Jeremy Hughes, *Secrets of the Times: Myth and History in Biblical Chronology*, JSOTSup 66 (Sheffield: JSOT Press, 1990), p. 234.
4. Jon D. Levenson, *Creation and the Persistence of Evil* (Princeton, NJ: Princeton University Press, 1988), pp. 78–99.
5. Ellen Van Wolde, *Stories of the Beginning: Genesis 1–11 and other Creation Stories* (London: SCM Press, 1996), pp. 132–6.
6. Robert Alter, *Genesis* (New York, NY: W. W. Norton & Company, 1996), p. 8.
7. Carol Ochs, *Song of the Self: Biblical Spirituality and Human Holiness* (Valley Forge, PA: Trinity Press International, 1994), p. 8.
8. Emmanuel Levinas, *Nine Talmudic Readings* (Bloomington, IN; Indiana University Press, 1990), p. 85.
9. Karl Barth, *Church Dogmatics III.4 The Doctrine of Creation* (Edinburgh: T. &T. Clark, 1978), p. 117.
10. Angela Tilby, *Let there be Light: Praying with Genesis* (London: Darton, Longman and Todd, 1989), p. 91.
11. Bernhard W. Anderson, *From Creation to New Creation: Old Testament Perspectives*, Overtures to Biblical Theology (Minneapolis, MN: Fortress Press, 1994), p. 72.
12. Van Wolde, *Stories of the Beginning*, pp. 158–62.
13. Michael Fishbane, *Biblical Text and Texture: A Literary Reading of Selected Texts* (Oxford: One World, 1998), p. 38.
14. Ralph W. Klein, *Israel in Exile*, Overtures to Biblical Theology (Philadelphia, PA: Fortress Press, 1979), see especially pp. 149–54.
15. Trevor Dennis, *Looking God in the Eye* (London: SPCK, 1998), p. 25.

[16] Walter Brueggemann, *Genesis* (Atlanta, GA: John Knox Press, 1982), p. 77.
[17] Brueggemann, *Genesis*, p. 81.
[18] Anonymous poem, quoted in Mark Link, *These Stones will Shout: A New Voice for the Old Testament* (Niles, IL: Argus Communications, 1975), pp. 28–9.
[19] Frank Moore Cross, *From Epic to Canon: History and Literature in Ancient Israel* (Baltimore, MD: Johns Hopkins University Press, 2000), p. 1.
[20] Cross, *From Epic to Canon*, p. 7.
[21] Jacques Ellul, *The Meaning of the City* (Grand Rapids, MI: Eerdmans, 1970).
[22] Jonathan Sacks, *The Dignity of Difference: How to Avoid the Clash of Civilizations* (London and New York, NY: Continuum [revised edition] 2003), p. 53.
[23] T. L. Thompson, *The Historicity of the Patriarchal Narratives: The Quest for the Historical Abraham* (Berlin: W. de Gruyter, 1974).
[24] J. Van Seters, *Abraham in History and Tradition* (New Haven, CT: Yale University Press, 1975).
[25] Adapted from an analysis in Jonathan Magonet, *Bible Lives* (London: SCM Press, 1992), p. 25.
[26] David J. A. Clines, *The Theme of the Pentateuch* (Sheffield: Sheffield Academic Press, second edn, 1997), p. 30.
[27] Elsa Tamez, quoted in John Goldingay, "The Place of Ishmael", in Philip R. Davies and David J. A. Clines (eds), *The World of Genesis: Persons, Places, Perspectives* (Sheffield: Sheffield Academic Press, 1998), p. 148.
[28] See e.g. Carole R. Fontaine, "Forgotten Voices of Earth: The Blessing subjects in Genesis 49", in Norman C. Habel and Shirley Wurst (eds), *The Earth Story in Genesis*, The Earth Bible 2 (Sheffield: Sheffield Academic Press, 2000), p. 207.
[29] W. Gross, *Glaubensgehorsam als Wagnis der Freiheit: Wir sind Abraham* (Mainz: Matthias-Grünewald-Verlag, 1980), p. 6, translated and quoted in Karl-Josef Kuschel, *Laughter: A Theological Reflection* (London: SCM Press, 1994), p. 51.
[30] Elie Wiesel, *Messengers of God* (New York, NY: Touchstone, 1994), p. 71.
[31] Edwin Good, *Irony in the Old Testament* (second edn, Sheffield: The Almond Press, 1981), p. 95.
[32] Trevor Dennis, *Sarah Laughed; Women's Voices in the Old Testament* (London: SPCK, 1994), pp. 58–9.

[33] Judah Goldin, "Introduction" in Shalom Spiegel (ed.), *The Last Trial: On the Legends and Lore of the Command to Abraham to Offer Isaac as a Sacrifice: The Akedah* (paperback edn: Woodstock, VT: Jewish Lights Publishing, 1993), p. xxi.

[34] Eric Auerbach, *Mimesis* (Princeton, NJ: Princeton University Press, 1953), p. 12.

[35] Good, *Irony in the Old Testament*, p. 96.

[36] Gerhard von Rad, *Genesis*, Old Testament Library (London: SCM, revised edition 1972), p. 240.

[37] J. P. Fokkelman, "Genesis", in Robert Alter and Frank Kermode (eds), *The Literary Guide to the Bible* (London: Fontana Press, 1989), p. 50.

[38] Michael E. W. Thompson, *I have heard your prayer: The Old Testament and Prayer* (Peterborough: Epworth Press, 1996), p. 17.

[39] Robert Alter, *The Art of Biblical Narrative* (New York, NY: Basic Books, 1981), pp. 52-3.

[40] Claus Westermann, *Genesis 12-36* (Minneapolis, MN: Augsburg Publishing House, 1985), p. 392.

[41] Clines, *The Theme of the Pentateuch*, e.g. pp. 114-19.

[42] W. Zimmerli, *Man and His Hope in the Old Testament* (London: SCM Press, 1971), p. 68.

[43] Clines, *The Theme of the Pentateuch*, p. 124.

[44] W. Zimmerli, "Promise and Fulfilment" in Claus Westermann (ed.), *Essays on Old Testament Interpretation* (London: SCM Press, 1963), p. 97.

[45] Gabriel Josipovici, *The Book of God: A Response to the Bible* (New Haven, CT: Yale University Press, 1988), pp. 269-70.

[46] Karl-Josef Kuschel, *Abraham: A Symbol of Hope for Jews, Christians and Muslims* (London: SCM Press, 1995), pp. 26-7.

[47] M. J. Bin-Gorion, *Die Sagen der Juden: Mythen, Legenden, Auslegungen* (Berlin: Avus Buch und Medien, 1935), p. 268, quoted and translated in Kuschel, *Abraham*, p. xi.

[48] Harvey Cox, *The Feast of Fools: A Theological Essay on Festivity and Fantasy* (Cambridge, MA: Harvard University Press, 1969), p. 157.

[49] Bernard Mandelbaum (editor), *Peskita de Rav Kahana* (New York, NY: Jewish Theological Seminary, 1962), 2.451.

[50] Elie Wiesel, *Messengers of God* (New York, NY: Touchstone, 1994), pp. 95-7.

51 Steven Saltzman, *A Small Glimmer of Light* (Hoboken, NJ: KTAV Publishing House, 1996), p. 56.
52 Carol Delaney, "Abraham and the seeds of patriarchy", in Athalya Brenner (ed.), *Genesis: A Feminist Companion to the Bible* (Sheffield: Sheffield Academic Press, 1998), p. 149.
53 Phyllis Trible, "Genesis 22: The Sacrifice of Sarah", in Jason P. Rosenblatt and Joseph C. Sitterson Jr (eds), *Not in Heaven: Coherence and Complexity in Biblical Narrative* (Bloomington, IN and Indianapolis, IN: Indiana University Press, 1991), pp. 189-91.
54 Trevor Dennis, *Imagining God: Stories from Creation to Heaven* (London: SPCK, 1997), pp. 78-9.
55 Naim S. Ateek, "Biblical perspectives on the Land", in Naim Ateek, Marc H. Ellis and Rosemary Radford Ruether (eds), *Faith and the Intifada* (Maryknoll, NY: Orbis, 1992), p. 108.
56 Clines, *The Theme of the Pentateuch*, pp. 99-126.
57 Norman C. Habel, *The Land is Mine: Six Biblical Land Ideologies*, Overtures to Biblical Theology (Minneapolis, MN: Fortress Press, 1995), see especially pp. 115-33.
58 Patricia Crone and Michael Cook, *Hagarism, The Making of the Islamic World* (Cambridge: Cambridge University Press, 1977), pp. 8-9.
59 See Pamela Tamarkin Reis, "Hagar requited" *Journal for the Study of the Old Testament* 87 (2000), pp. 75-109.
60 Shin Shalom (Joseph Shapira Shalom) as translated in *Forms of Prayer for Jewish Worship*, The Assembly of Rabbis of the Reform Synagogues of Great Britain, Vol.III (Prayers for the High Holy Days) (London, 1985), p. 891.
61 David M. Gunn and Danna Nolan Fewell, *Narrative in the Hebrew Bible* (Oxford: Oxford University Press, 1993), p. 109.
62 Robert Alter, *The Art of Biblical Narrative*, p. 53.
63 Karen Armstrong, *In the Beginning: A New Reading of the Book of Genesis* (London: HarperCollins Publishers, 1996), p. 77.
64 Robert Alter, *Genesis* (New York, NY and London: W. W. Norton & Company, 1996), p. 158.
65 Heather A. McKay, "Jacob makes it across the Jabbok. An attempt to solve the Success/Failure ambivalence in Israel's self-consciousness", *Journal for the Study of the Old Testament* 38 (1987), pp. 3-13.

66   J. P. Fokkelman, *Narrative Art in Genesis* (Amsterdam: Van Gorcum, Assen, 1975), p. 188.
67   von Rad, *Genesis*, p. 325.
68   Roland Barthes, "The Struggle with the Angel: Textual Analysis of Genesis 32:23–33", in Roland Barthes et al. (eds), *Structural Analysis and Biblical Exegesis: Interpretational Essays* (Pittsburgh, PA: Pickwick, 1974), pp. 21–33.
69   J. P. Fokkelman, "Genesis", in Robert Alter and Frank Kermode (eds), *The Literary Guide to the Bible*, p. 51.
70   Carl Gustav Jung, *Answer to Job*, tr. R. F. C. Hull (London and New York, NY: Routledge, 2002), p. 115.
71   Alter, *Genesis*, p. 187.
72   Lyn M. Bechtel, "What if Dinah is not Raped? (Genesis 34)", in John W. Rogerson (ed.), *The Pentateuch: A Sheffield Reader* (Sheffield: Sheffield Academic Press, 1996), pp. 263–80.
73   Elie Wiesel, *Messengers of God* (New York, NY: Touchstone, 1994), pp. 106–7.
74   J. Neville Ward, *The Use of Praying* (London: Epworth Press, 1967), p. 158.
75   C. S. Lewis, *The Lion, the Witch and the Wardrobe* (London: Geoffrey Bles, 1950), p. 75.
76   Dennis, *Looking God in the Eye*, pp. 81–2.
77   Wiesel, *Messengers of God*, p. 132.
78   <https://paxchristi.org.uk/resources/pax-christi-icon-of-peace/>, accessed 19 June 2021.
79   This story is generally ascribed to "Jewish tradition", although it is impossible to link definitively to any rabbinic source. However, Professor Alexander Scheiber of Budapest devoted a number of special studies to the history of the legend. According to Scheiber's research, the earliest attestation of the story appears in the writings of Alphonse de Lamartine, a French author who claims to have heard it from the mouth of an Arab peasant during a journey through the Holy Land in 1832. It may therefore in fact originate in Muslim or Christian circles. See comments by Eliezer Segal <http://www.acs.ucalgary.ca/~elsegal/Shokel/940505_Pal_Midrash.html>, accessed 19 June 2021.
80   Elias Chacour, *We Belong to the Land* (Collegeville, MN: University of Notre Dame Press, 2001), pp. 46–7.
81   The "Tale of the Two Brothers" is an ancient Egyptian story, probably originally dating from c. 1200 BC, preserved on the Papyrus D'Orbiney, now in the British Museum.

[82] Brueggemann, *Genesis*, pp. 328–9.
[83] Jon Levenson, *The Death and Resurrection of the Beloved Son: The Transformation of Child Sacrifice in Judaism and Christianity* (New Haven, CT and London: Yale University Press, 1993), p. 163.
[84] Aaron Wildavsky, *Assimilation versus Separation* (New Brunswick and London: Transaction Publishers, 1993), p. 159.
[85] Wildavsky, *Assimilation versus Separation*, p. 163.
[86] Nahum M. Sarna, *Genesis*, JPS Torah commentary (Philadelphia, PA: Jewish Publication Society, 1989), p. 343.
[87] Armstrong, *In the Beginning*, p. 113.
[88] Rabbi Naftali Zvi Yehudah Berlin, quoted in Sacks, *The Dignity of Difference*, p. 52.
[89] Kenneth Cragg, *Readings in the Qur'an* (London: Collins, 1988), p. 130.
[90] Cragg, *Readings in the Qur'an*, pp. 136–7.
[91] Thomas Mann, *Joseph and His Brothers* (London: Vintage, 1999), pp. 415–16.
[92] Tim Rice (words), Andrew Lloyd Webber (music), *Joseph and the Amazing Technicolor Dreamcoat* (London: The Really Useful Group Ltd, 1991), pp. 31–42.
[93] Janet Morley, in *Bread of Tomorrow: Praying with the World's Poor*, edited by Janet Morley (London: SPCK/Christian Aid, 1992), p. 101.
[94] Robert L. Cohn, "Narrative Structure and Canonical Perspective in Genesis", in Rogerson (ed.), *The Pentateuch*, p. 102.
[95] Mann, *Joseph and His Brothers*, p. 1207.